PAUL PRESTON is the world's foremost historian of twentieth-century Sp⸺ ⸺ book⸺ ⸺andard biographies ⸺ Franco and King Juan Carlos. *The Spanish Civil War* was hailed by *The Times* as 'the definitive work'. *The Spanish Holocaust* was shortlisted for the 2012 Samuel Johnson Prize and named *Sunday Times* History Book of the Year. He is the Príncipe de Asturias Professor of Spanish History at the London School of Economics, a Fellow of the British Academy and lives in London.

From the reviews for *The Last Stalinist*:

'Enormously engaging ... authoritative ... fascinating ... *The Last Stalinist* is yet another reminder that Paul Preston remains the most reliable historian in the English-speaking world for anyone wishing to understand the complicated power struggles between left and right in Spanish politics over the course of the 20th century'

J. P. O'MALLEY, *Spectator*

'In taking a scalpel to his morally questionable subject, Preston sheds light on the Francoist past, with all its deficiencies and horrors. *The Last Stalinist* will appeal to devotees of 20th-century Spanish history'

IAN THOMSON, *Independent*

'Carrillo's part in helping to usher his country back into the European democratic fold made him an unlikely hero to many in Spain and beyond ... In truth, as Paul Preston makes clear in this exhaustive and admirable biography, it was the only decent thing Carrillo did in a long and eventful political life characterised by treachery, lies, opportunism, ruthlessness, self-delusion, and almost certainly mass murder ... Paul Preston has no rival as historian of contemporary Spain'

ROBERT LOW, *Standpoint*

'Fluent, ⸺ sobering and we⸺ ⸺conomist

'Though he behaved bravely during the attempted coup of 1981, Carrillo is given short shrift in this merciless biography as an exemplar of moral virtue. His priority, Preston says, was always his own eminence. On that altar of ambition, all truth, decency, friends and allies were sacrificed'
IAIN FINLAYSON, The Times

'a fascinating if disturbing read … The Last Stalinist is filled with betrayals, double-dealings and vicious feuds that often ended in murder'
GILES MILTON, Mail on Sunday

BY THE SAME AUTHOR

THE LAST STALINIST

The Life of Santiago Carrillo

PAUL PRESTON

WILLIAM
COLLINS

William Collins
An imprint of HarperCollins Publishers
1 London Bridge Street
London SE1 9GF
WilliamCollinsBooks.com

First published in Great Britain by William Collins in 2014
This paperback edition first published in Great Britain by William Collins in 2015

1

ISBN 978-0-00-810621-8

Printed and bound in Great Britain by
Clays Ltd, St Ives plc

MIX
Paper from
responsible sources
FSC® C007454

FSC is a non-profit international organisation established to promote
the responsible management of the world's forests. Products carrying the
FSC label are independently certified to assure consumers that they come
from forests that are managed to meet the social, economic and
ecological needs of present or future generations,
and other controlled sources.

Find out more about HarperCollins and the environment at
www.harpercollins.co.uk/green

In memory of Michael Jacobs

CONTENTS

ACKNOWLEDGEMENTS

In a sense, the origins of this book date back to the 1970s when I first began to collect information about the anti-Francoist resistance. At the time and subsequently, I had long conversations with many of the protagonists of the book, including Santiago Carrillo himself. Many of those who shared their opinions and memories with me have since died. However, I would like to put on record my gratitude to them: Santiago Álvarez, Manuel Azcárate, Rafael Calvo Serer, Fernando Claudín, Tomasa Cuevas, Carlos Elvira, Irene Falcón, Ignacio Gallego, Jerónimo González Rubio, Carlos Gurméndez, Antonio Gutiérrez Díaz, K. S. Karol, Domingo Malagón, José Martinez Guerricabeitia, Miguel Núñez, Teresa Pàmies, Javier Pradera, Rossana Rossanda, Jorge Semprún, Enrique Tierno Galvan, Manuel Vázquez Montalbán, Francesc Vicens and Pepín Vidal Beneyto.

Over the years, I discussed the issues raised in the book with friends and colleagues who have worked on the subject, some of whom played a part in the events related therein. I am grateful for what I have learned from Beatriz Anson, Emilia Bolinches, Jordi Borja, Natalia Calamai, William Chislett, Iván Delicado, Roland Delicado, Carlos García-Alix, Dolores García Cantús, David Ginard i Féron, María Jesús González, Carmen Grimau, Fernando Hernández Sánchez, Enrique Líster López, Esther López Sobrado, Aurelio Martín Nájera, Rosa Montero, Silvia Ribelles de la Vega, Michael Richards, Ana Romero, Nicolás Sartorius, Irène Tenèze, Miguel Verdú and Ángel Viñas Martín.

Finally, this book would not have been possible without the friends who helped with documentation and who read all or part of the text: Javier Alfaya, Nicolás Belmonte Martínez, Laura Díaz

Herrera, Helen Graham, Susana Grau, Fernando Hernández Sánchez, Michel Lefevbre, Teresa Miguel Martínez, Gregorio Morán, Linda Palfreeman, Sandra Souto Kustrin and Boris Volodarsky. I am immensely grateful to them all.

PREFACE

This is the complex story of a man of great importance. From 1939 to 1975, the Spanish Communist Party (the Partido Comunista de España, or PCE) was the most determined opponent of the Franco regime. As its effective leader for two decades, Santiago Carrillo was arguably the dictator's most consistent left-wing enemy. Whether Franco was concerned about the left-wing opposition is another question. However, the lack of a comparable figure in either the anarchist or Socialist movements means that the title belongs indisputably to Carrillo.

Carrillo's was a life of markedly different and apparently contradictory phases. In the first half of his political career, in Spain and in exile, from the mid-1930s to the mid-1970s, Santiago Carrillo was admired by many on the left as a revolutionary and a pillar of the anti-Franco struggle and hated by others as a Stalinist gravedigger of the revolution. For many on the right, he was a monster to be vilified as a mass murderer for his activities during the Civil War. He came to prominence as a hot-headed leader of the Socialist Youth whose incendiary rhetoric contributed in no small measure to the revolutionary events of October 1934. After sixteen months in prison, he abandoned, and betrayed, the Socialist Party by taking its youth movement into the Communist Party. This 'dowry' and his unquestioning loyalty to Moscow were rewarded during the Civil War by rapid promotion within the Communist ranks. Not yet twenty-two years old, he became public order chief in the besieged Spanish capital and acquired enduring notoriety for his alleged role in the episodes known collectively as Paracuellos, the elimination of right-wing prisoners. After the war, he was a faithful apparatchik, who by dint of skill and ruthless ambition rose to the leadership of the Communist Party.

Then, in the course of the second half of his political career, from the mid-1970s until his death in 2012, he came to be seen as a national treasure because of his contribution to the restoration of democracy. From his return to Spain in 1976 until 1981, his skills, honed in the internal power struggles of the PCE, were applied in the national political arena. During the early years of the transition, it appeared as if the interests of the PCE coincided with those of the population. He would be canonized as a crucial pillar of Spanish democracy as a result of his moderation then. He was particularly lauded for his bravery on the night of 23 February 1981 when the Spanish parliament was seized as part of a failed military coup. After that time, his role reverted to that of Party leader and he was undone by generational conflict. Between 1981 and 1985, he presided over the destruction of the Communist Party, which he had spent forty years shaping in his own image. Accordingly, in later life and on his death, he was the object of many tributes and accolades from members of the Spanish establishment ranging from the King to right-wing heavyweights.

The chequered nature of Carrillo's political career poses the question of whether he was simply a cynical and clever chameleon. In 1974, denying the existence of a personality cult within the PCE, he proclaimed: 'I will never permit propaganda being made about myself.'[1] Then, in an interview given two years later, he announced: 'I will never write my memoirs because a politician cannot tell the truth.'[2] He had already contradicted the first of these denials by dint of speeches and internal Party reports in which he constructed the myth of a selfless fighter for democracy. Then, in his last four decades, he propagated numerous accounts of his life in countless interviews, in more than ten of the many books that he wrote himself and in two others that he dictated.[3] In this regard, he shared with Franco a dedication to the constant rewriting and improving of his own life story.

Accordingly, this account of a fascinating life differs significantly from the many versions produced by the man himself which are contrasted here with copious documentation and the interpretations of friends and enemies. There can be little here about Carrillo's personal life. From the time that he entered employment at the printing works of the Socialist Party aged thirteen until his retirement from active politics in 1991, he seems not to have had much of one. Certainly, his life was dominated by his political activity, but he surrounded accounts about his existence outside politics with a web of contradictory statements and downright untruth.[4] Despite his apparent gregariousness and loquacity, this is the story of a solitary man. One by one he turned on those who helped him: Largo Caballero, his father Wenceslao Carrillo, Segundo Serrano Poncela, Francisco Antón, Fernando Claudín, Jorge Semprún, Pilar Brabo, Manuel Azcárate, Ignacio Gallego – the list is very long. In his anxiety for advancement, he was always ready to betray or denounce comrades. Such ruthlessness was another characteristic that he shared with Franco. What will become clear is that Carrillo had certain qualities in abundance – a capacity for hard work, stamina and endurance, writing and oratorical skills, intelligence and cunning. Unfortunately, what will become equally clear is that honesty and loyalty were not among them.

AUTHOR'S NOTE

Although I hope the context always makes the meaning clear, I have used the word 'guerrilla' in its original Spanish meaning.

The Spanish word does not mean, as in English usage, 'a guerrilla fighter', but rather something closer to 'campaign of guerrilla warfare'. See page 124: 'On 20 September, Pasionaria herself had published a declaration hailing the guerrilla as the way to spark an uprising in Spain.' For the guerrilla fighters themselves, I have used the singular *guerrillero* or the plural *guerrilleros*.

1

The Creation of a Revolutionary: 1915–1934

Santiago Carrillo was born on 18 January 1915 to a working-class family in Gijón on Spain's northern coast. His grandfather, his father and his uncles all earned their living as metalworkers in the Orueta factory. Prior to her marriage, his mother, Rosalía Solares, was a seamstress. His father Wenceslao Carrillo was a prominent trade unionist and member of the Socialist Party who made every effort to help his son follow in his footsteps. As secretary of the Asturian metalworkers' union, Wenceslao had been imprisoned after the revolutionary strike of August 1917. Indeed, Santiago claimed later that his most profound memory of his father was seeing him regularly being taken away by Civil Guards from the family home. It was there, and later in Madrid, that he grew up within a warm and affectionate extended family in an atmosphere soaked in a sense of the class struggle. Such a childhood would help account for the impregnable self-confidence that was always to underlie his career. He asserted in his memoirs that family was always tremendously important to him.[1] That, however, would not account for the viciousness with which he renounced in father in 1939. Then, as throughout his life, at least until his withdrawal from the Communist Party in the mid-1980s, political loyalties and ambition would count for far more than family.

Santiago was one of seven children, two of whom died very young. His brother Roberto died during a smallpox epidemic in Gijón that Santiago managed to survive unscathed thanks to the efforts of his paternal grandmother, who slept in the same bed to stop him scratching his spots. A younger sister, Marguerita, died of meningitis only two months after being born. A brother born subsequently was also named Roberto. Coming from a left-wing family, Santiago was not short of rebellious tendencies and, perhaps inevitably, they were exacerbated when he attended Catholic primary school. By then the family had moved to Avilés, 12 miles west of Gijón. For an inadvertent blasphemy, he was obliged to spend an hour kneeling with his arms stretched out in the form of a cross while holding extremely heavy books in each hand. In reaction to the bigotry of his teachers, his parents took him out of the school. Shortly afterwards, the local workers' centre opened, in the attic of its headquarters, a small school for the children of trade union members. A non-religious teacher was difficult to find and the task fell to a hunchbacked municipal street-sweeper who happened to be slightly more cultured than most of his comrades. Carrillo later remembered with regret the cruel mockery to which he and his fellow urchins subjected the poor man.

Not long afterwards, in early 1924, with Wenceslao now both a full-time trade union official of the General Union of Workers (Unión General de Trabajadores) and writing for *El Socialista*, the newspaper of the Socialist Party (Partido Socialista Obrero Español, or PSOE), the family moved to Madrid. There, on the exiguous salary that the UGT could afford to pay Wenceslao, they lived in a variety of poor working-class districts. At first, they endured appalling conditions and Santiago later recalled that he witnessed suicides and crimes of passion. In the barrio of Cuatro Caminos, he had the good luck to gain entry to an excellent school, the Grupo Escolar Cervantes.[2] He later attributed to its committed teachers and its twelve-hour schoolday enormous influence in his development, in particular his indubitable work ethic. Whatever criticisms might be made of Carrillo, an accusation of laziness would never be one of them. He was also toughened up by the constant fist-fights with a variety of school bullies.

As a thirteen-year-old his ambition was to be an engineer. However, neither the school nor his family could afford the cost of the examination entry fee for each of the six subjects of the school-leaving certificate. Accordingly, without being able to pursue further studies, he left school with a burning sense of social injustice. Thanks to his father, he would soon embark on a meteoric rise within the Socialist movement. Wenceslao managed to get him a job at the printing works of *El Socialista* (la Gráfica Socialista). This required him to join the UGT and the Socialist youth movement (Federación de Juventudes Socialistas). As early as November 1929, the ambitious young Santiago, not yet fifteen years of age, published his first articles in *Aurora Social* of Oviedo, calling for the creation of a student section of the FJS. Helped by the position of his father, he enjoyed a remarkably rapid rise within the FJS, almost immediately being voted on to its executive committee. Of key importance in this respect was the patronage that derived from Wenceslao Carrillo's close friendship with the hugely influential union leader Francisco Largo Caballero. An austere figure in public life, Largo Caballero was affectionately known as 'Don Paco' in the Carrillo household.

The two families used to meet socially for weekly picnics in Dehesa de la Villa, a park outside Madrid. Along with the food and wine, they used to bring a small barrel-organ (*organillo*). It was used to accompany Don Paco and his wife Concha as they showed off their skill in the typical Madrid dance, the *chotis*. This family connection was to constitute a massive boost to Santiago's career within the PSOE. Indeed, the veteran leader had often given the baby Santiago his bottle and felt a paternalistic affection for him that would persist until the Civil War. Later, when he was old enough to understand, Santiago would avidly listen to the conversations of his father and Largo Caballero about the internal disputes within both the UGT and PSOE. There can be little doubt that the utterly pragmatic, and hardly ideological, stances of these two hardened union bureaucrats were to be a deep influence on Santiago's own political development. Their tendency to personalize union conflicts would also be reflected in his own later conduct of polemics in both the Socialist and Communist parties.[3]

Santiago was soon publishing regularly in *Renovación*, the weekly news-sheet of the FJS. This brought him into frequent contact with his almost exact contemporary, the famous intellectual prodigy Hildegart Rodríguez, who as a teenager was already giving lectures and writing articles on sexual politics and eugenics. She spoke six languages by the age of eight and would have a law degree at the age of seventeen. Just as she was rising to prominence within the Socialist

Youth, she was shot dead by her mother, Aurora, jealous of Hildegart's growing independence.

In early 1930, the editor of *El Socialista*, Andrés Saborit, offered Santiago the chance to leave the machinery of the printing works and work full time in the paper's editorial offices. It was a promotion that suggested the hands of his father and Don Paco. He started off modestly enough, cutting and pasting agency items and then writing headlines for them. However, he was soon a cub journalist and given the town-hall beat.[4]

The end of January 1930 saw the departure of the military dictator General Miguel Primo de Rivera. Between then and the establishment of the Second Republic on 14 April 1931, there was intense ferment within the Socialist movement. Certainly, there were as yet few signs of the radicalization that would develop after 1933 and catapult Santiago Carrillo into prominence on the left. The issues in those early days of the Republic revolved around the validity and value of Socialist collaboration with government. In the late 1920s, just as Santiago Carrillo was becoming involved in the Socialist Youth, there were basically three factions within both the Unión General de Trabajadores and the Socialist Party. The most moderate of the three was the group led by the academic Julián Besteiro, president since 1926 of both the party and the union and Professor of Logic at the University of Madrid.[5] In the centre, at this stage the most realistic although paradoxically, in the context of the time, the most radical, was the group associated with Indalecio Prieto, the owner of the influential Bilbao newspaper *El Liberal*.[6] The third, and the one to which Carrillo's father Wenceslao was linked, was that of Largo Caballero, who was vice-president of the PSOE and secretary general of the UGT.[7] Given his junior position on the editorial staff of *El Socialista*, which brought him into daily contact with Besteiro's closest collaborator, Andrés Saborit, and given his links to Largo Caballero via his father, Santiago Carrillo found it easy to follow the internal polemics even if, to protect his job, he did not yet publicly take sides.

Although extremely conservative, Besteiro seemed to be the most extremist of the three leaders because of his rigid adherence to Marxist theory. The Spanish Socialist movement was essentially reformist and had, with the exception of Besteiro, little tradition of theoretical Marxism. In that sense, it was true to its late nineteenth-century origins among the working-class aristocracy of Madrid printers. Its founder, the austere Pablo Iglesias Posse, was always more concerned with cleaning up politics than with the class struggle. Julián Besteiro, his eventual successor as party leader, also felt that a highly moral political isolationism was the only viable option in the corrupt political system of the constitutional monarchy. In contrast, and altogether more realistically, Indalecio Prieto, who was unusual in that he did not have a trade union behind him, believed that the Socialist movement should do whatever was necessary to defend workers' interests. His experiences in Bilbao politics had convinced him of the prior need for the establishment of liberal democracy. His early electoral alliances with local middle-class Republicans there led to him advocating a Republican–Socialist coalition as a step to gaining power.[8] This had brought him into conflict with Largo Caballero, who distrusted bourgeois politics and believed that the proper role of the workers' movement was strike action. The lifelong hostility of Largo Caballero towards Prieto would eventually be assumed by Santiago Carrillo and, from 1934, become part of his political make-up.

In fact, the underlying conflict between Prieto and Largo Caballero had been of little consequence before 1914. That was largely because in the two decades before the boom prompted by the Great War, prices and wages remained relatively stable in Spain – albeit they were among the highest prices and lowest wages in Europe. As a result, there was little meaningful debate in the Socialist Party over whether to attain power by electoral means or by revolutionary strike action. In 1914, those circumstances began to change. As a non-belligerent, Spain was able to supply food, uniforms, military equipment and shipping to both sides. A frenetic and vertiginous industrial boom accompanied by a fierce inflation reached its peak in 1916. In response to a dramatic deterioration of social conditions, the PSOE and the UGT took part in a national general strike in mid-August 1917. Even then, the maximum ambitions of the Socialists were anything but revolutionary, concerned rather to put an end to political corruption and government inability to deal with inflation. The strike was aimed at supporting a broad-based movement for the establishment of a provisional government that would hold elections for a constituent Cortes to decide on the future form of state. Despite its pacific character, the strike that broke out on 10 August 1917 was easily crushed by savage military repression in Asturias and the Basque Country, two of the Socialists' three major strongholds – the third being Madrid. In Asturias, the home province of the Carrillo family, the Military Governor General Ricardo Burguete y Lana declared martial law on 13 August. He accused the strike organizers of being the paid agents of foreign powers. Announcing that he would hunt down the strikers 'like wild beasts', he sent columns of regular troops and Civil Guards into the mining valleys where they unleashed an orgy of rape, looting, beatings and torture. With 80 dead, 150 wounded and 2,000 arrested, the failure of the strike was guaranteed.[9] Manuel Llaneza, the moderate leader of the Asturian mineworkers' union, referring to the brutality of the Spanish colonial army in Morocco, wrote at the time of the 'African hatred' during an action in which one of Burguete's columns was under the command of the young Major Francisco Franco.[10] As a senior trade unionist who took part in the strike and had experienced the severity of the consequent repression in Asturias, Wenceslao Carrillo was notable thereafter for his caution in any decision that could lead the Socialist movement into perilous conflict with the state apparatus.

The four-man national strike committee was arrested in Madrid. It consisted of the PSOE vice-president, Besteiro, the UGT vice-president, Largo Caballero, Andrés Saborit, leader of the printers' union and already editor of *El Socialista*, and Daniel Anguiano, secretary general of the Railway Workers' Union (Sindicato Ferroviario Nacional). Very nearly condemned to summary execution, all four were finally sentenced to life imprisonment and spent several months in jail. After a nationwide amnesty campaign, they were freed as a result of being elected to the Cortes in the general elections of 24 February 1918. The entire experience was to have a dramatic effect on the subsequent trajectories of all four. In general, the Socialist leadership, particularly the UGT bureaucracy, was traumatized, seeing the movement's role in 1917 as senseless adventurism. Largo Caballero, like Wenceslao Carrillo, was more concerned with the immediate material welfare of the UGT than with possible future revolutionary goals. He was determined never again to risk existing legislative gains and the movement's property in a direct confrontation with the state. Both Besteiro and Saborit also became progressively less radical. In different ways, all three perceived the futility of Spain's weak Socialist movement undertaking a frontal assault on the state. Anguiano, in contrast, moved to more radical positions and was eventually to be one of the founders of the Communist Party.

In the wake of the Russian revolution, continuing inflation and the rising unemployment of the post-1918 depression fostered a revolutionary group within the Socialist movement, particularly in Asturias and the Basque Country. Anguiano and others saw the events in Russia and the failure of the 1917 strike as evidence that it was pointless to work towards a bourgeois democratic stage on the road to socialism. Between 1919 and 1921, the Socialist movement was to be divided by a bitter three-year debate on the PSOE's relationship with the Communist International (Comintern) recently founded in Moscow. The fundamental issue being worked out was whether the Spanish Socialist movement was to be legalist and reformist or violent and revolutionary. The pro-Bolshevik tendency was defeated in a series of three party congresses held in December 1919, June 1920 and April 1921. In a closely fought struggle, the PSOE leadership won by relying on the votes of the strong UGT bureaucracy of paid permanent officials. The pro-Russian elements left to form the Spanish Communist Party.[11] Numerically, this was not a serious loss but, at a time of grave economic and social crisis, it consolidated the fundamental moderation of the Socialist movement and left it without a clear sense of direction.

Indalecio Prieto had become a member of the PSOE's executive committee in 1918.[12] He represented a significant section of the movement committed to seeking reform through the electoral victory of a broad front of democratic forces. He was appalled when the paralysis within the Socialist movement was exposed by the coming of the military dictatorship of General Primo de Rivera on 13

September 1923. The army's seizure of power was essentially a response to the urban and rural unrest of the previous six years. Yet the Socialist leadership neither foresaw the coup nor showed great concern when the new regime began to persecute other workers' organizations. A joint PSOE–UGT note simply instructed their members to undertake no strikes or other 'sterile' acts of resistance without instructions from their two executive committees lest they provoke repression. This reflected the determination of both Besteiro and Largo Caballero never again to risk the existence of the UGT in direct confrontation with the state, especially if doing so merely benefited the cause of bourgeois liberalism.[13]

It soon became apparent that it would be a short step from avoidance of risky confrontation with the dictatorship to active collaboration. In view of the Socialist passivity during his coup, the dictator was confident of a sympathetic response when he proposed that the movement cooperate with his regime. In a manifesto of 29 September 1923, Primo thanked the working class for its attitude during his seizure of power. This was clearly directed at the Socialists. It both suggested that the regime would foster the social legislation longed for by Largo Caballero and the reformists of the UGT and called upon workers to leave those organizations which led them 'along paths of ruin'. This unmistakable reference to the revolutionary anarcho-syndicalist CNT (Confederación Nacional del Trabajo) and the Spanish Communist Party was a cunning and scarcely veiled suggestion to the UGT that it could become Spain's only working-class organization. In return for collaborating with the regime, the UGT would have a monopoly of trade union activities and be in a position to attract the rank and file of its anarchist and Communist rivals. Largo Caballero was delighted, given his hostility to any enterprise, such as the revolutionary activities of Communists and anarchists, that might endanger the material conditions of the UGT members. He believed that under the dictatorship, although the political struggle might be suspended, the defence of workers' rights should go on by all possible means. Thus he was entirely open to Primo's suggestion.[14] In early October, a joint meeting of the PSOE and UGT executive committees agreed to collaborate with the regime.

There were only three votes against the resolution, among them those of Fernando de los Ríos, a distinguished Professor of Law at the University of Granada, and Indalecio Prieto, who argued that the PSOE should join the democratic opposition against the dictatorship.[15]

Besteiro, like Largo Caballero, supported collaboration, albeit for somewhat different reasons. His logic was crudely Marxist. From the erroneous premise that Spain was still a semi-feudal country awaiting a bourgeois revolution, he reasoned that it was not the job of the Spanish working class to do the job of the bourgeoisie. In the meantime, however, until the bourgeoisie completed its historic task, the UGT should seize the opportunity offered by the dictatorship to have a monopoly of state labour affairs. His argument was built on shaky foundations. Although Spain had not experienced a political democratic revolution comparable to those in England and in France, the remnants of feudalism had been whittled away throughout the nineteenth century as the country underwent a profound legal and economic revolution. Besteiro's contention that the working class should stand aside and leave the task of building democracy to the bourgeoisie was thus entirely unrealistic since the landowning and financial bourgeoisie had already achieved its goals without a democratic revolution. His error would lead to his ideological annihilation at the hands of extreme leftist Socialists, including Santiago Carrillo, in the 1930s.

Prieto and a number of others within the Socialist Party, if not the UGT, were shocked by the opportunism shown by the leadership of the movement. They accepted that strike action against the army would have been self-destructive, sentimental heroics that would have risked the workers' movement merely to save the degenerate political system that sustained the monarchy re-established in 1876 after the collapse of the First Republic. However, they could not admit that this justified close collaboration with it. They went largely unheard and the integration of the national leadership with the dictatorship was considerable, the UGT having representatives on several state committees. Wenceslao Carrillo was the Socialist representative on one of the most important, the State Finances Auditing Commission (Consejo Interventor de Cuentas del Estado).[16] Most

UGT sections were allowed to continue functioning and the UGT was well represented on a new Labour Council. In contrast, anarchists and Communists suffered a total clampdown on their activities. In return for refraining from strikes and public protest demonstrations, the UGT was offered a major prize. On 13 September 1924, the first anniversary of the military coup, a royal decree allowed for one workers' and one employers' representative from the Labour Council to join the Council of State. The UGT members of the Labour Council chose Largo Caballero. Within the UGT itself this had no unfavourable repercussions – Besteiro was vice-president and Largo himself secretary general. The president, the now ageing and infirm Pablo Iglesias, did not object. However, there was a certain degree of outrage within the PSOE.

Prieto was appalled, rightly fearing that Largo Caballero's opportunism would be exploited by the dictator for its propaganda value. In fact, on 25 April 1925, Primo did cite Largo Caballero's presence on the Council of State as a reason for ruling without a parliament, asking rhetorically, 'why do we need elected representatives?'[17] When Prieto and De los Ríos wrote to the PSOE executive committee urging the need for distance between party leaders and the military directorate, they were told that Largo Caballero's nomination was a UGT matter. This was utterly disingenuous since the same individuals made up the executive committees of both bodies which usually held joint deliberations on important national issues. In the face of this dishonesty, Prieto resigned from the committee.[18] Inevitably, given Largo Caballero's egoism, his already festering personal resentment of Prieto was cast in stone.[19] It would continue throughout the years of the Republic and into the Civil War and would later influence Santiago Carrillo. When his own political positions came to be opposed to those of Prieto from late 1933 onwards, Carrillo would adopt an aggressive hostility towards him that fed off that of his mentor. This was to be seriously damaging to the Republic at the time and to the anti-Francoist cause after the Civil War.

Within four years of the establishment of Primo de Rivera's dictatorship, the economic boom that had facilitated Socialist collaboration was coming to an end. By the beginning of 1928, significant increases in unemployment were accompanied by growing evidence of worker unrest. The social democratic positions of Prieto and De los Ríos were gaining support. They constituted just one of the three tendencies within the Socialist movement whose divisions had been exacerbated by the dictatorship. The deteriorating economic situation confirmed both Prieto and the deeply reformist and rigidly orthodox Marxist Besteiro and Saborit in their respective positions. However, as the recession changed the mood of the Socialist working masses, it inevitably affected the views of the pragmatic trade unionists under Largo Caballero. That necessarily included his lieutenant Wenceslao Carrillo. They had gambled on securing for the UGT a virtual monopoly within the state industrial arbitration machinery, but it had done little to improve recruitment. Indeed, the small overall increase in membership was disappointing relative to the UGT's privileged position. Moreover, there was a drop in the number of union members paying their dues in two of the UGT's strongest sections, the Asturian miners and the rural labourers.[20] Always sensitive to shifts in rank-and-file feeling, Largo Caballero began to rethink his position and reconsider the advantages of a rhetorical radicalism. Since Wenceslao Carrillo spoke freely with his thirteen-year-old son, it is to be supposed that the beginnings of Santiago's own extremism in the period between 1933 and 1935 may be traced to this period. The difference would be that he believed in revolutionary solutions whereas Largo Caballero merely used revolutionary language in the hope of frightening the bourgeoisie.

At the Twelfth Congress of the PSOE, held in Madrid from 9 June to 4 July 1928, Prieto and others advocated resistance against the dictatorship, and a special committee created to examine the party's tactics rejected collaboration by six votes to four. Nevertheless, the wider Congress majority continued to support collaboration. This was reflected in the elections for party offices at the Congress and for those in the UGT at its Sixteenth Congress, held from 10 to 15 September. Pablo Iglesias had died on 9 December 1925. Having already replaced him on an interim basis, Besteiro was now formally elected to succeed him as president of both the PSOE and the UGT. All senior offices went to followers either of Besteiro or of Largo

Caballero. In the PSOE, Largo Caballero was elected vice-president, Saborit treasurer, Lucio Martínez Gil of the land workers secretary general and Wenceslao Carrillo minutes secretary. In the UGT, Saborit was elected vice-president, Largo Caballero secretary general and Wenceslao Carrillo treasurer.[21] Despite a growth in unemployment towards the end of the decade and increasing numbers of strikes, as late as January 1929 Largo Caballero was still arguing against such direct action and in favour of government legislation.[22] However, with the situation deteriorating, it can have been with little conviction. Opposition to the regime was growing in the universities and within the army. Intellectuals, Republicans and even monarchist politicians protested against abuses of the law. The peseta was falling and, as 1929 advanced, the first effect of the world depression began to be felt in Spain. The Socialists were gradually being isolated as the dictator's only supporters outside his own single party, the Unión Patriótica.

Matters reached a head in the summer when General Primo de Rivera offered the UGT the chance to choose five representatives for a proposed non-elected parliament to be known as the National Assembly. When the National Committees of the PSOE and the UGT held a joint meeting to discuss the offer on 11 August, Largo Caballero called for rejection of the offer while Besteiro, with support from Wenceslao Carrillo, was in favour of acceptance. Largo Caballero won, having changed his mind about collaboration with the dictatorship for the purely pragmatic reason that the tactic was now discredited in the eyes of the rank and file.[23] Since Besteiro regarded the dictatorship as a transitional stage in the decomposition of the monarchical regime, he thought it logical to accept the privileges offered by the dictator. According to his simplistically orthodox Marxist analysis, the monarchy had to be overthrown by a bourgeois revolution, and therefore the job of the UGT and PSOE leadership was to keep their organizations intact until they would be ready to work for socialism within a bourgeois regime.[24]

Largo Caballero made a number of speeches in late 1929 and early 1930 which indicated a move towards the stance of Prieto and De los Ríos in favour of Socialist cooperation with middle-class Republicans against the monarchy.[25] Pragmatic and opportunist, concerned always with the material interests of the Socialist movement and the maintenance of the union bureaucracy's control over the rank and file, he was prone to sudden and inconsistent shifts of position. Primo de Rivera resigned on 28 January 1930 to be replaced for three weeks by General Dámaso Berenguer. Just at the moment that the young Santiago Carrillo was being promoted from the printing works of *El Socialista* to the editorial staff, the Socialists seemed to be in a strong position despite the failures of collaboration. Other left-wing groups had been persecuted. Right-wing parties had put their faith in the military regime and allowed their organizations, and more importantly their networks of electoral falsification, to fall into decay. Inevitably, the growing opposition to the monarchy looked to the Socialists for support. With the Socialist rank and file increasingly militant, especially as they followed the examples set by the resurgent anarcho-syndicalist CNT and, to a much lesser extent, by the minuscule Communist Party, Largo Caballero moved ever more quickly towards Prieto's position. The Director General of Security, General Emilio Mola, was convinced that what he called the CNT's 'revolutionary gymnastics' were forcing the UGT leadership to follow suit for fear of losing members.[26]

Prieto and De los Ríos attended a meeting of Republican leaders in San Sebastián on 17 August. From this meeting emerged the so-called Pact of San Sebastián, the Republican revolutionary committee and the future Republican–Socialist provisional government. The National Committees of the UGT and the PSOE met on 16 and 18 October (respectively) to discuss the offer of two ministries in the provisional government in return for Socialist support, with a general strike, for a coup d'état. The Besteiristas were opposed but the balance was swung by Largo Caballero. His change of mind reflected that same opportunistic pragmatism that had inspired his early collaboration with, and later opposition to, the dictatorship. He said himself at the time, 'this is a question not of principles but of tactics'.[27] In return for UGT support for a military insurrection against the monarchy, the Republicans' original offer was increased to three ministries. When the executive committee of the PSOE met to examine the offer, it was accepted by eight votes to six. The three Socialist ministers in the provisional government were designated as Largo Caballero in the Ministry of Labour, and, to the latter's barely concealed resentment, Prieto in the Ministry of Public Works and De los Ríos in Education.[28]

All of these issues were discussed by Santiago and his father as they walked home each day from Socialist headquarters in Madrid, housed in the members' meeting place, the Casa del Pueblo. Inevitably, Wenceslao propounded a version that entirely justified the positions of Largo Caballero. There can be little doubt that, at least from this time onwards, if not before, the young Santiago Carrillo began to venerate Largo Caballero and to take his pronouncements at face value.[29] It would not be until the early months of the Civil War that he would come to realize the irresponsible opportunism that underlay his hero's rhetoric. Now, however, in his early teens and on the threshold of his political career, he absorbed the views of these two mentors, his father and Largo Caballero. These close friends were both practical union men whose central preoccupation was always to foster the material welfare of the Socialist Unión General de Trabajadores. They put its finances and its legal position, its recruitment and the collection of its members' dues and subscriptions ahead of all theoretical considerations. In long conversations with his father and at gatherings of both families, the young Santiago learned key lessons that were to be apparent in his later career. He learned about pragmatism and opportunism, about how an organization works, about how to set up and pack meetings and congresses to ensure victory. He learned that, while theoretical polemics might rage, these organizational lessons were the immutable truths that mattered. They were to be of inestimable value to him in his rise to power within the Communist Party, within the internal struggles that divided the Party throughout the 1960s and in the transition to, and the early years of, democracy in Spain. Parallels might be drawn between the collaboration of Largo Caballero's UGT with the dictatorship of General Miguel Primo de Rivera in the 1920s and Santiago's own moderation during the transition to democracy symbolized by his adoption of the monarchist flag in 1977.

Apart from sporadic strike action, the Socialist movement had taken no official part in the varied resistance movements to the dictatorship, at least until its later stages. The Pact of San Sebastián changed things dramatically. The undertaking to help with the revolutionary action would further divide both the UGT and the PSOE. Strike action in support of a military coup was opposed by Besteiro, Saborit and their reformist supporters within the UGT, Trifón Gómez of the Railway Workers' Union and Manuel Muiño, president of the Casa del Pueblo, where Socialist Party and union members would gather. Largo Caballero and Wenceslao Carrillo were firmly in favour. Santiago was an enthusiastic supporter of revolutionary action, having just read his first work by Lenin, the pamphlet *Two Tactics of Social Democracy in the Democratic Revolution*, which outlined the theoretical foundation for the strategy and tactics of the Bolshevik Party and criticized the role of the Mensheviks during the 1905 revolution. He equated the position of Besteiro with that of the Mensheviks. He was also influenced by both his father and Largo Caballero. Inevitably, he faced an uncomfortable time in the office that he shared with Saborit at the Gráfica Socialista.[30]

Santiago saw his first violent action in mid-November 1930. On 12 November, the collapse of a building under construction in the Calle Alonso Cano of Madrid killed four workers and badly injured seven others. The large funeral procession for the victims was attacked by the police, and in consequence the UGT, seconded by the CNT, called a general strike for 15 November. Santiago was involved in the subsequent clashes with youths who were selling the Catholic newspaper *El Debate*, the only one that had ignored the strike call.[31] He was also involved peripherally when the UGT participated, in a small way, in the revolutionary movement agreed upon in October. It finally took place in mid-December. The Republican 'revolutionary committee' had been assured that the UGT would support a military coup with a strike. Things were complicated somewhat when, in the hope of sparking off a pro-Republican movement in the garrisons of Huesca, Zaragoza and Lérida, Captains Fermín Galán, Angel García Hernández and Salvador Sediles rose in Jaca (Huesca) on 12 December, three days before the agreed date. Galán and García

Hernández were shot after summary courts martial on 14 December which led to the artillery withdrawing from the plot. And, although forces under General Queipo de Llano and aviators from the airbase at Cuatro Vientos went ahead, they realized that they were in a hopeless situation when the expected general strike did not take place in Madrid.[32]

This was largely the consequence of the scarcely veiled opposition of the Besteirista leadership. Madrid, the stronghold of the Besteiro faction of the UGT bureaucracy, was the only important city where there was no strike. That failure was later the object of bitter discussion at the Thirteenth Congress of the PSOE, in October 1932, where the Besteiristas in the leadership were accused of dragging their feet, if not actually sabotaging the strike. When, on 10 December 1930, Julio Álvarez del Vayo, one of the Socialists involved in the conspiracy, tried to have the revolutionary manifesto for the day of the proposed strike printed at the Gráfica Socialista, Saborit refused point-blank. General Mola, apparently on the basis of assurances from Manuel Muiño, was confident on the night of the 14th that the UGT would not join in the strike on the following day. Despite being given the strike orders by Largo Caballero, Muiño did nothing. This was inadvertently confirmed by Besteiro when he told the Thirteenth Congress of the PSOE that he had finally told Muiño to go ahead only after having been pressed by members of the Socialist Youth Federation to take action. One of those FJS members was Santiago Carrillo, whose later account casts doubt on that of Besteiro. The fact is that none of the powerful unions controlled by the Besteirista syndical bureaucracy stopped work. The group from the FJS, including Santiago Carrillo (who had been given a pistol which he had no clue how to use), had gone to the Conde Duque military garrison on the night of 14 December in the hope of joining the rising that never materialized. After being dispersed by the police, but seeing planes dropping revolutionary propaganda over Madrid, this group of teenage Socialists went to the Casa del Pueblo at Calle Carranza 20 to demand to know why there was no strike. They got no explanation but only a severe dressing-down from Besteiro himself.[33]

Not long afterwards, the barely sixteen-year-old Santiago was elected on to the executive committee of the FJS. In the wake of the failed uprising in December, the government held municipal elections on 12 April 1931 in what it hoped would be the first stage of a controlled return to constitutional normality. However, Socialists and liberal middle-class Republicans swept the board in the main towns while monarchists won only in the rural areas where the social domination of the local bosses, or *caciques*, remained intact. On the evening of polling day, as the results began to be known, people started to drift on to the streets of the cities of Spain and, with the crowds growing, Republican slogans were shouted with increasing excitement. Santiago Carrillo and his comrades of the FJS took part in demonstrations in favour of the Republic which were fired on by Civil Guards on the evening of 12 April and dispersed by a cavalry charge the following day.[34] Nevertheless, General José Sanjurjo, the commander of the Civil Guard, made it clear that he was not prepared to risk a bloodbath on behalf of the King, Alfonso XIII. General Dámaso Berenguer had been replaced as head of the government by Admiral Juan Bautista Aznar. Berenguer, now Minister of War, was equally pessimistic about army morale but was constrained by his loyalty to the King. Despite his misgivings, on the morning of 14 April Berenguer told Alfonso that the army would fight to overturn the result of the elections. Unwilling to sanction bloodshed, the King refused, believing that he should leave Spain gracefully and thereby keep open the possibility of an eventual return.[35] As news of his departure spread, a euphoric multitude, including Santiago Carrillo, gathered in Madrid's Puerta del Sol to greet the Republican–Socialist provisional government.

Despite the optimism of the crowds that danced in the streets, the new government faced a daunting task. It consisted of three Socialists and an ideologically disparate group of petty-bourgeois Republicans, some of whom were conservatives, some idealists and several merely cynics. That was the first weakness of the coalition. They had shared the desire to rid Spain of Alfonso XIII, but each then had a different agenda for the future. The conservative elements wanted to go no further than the removal of a corrupt monarchy. Then there was the

Radical Party of Alejandro Lerroux whose principal ambition was merely to enjoy the benefits of power. The only real urge for change came from the more left-leaning of the Republicans and the Socialists, whose reforming objectives were ambitious but different. They both hoped to use state power to create a new Spain. However, that required a vast programme of reform which would involve weakening the influence of the Catholic Church and the army, establishing more equitable industrial relations, breaking the near-feudal powers of the owners of the *latifundios*, the great estates, and satisfying the autonomy demands of Basque and Catalan regionalists.

Although political power had passed from the oligarchy to the moderate left, economic power (ownership of the banks, industry and the land) and social power (control of the press, the radio and much of the education system) were unchanged. Even if the coalition had not been hobbled by its less progressive members, this huge programme faced near-insuperable obstacles. The three Socialist ministers realized that the overthrow of capitalism was a distant dream and limited their aspirations to improving the living conditions of the southern landless labourers (*braceros*), the Asturian miners and other sections of the industrial working class. However, in a shrinking economy, bankers, industrialists and landowners saw any attempts at reform in the areas of property, religion or national unity as an aggressive challenge to the existing balance of social and economic power. Moreover, the Catholic Church and the army were equally determined to oppose change. Yet the Socialists felt that they had to meet the expectations of those who had rejoiced at what they thought would be a new world. They also had another enemy – the anarchist movement.

The leadership of the anarchist movement expected little or nothing from the Republic, seeing it as merely another bourgeois state system, little better than the monarchy. At best, their trade union wing wanted to pursue its bitter rivalry with the Union General de Trabajadores, which they saw as a scab union because of its collaboration with the Primo de Rivera regime. They thirsted for revenge for the dictatorship's suppression of the Confederación Nacional del Trabajo throughout the 1920s. The hard-line activist wing of the anarchist movement, the Federación Anarquista Ibérica, aspired to greater liberty with which to propagate its revolutionary objectives. The situation could not have been more explosive. Mass unemployment was swollen by the unskilled construction workers left without work by the collapse of the ambitious public works projects of the dictatorship. The brief honeymoon period came to an end when CNT–FAI demonstrations on 1 May were repressed violently by the forces of order. It was the trigger for an anarchist declaration of war against the Republic and the beginning of a wave of strikes and minor insurrections over the next two years.[36]

Needless to say, anarchist activities against the Republic were eagerly portrayed by the right-wing media, and from church pulpits, as proof that the new regime was itself a fount of godless anarchy.[37] Despite these appalling difficulties, the Federación de Juventudes Socialistas shared the optimism of the Republican–Socialist coalition. When the Republic was proclaimed on 14 April, FJS militants had guarded buildings in Madrid associated with the right, including the royal palace. On 10 May, when churches were burned in response to monarchist agitation, the FJS also tried to protect them.[38] However, as the obstacles to progress mounted, frustration soon set in within the Socialist movement as a whole.

The first priority of the Socialist Ministers of Labour, Francisco Largo Caballero, and of Justice, Fernando de los Ríos, was to ameliorate the appalling situation in rural Spain. Rural unemployment had soared thanks to a drought during the winter of 1930–1 and thousands of emigrants were forced to return to Spain as the world depression affected the richer economies. De los Ríos established legal obstacles to prevent big landlords raising rents and evicting smallholders. Largo Caballero introduced four dramatic measures to protect landless labourers. The first of these was the so-called 'decree of municipal boundaries' which made it illegal for outside labour to be hired while there were local unemployed workers in a given municipality. It neutralized the landowners' most potent weapon, the import of cheap blackleg labour to break strikes and depress wages. He also introduced arbitration committees (*jurados mixtos*) with union representation to adjudicate rural wages and working conditions which had previously been decided at the whim of the owners. Resented even more bitterly by the landlords was the introduction of the eight-hour day. Hitherto, the *braceros* had worked from sun-up to sun-down. Now, in theory at least, the owners would either have to pay overtime or else employ more men to do the same work. A decree of obligatory cultivation prevented the owners sabotaging these measures by taking their land out of operation to impose a lock-out. Although these measures were difficult to implement and were often sidestepped, together with the preparations being set in train for a sweeping law of agrarian reform, they infuriated the landowners, who claimed that the Republic was destroying agriculture.

While the powerful press and radio networks of the right presented the Republic as the fount of mob violence, political instruments were being developed to block the progressive project of the newly elected coalition. First into action were the so-called 'catastrophists' whose objective was to provoke the outright destruction of the new regime by violence. The three principal catastrophist organizations were the monarchist supporters of Alfonso XIII who would be the General Staff and the paymasters of the extreme right; the ultra-reactionary Traditionalist Communion or Carlists (so called in honour of a nineteenth-century pretender to the throne); and lastly a number of minuscule openly fascist groups, which eventually united between 1933 and 1934 under the leadership of the dictator's son, José Antonio Primo de Rivera, as Falange Española. Within hours of the Republic being declared, the 'Alfonsine' monarchists had met to create a journal to propagate the legitimacy of a rising against the Republic particularly within the army and to establish a political party merely as a front for meetings, fund-raising and conspiracy against the Republic. The journal *Acción Española* would peddle the idea that the Republican–Socialist coalition was the puppet of a sinister alliance of Jews, Freemasons and leftists. In the course of one month, its founders had collected substantial funds for a military coup. Their first effort would take place on 10 August 1932 and its failure would lead to a determination to ensure that the next attempt would be better financed and entirely successful.[39]

In contrast, the other principal right-wing response to the Republic was to be legal obstruction of its objectives. Believing that forms of government, republican or monarchical, were 'accidental' as opposed to fundamental and that only the social content of a regime mattered, they were prepared to work within the Republic. The mastermind of these 'accidentalists' was Ángel Herrera, head of the Asociación Católica Nacional de Propagandistas (ACNP), an elite Jesuit-influenced organization of about 500 prominent and talented Catholic rightists with influence in the press, the judiciary and the professions. They controlled the most modern press network in Spain whose flagship daily was *El Debate*. A clever and dynamic member of the ACNP, the lawyer José María Gil Robles, began the process of creating of a mass right-wing party. Initially called Acción Popular, its few elected deputies used every possible device to block reform in the parliament or Cortes. A huge propaganda campaign succeeded in persuading the conservative Catholic smallholding farmers of northern and central Spain that the Republic was a rabble-rousing instrument of Soviet communism determined to steal their lands and submit their wives and daughters to an orgy of obligatory free love. With their votes thereby assured, by 1933 the legalist right would be able to wrest political power back from the left.[40]

The efforts of Gil Robles in the Cortes to block reform and provoke the Socialists was witnessed, on behalf of *El Socialista*, by Santiago Carrillo, who had been promoted from the town-hall beat to the arduous task of the verbatim recording of parliamentary debates. This could be done only by dint of frantic scribbling. The job did, however, bring him into contact with the passionate feminist Margarita Nelken, who wrote the parliamentary commentary for *El Socialista*. Herself a keen follower of Largo Caballero at this time, she would encourage Santiago in his process of radicalization and indeed in his path towards Soviet communism.[41]

In the first months of the Republic, Santiago won his spurs as an orator, speaking at several meetings of the FJS around the province of Madrid. This culminated at a meeting in the temple of the PSOE, the Casa del Pueblo. Opening a bill that included the party president, Julián Besteiro, he was at first tongue-tied. However, he recovered his nerve and made a speech whose confident delivery contrasted with his baby-faced appearance. In it, he betrayed signs of the radicalism that would soon distinguish members of the FJS from their older comrades. He declared that the Socialists should not be held back by their Republican allies and that, in a recent assembly, the FJS had resolved that Spain should dispense with its army. His rise within the FJS was meteoric. He would become deeply frustrated as he closely followed the fate of Largo Caballero's decrees and even liaised with strikers in villages where the legislation was being flouted. At the FJS's Fourth Congress, held in February 1932 when he had just turned seventeen, he was elected minutes secretary of its largely Besteirista executive committee. This was rather puzzling since his adherence to the view of Largo Caballero about the importance of Socialist participation in government set him in opposition to the president of the FJS, José Castro, and its secretary general, Mariano Rojo.

Carrillo's election was probably the result of two things – the fact that he was able to reflect the frustrations of many rank-and-file members and, of course, the known fact of his father's links to Largo Caballero. Not long afterwards, he became editor of the FJS weekly newspaper, *Renovación*, which had considerable autonomy from the executive committee. From its pages he promoted an ever more radical line with a number of like-minded collaborators. The most senior were Carlos Hernández Zancajo, one of the leaders of the transport union, and Amaro del Rosal, president of the bankworkers' union. Among the young ones was a group – Manuel Tagüeña, José Cazorla Maure, José Laín Entralgo, Segundo Serrano Poncela (his closest comrade at this time) and Federico Melchor (later a lifelong friend and collaborator) – all of whom would attain prominence in the Communist Party during the Civil War. Greatly influenced by their superficial and rather romantic understanding of the Russian revolution, they argued strongly for the PSOE to take more power. Their principal targets were Besteiro and his followers, who still advocated that the Socialists abstain from government and leave the bourgeoisie to make its democratic revolution.[42]

Carrillo's intensifying, and at this stage foolhardy, radicalism saw him risk his life during General Sanjurjo's attempted military coup of

10 August 1932. When the news reached Madrid that there was a rising in Seville, Carrillo – according to his memoirs – abandoned his position as the chronicler of the Cortes debates and joined a busload of Republican officers who had decided to go and combat the rebels. In this account of this youthful recklessness, he says that he left his duties spontaneously without seeking permission from the editor. However, El Socialista published a more plausible and less heroic version at the time. The paper reported that he had been sent to Seville as its correspondent and had actually gone there on the train carrying troops sent officially to repress the rising. Whatever the truth of his mission and its method of transport, by the time he reached Seville Sanjurjo and his fellow conspirators had already given up and fled to Portugal. The fact that Carrillo stayed on in Seville collecting material for four articles on the rising that were published in El Socialista suggests that he was there with his editor's blessing.[43]

A close reading of the lucid prose that characterized the articles suggests that the visit to Seville was an important turning point in the process of his radicalization. In the first, he recounted the involvement of an alarming number of the officers in the Seville garrison. In the second, he described the indecision, not to say collusion, of the Republican Civil Governor, Eduardo Valera Valverde. He went on to comment on the role of the local aristocracy in the failed coup. In the third, after some sarcastic comments on the inactivity of the police, he praised the workers of the city. As far as he was concerned, the coup had been defeated because the Communist and anarchist workers who dominated the labour movement in the city had unanimously joined in the general strike called by the minority UGT. In the fourth, he reiterated his conviction that it was the workers who had saved the day, whether they were the strikers in the provincial capital or the landless labourers from surrounding villages who had readied themselves to intercept any column of rebel troops that Sanjurjo might have sent against Madrid.[44]

The entire experience consolidated Carrillo's growing conviction that the gradualism of the Republic, particularly as personified by its ineffectual provincial governors, could never overcome the entrenched social and economic power of the right. His belief that what was needed was an outright social revolution was shared by an increasing number of his comrades in the Socialist Youth but not by its executive committee. Around this time, he undertook a propaganda tour of the provinces of Albacete and Alicante. He later believed that the itinerary chosen for him by the Besteirista executive was a dirty trick designed to cause him considerable discomfort. While some of the villages selected were Socialist-dominated, most were controlled by the CNT. In Elda and Novelda, heavily armed anarchists prevented his meetings going ahead. In Alcoy, he started but the meeting was disrupted and he had to flee by hitchhiking to Alicante. Such experiences were part of the toughening up of a militant.[45]

Yet another stage in the process took place when he was imprisoned after falling foul of the Law for the Defence of the Republic. Ironically, his mentor Largo Caballero had enthusiastically supported the introduction of the law on 22 October 1931 because he perceived it as directed against the CNT. Its application saw Carrillo and Serrano Poncela arrested in January 1933, and then tried for subversion because of inflammatory articles published in *Renovación* during the state of emergency that had been decreed in response to an anarchist insurrection. This was the uprising in the course of which there took place the notorious massacre of Casas Viejas in Cádiz. While Carrillo and Serrano Poncela were in the Cárcel Modelo in Madrid, anarchist prisoners were brought in. They aggressively rebuffed the attempts at communication made by the two young Socialists. Carrillo later regarded that first short stay in prison as a kind of baptism for a nascent revolutionary.[46]

Carrillo might have been in the vanguard of radicalism, but he was not alone. Given that the purpose of his reforms had been humanitarian rather than revolutionary, Largo Caballero was profoundly embittered by the ferocity and efficacy of right-wing obstacles to the implementation of his measures. The hatred of capitalism so powerful in his youth was reignited. Largo Caballero's closest theoretical adviser was Luis Araquistáin, who, as his under-secretary at the Ministry of Labour, had shared his frustration at rightist obstruction. Greatly influenced by Araquistáin, Largo Caballero began to doubt the efficacy of democratic reformism in a period in which economic depression rendered capitalism inflexible. It was inevitably those Socialist leaders who were nearest to the problems of the workers – Largo Caballero himself, Carlos de Baraibar, his Director General of Labour, and Araquistáin – who were eventually to reject reformism as worse than useless. Writing in 1935, Araquistáin commented on the Socialist error of thinking that, just because a law was entered on the statute book, it would be obeyed. He recalled, 'I used to see Largo Caballero in the Ministry of Labour feverishly working day and night in the preparation of far-reaching social laws to dismantle the traditional clientalist networks [caciquismo].' It was useless. While the Minister drafted these new laws, Araquistáin had to deal with 'delegations of workers who came from the rural areas of Castille, Andalusia, Extremadura to report that existing laws were being flouted, that the bosses [caciques] still ruled and the authorities did nothing to stop them.' The consequent fury and frustration inevitably fed into a belief that the Socialists needed more power.[47]

By the autumn of 1932, verbally at least, Largo Caballero was apparently catching up with the radicalism of his young disciple. The scale of his rhetorical radicalization was revealed by his struggle against the moderate wing of the Socialist movement led by Julián Besteiro. At the Thirteenth Congress of the PSOE, which opened on 6 October, Besteiro's abstentionist positions were defeated by the combined efforts of Prieto and Largo Caballero, and Largo Caballero was elected party president.[48] In fact, the Thirteenth PSOE Congress represented the last major Socialist vote of confidence in the efficacy of governmental collaboration. It closed on 13 October. The following day, the Seventeenth Congress of the UGT began. It would be dominated by the block votes of those unions whose bureaucracy was in the hands of Besteiro's followers, the printers (Andrés Saborit), the railway workers (Trifón Gómez) and the landworkers' Federación Nacional de Trabajadores de la Tierra (Lucio Martínez Gil). Accordingly, and despite the growing militancy of the rank and file of those unions, the Seventeenth Congress elected an executive committee with Besteiro as president, and all his senior followers in key positions. Largo Caballero was in fact elected secretary general, but he immediately sent a letter of resignation on the grounds that the congress's vindication of the role of Besteiro and Muiño in the December 1930 strike constituted a criticism of his own stance. He was convinced that the mood of the rank and file demanded a more determined policy.[49]

Largo Caballero's position was influenced by events abroad as well as by those within Spain. He and indeed many others in the party, the union and particularly the youth movement were convinced that the Republic was seriously threatened by fascism. Aware of the failure of German and Italian Socialists to oppose fascism in time, they advocated a seizing of the initiative. Throughout the first half of 1933 the Socialist press had fully registered both its interest in events in Germany and its belief that Gil Robles and his followers intended to follow in the footsteps of Hitler and Mussolini. Largo Caballero received frequent letters from Araquistáin, now Spanish Ambassador in Berlin, describing with horror the rise of Nazism.[50]

In the summer of 1933, Largo Caballero and his advisers came to believe that the Republican–Socialist coalition was impotent to resist the united assault by both industrial and agricultural employers on their social legislation. In consequence, Largo Caballero set about trying to regain his close contact with the rank and file, which had faded somewhat during his tenure of a ministry. The first public revelation of his newly acquired radical views began with a speech, in the Cine Pardiñas in Madrid on 23 July, as part of a fund-raising event for *Renovación*. In fact, the first part of the speech was essentially moderate and primarily concerned with defending ministerial collaboration against the criticisms of Besteiro. However, a hardening of attitude was apparent as he spoke of the increasing aggression of the right. Declaring that fascism was the bourgeoisie's last resort at a time of capitalist crisis, he accepted that the PSOE and the UGT had a duty to prevent the establishment of fascism in Spain. Forgetting that, in the wake of the defeat in 1917, he had resolved never to risk conflict with the apparatus of the state, he now announced that if the defeat of fascism meant seizing power and establishing the dictatorship of the proletariat, then the Socialists, albeit reluctantly, should be prepared to do so. Enthusiastic cheers greeted the more extremist portions of his speech, which confirmed his belief in the validity of his approach towards a revolutionary line. Serrano Poncela and Carrillo and others regarded Largo Caballero as their champion and themselves as the 'pioneers' of his new line. 'The emblematic figure of Largo Caballero' was described, in terms that recalled the sycophancy of the Stalinist Bolshevik Party, as 'the highest representative of a state of consciousness of the masses in the democratic republic, as the life force of a class party'.[51]

With the FJS experiencing a growth in numbers, many of them poorly educated, it was decided in 1932 to hold an annual summer school to train cadres. The sessions were to take place at Torrelodones to the north-west of Madrid. The second school was held in the first half of August 1933 with appearances by the major barons of the PSOE. Besteiro spoke first on 5 August with a speech entitled 'Roads to Socialism'. It was obvious that his aim was to discredit the new extremist line propounded by Largo Caballero in the Cine Pardiñas. Insinuating that it was merely a ploy to gain cheap popularity with the masses, he condemned the idea of a Socialist dictatorship to defeat fascism as 'an absurdity and a vain infantile illusion'. Without naming Largo Caballero, he spoke eloquently about the dangers of a cult of personality – which was precisely what Carrillo and the radical group within the FJS were creating around their champion. This might have been the fruit of genuine wide-eyed admiration on Carrillo's part, but it also served his ambition. Moreover, this approach would later be repeated in his relationship with Dolores Ibárruri, better known as 'Pasionaria'. Besteiro's speech was received with booing and jeers. *El Socialista* refused to publish it. This was a reflection of the fact that the paper was now edited by Julián Zugazagoitia, a follower of Prieto who was sympathetic to the FJS and, for the moment, loyally followed the line of the PSOE's president, Largo Caballero.[52]

The following day, 6 August, Prieto spoke. His language was neither as patronizing nor as confrontational as that of Besteiro, although he too warned against the dangers of easy radicalism. While defending, as Largo Caballero had done, the achievements of the Republic so far, he also spoke of the savage determination of the economic establishment to destroy the Republic's social legislation. Nevertheless, he called upon the 200 young Socialists in his audience who dreamed of a Bolshevik revolution to consider that the weakness of the ruling classes and of the state and military institutions in the war-torn Russia of 1917 was simply not present in the Spain of 1933. He also warned that, even if a Socialist seizure of power were possible, capitalists in other parts of Europe were unlikely to stand idly by. It was a skilful speech, acknowledging that the FJS was morally justified in hankering after a more radical line, but rejecting such radicalism as practical PSOE policy. This was not what the assembled would-be cadres wanted to hear. Prieto was received with less outright hostility than Besteiro but the response was nonetheless cool, and his speech was also ignored by *El Socialista*.[53]

Largo Caballero was not at first scheduled to speak at the summer school. However, Carrillo informed him that the speeches by Besteiro and Prieto had caused great dissatisfaction and invited him to remedy the situation. Largo Caballero accepted readily, convinced that he had a unique rapport with the rank and file. In a somewhat embittered speech, he revealed his dismay at the virulence of rightist attacks on Socialist legislation and suggested that the reforms to which he aspired were impossible within the confines of bourgeois democracy. He claimed to have been radicalized by the intransigence of the bourgeoisie during his twenty-four months in government: 'I now realize that it is impossible to carry out a Socialist project within bourgeois democracy.' Although he affirmed a continuing commitment to legality, he asserted that 'in Spain, a revolutionary situation that is being created both because of the growth of political feeling among the working masses and of the incomprehension of the capitalist class will explode one day. We must be prepared.' Just as it alarmed the right, the speech delighted the young Socialists and shouts could be heard of '¡Viva el Lenin Español!' The coining of the nickname has been attributed variously to the Kremlin, to Araquistáin and to Carrillo.[54]

Less than a month after the summer school, on 11 September, the Republican–Socialist coalition had fallen. Largo Caballero was interviewed by Carrillo for *Renovación*. Among other incendiary statements, he declared that 'we are at the gates of an action that will lead the proletariat to social revolution ... Socialism will have to resort to the maximum violence to displace capitalism ... It is the task of the youth movement to firm up those who are indecisive and to push aside the passive elements who are of no use for the revolution.'[55] A new government was formed by the leader of the corrupt Radical Party, Alejandro Lerroux. Lacking adequate parliamentary support, Lerroux was rapidly obliged to resign. He was replaced at the beginning of October by his deputy, Diego Martínez Barrio, who governed with the Cortes closed. Elections were called for 19 November.

In the run-up to the November 1933 elections, Carrillo's editorial line in *Renovación* increasingly adopted an extremist rhetoric of violence intermingled with frequent quotations from Lenin. Carrillo himself wrote on 7 October that a general strike would not be sufficient for a revolution and that other 'techniques' were required, a veiled reference to his desire to see the workers armed.[56] A voracious reader at this period of his life, he was starting to devour the more accessible works of Marx, Engels and, above all, Lenin, as well as the few works by Stalin that had been translated into Spanish. He read novels and personal accounts of the Russian revolution and was an enthusiast of Soviet cinema. In later life, he would recall his romantic view of what it meant to be an heroic Bolshevik revolutionary.[57]

Embittered by the frustrations of the previous two years, Largo Caballero ensured that the electoral coalition with the Republicans was not renewed and the Socialists went into the elections alone – a fatal tactical error. Intoxicated by the adulation of the FJS and influenced by the distress of the landless labourers, Largo Caballero irresponsibly blamed the Left Republicans for all the deficiencies of the Republic while confidently assuming that all the votes cast in 1931 for the victorious Republican–Socialist coalition would stay with the PSOE. There was little basis for such a belief. To make matters worse, during the campaign he alienated many of the liberal middle-class progressives who had previously voted for the coalition. His refrain that only the dictatorship of the proletariat could carry out the necessary economic disarmament of the bourgeoisie might have delighted his youthful supporters and the rural sectors of the UGT, but it frightened many potential voters.

In the course of the election campaign, the openly fascist Falange Española was launched on Sunday 29 October at the Teatro de la Comedia in Madrid. Recruits were issued with truncheons (*porras*). In his inaugural speech, the leader, José Antonio Primo de Rivera, made much of his commitment to violence: 'if our aims have to be achieved by violence, let us not hold back before violence ... The dialectic is all very well as a first instrument of communication. But the only dialectic admissible when justice or the Fatherland is offended is the dialectic of fists and pistols.'[58]

Since the existing electoral law favoured coalitions, Gil Robles eagerly sought allies across the right-wing spectrum, particularly with the Radical Party. The election results brought bitter disappointment to the Socialists, who won only fifty-eight seats. After local deals designed to exploit the electoral law, the CEDA (Confederación Española de Derechas Autónomas – or Spanish Confederation of Autonomous Right-Wing Groups) won 115 seats and the Radicals 104. The right had regained control of the apparatus of the state and was determined to use it to dismantle the reforms of the previous two years. The President, Niceto Alcalá Zamora, did not invite Gil Robles to form a government despite the fact that the CEDA had most seats in the Cortes although not an overall majority. Alcalá Zamora feared that the Catholic leader harboured more or less fascist ambitions to establish an authoritarian, corporative state. So Alejandro Lerroux, as leader of the second-largest party, became Prime Minister. Dependent on CEDA votes, the Radicals were to be Gil Robles's puppets. In return for dismantling social legislation and pursuing harsh anti-labour policies in the interests of the CEDA's wealthy backers, the Radicals would be permitted to enjoy the spoils of office. Once in government, they set up an office to organize the sale of state favours, monopolies, government procurement orders, licences and so on. The PSOE view was that the Radicals were hardly the appropriate defenders of the basic principles of the Republic against rightist assaults.

Thus the November 1933 elections put power in the hands of a right wing determined to overturn what little reforming legislation had been achieved by the Republican–Socialist coalition. Given that many industrial workers and rural labourers had been driven to desperation by the inadequacy of those reforms, a government set on destroying these reforms could only force them into violence. At the end of 1933, in a country with no welfare safety-net, 12 per cent of Spain's workforce was unemployed, and in the south the figure was nearer 20 per cent. Now employers and landowners celebrated the victory by cutting wages, sacking workers, evicting tenants and raising rents. Even before a new government had taken office, labour legislation was being blatantly ignored.

Outrage across the Socialist movement knew no bounds but nowhere more vehemently than in the FJS. Carrillo's response in *Renovación* took the form of a banner headline 'ALL POWER FOR THE SOCIALISTS'. His editorial came under the sub-heading 'They stole our election victory'. The tactical error of Largo Caballero in rejecting a coalition with the Republicans was a key element in the PSOE's electoral defeat, but that did not prevent Carrillo from laying the blame at the door of the Republicans. He trumpeted the general view within the party that the elections had been fraudulent.[59] In the south, it is certainly true that the Socialists had been swindled out of seats by the power over the starving *braceros* of the local bosses, the *caciques*. In rural areas where hunger, insecurity and unemployment were endemic, it had been easy to get votes by the promise of jobs or the threat of dismissal. Armed thugs employed by the *caciques* frequently prevented Socialist campaigners reaching meetings and disrupted others. They were a threatening presence standing next to the glass voting urns on election day.

In Spain as a whole, the PSOE's 1,627,472 votes had won it 58 seats in the Cortes, while the Radicals' 806,340 votes had been rewarded with 104 seats. The united parties of the right had together got 3,345,504 votes and 212 seats at 15,780 votes per seat, while the disunited left had received 3,375,432 votes and only 99 seats at 34,095 votes per seat.[60] In some southern provinces, such as Badajoz, Córdoba and Málaga, the margin of right-wing victory was small enough for electoral fraud to have swung the result. The bitterness of the Socialist rank and file at losing the elections unfairly was compounded by dismay at the subsequent untrammelled offensive of the employers. Popular outrage was all the greater because of the restraint and self-sacrifice that had characterized Socialist policy between 1931 and 1933. According to Largo Caballero, delegations of workers' representatives from the provinces came to Madrid to beg the PSOE executive committee to organize a counter-offensive. Efforts were made by the Caballerista party executive to reach an agreement with the Besteirista executive of the UGT on action to block any attempt to establish fascism, to restore the monarchy or to establish a dictatorship. At a joint meeting of the PSOE and UGT executives on 25 November, Besteiro, Saborit and Trifón Gómez made it clear that the UGT executive was hostile to any kind of adventurism. A furious Largo Caballero declared that 'the workers themselves were calling for rapid and energetic action'. Even Prieto finally agreed with Largo on the need for 'defensive action'. Eventually, a joint committee of the PSOE and the UGT would be set up to elabo-rate this 'defensive action'.[61]

Needless to say, the FJS was not slow with a radical rhetoric in response to the changed situation. Pushing the logic of Largo Caballero's declarations to their logical extremes, Carrillo declared in that first editorial after the elections: 'the proletariat knows where it stands and has understood that it must take the road of insurrection'. By the following week, the main headline in *Renovación* was 'LONG LIVE SOCIAL REVOLUTION', and Largo Caballero was quoted as saying that a social revolution was necessary to secure all power for the Socialists. Such overt militancy broadcast in *Renovación* and also in *El Socialista* led to a police raid on the Gráfica Socialista printing works and the temporary banning of both papers.[62]

The accentuation of revolutionary rhetoric was a response to the growing wave of militancy and, in Largo Caballero's case, a merely verbal extremism intended to calm rank-and-file desperation. Largo Caballero's vain hope was that his threats could both scare the right into limiting its belligerency and persuade the President of the Republic, Niceto Alcalá Zamora, to call new elections. In Carrillo's case, it was more genuinely revolutionary. The following – and equally provocative – issue of *Renovación* had to be submitted to government censorship, as a result of which it was not permitted to appear and both Carrillo and his closest ally Segundo Serrano Poncela were arrested and imprisoned in the Cárcel Modelo. After a few days, they were tried for subversion but found not guilty by an emergency court. When *Renovación* reappeared, Carrillo's editorial line was slightly more restrained. Under the headline 'Another Fascist Shriek', he responded to a speech made in the Cortes on 19 December in which Gil Robles had laid out the policies that the new Radical government would have to implement in order to stay in power with CEDA votes. His demands revealed the narrow interests defended by the CEDA. They included amnesty for those imprisoned for the military rising of August 1932, a revision of the religious legislation of the Constituent Cortes and a sweeping attack on social reforms. All the decrees that had been most welcomed by the landless peasantry – the law of municipal boundaries, that of obligatory cultivation and the introduction of mixed juries – were to be revised. He also called for a reduction of the area of land subject to expropriation under the agrarian reform bill. Carrillo's editorial ended with a perspicacious comparison of Gil Robles's tactics with those of the authoritarian Austrian Prime Minister Engelbert Dollfuss, a call for an energetic response and a threat that the FJS would not go down without a fight.[63]

On 13 December 1933, the UGT's National Committee discussed the PSOE's calls for action in response to the deteriorating position of the working class in both rural and urban Spain. Against the calls for calm from Saborit and Trifón Gómez, Carrillo's ally Amaro del Rosal, the hot-headed president of the Federation of Bank and Stock Exchange Workers, proposed that the UGT join the PSOE in organizing a revolutionary movement to seize power and establish socialism. He was supported by, among others, Carlos Hernández Zancajo, leader of the transport workers. Del Rosal's proposal was defeated, but further acrimonious debate led to a decision to call an extraordinary congress of the UGT to resolve the bitter divisions between the moderate Besteiristas and the young revolutionary supporters of Largo Caballero.[64] When that meeting took place on 31 December, one after another the leaders of the major federations of the UGT – the mineworkers, the textile workers, the bakery workers, the hotel workers, the metalworkers, the bank workers and the transport work-ers – rose to declare that they supported the line of the PSOE execu-tive and not that of the UGT. They were opposed only by the representatives of the Besteirista strongholds, the printers, the land-workers' Federación Nacional de Trabajadores de la Tierra (FNTT) and the railwaymen. Amaro del Rosal proposed that the UGT join with the PSOE in organizing 'a national revolutionary movement to seize power and establish socialism'. When he and Carlos Hernández Zancajo talked of establishing the dictatorship of the proletariat, the proposal was defeated by twenty-eight votes to seventeen.[65]

As their mouthpiece *Renovación* was in constant difficulties with the authorities, receiving fines and, on some days, the entire print-run being seized, Carrillo understandably saw this as a deliberate attempt to destroy the paper economically. As a result, under the headline 'They are pushing us into clandestinity', he wrote that, as a revolutionary group, the FJS might have to go underground. Indeed, the FJS began tentatively to organize its own militias. Carrillo's efforts in this regard were central to what passed for the creation of Socialist militias prior to the general strike of October 1934 in Madrid. Both through the pages of *Renovación* and via numerous circulars, the FJS issued instructions about the creation of a paramilitary organization.[66]

Not fully perceiving the emptiness of Largo Caballero's rhetoric, Carrillo could legitimately feel that he had full backing for this from the senior party leadership. The PSOE had named a special commis-sion, presided over by Largo Caballero, to examine the practical side of organizing a revolutionary movement and, after another tense meeting on 9 January 1934, the UGT's National Committee had reluctantly agreed to participate. Largo Caballero then insisted that the PSOE's policies be submitted to the UGT's National Committee. This was to meet on 27 January.[67] In the meanwhile, on 13 January, the PSOE executive approved a five-point programme of immediate action, drawn up by Largo Caballero himself. This called for (1) the organization of a frankly revolutionary movement; (2) the declara-tion of such a movement at the right moment, preferably before the enemy could take definitive precautions; (3) contacts to be made between the PSOE and the UGT and any other groups ready to co-operate in the movement; and, in the event of triumph, (4) the PSOE and the UGT, in collaboration with other participants in the revolution, to take political power, and (5) the implementation of a ten-point reform programme drawn up by Prieto.[68]

When the UGT's National Committee met on 27 January to discuss the various projects, against the fierce opposition of Besteiro, the PSOE's revolutionary project was approved by thirty-three members of the committee. Only Trifón Gómez of the Railway Workers' Union and Lucio Martínez Gil of the FNTT voted for the executive, which immediately resigned en masse. Two days later, a new UGT executive was elected, with Largo Caballero as secretary general and including some of the most radical members of the FJS: Ricardo Zabalza of the FNTT, Carlos Hernández Zancajo and Amaro del Rosal. On 30 January, the National Committee of the FNTT had also met to debate the revolutionary proposals. An identical situation had arisen within its ranks. The entire executive, all Besteiristas, resigned, and a new committee of young Caballeristas was elected under Zabalza's presidency. The organizations of the Socialist movement were falling in quick succession to the extremist youth. A meeting of the most influential section within the PSOE, the Agrupación Socialista Madrileña, was packed by young Socialists, who passed a motion of censure against its president, Trifón Gómez, obliging him to resign. He was replaced by supporters of Largo Caballero, with Rafael Henche as president and Julio Álvarez del Vayo as vice-president backed by a group of the most fervent 'bolshevizers', including Hernández Zancajo and Santiago Carrillo.

With Largo Caballero now controlling both the UGT and PSOE executives and the FJS in the hands of his most fervent supporters, a joint committee was immediately established to make preparations for a revolutionary movement. It consisted of Juan Simeón Vidarte, Pascual Tomás and Enrique de Francisco for the Socialist Party, Felipe Pretel, José Díaz-Alor and Carlos Hernández Zancajo for the UGT and Santiago Carrillo for the FJS. Carrillo was thrilled and would take the appointment more seriously than most of the others on the committee. It was a remarkable appointment for someone who had only recently had his nineteenth birthday. With his large glasses and chubby, beardless cheeks, he looked even younger. Operating from UGT headquarters in Madrid, the committee contacted the PSOE, UGT and FJS organizations in each province and issued seventy-three instructions for the creation of militias, the acquisition of arms, the establishment of links with sympathetic local units of the army and the Civil Guard and the organization of squads of technicians able to take over the running of basic services. The response from the provinces was deeply discouraging and there is little evidence, apart from the flurry of communications generated by the committee, that any practical action was taken.[69]

Since all sections of the Socialist movement were outraged at the perceived injustice of the election results and the rapid dismantling of the few social advances made from 1931 to 1933, a resort to revolutionary verbalism was understandable. However, when it came to organizing real confrontation with the apparatus of the state, despite the Caballeristas' sweeping conquest of the leadership positions in the PSOE, the UGT and the FJS, there was considerable trepidation. Most union functionaries and militants remained cautious, and even Largo Caballero and his older trade union supporters were far from comfortable with the bolshevizing policies of Carrillo and the other young radicals. Largo Caballero might call for the dissolution of the army and the Civil Guard and for the arming of the workers.[70] However, for him and for the older trade unionists, revolutionary threats were little more than that: threats that they had neither the inclination nor the expertise to implement. The young bolshevizers, in contrast, felt an intense exhilaration about the ideas expressed in the pages of *Renovación*. They too had little idea of how to implement their rhetoric and were thus united with Largo Caballero only in irresponsibility and incompetence.

The provincial sections barely responded to the hopeful missives of the revolutionary committee. That, together with Largo Caballero's cautious trade union instincts, ensured that, except in the mining districts of Asturias, the activities of the revolutionary committee never went much beyond rhetoric. The committee issued a 'secret' instruction that a revolutionary movement would be launched in the event of the CEDA joining the government. Since it was meant to be a warning to the President of the Republic, Alcalá Zamora was told about it and Gil Robles and other leaders of the right were fully aware of its existence. The lack of secrecy and the lack of any link between the chosen 'revolutionary moment' and any real working-class struggles effectively gave all the cards to the government. On 3 February, the new UGT executive met to decide whether to try to stop all strike action so that the movement could harness its energies for the projected revolution. Revealingly, it was decided, at the urging of Largo Caballero, that UGT members should not be asked to abstain from strike action in defence of their economic interests.[71] Nevertheless, in issue after issue, the FJS gave ever more coverage to the achievements of the Soviet Union while calling for social revolution, armed insurrection and the dictatorship of the proletariat.[72] Such indiscreet, not to say strident, revolutionism provided the perfect excuse throughout the spring and summer of 1934 for the government's uncompromising repression of strikes that were not revolutionary but rather had only limited economic objectives.

Concern about the intentions of the right had intensified with the appointment at the beginning of March of a new Minister of the Interior, the thirty-nine-year-old Rafael Salazar Alonso. Although a member of the Radical Party, he was effectively the representative of the landowners of Badajoz, with whom he had many personal connections.[73] Shortly after taking up his post, Salazar Alonso told the Director General of the Civil Guard that his forces need not be inhibited in their interventions in social conflicts.[74] Gil Robles was delighted with Salazar Alonso who, on 7 March, declared a state of emergency and closed down the headquarters of the FJS, the Communist Party and the anarcho-syndicalist CNT. *Renovación* was banned and did not reappear until early April.

Santiago Carrillo's own ever more vehement advocacy of ultra-revolutionary positions saw him arrested again in February 1934 for a speech made at the small town of Campo de Criptana in the province of Ciudad Real. His offence was to have insulted the President of the Republic, whom he accused of opening the way to fascism by dissolving the Constituent Cortes. During his short stay in the prison of Ciudad Real, Carrillo heard the news of the Austrian Socialist uprising against Dollfuss. It fired his growing enthusiasm for violence as the only valid means to combat fascism. Although the Austrian insurrection was crushed, he would incessantly cite it as an example for Spanish Socialists.[75] At the Fifth Congress of the FJS held in the third week of April 1934, an airy commitment to an armed insurrection was made. A new executive committee was elected with Hernández Zancajo as president and Carrillo as secretary general. Carrillo's closest friends among the bolshevizers – José Laín Entralgo, Federico Melchor, Serrano Poncela, José Cazorla and Aurora Arnaiz, all of whom later joined the Communist Party – were elected on to the committee. There was much talk of armed insurrection and the dictatorship of the proletariat. *Espartaco*, a theoretical journal, was created. Its first issue appeared three months later and contained an attack on the PSOE's parliamentary group (*minoría*). Over the next few months, Prieto and those Socialists who believed in parliamentary action would be denigrated in the belief that they constituted an obstacle to the inevitable revolution.[76]

The extent to which the FJS was moving ahead of its idol Largo Caballero was illustrated by the decision of the new FJS executive, without consultation with the leadership of either the PSOE or the UGT, to call a general strike in Madrid. This was a response to the passage through the Cortes, while the FJS congress was in session, of the CEDA's amnesty law for right-wing attacks on the Republic, which encompassed the plotters responsible for the military coup of August 1932. While the President dithered about signing it into law, the CEDA made a sinister gesture in the form of a large rally of its youth movement, the JAP (Juventud de Acción Popular). It had been planned since January, and *Renovación* had warned that it might culminate in a fascist 'march on Madrid'. The JAP held hundreds of meetings to drum up support and arranged special trains with subsidized tickets. Coinciding with the political crisis over the amnesty, the rally inevitably had the appearance of an attempt to pressurize Alcalá Zamora into signing the law. The choice of Philip II's monastery of El Escorial as venue was an obviously anti-Republican gesture. In order to prevent the rally being the starting point for a 'march on

Madrid', the FJS committee called a general strike. In the event, despite the giant publicity campaign and the large sums spent, torrential rain and the impact of the strike on the transport facilities offered by the organizers ensured that fewer than half of the expected 50,000 actually took part.[77] The real initiative for the strike was probably taken not by Carrillo and the FJS but by the Izquierda Comunista. This Trotskyist group had been founded by Trotsky's one-time friend and collaborator Andreu Nin and was led in Madrid by Manuel Fernández Grandizo, who used the pseudonym Grandizo Munis. Nevertheless, the strike order was actually issued by the FJS.[78]

The Izquierda Comunista was, like the FJS, part of the Alianza Obrera (Workers' Alliance). It was the brainchild of Joaquín Maurín, leader of the quasi-Trotskyist Bloc Obrer i Camperol (Worker and Peasant Bloc), who argued that only a united working class could resist the great advances of the authoritarian right.[79] For Largo Caballero, the Alianza Obrera was just a possible means of dominating the workers' movement in areas where the UGT was relatively weak, less an instrument of rank-and-file working-class unity than a liaison committee dominated by Socialists linking existing organizations.[80] In Madrid, the Socialist leadership effectively imposed its own policy on the Alianza. Throughout the spring and into the early part of the summer of 1934, the Socialist members blocked every revolutionary initiative proposed by the Izquierda Comunista representative, Fernández Grandizo, claiming cynically that the UGT had to avoid partial strike actions and save itself for the ultimate struggle against fascism. The one exception seems to have been the general strike in protest against the JAP rally at El Escorial. Nevertheless, Carrillo was an enthusiast for the Alianza Obrera, since he was deeply committed to the idea of working-class unity.

Leaving aside the anarchists, there were effectively two processes going on within the workers' movement in 1934. On the one hand, there were the young revolutionaries of the Socialist and Communist youth movements and the Alianza Obrera. On the other, there were the traditional trade unionists of the UGT who were trying to protect living standards against the assault of the landowners and industrialists. In a way that was damaging to both, Largo Caballero spanned the two, giving the erroneous impression that entirely economic strikes had revolutionary ends. Repression had intensified since the appointment as Minister of the Interior of Salazar Alonso. Deeming all strikes to be political, he deliberately provoked several throughout the spring and summer of 1934 which enabled him to pick off the most powerful unions one by one, beginning with the printers in March. He seized the flimsiest excuses for heavy-handed action and defeated the printers, construction workers and metalworkers one after the other.

Salazar's greatest victory, which to his great satisfaction pushed the Socialists ever nearer to having to implement their revolutionary threats, took place in June. After much agonized debate, the leaders of the landworkers' union concluded that a general strike was the only way to halt the owners' offensive. Under extreme pressure from a hungry rank and file pushed beyond endurance by the constant provocation of *caciques* and Civil Guard, the FNTT's newly elected general secretary Ricardo Zabalza called for a series of strikes, to be carried through in strict accordance with the law. Although the strike action was economic in motivation, Salazar Alonso seized the chance to strike a blow at the most numerous section of the UGT. His measures were swift and ruthless. He undermined compromise negotiations between the FNTT and the Ministers of Agriculture and Labour by criminalizing the actions of the FNTT with a decree declaring the harvest a national public service and the strike a 'revolutionary conflict'. Several thousand peasants were loaded at gunpoint on to lorries and deported hundreds of miles from their homes and then left without food or money to make their own way back. Much was made by *Renovación* of the arrival in Madrid of hundreds of bedraggled rural workers en route to their homes in the south. Workers' centres were closed down and many town councils were removed, to be replaced by government nominees. Emergency courts sentenced prominent workers' leaders to four or more years of imprisonment. The workers' societies in each village, the Casas del Pueblo, were closed and the FNTT was effectively crippled until 1936.[81]

The FJS was also subjected to various obstacles to its normal functioning. *Renovación* received a crippling fine at the beginning of July. The following week, Salazar Alonso issued a decree prohibiting the use of the clenched-fist salute. Inevitably, this hardened the FJS revolutionary rhetoric and pushed the organization close to the Communist Youth.[82] On 26 July 1934, attracted by the incessant praise for the USSR in the pages of *Renovación*, the leadership of the Communist Youth proposed negotiations with the FJS with a view to a possible unification. Although the invitation was preceded by patronizing remarks which described the FJS as reformist social democrats, the conversations went ahead. The FJS was represented by Carrillo, Melchor, Serrano Poncela and Cazorla; the Unión de Juventudes Comunistas by Trifón Medrano, Segismundo Álvarez and Fernando Claudín (Claudín would later develop into the most sophisticated thinker in the Spanish Communist Party). The talks were dominated by Carrillo, who presented the FJS as the revolutionary vanguard of the Socialist movement while the UJC was merely a very junior offshoot of the tiny Communist Party.

The meetings were tense, if slightly more cordial than might have been expected given the organizations' history of mutual criticism. No concrete plans were made for formal unification. As Carrillo made clear, the FJS was already preparing a revolutionary action and this would take place within the Alianza Obrera. Nevertheless, Carrillo also indicated that he believed that the FJS should be prepared to make compromises in order to hasten the revolution. Thereafter there was ever more united action on the ground. At a local level, militants of both organizations were already acting together, particularly in cooperation against the JAP. They held joint demonstrations such as that which followed the murder by Falangists on 10 June of the young militant Juanita Rico. Their two news-sheets, *Renovación* and *Juventud Roja*, henceforth carried news of each other's activities. Claudín was deeply impressed by the nineteen-year-old Carrillo's remarkable self-confidence, the powerful and lucid way in which he presented his arguments, and his profound knowledge of the Bolshevik revolution. Amaro del Rosal was every bit as impressed with the talent, energy and capacity for work of his young comrade.[83]

Carrillo had also been noticed by others outside the FJS. After the talks with the UJC, Trifón Medrano invited him to meet a representative of KIM – the Communist Youth International – which effectively meant with a Soviet agent. He consulted with his comrades on the FJS executive committee and they agreed that he should go ahead with the encounter. He was excited by the idea of meeting someone whom he imagined to be linked with the assault on the Winter Palace in St Petersburg. Indeed, such was his admiration of the Soviet Union that his office as secretary general of the FJS was dominated by a large portrait of Stalin. Forty years later, he was to tell Fernando Claudín that, in the internal conflict within the PSOE and the UGT, he associated the workers' champion Largo Caballero with Stalin and the intellectual Besteiro with Trotsky. When he got to the park where he was to meet the Russian agent, he was bitterly disappointed to be introduced not to a hardened Bolshevik revolutionary but to 'fat Carmen' ('Carmen la gorda'), the pseudonym of a portly German woman who was a Soviet agent within the Spanish KIM Bureau. This first meeting with a representative of the fortress of world communism went from bad to worse. She accused the FJS of being potential Trotskyists. Then, believing erroneously that they had been followed by the police, she suddenly proposed that they flee from the bar where they were having a cold drink. Jumping on a moving tram, she tripped and collapsed on the platform to the immense hilarity of passers-by.[84]

As the summer wore on, Carrillo continued to push the insurrectionary line in *Renovación*, whose pages, when the entire issue was not seized by the police, carried more and more sections blacked out by the censor.[85] In contrast, Largo Caballero was moving in the opposite direction. The UGT's National Committee met on 31 July to hold an inquest into the failure of the peasant strike. The representative of the schoolteachers' union criticized the UGT executive for its failure to go to the aid of the peasants and virtually accused Largo Caballero of being a reformist. He responded by condemning such rhetoric as frivolous extremism and by declaring that the Socialist movement must abandon its dangerous verbal revolutionism. He had apparently forgotten his own rhetoric of four months previously and the existence of the joint revolutionary committee. When the schoolteachers' leader read out texts by Lenin, Largo Caballero replied that the UGT was not going to act in accordance with Lenin or any other theorist. Reminding his young comrade that Spain in 1934 was not Russia in

1917, he stated rightly that there was no armed proletariat and that the bourgeoisie was strong. It was exactly the opposite of his own recent speeches and of the line being peddled by Carrillo and the young hotheads of the FJS. In fact, Largo Caballero seems to have become increasingly annoyed by their facile extremism, complaining that 'they did just what they felt like without consulting anyone'. Nevertheless, Carrillo was later to write that, as far as he knew at the time, Largo Caballero was forging ahead with detailed revolutionary preparations, for some of which he was using the FJS.[86]

In fact, Largo Caballero's PSOE–UGT–FJS revolutionary liaison committee had not done much beyond compiling a large collection of file-cards with details of potential local revolutionary committees and militias. That filing system was the only place where there existed an infrastructure of revolution. Each UGT, PSOE or FJS section made its own arrangements for creating militias, which usually went no further than drawing up lists of names of those who might be prepared to take to the streets. Whatever Carrillo fondly believed, there was no central coordination. Largo Caballero himself admitted that the majority of local party and union leaders thought that 'the revolution was inevitable but feared it and just hoped that some initiative or incident might see it avoided and so they invested only the minimum effort in its preparation, not wanting to appear to be hostile to it in order to keep the loyalty of their members'. He thus perfectly summed up his own attitude. For the bulk of the Socialist leadership, if not for the bolshevizing youth, there was never any real intention of making a revolution. Largo Caballero was convinced that President Alcalá Zamora would never invite the CEDA to join the government because its leaders had never declared their loyalty to the Republic.[87]

The loud revolutionary rhetoric of the FJS was followed with relish by both Gil Robles and Salazar Alonso. They were aware that the revolutionary committee had linked its threats of revolution specifically to the entry of the CEDA into the cabinet. They also knew – as did Largo Caballero but apparently not Carrillo – that the left was in no position to succeed in a revolutionary attempt. Thorough police activity throughout the spring and summer of 1934 had undermined most of the uncoordinated preparations made by the revolutionary committee. Most of the few weapons acquired by the left had been seized. Gil Robles admitted later that he was anxious to enter the government because of, rather than in spite of, the violent reaction that could be expected from the Socialists: 'Sooner or later, we would have to face a revolutionary coup. It would always be preferable to face it from a position of power before the enemy were better prepared.'[88] Speaking in the Acción Popular offices in December, he recalled complacently:

> I was sure that our arrival in the government would immediately provoke a revolutionary movement ... and when I considered that blood which was going to be shed, I asked myself this question: 'I can give Spain three months of apparent tranquillity if I do not enter the government. If we enter, will the revolution break out? Better let that happen before it is well prepared, before it can defeat us.' This is what Acción Popular did: precipitated the movement, confronted it and implacably smashed the revolution within the power of the government.[89]

In similar terms, Salazar Alonso wrote: 'The problem was simply to begin a counter-revolutionary offensive to establish a government determined to put an end to the evil.' It was not just a question of smashing the immediate revolutionary bid but of making sure that the left did not raise its head again.[90]

The moment of truth was coming nearer, but the reality would be very different from the Leninist dreams of armed insurrection nurtured by Carrillo and the other young bolshevizers. They had little or no idea of how to convert their threats into action. Largo Caballero and his hardened trade union followers were now using revolutionary phrases less frequently and with decreasing conviction. Their outrage in the wake of the November 1933 elections had given way to alarm at the way in which Salazar Alonso had managed to decimate the organized labour movement during the strikes of the spring and early summer of 1934. Throughout September, there were numerous minor strikes and waves of police activity. On 8 September, in response to a twenty-four-hour strike in Madrid, Salazar Alonso had ordered the Casa del Pueblo to be closed. It was searched, to no avail, by the police. When it was reopened six days later, the police went in again and allegedly found a substantial cache of bombs and firearms. This unlikely discovery was the excuse needed for the Socialist headquarters to be closed again.

The next day, 14 September, there took place an event which symbolized the naive hopes of the bolshevizers. Eighty thousand people attended a spectacular joint rally of the FJS and the Communist Youth at the Madrid Metropolitan Stadium. It was in response to a decree by Salazar Alonso, prohibiting those under the age of twenty-one from joining political organizations without written permission from their parents. Although there were speeches by members of the PSOE and the Communist Party, the main speakers were Carrillo for the FJS and Trifón Medrano for the UJC. All spoke of the imminent seizure of power. Greeted by a sea of raised fists, Carrillo declared that 'if this government at the service of the right does not withdraw the decree, these youth movements will assault the citadels of power and establish a class dictatorship'. He spoke of the identification of the FJS with 'the chief of the Spanish revolution', an obvious reference to Largo Caballero. Intoxicated by the moment, he closed his intervention with cries of 'Death to the Government! Death to the Bourgeoisie! Long live the Revolution! Long Live the Dictatorship of the Proletariat!' The event ended with the militants marching out 'military style' while waving a profusion of red flags. *El Socialista* rather ingenuously described the event as 'a show of strength by the proletariat of Madrid'.[91]

The crunch came on 26 September, when the CEDA sparked off the crisis by announcing that it could no longer support a minority government. The only solution was either the calling of new elections or the entry into the government of the CEDA. Lerroux's new cabinet, announced in the early hours of the morning of 4 October, included three CEDA ministers. The arrival in power of the CEDA had been denominated the first step towards the imposition of fascism in Spain. It was the moment for the much threatened revolutionary insurrection. In the event, the efficacy of the threatened revolution was to be in inverse proportion to the scale of the bolshevizers' bombast. Much of the Socialist movement was paralysed with doubt. The executives of the PSOE and the UGT met and agreed that, if indeed the President did what they were sure he would not do – invite the CEDA to join the government – then the revolution must be launched. Coded telegrams – with messages like 'I arrive tomorrow', 'Angela is better', 'Pepe's operation went well' – were sent to local committees in every province.

However, having hoped that threats of revolution would suffice to make Alcalá Zamora call new elections, Largo Caballero simply could not believe that he had failed. The revolutionary committee thus did nothing about making the final preparations for the threatened seizure of power. Instead, they spent the next three days in Prieto's apartment 'anxiously awaiting' news of the composition of the cabinet. Largo still believed that Alcalá Zamora would never hand over power to the CEDA. Similarly, the FJS's revolutionary militias were also lacking leadership and organization. At 11 p.m. on 3 October, two Socialist journalists, Carlos de Baraibar and José María Aguirre, arrived with the unofficial news that a government had been formed with CEDA participation. Several members of the revolutionary committee declared that the time had come to start the movement. Largo, however, stated flatly that 'until I see it in the *Gaceta*, I won't believe it'. He was finally convinced only by the arrival of some soldiers who brought news that the new cabinet had declared martial law. Even then, it was with reluctance that the Socialists prepared for action. They felt that they had no choice. 'The die was cast,' wrote Largo.[92]

Now the extent of his revolutionary intentions was revealed when the UGT gave the government twenty-four hours' notice of a pacific general strike. He hoped that the President would change his mind, but he succeeded merely in giving the police time to arrest working-class leaders. In most parts of Spain, the strike was a failure largely because of the prompt action of the government in declaring martial law and bringing in the army to run essential services.

The entry of the CEDA into the cabinet revealed the emptiness of the revolutionary bombast of the previous months. It was followed by the creation of an independent Catalan Republic, though it lasted only for ten hours; a desultory general strike in Madrid; and the establishment of a workers' commune in Asturias. With the exception of the Asturian revolt, which held out against the armed forces during two weeks of fierce fighting and owed its 'success' to the mountainous terrain and the special skills of the miners, the keynote of the Spanish October was its half-heartedness. There is nothing about the events of that month, even those in Asturias, to suggest that the left had thoroughly prepared a rising. Indeed, the scale of failure was in direct proportion to the scale of the optimistic rhetoric that had preceded it. In fact, throughout the crisis, Socialist leaders were to be found restraining the revolutionary zeal of their followers.[93] Accordingly, the new government was able with considerable ease to arrest workers' leaders and detain suspect members of the police and the army. Without instructions to the contrary, Socialist and anarchist trade unionists in Madrid simply stayed away from work rather than mounting any show of force in the streets. The army took over basic services – conscripts were classified according to their peacetime occupations – and bakeries, right-wing newspapers and public transport were able to function with near normality. Those Socialist leaders who managed to avoid arrest either went into hiding, as did Largo Caballero, or into exile, as did Prieto. Their followers were left standing on street corners awaiting instructions, and within a week the strike had petered out. All the talk of a seizure of power by revolutionary militias came to nothing. Hopes of collaboration by sympathizers in the army did not materialize and the few militants with arms quickly abandoned them. In the capital, some scattered sniper fire and many arrests was the sum total of the revolutionary war unleashed.[94]

Carrillo was arrested late at night on 7 October. He and several other prominent members of the UGT and the FJS were hiding in the Madrid studio belonging to the artist Luis Quintanilla, who was a friend of most of the PSOE top brass. According to Quintanilla, while awaiting the instructions that never came they had idled away the day by making and consuming an enormous paella. According to Carrillo, they had merely shared a French omelette. Quintanilla went to bed around 10.00 p.m. but was awakened shortly afterwards by the arrival of the police. They had been betrayed because Carrillo and other FJS comrades had gone out to enjoy the warm October evening on the studio's wide terrace. Quintanilla had warned them not to do so because he had a neighbour whom he described as 'a witch who spent all day snooping'. They sat heatedly discussing the bad news that they were hearing, whether it was about the failure to materialize of the promised military participation or the arrest of sections of the FJS. As expected, the neighbour overheard them and reported them to the police. The officers who arrived were extremely nervous and pointed rifles at the would-be revolutionaries as they were handcuffed and led away. Each one was put in a car with two policemen, one of whom kept a revolver pressed against their side. After a cursory interrogation, Carrillo was transferred the next morning to the Cárcel Modelo and locked in a malodorous cell.[95] His dreams of revolutionary glory were shattered. Over the next seventeen months in prison, his reflections on the reasons for that failure would profoundly change the direction of his political life.

2

The Destruction of the PSOE: 1934–1939

The performance of the revolutionary committee and the Socialist Youth in Madrid can best be described as pathetic. Once it was clear that revolutionary threats had not diverted Alcalá Zamora from bringing the CEDA into the cabinet, the Socialist leaders went to ground. No arms were distributed and the masses were left without instructions. No serious plans for a rising had been made. The only militia group with arms, led by Manuel Tagüeña of the FJS, clashed with Assault Guards in the La Guindalera district of Madrid. After a skirmish, they were quickly disarmed and arrested.[1] Amaro del Rosal, one of Carrillo's more extremist comrades on the revolutionary committee, denied participation. In a sense, he was telling the truth. When Manuel Fernández Grandizo of the Izquierda Comunista met Del Rosal in a Madrid street on 5 October, he asked him what the revolutionary committee planned. Del Rosal allegedly replied, 'if the masses want arms, they had better go and look for them, then do what they like'. In his own account, he complained that the crisis had come too soon, that the CNT had failed to collaborate and that the authorities had blocked any military assistance by confining troops to their barracks.[2]

The October issues of *Renovación* were confiscated by the police and the paper was shut down until 1936. After the failure of the 'revolution', Amaro del Rosal escaped to Portugal but was repatriated by Salazar's police. Carrillo was imprisoned in the Cárcel Modelo in Madrid along with his father and most of the leadership of the revolutionary committee, including Largo Caballero. The editor of *El Socialista*, Julián Zugazagoitia, was also imprisoned and the entire Socialist press was silenced. The clandestine life of the movement was, in fact, directed from the prison.[3] Tens of thousands of workers were imprisoned. Many more lost their jobs. In Asturias, torture was used in interrogations, and military courts passed out many death sentences against miners' leaders. All over Spain, Socialist local councils (*ayuntamientos*) were replaced by government nominees. The Casas del Pueblo were closed and the unions were unable to function.[4]

Many Socialist trade unionists, including the Asturian miners' leaders, believed that the lesson of October and the subsequent repression was the same as that of the events of 1917. The movement would always lose in direct confrontation with the apparatus of the state. The members of the revolutionary committee, however, did not view the 1934 events as a defeat. Whether this was merely self-deception or a cynical ploy to cover their own ineptitude is not clear. Carrillo in particular, showing a capacity for unrealistic optimism that would characterize his entire political life, was convinced that the overall balance had been positive. His logic was that Gil Robles had been shown that the peaceful establishment of fascism would not be permitted by the working class. The brief success of the Alianza Obrera in Asturias profoundly strengthened his conviction that eventual revolution required a united working class. This view briefly brought him closer to the Trotskyists and inevitably fed the suspicions of 'fat Carmen', the KIM representative who was watching him closely. The Spanish Communist Party, the Partido Comunista de España, was also calling for proletarian unity. Hitherto, as part of its 'class against class' line, it had denounced Socialists as 'social fascists' because, so the logic went, reformism perpetuated bourgeois society. In the aftermath of the triumph of Nazism which had been facilitated by the reformism of the German Socialists, the line was softened and the PCE had entered the Alianza Obrera. Now the PCE sought to derive – largely undeserved – credit for Asturias and, with it, ownership of the most powerful symbol of working-class unity. The Communist fabrication of its own revolutionary legend would increase its attractiveness to the FJS.[5]

After his arrest on 14 October, Largo Caballero assured the military judge investigating his case that he had taken no part in the organization of the rising. Later, on 7 November, he told the Cortes committee that had to decide whether his parliamentary immunity could be waived for him to be prosecuted: 'I was in my house ... and I issued an instruction that anyone who came looking for me should be told that I was not there. I gave that order, as I had done in the past, because I was playing no part in what was going on, I was having nothing to do with anything that might happen; I did not want to have any contact with anyone, with anyone at all.'[6] The scale of the repression provided some justification. Araquistáin later claimed that 'only a madman or an agent provocateur' would have admitted participation in the preparation of the rising because such an admission of guilt would have been used by the CEDA to justify carrying through its determination to smash both the PSOE and the UGT.[7]

Nevertheless, what Largo Caballero said in his defence was completely plausible in the light of the total failure of the movement in Madrid. Shortly before he was arrested, Carrillo had asked him, 'What shall I tell the militias?' To the young revolutionary's surprise, Largo Caballero had replied, 'Tell them anything you like,' adding, 'If you get arrested, say that this was spontaneous and not organized by the party.'[8] However, Largo Caballero's memoirs suggest that he continued to see himself as a revolutionary leader who had merely set out to deceive the bourgeois authorities. Initially, Carrillo was deeply disappointed both by Largo Caballero's passivity in October and by public denials being made by the man now hailed as 'the Spanish Lenin'. However, in their frequent conversations walking around the exercise yard, he was flattered by the apparent pleasure with which Largo listened to his harangues about the need to bolshevize the PSOE. That and his own optimism reconciled him to his hero. At this stage, they were still extremely close. Harking back to the warm relations between the two families, Largo Caballero called him 'Santiaguito' and other prisoners referred to him as 'the boss's spoiled child'.[9] Certainly, Largo Caballero's denials played directly into the hands of the Communists, who were only too glad to assume the responsibility. The secretary general of the Spanish Communist Party, José Díaz Ramos, visited him in prison and suggested that the PCE and the PSOE jointly claim to have organized the revolution. Largo

Caballero refused. His denial of any responsibility was a potentially counter-productive tactic. It gave credibility to Communist claims that the October events showed that the PSOE and Largo Caballero were incapable of making a revolution. It ensured that 1935 was the period of 'the great harvest' for the Communists.[10] Santiago Carrillo was to be an important part of that harvest, yet at the time he seems to have taken Largo Caballero's excuses at face value.

Carrillo and the other prisoners lived in a kind of euphoric isolation, able to discuss politics all day without the preoccupations of daily life. Carrillo's main concern was the health of his mother, who had serious heart problems, and he missed his girlfriend, Asunción 'Chon' Sánchez Tudela, a beautiful nineteen-year-old Asturian brunette whom he had met earlier in the year. Otherwise, he and the other political prisoners enjoyed relatively pleasant conditions. Carrillo had a typewriter and plenty of books in his cell. He claimed later to have spent most of his time reading the classics of Marxism until the early hours of every morning. He was particularly impressed by Trotsky. Indeed, he later described this period as his 'university'. The warders put no obstacles in the way of the sending and receiving of correspondence or the virtually unlimited visits from comrades who brought them the legal press. To his surprise, the normally dour Largo Caballero was very good humoured.[11]

It was not long before Carrillo and the other imprisoned revolutionaries were blaming the less radical sections of the Socialist movement for the defeat of October. From that it was a short step to trying to hound the reformists out in order to build a 'proper' Bolshevik party. Initially, they were not concerned about the Besteiristas since they had already been defeated within the UGT and many affiliated trade union federations in early 1934. Besteiro had opposed the revolutionary project and had stood aside in October. Nevertheless, during the October events, a group of extremists from the FJS had stoned Besteiro's home. In consequence, he virtually withdrew from the political stage for a time.[12] However, renewed calls for his expulsion from the PSOE finally provoked his followers to take up his defence against the youthful bolshevizers. That was not to be until June 1935. In the meantime, Carrillo and his allies concentrated their fire on Indalecio Prieto. The irony of that was that it had been Prieto's followers in Asturias who had taken the most active part in the events of October.

Egged on by Carrillo, Largo Caballero began to take up ever more revolutionary positions. In part, this reflected his acute personal resentment of Prieto, who with backing from the Asturian miners and the Basque metalworkers hoped to rebuild the democratic Republic of 1931–3. In the view of both Prieto and the Republican leader and ex-Prime Minister Manuel Azaña, the vindictive policies of the Radical–CEDA coalition were provoking a great national resurgence of support for the Republic. Accordingly, Prieto argued that the immediate goal for the left had to be the recapture of state power by a broad coalition that could ensure electoral success and thus bring working-class suffering to an end. In contrast, Carrillo and Largo Caballero believed that the repressive policies of the Radical–CEDA cabinet had dramatically undermined all working-class faith in the reforming possibilities of the Republic.[13]

In early 1935, those members of the PSOE executive committee not in prison were highly receptive to the arguments sent out by Prieto from his exile in Belgium in favour of a broad coalition with the Left Republicans. Their views were publicized within the Socialist movement in April by means of a circular which made an intelligent plea for the use of legal possibilities to defend the working class.[14] The imprisoned Largo Caballero was informed about this initiative but did not object. Nevertheless, it infuriated Carrillo and the bolshevizers who advocated an exclusively proletarian revolutionary bloc. Prieto, thinking in terms only of a legal road to power, knew that not to ally with the Republicans would result in a disastrous three-sided contest as had happened in the elections of 1933. He was determined not to let the party fall into the hands of the extremist youth who, he believed, had to be obliged to accept party discipline.[15]

Prieto could count on support from the Asturian miners' leader Ramón González Peña, who was widely considered to be the hero of October and had recently escaped a death sentence. In a letter to Prieto, González Peña called for a broad anti-fascist front for the next elections. He bitterly criticized Largo Caballero and his imprisoned comrades for denying participation in the events of October. His greatest outrage was reserved for 'the kids of the FJS' for their demands that the PSOE be bolshevized, that Besteiro and his followers be expelled and that Prieto and the 'centrists' be marginalized: 'It would be an enormous shame if we were to suffer the misfortune of being led by the son of [Wenceslao] Carrillo and company.' Copies of the letter, along with a similar letter from young Asturian members of the FJS imprisoned in Oviedo, were circulated throughout the Socialist Party, much to the annoyance of the imprisoned Caballeristas. Carrillo and others had sent González Peña a set of questions with the intention of getting his support for their plans. When they saw his answers in favour of electoral coalition and against the purging of the party, they refused to publish them.[16] To their chagrin, Prieto had at his disposal his own newspaper, El Liberal de Bilbao, within whose pages he and Republicans could advocate an electoral alliance.[17]

The fact that the reformist policies of the Republican–Socialist coalition had provoked the fury of the right convinced Carrillo that Spain's structural problems required a revolutionary solution. However, Prieto was correct that most of the Socialists' problems derived from Largo Caballero's tactical error before the elections of 1933. Out of government, no change, reformist or revolutionary, could be introduced. October had exposed the Socialists' inability to organize a revolution. Thus two valid positions were possible: Prieto's advocacy of the electoral return to power and the gradualist road to socialism; and the one principally advocated by the Trotskyists, which recognized the revolutionary incompetence of both the PSOE and the PCE and aimed at the long-term construction of a genuine Bolshevik party. This was a position that Carrillo found attractive. However, both these strategies required a prior electoral victory.[18]

The radical youth's counter-attack against Prieto took the form of a long pamphlet, signed by the FJS president, Carlos Hernández Zancajo, entitled Octubre: segunda etapa. In fact, it had been written largely by Amaro del Rosal and Santiago Carrillo.[19] The purpose was threefold: to cover up the FJS's failures in the October events in Madrid, to combat Prieto's interpretation of the Asturian rising as an attempt to defend the Republic, and to eradicate the influence of both

Besteiro and Prieto from the Socialist movement as a first step to its bolshevization. The pamphlet began with a largely mendacious interpretation of the activities of the workers' movement during 1934. Its authors pointed out correctly that the strikes of the construction workers, metalworkers and peasants had dissipated working-class energies while failing to mention that the 'union organization' blamed for these tactical errors was actually dominated at the time by members of the FJS. They blamed the defeat of October on Besteiro's reformists, which was absurd. This was used to justify the 'second stage' announced in the pamphlet's title, the expulsion of the reformists and the bolshevization of the PSOE, which signified the adoption of a rigidly centralized command structure and the creation of an illegal apparatus to prepare for an armed insurrection. Inhibited by Asturian backing for Prieto, the authors did not dare call for his expulsion but aggressively demanded the abandonment of his 'centrist' line in favour of their revolutionary one.[20]

Prieto and others were convinced that the pamphlet had been concocted during the authors' walks around the prison patio or courtyard with Largo Caballero. Years later, despite being the subject of rapturous praise in the pamphlet, Largo Caballero claimed that it had been published without his permission and that, deeply annoyed, he had protested to Carrillo. Carrillo himself was to admit later that his group had acted without the boss's authorization. Later still, he categorized the view expressed in the pamphlet as puerile, deriving from 'infantile leftism'.[21] In an interview published in December 1935, however, Largo Caballero agreed with much of the pamphlet, albeit not with its demand for expulsions and for entry into the Comintern.[22]

In response to the insulting attacks of the FJS pamphlet, the Besteiristas were emerging from their silence.[23] They founded a publication to defend their ideas. Called *Democracia*, it appeared weekly from 15 June to 13 December. Its lawful appearance was taken by Carrillo's crony Segundo Serrano Poncela as proof of the Besteirista treachery to the Socialist cause.[24] This point of view was given some credibility by Besteiro's inaugural lecture, 'Marxism and Anti-Marxism', on being elected to the Academy of Political and Moral Sciences. In this long and tortuous lecture, given on 28 April 1935,

Besteiro set out to prove that Marx had been hostile to the notion of the dictatorship of the proletariat. He infuriated the imprisoned bolshevizers with his insinuations that the violence of the Socialist left was hardly distinguishable from fascism.[25] A devastating reply to Besteiro's lecture by Largo's most competent adviser, Luis Araquistáin, appeared in the doctrinal journal *Leviatán*, which had survived the repression of the Socialist media. Araquistáin's articles were of a notably higher level of theoretical competence than *Octubre: segunda etapa* and their demolition of the inaugural lecture ensured Besteiro's withdrawal from the PSOE leadership stakes.[26]

With Besteiro eliminated, in late May Prieto returned to the fray with a series of highly influential articles. Collectively entitled *Posiciones socialistas*, they were published shortly afterwards as a book. The first two restated the need to avoid the great tactical error of 1933, arguing that the right would be united at the next elections and an exclusively workers' coalition would be the victim of anarchist indiscipline. For Prieto, only a Republican–Socialist coalition could guarantee an amnesty for political prisoners. The last three articles set out, in mild yet firm language, to expose some of the more absurd contradictions of *Octubre: segunda etapa*. Prieto indignantly dismissed the right of untried youngsters to call for the expulsion of militants who had dedicated their lives to the PSOE and pointed out that the accusations made against various sections of the Socialist movement by the pamphlet were most applicable to the FJS itself. Above all, he denounced the bolshevizers' dictatorial tendencies and proposed a party congress to settle the direction that the movement was to take.[27]

With Carrillo's name on the cover, *Octubre* was reissued with a reply to Prieto. Largo Caballero's friend Enrique de Francisco wrote to Prieto to say that he had no right to make party policy in bourgeois newspapers. Prieto replied that the same moralistic view had not inhibited the Socialist Youth from advocating bolshevization. More stridently, the journalist Carlos de Baraibar, in consultation with Largo Caballero, prepared a book attacking the 'false socialist positions' of Prieto. In criticizing him for breaking party discipline by publicizing his ideas, Baraibar conveniently forgot that the FJS had not hesitated to broadcast its controversial views.[28] The extremism of the FJS was seriously dividing Spanish socialism. While the repressive policies of the CEDA–Radical government and the existence of thousands of political prisoners made revolutionary propaganda attractive, they also ensured a sympathetic mass response to Prieto's call for unity and a return to the progressive Republic of 1931–3. An indication of the bitterness being engendered was shown in the summer of 1935 when the Caballeristas produced a legal weekly newspaper called *Claridad*. Its pages loudly backed the FJS call for the expulsion of the Besteiristas and the marginalization of the Prietistas.[29] *Democracia* responded by arguing that the bolshevization campaign was just a smokescreen to divert attention from the FJS's failures in October 1934. When Saborit made the gracious gesture of visiting the prisoners in the Cárcel Modelo, Largo Caballero rudely refused to shake his hand or even speak to him.[30]

Everything changed after the Seventh Congress of the Comintern was held in Moscow in August 1935. The secretary general, Giorgi Dimitrov, launched a call for proletarian unity and a broad popular front of all anti-fascist forces. Already, in a speech on 2 June, the PCE secretary general, José Díaz, had openly called for union with the PSOE. On 3 November, he declared that the Seventh Congress showed the need for a Popular Front.[31] Carrillo was delighted. In prison, he and Hernández Zancajo lived in close proximity to their comrades from the UJC, Trifón Medrano and Jesús Rozado. They were aware that in October 1934 there had been some collaboration on the ground between the rank-and-file militants of their respective organizations. Now their daily encounters and discussions favoured the eventual unification of their organizations.[32]

The FJS delegate at the Comintern congress, José Laín Entralgo, reported back enthusiastically that the Communist union, the Confederación General de Trabajo Unitaria (CGTU), would amalgamate with the UGT. He also claimed that the switch of tactics meant that Moscow had returned sovereignty to the various national parties and that there was therefore no longer any reason why the FJS should not join the Comintern.[33] Carrillo was already trying to secure the incorporation of the Trotskyist Bloc Obrer i Camperol and the

Communist Youth into the PSOE as part of the process of bolsheviz-ing the party. Writing in *Leviatán*, Araquistáin rightly suggested that Moscow's fundamental objective with the Popular Front tactic was to ensure that liberal and left-wing anti-fascist governments would be in power in the West to ensure favourable alliances should Germany declare war on the USSR. Far from breaking with the old Comintern habit of dictating the same policy for each country, as the FJS fondly thought, the new tactic confirmed the dictatorial customs of the Third International. Araquistáin accepted the need for proletarian unity but rejected the notion of alliance with the bourgeois left.[34]

Largo Caballero was keen on working-class unity as long as it meant the absorption of the Communist working-class rank and file into the UGT. However, he remained hostile to an electoral coalition with the Left Republicans and, like Araquistáin, he opposed the idea of the PSOE joining the Comintern.[35] For this reason, Carrillo had to be circumspect in all the negotiations with the imprisoned UJC members and crucially with the most senior Comintern representa-tive in Spain, the Argentinian Vittorio Codovila, codenamed 'Medina'. The director of the Cárcel Modelo turned a blind eye as Codovila was smuggled into the prison as part of a family party visiting Carrillo. Codovila was surprised by Carrillo's readiness to accept all of the conditions requested by the Communists. All he wanted in return was for the name of the new organization to be the Juventudes Socialistas Unificadas. His reasoning was that if the FJS lost the word 'Socialista' from its title, it would lose its seat on the PSOE executive and be less able to continue the struggle to purge Prieto and bolshe-vize the party.[36]

On the first anniversary of the October insurrection, the FJS had issued a circular signed by Santiago Carrillo authorizing its local sections to draft joint manifestos with the UJC but not to organize joint commemorations since the PSOE had decreed that the FJS could hold joint events only with other Socialist organizations. The circular noted regretfully that the PSOE had in fact made no arrange-ments to celebrate the anniversary. However, it recommended that local FJS sections organize their own publicity for the anniversary and to do so stressing that 'October had been a proletarian movement to conquer power', that the Socialist Party had been its only leader (something that the PSOE leadership never acknowledged) and that October had halted 'the rise of fascism'.[37]

In mid-November, Carrillo received a letter from the left-wing Socialist and feminist Margarita Nelken, who was exiled in Russia. She enclosed some Soviet pamphlets including a Spanish translation of Dimitrov's speech to the Seventh Congress of the Comintern. He thought the speech 'magnificent', although he still had doubts about the Comintern leader's readiness to make an alliance with the bourgeoisie without first securing the broad unity of the working class. In the package was a copy of a photograph of Largo Caballero that had been distributed among the crowd during an event in Moscow's Red Square. When Carrillo showed him the photo, Largo Caballero was suitably flattered. Carrillo reported back that 'the boss is in magnificent form, without any hesitation going further every day in the same direction as the Juventudes'.[38]

Meanwhile, on 14 November, Manuel Azaña, writing on behalf of the various Left Republican groups, formally proposed an electoral alliance to the PSOE executive. Faced with a dramatic choice, Largo Caballero quickly convoked a joint session of the PSOE, UGT and FJS executives for 16 November. Azaña's proposal was accepted after Largo Caballero had acknowledged the absurdity of repeating the error of 1933. Carrillo and Amaro del Rosal followed the Comintern line and also spoke strongly in favour of the electoral alliance. Carlos Hernández Zancajo, however, opposed it. He thereby anticipated divisions inside Caballerista ranks that would seriously damage the Socialist movement during the Civil War, between those unswervingly committed to the Soviet Union and those, like Hernández Zancajo, for whom revolutionary politics were not understood as synonymous with Soviet interests. Determined that dealings with the bourgeois Republicans should not strengthen the Prietista wing of the Socialist movement, Largo Caballero insisted that any coalition should extend to other working-class organizations including the Communist Party. Carrillo was delighted. The UGT executive decided to open negotiations with the PCE for the incorporation of the Communist CGTU into the UGT. Moreover, Largo Caballero insisted

that the Popular Front electoral programme should be approved by
the PCE and the CGTU as well as by the FJS, the PSOE and the
UGT.[39] In contrast, Prieto feared that the disproportionate weight to
be given to the Communist Party would damage the interests of the
PSOE. He was also opposed to the idea that the programme required
FJS approval since he was adamant that to consider it as an autonomous organization was entirely contrary to the PSOE's statutes.[40]

Two weeks later, Carrillo published a typically triumphalist article
that crowed over the defeat of reformist elements in the Socialist
movement. He stated that the changes of strategy effected by the
Comintern placed the FJS on 'a similar political plane to the
Communists'. His statement that 'prior negotiations' were moving
ahead made it clear that the FJS was drawing ever nearer to the UJC.
He dismissed as groundless any suspicion that unification would
effectively mean a take-over of the Socialist Youth by the Communists.
He argued that, if there was unity of purpose of the revolutionary
elements on both sides, only the reformists could have any grounds
for concern. He ended with the resounding declaration that 'the knots
that tie us to the affiliates of the Moscow International will end up
untying those that still link us to certain "socialists".[41]

He crowed too soon. On 16 December, there was a meeting of the
PSOE National Committee, at which Largo Caballero reiterated his
view that any electoral coalition should be dominated by the workers'
organizations. Before a full-scale discussion could take place, Prieto
criticized the activities of Carrillo and the FJS leadership. More
importantly, he raised a procedural issue about the relationship of the
parliamentary group to the PSOE executive. In immensely complicated circumstances, Largo Caballero resigned as president of the
PSOE. After Largo Caballero had stormed out of the meeting, Prieto
was able successfully to propound his moderate vision of the
Republican–Socialist electoral coalition. The Caballerista desire that
negotiations with the Republicans be carried out by a workers' bloc
including the FJS, the PCE and the CGTU was stymied. The resig-
nations of Largo Caballero and three of his closest lieutenants,
Enrique de Francisco, Wenceslao Carrillo and Pascual Tomás, meant
that there would have to be a party congress in the spring to elect a

new National Committee. This was clearly conceived as the first step to clearing out the centrists from the party and securing the bolshevizing objective of a centralized party hierarchy. However, it was a gamble that, in immediate terms, broke the control of both the party and the union established by the Caballeristas after the defeat of Besteiro in January 1934. Now the movement was divided, with the UGT in the hands of the Caballeristas and the PSOE in the hands of the Prietistas. In his formal letter of resignation, Largo Caballero revealed his motives. It was a step to securing a unanimous executive, as the 'homogeneous organ of an iron leadership': 'We have resolved to keep on the October road.' The gamble failed because, for a variety of complex reasons related to the tense political situation, that congress never materialized.[42]

This development in the higher echelons of the Socialist movement may have pushed an impatient Carrillo nearer to thinking that his revolutionary ambitions would be better fulfilled within the Communist Party. In the meantime, at the end of December 1935, in the first issue of the newly legalized *Renovación,* the FJS justified its acceptance of the Popular Front in terms of securing an electoral victory to put an end to 'this painful situation'. Nevertheless, as might have been expected, Carrillo did not renounce the maximalist objectives of revolution and dictatorship of the proletariat, calling for proletarian organizations to prepare their cadres for the coming struggle and urging them to intensify the work of purging the PSOE of reformist elements.[43] During the Socialist election campaign, Largo Caballero harped on the need for proletarian unity and for the transformation of capitalist society. His superficially revolutionary rhetoric delighted his working-class audiences all over Spain. At one point, on 11 February 1936, with José Díaz he addressed a joint PSOE–PCE meeting on the subject of unity, by which both orators meant the take-over of the entire working-class movement by their own organizations.[44]

During the night of 16 February, Carrillo and his comrades waited anxiously for the election results and news as to whether there would be an amnesty. The next morning they heard the first rumours of the Popular Front victory and the noise of a huge crowd approaching the prison. It was a demonstration demanding their release. He and the others who, like him, were still awaiting trial were freed on the evening of 17 February.[45] Carrillo immediately applied for a passport to travel to Russia, which was issued on 24 February in Madrid. He was going to Moscow as part of a joint delegation of the FJS and the UJC to attend a congress of the Communist Youth International and to discuss the forthcoming unification with the leadership of the KIM. Before leaving, he had several meetings with Vitorio Codovila at the apartment of Julio Álvarez del Vayo, Araquistáin's brother-in-law. The Comintern representative was now grooming him and chose intelligently not to reprimand him for the near-Trotskyist views expressed in *Octubre: segunda etapa*. Carrillo himself said later of Codovila, 'I am indebted to him for becoming a Communist.'[46]

On the trip to Moscow, he was accompanied by Federico Melchor and the two UJC representatives, Trifón Medrano and Felipe Muñoz Arconada. In the Soviet capital, he was utterly bedazzled. After a year incarcerated with Largo Caballero, despite his residual affection for his father's friend, Carrillo was beginning to suspect that the PSOE was yesterday's party. The Socialist leadership of middle-aged men rarely allowed young militants near powerful positions in its sclerotic structures. He might be Largo Caballero's spoilt favourite, but other senior Socialists treated him with suspicion. In Moscow, he was inspired by the sight of armed workers marching in the streets. Moreover, he was fêted as a celebrity. He described as a 'fairy tale' being accommodated in the luxurious Savoy Hotel and transported everywhere in a chauffeur-driven limousine to see the sights – Red Square, Lenin's mausoleum, the Kremlin and the Bolshoi. He was even more impressed to be presented to the leaders of the Comintern, Giorgi Dimitrov and Dimitry Manuilsky, and to the secretary general of the KIM, Raymond Guyot, and his deputy, the Hungarian Mihály Farkas ('Michael Wolf'). Barely two months after his twenty-first birthday, Carrillo was thrilled to be addressed as an equal by his heroes, especially the giant Dimitrov, who had been arrested in Berlin in March 1933 for his alleged part in the burning down of the Reichstag and then became an international hero after his courageous defence at the subsequent trial. Carrillo was entranced when Dimitrov modestly waved away talk of his exploits in the Reichstag trial. Apparently on this trip, Carrillo acquired a taste for vodka and caviar.[47]

He admitted later that the fusion with the UJC was merely the opening step of a project to take first the FJS and then the entire Socialist movement into the Communist International. In his submission to the KIM, he declared that the maintenance of the organizational structure of the Socialist Youth was a necessary interim measure dictated by the need first to complete the purging of the PSOE. This trip inevitably had a crucial influence on his subsequent development. The KIM, with its headquarters in Moscow, was closely invigilated by the Russian intelligence service, the NKVD (the People's Commissariat for Internal Affairs), and Soviet Military Intelligence (Glavnoe Razvedupravlenie, or GRU). Having been identified by Codovila as a potential Comintern star, Carrillo would have been vetted anyway, but the process was probably more rigorous because of suspicions of his Trotskyist leanings reported by 'fat Carmen'.[48] Like all prospective Comintern leaders, Carrillo would have been obliged to convince his Moscow bosses, particularly the hard-line Stalinist Farkas/Wolf, that he would fully collaborate with the Soviet security services.[49] It seems to have been no hardship. Seduced by Dimitrov, Manuilsky and other heroes, the young man who had presumed to argue that the FJS should dictate Socialist strategy would happily accept the diktats of the Kremlin. His first lesson was to accept that Trotsky was a traitor. The second was that the mission of a united youth movement was not to forge an elite revolutionary vanguard but to recruit a mass youth organization.

Even though it had been long coming, Carrillo's change of position was breathtaking. He had played a significant part in encouraging the capricious and vacuous revolutionary rhetoric of Largo Caballero that had contributed to the disaster of October 1934. He had been a central figure in the project to bolshevize the PSOE and had done significant damage to the moderate and more realistic wings of the Socialist movement. Gil Robles and Salazar Alonso knew that Largo Caballero's revolutionary threats were meaningless. In contrast, the insistent demands of Carrillo and the FJS leadership in *Renovación* for the conquest of power and the dictatorship of the proletariat can only have terrified moderates on the Spanish right and played into the hands of the conspiratorial extremists. The same can be said about *Octubre: segunda etapa*. Yet now he put all that behind him without apology or regret. He used to say in later life, 'Repentence does not exist.' Having contributed to the intensification of hatreds in Spain and thus weakened the Republic, he had now initiated a process that would mortally wound the party of his father and his patron. In doing so, he demonstrated a poisonous cocktail of vaulting ambition, supreme self-confidence and irresponsibility.

After the Civil War Carlos de Baraibar commented bitterly on the manic enthusiasm of Carrillo and Melchor for everything they had seen in the Soviet Union. On their return, 'they spoke extravagantly about the people, their achievements, their laboratories and even their toilets'. He believed that, in a sense, they had been corrupted by the experience. 'In Moscow,' he wrote,

> they, like many simple souls before them, had found their road to Damascus and, on their return, began to sketch wild plans for the reorganization of the youth movement that signified the undermining of its revolutionary essence. They brought back with them a confused mixture of totalitarian illusions of recruiting the entire young population of Spain, ambition to create a colossal organization and sheer village idiocy. They were seduced by the bewildering panoply of figures, tables and statistics cleverly put before them.[50]

Shortly after Carrillo's return to Madrid, a joint meeting was held of the FJS and UJC executive committees to consider the report that the delegation had elaborated in Moscow in favour of a new mass united movement. The report was approved as the basis for unification and a joint national committee set up to implement the fusion process. Much effort had been made to combat suspicions that the Socialist movement was about to lose its youth movement to the Communists. Rather, it was hoped to reassure Largo Caballero that the UJC would be absorbed into the FJS. However, in practice, as could have been anticipated, that was not what happened, given Carrillo's ever closer links to Moscow. Public meetings were held in local sections of both organizations to propagate the unification. They culminated in a mass gathering at the Las Ventas bull-ring in Madrid on Sunday 5 April 1936. In his speech on that occasion, Carrillo declared that what was happening repaired the schism of 1921 which had seen the radical wing of the PSOE depart to form the PCE. The event at Las Ventas was followed throughout May and July 1936 by meetings of the provincial sections of the FJS and UJC to prepare for a great national conference of unification which, because of the outbreak of civil war, never took place. In those months, the joint membership of 100,000 was swollen to 140,000.[51]

Retrospectively, Largo Caballero recalled his reaction in similar terms to those of Baraibar. He claimed that when Carrillo and others came to explain the proposed organizational plans, he told them that their plans for a mass youth movement undermined the purpose of the FJS as an elite training school for future PSOE leaders. He declared uncompromisingly that he now considered the FJS to be dead and, with it, the hope that it would be a bulwark for the Socialist Party. Carrillo tried to convince him of his good faith and his loyalty. He made 'a solemn promise that he would create a formidable organization that was totally socialist'.[52]

Amaro del Rosal, who was one of those present when Largo Caballero was informed of the unification, recalled his distress: 'his eyes filled with tears'. Carrillo had effectively delivered a shattering blow to the PSOE, undermining its political future. As Largo Caballero perceived, he was delivering to the PCE, in the words of Helen Graham, 'a political vanguard which undoubtedly included many potential national and provincial leaders'. There were those, Serrano Poncela among them, who were alarmed that Carrillo now talked of creating a mass organization contrary to the traditional perception of the FJS as an elite training ground for the PSOE. Although Carrillo made a speech in which he paid tribute to Largo Caballero, the damage had been done.[53]

Carrillo took part in a meeting of the Communist Party Central Committee on 31 March, at which he suggested that the new JSU, the

Juventudes Socialistas Unificadas, should seek membership of the KIM and that the PSOE should unite with the PCE and join the Comintern. Attendance at Central Committee meetings was a privilege not normally extended to outsiders.[54] Carrillo would not formally join the Communist Party for another six months, but there is reason to believe that he was already a Communist in all but name. In 1974, he admitted that, on his return from Moscow, 'I had begun to become a Communist. I did not join the Party immediately, although I began to collaborate with the Communists and was even invited to take part in meetings of the Central Committee. I had not yet joined because I was still hopeful of bringing about the unification of the Socialist and Communist parties.'[55]

The procedure whereby the new executive committee of the JSU was appointed in September 1936 was extremely opaque. There were fifteen members, of whom seven were Communists, although several of the eight Socialists were so close to the PCE as made little difference. Carrillo became secretary general of an organization that, despite its name, constituted a massive advance of Communist influence.[56] Those who perceived the creation of the Juventudes Socialistas Unificadas as the loss of the FJS to the Third International coined the nickname 'Juventudes Socialistas Urssificadas' (USSR in Spanish being URSS).[57]

When the military coup in Spain began on 18 July, Carrillo was in Paris where he had gone with Trifón Medrano and José Laín Entralgo to discuss with Raymond Guyot, the secretary general of the Communist Youth International, the problems posed by the meeting in Madrid with the comical German woman delegate of the Comintern, Carmen. In his memoirs, he recounted his heroic response to hearing of the military coup. In this version, for which there is no corroboration, all three immediately set off for the border. Crossing into Spain at Irún, they headed for San Sebastián and immediately got involved in an assault on an hotel where some rebel supporters had barricaded themselves in. Later, in a vain effort to reach Madrid, Carrillo and his companions spent some weeks fighting on the Basque front with a unit organized by the Basque Communist Party. Being extremely short-sighted, Carrillo was anything but a natural soldier. Eventually, they were able to cross into France and then back into Spain via Puigcerdà. The Communist veteran Enrique Líster claimed that the entire account was pure invention and that, during this period, Carrillo remained in Paris. Whatever the truth, it is clear that already, in those early weeks of the war, he was convinced that the only party with the sense of direction to take control of events was the PCE.[58]

When he got back to Madrid at the beginning of August, the JSU was already trying to turn its pre-war militia structure into proper fighting units. Carrillo claims that he was made political commissar of the JSU's 'Largo Caballero' battalion which was fighting in defence of the city in the sierras to the north. His heroic picture of that period of his life is somewhat undermined by Manuel Tagüeña, a much more reliable witness, who suggested that Carrillo was involved in political rivalries that undermined the efforts of the Italian Fernando De Rosa to link the various units.[59] Certainly, his military career, if it took place at all, was brief. Given the vertiginous growth of the JSU, it was clear that Carrillo could be of most use in a political rather than a military capacity.

The JSU was being inundated with new recruits and soon had more militants than the adult membership of the PSOE and PCE combined.[60] At every level of society, the economy and the war effort, in industry and the nascent armed forces, JSU members were playing a key role. Accordingly, Carrillo was now working in Madrid on the practicalities of consolidating Communist control over this powerful new instrument. After prolonged hesitation, on 4 September 1936 Largo Caballero finally succumbed to Prieto's arguments that the survival of the Republic required a cabinet backed by the working-class parties as well as the bourgeois Republicans. A true Popular Front government was formed in which Largo Caballero was both Prime Minister and Minister of War. It contained Communists as well as Socialists and Republicans. Two months later, on 4 November, with the Nationalist rebels already at the gates of Madrid, four representatives of the anarcho-syndicalist CNT would also join the cabinet.

By then, rebel air raids were intensifying. Far from undermining the morale of the Madrileños, they did the opposite and provoked a deep loathing of the self-styled 'Nationalists'. Virtually every left-wing political party and trade union had established squads to eliminate suspected fascists. With their tribunals, their prisons and their executioners, they were known loosely as *checas*. Their targets were those assumed to be rebel supporters within the capital. This included both imprisoned and as yet undetected right-wingers, all of whom in the frantic conditions of the besieged capital were indiscriminately regarded as 'fifth columnists'. The name was inadvertently coined by General Mola, who in early October had infamously stated that he had four columns poised to attack Madrid but that the attack would be initiated by a fifth column already inside the city.[61] On the basis of the massacres perpetrated in southern Spain by Franco's African columns, it was believed that the rebels planned to kill anyone who had been a member of any party or group linked to the Popular Front, held a government post or was an affiliate of a trade union. Spine-chilling broadcasts from Seville made by General Gonzalo Queipo de Llano propagated fear and hatred.

In the claustrophobia generated by the siege, popular rage focused on the prison population. Among those detained were many who were considered potentially very dangerous. As rebel columns came ever nearer to the capital throughout October, there was growing concern about the many experienced right-wing army officers who had refused to honour their oath of loyalty to the Republic. These men boasted that they would form new units for the rebel columns once they were, as they expected, liberated. Anarchist groups were already randomly seizing prisoners and shooting them. On 4 November, Getafe to the south of Madrid fell and the four anarchist ministers joined the government. Advancing through the University City and the Casa de Campo, by 6 November the rebels were only 200 yards from the largest of the prisons, the Cárcel Modelo, in the Argüelles district.

In this context, the decision that Largo Caballero's cabinet should leave for Valencia was finally taken in the early afternoon of 6 November. The two Communist ministers in the government, Jesús Hernández (Education) and Vicente Uribe (Agriculture), had argued the Party line that, even if the government had to be evacuated,

Madrid could still be defended.[62] General José Miaja Menent, head of the 1st Military Division, that is to say, Military Governor of Madrid, was placed in charge of the defence of the capital and ordered to establish a body, to be known as the Junta de Defensa, which would have full governmental powers in Madrid and its environs. In fact, Largo Caballero and the fleeing cabinet believed that the capital was doomed anyway. In their view, the Junta was there merely to administer its surrender. Indeed, when Largo Caballero informed him of his new responsibilities, Miaja turned pale, sure that he was being sacrificed in a futile gesture.[63] Whether or not that was the intention, Madrid would survive the siege for another twenty-nine months.

Until the battle for the capital was resolved, Miaja's awesome task was to organize the city's military and civil defence at the same time as providing food and shelter for its citizens and the refugees who thronged its streets. In addition, he had to deal with the violence of the *checas* and the snipers and saboteurs of the 'fifth column'.[64] The Junta de Defensa would thus be a localized mini-government made up of 'ministers' (whose title was Councillor – Consejero) chosen from all those parties that made up the central government. However, Miaja would turn first to the Communists in search of help. And they were ready and waiting.

The two Communist ministers had immediately reported the cabinet's decision to the PCE top brass, Pedro Fernández Checa and Antonio Mije. They were effectively leading the Party in the frequent absences of the secretary general, José Díaz, who was seriously ill with stomach cancer. Pedro Checa was already collaborating closely with the NKVD.[65] The implications were discussed and plans made. Astonishingly, present at this historic meeting were Santiago Carrillo and José Cazorla, who were both, theoretically at least, still members of the Socialist Party. Their presence demonstrates the enormous importance of the now massive JSU and also suggests that they were already in the highest echelons of the PCE.

Late in the afternoon, Checa and Mije went to negotiate with Miaja the terms of the Communist participation in the Junta de Defensa. A grateful Miaja eagerly accepted their offer that the PCE run the two 'ministries' (*consejerías*) of War and Public Order in the Junta de

Defensa. He also accepted their specific nominations of Antonio Mije as War Councillor and of Carrillo as Public Order Councillor with Cazorla as his deputy. While Mije and Checa were negotiating with Miaja, Carrillo and Cazorla had gone to ask Largo Caballero for a statement to explain to the people of Madrid why the government was leaving. The Prime Minister denied that the government was being evacuated, despite the suitcases piled outside his office. Further disillusioned by the lies of their already broken hero, Carrillo and Cazorla went back to the Central Committee of the PCE.[66]

At about eight in the evening, Mije and Carrillo went to see Miaja to discuss their future roles. Shortly before his death, in discussing the Spanish edition of my book *The Spanish Holocaust*, Carrillo claimed that, at the end of this meeting, he had asked Miaja what he was expected to do about the fifth column and that the General had replied, 'Smash it.' In this account, Miaja allegedly said that victory would go to the army that annihilated the other and that this would be done with bullets and bayonets. He said that the fifth column must be prevented at all costs from attacking from behind. Looking at Carrillo, he said, 'That is your job and you will have our help.' It is curious that, in his innumerable statements about his role in the executions of right-wing prisoners in Madrid, Carrillo had never previously mentioned Miaja. In *The Spanish Holocaust* reference was made to a later Republican police report on collaboration between NKVD agents and the public order apparatus, an ambiguity of whose wording raised the possibility that Miaja may have approved of Carrillo's activities. That Carrillo should seize upon this was a way of saying that, whatever he did subsequently, he was only obeying orders.[67] There is an irony about this, since elsewhere he denied all knowledge of the massacres committed on his watch.

In Carrillo's own words, 'on that same night of 6 November, I began to discharge my responsibilities along with Mije and others'.[68] He was able to nominate his subordinates in the Public Order Council and assign them tasks immediately after this meeting with Miaja late on the night of 6–7 November. He set up a sub-committee, known as the Public Order Delegation, under Serrano Poncela, who was effectively given responsibility for the work in Madrid of the Dirección General de Seguridad, the national police headquarters. The Delegation was taking decisions from the very early hours of 7 November.[69] The anarchist Gregorio Gallego highlighted the Communists' ability to hit the ground running: 'we realized that the operation was far too well prepared and manipulated to have been improvised'.[70]

Overall operational responsibility for the prisoners lay with three men: Carrillo, Cazorla and Serrano Poncela. They took key decisions about the prisoners in the vacuum between the evacuation of the government late on the night of 6 November and the formal constitution of the Junta de Defensa twenty-four hours later. However, it is inconceivable that those decisions were taken in isolation by three inexperienced young men aged respectively twenty-one (Carrillo), thirty (Cazorla) and twenty-four (Serrano Poncela). The authorization for their operational decisions, as will be seen, had to have come from far more senior elements. Certainly, it required the go-ahead from Checa and Mije who, in turn, needed the approval of Miaja and of the Soviet advisers, since Russian aid in terms of tanks, aircraft, the International Brigades and technical expertise had started to arrive over the previous weeks. How much detail, other than airy references to 'controlling the fifth column', Miaja received is impossible to say. The implementation of the operational decisions also required, and would get, assistance from the anarchist movement.

Thus the authorization, the organization and the implementation of what happened to the prisoners involved many people. However, Carrillo's position as Public Order Councillor, together with his later prominence as secretary general of the Communist Party, saw him accused of sole responsibility for the deaths that followed. That is absurd, but it does not mean that he had no responsibility at all. The calibration of the degree of that responsibility must start with the question of why the twenty-one-year-old leader of the Socialist Youth was given such a crucial and powerful position. Late on the night of 6 November, after the meeting with Miaja, Carrillo, along with Serrano Poncela, Cazorla and others, was formally incorporated into the Communist Party. They were not subjected to stringent membership requirements. In what was hardly a formal ceremony, they simply informed José Díaz and Pedro Checa of their wish to join and were incorporated into the Party on the spot. The brevity of the proceedings confirms that Carrillo was already an important Communist 'submarine' within the Socialist Party. After all, he had brought into the PCE's orbit the 50,000 members of the FJS and the further 100,000 who had subsequently joined the JSU. He was already attending meetings of the PCE's politburo, its small executive committee, which indicated that he was held in high esteem. He had long since been identified by Comintern agents as a candidate for recruitment. If he had not publicly made the switch before, it was because of his, and presumably their, hope that he could help bring about the unification of the PSOE and the PCE. Largo Caballero's determined opposition to unity combined with his poor direction of the war effort had made this seem a futile aspiration. Moreover, the prestige accruing to the Communist Party from Soviet aid suggested that there was little advantage in delaying the leap. It was an eminently practical decision, although Fernando Claudín argued implausibly that Carrillo was brave to sever his links with a party within which he was so prominently placed.[71]

Oddly, Carrillo claimed that his membership of the PCE was not public knowledge as late as July 1937.[72] Certainly, in late December 1936 in Valencia, Carrillo, Cazorla, Melchor and Serrano Poncela had all informed Largo Caballero of what they had done. The 'boss' was devastated, as were others in his entourage. It finally dawned on him that he had let the future of the PSOE slip into the hands of the Communists. According to Carrillo, he said with tears in his eyes, 'As of now, I no longer believe in the Spanish revolution.'[73] Not long afterwards, he said of Carrillo to a close collaborator, perhaps Amaro del Rosal, 'He was more than a son to me. I shall never forgive the Communists for stealing him from me.'[74] Largo Caballero's later reflections were altogether more vitriolic. In his unpublished memoirs, he wrote, 'In the Socialist Youth, there were Judases like Santiago Carrillo and others who managed to simulate a fusion which they called the JSU. Later, they revealed their treachery when they joined the Communist International.'[75]

Carlos de Baraibar, who had replaced Carrillo as the old leader's favourite, recalled sarcastically that:

a group of leaders of the JSU visited me to let me know that they had decided en masse to join the Communist Party. I knew nothing about it, but they made their case so eloquently that I was left with the impression that their lives had been rendered so impossible within the Socialist movement that, to be able to go on fighting effectively for the cause, the poor creatures had had no alternative but to join the Communists. Nevertheless, it seemed to me monstrous that this had been done without them consulting with senior comrades other than, as I later discovered, Álvarez del Vayo. They had been advised throughout by the man we called 'the eye of Moscow', the secret representative of the Comintern or rather of Stalin.

Largo Caballero also referred to 'Medina'/Codovila as 'el ojo de Moscú'.[76]

When Serrano Poncela began to run the Public Order Delegation, in the early hours of 7 November, he used written orders for the evacuation of prisoners left by the Director General of Security, Manuel Muñoz, before leaving Madrid for Valencia.[77] The Norwegian Consul, the German Felix Schlayer, claimed that the preparation of the necessary document was the price paid by Muñoz to Communist militiamen who were preventing him joining the rest of the government in Valencia.[78] Evacuation orders were not the equivalent of specific instructions for murder – as was shown by the safe arrival of some evacuated prisoners at their destinations. Whoever signed the orders, in the midst of administrative collapse and widespread popular panic, the evacuation of 8,000 prisoners seemed impossible. Nevertheless, Carrillo's Public Order Council would undertake the task.[79]

Among those pushing for the evacuation of the prisoners were the senior Republican military authorities in the capital, General Miaja and his chief of staff, Vicente Rojo, the senior Russians present in Madrid and the Communist hierarchy. Given the crucial military assistance being provided by the Soviet personnel, and their own experience of the siege of St Petersburg in the Russian Civil War, it was natural that their advice should be sought. The most senior of the Soviet military personnel were Generals Ian Antonovich Berzin, the overall head of the Soviet military mission, and Vladimir Gorev. Berzin, along with Soviet diplomats, had gone to Valencia with the government, while Gorev, officially the military attaché but actually Madrid station chief of Soviet Military Intelligence (GRU), remained. Gorev would thus play a crucial role, alongside Rojo, in the defence of Madrid. Also involved were Mikhail Koltsov, the *Pravda* correspondent, perhaps the most powerful Russian journalist of the day, and Lev Lazarevich Nikolsky, the acting NKVD station chief in Madrid who went by the name Aleksandr Orlov. In fact, according to the principal expert on Soviet security services in Spain, Orlov was away from Madrid from 13 October to 10 November in Cartagena.[80] However, his subordinate, Josif Grigulevich, was his liaison with Carrillo. They became active collaborators and friends. Grigulevich would certainly have transmitted to Carrillo the Russian view that the captive military officers who had refused to fight for the Republic should simply be liquidated.

Other influential figures in the defence of Madrid were the senior Comintern personnel, Codovila and the Italian Vittorio Vidali. Known by his pseudonym of 'Carlos Contreras', Vidali had been instrumental in the founding of the Fifth Regiment, from which the Republic's Popular Army evolved. He was the Fifth Regiment's political commissar, and his conviction that rebel supporters within Madrid should be eliminated was reflected in his vehement articles and speeches. Conscious that the prisoners were already boasting that they would soon join their rebel comrades, Gorev and other Soviet advisers, including Vidali, insisted that it would be suicidal not to evacuate them. As the rebel siege tightened, Vicente Rojo and Miaja fully concurred.[81]

Miaja soon established a close relationship with Carrillo's deputy, José Cazorla, one of the key players in the organization of the fate of the prisoners.[82] Taciturn and efficient, Cazorla believed that rebel supporters had to be eliminated. To carry out this task, as will be seen, he frequently relied on the advice of Russian security personnel. As concerned as Miaja about the prisoners was the forty-two-year-old Vicente Rojo, recently promoted lieutenant colonel. Rojo believed that the fifth column was made up of spies, saboteurs and agitators and feared that they could play a decisive role in the fate of the capital. Accordingly, he wrote, the military authorities had to take the decision to eliminate it.[83]

The public order set-up of the Junta de Defensa under the command of Santiago Carrillo answered to Pedro Checa and Antonio Mije, and it is clear that they were in constant touch with the Russians. In the Ministry of War, there were meetings between Mije, Gorev and Rojo. Pedro Checa also had a key meeting at PCE headquarters with Gorev's messenger Mikhail Koltsov.[84] This was almost certainly the same encounter described in Koltsov's diary as being between Checa and 'Miguel Martínez'. In Koltsov's version, 'Miguel Martínez' urged Checa to proceed with the evacuation of the prisoners. Koltsov/Martínez pointed out that it was not necessary to evacuate all of the 8,000 but that it was crucial to select the most dangerous elements and send them to the rearguard in small groups. Accepting this argument, Checa despatched three men to 'two big prisons', which almost certainly meant San Antón and the Cárcel Modelo – from which prisoners were indeed taken away on the morning of 7 November.[85] The removal of prisoners was known as a *saca*. Clearly, three men alone could not organize a large-scale *saca*, which required written authorizations, means of transport, escorts and other facilities.

Accordingly, Koltsov's account seems to confirm Carrillo's statement that the Consejería de Orden Público had begun to function late on the night of 6 November or in the early hours of 7 November and started the process of evacuation of prisoners. This required committed personnel, and Carrillo, Cazorla and Serrano Poncela turned to 'Carlos Contreras' (Vittorio Vidali). Although in Spain as an emissary of the Comintern, Vidali was also an agent of the NKVD. Both Vidali and Josif Grigulevich, who was briefly his assistant at the Fifth Regiment, belonged to the NKVD Administration for Special Tasks (assassination, terror, sabotage and abductions) commanded by Yakov Isaakovich Serebryansky. Grigulevich was a twenty-three-year-old Lithuanian who spoke fluent Spanish as a result of having lived in Argentina.[86]

Enrique Castro Delgado, the Communist commander of the Fifth Regiment, described how, on the night of 6 November, he and Vidali/

Contreras gave orders to the head of a special unit: 'The massacre starts. No quarter to be given. Mola's fifth column must be destroyed before it begins to move.'[87] The clear implications of the encounter between Contreras/Vidali and Castro Delgado are that elements of both the Fifth Regiment and the NKVD were involved in what happened to the prisoners in November. There were many JSU members in the Fifth Regiment. In a revealing interview in 1986, two years before his death, Grigulevich stated that, in Madrid, he had worked under the orders of Santiago Carrillo, heading a special squad (*brigada especial*) of Socialist militants in the Dirección General de Seguridad dedicated to 'dirty' operations. The squad was formed by Grigulevich from what he called 'trusted elements' recruited from members of the JSU who had been part of the unit responsible for the security of the Soviet Embassy in Madrid.[88]

Grigulevich's assertion is sustained by the record in the Francoist archive, the Causa General, of the post-war interrogations of JSU members of what came to be three *brigadas especiales*. Grigulevich had arrived in Spain in late September and worked for Contreras for some weeks before beginning to collaborate with Carrillo in late October or early November. Carrillo, Cazorla and the unit's members knew Grigulevich as 'José Escoy', although he was known to others as 'José Ocampo'.[89] The documents in the Causa General are further corroborated by a report, written in the autumn of 1937, by the Republican police that referred to the frequent visits made to Carrillo's office by Russian technicians specializing in security and counter-espionage matters. The report stated that these technicians had offered their 'enthusiastic collaboration to the highest authority in public order in Madrid', which would seem at first sight to have been a reference to Carrillo although it might have referred to Miaja since he was the authority under whom Carrillo worked. If the latter, it would mean that Carrillo's activities were covered by Miaja's approval, as he was quick to emphasize shortly after the publication of *The Spanish Holocaust*. Of course, his collaboration with the Russians would have happened anyway given the Soviet links with the Communist Party. The report went on to state that Carrillo had directed these technicians to 'the chief and the officers of the *brigada especial*.[90] This was confirmed by Grigulevich, who later described himself as 'the right hand of Carrillo' in the Consejería de Orden Público.[91] According to the records of the Soviet security services, their friendship was so close that years later Carrillo chose Grigulevich to be secular 'godfather' to one of his sons. Carrillo's three sons were born in Paris between early 1950 and late 1952. During those years, Grigulevich was living in Rome under the name Teodoro Bonnefil Castro. The Russian security services had managed to create an identity for him as a Costa Rican businessman and his success in this role had seen him named as first secretary in the country's Embassy to Italy. The ease of connections between Rome and Paris certainly made it possible for him and Carrillo to meet.[92]

It is clear that Miaja, Rojo, Gorev and the senior leadership of the Communist Party were all anxious to see the prisoner question resolved with the greatest urgency. There is no doubt that Miaja and Rojo approved of prisoner evacuations although not necessarily of executions. What is likely is that, in the meetings immediately following the creation of the Junta de Defensa, they delegated responsibility to the two-man leadership of the PCE. Checa and Mije, who, like the Russians, certainly did approve of the execution of prisoners, passed organizational responsibility to Carrillo, Cazorla and Serrano Poncela. To implement their instructions, the trio drew on members of the JSU who were given posts in the Public Order Delegation headed by Serrano Poncela, effectively head of the Dirección General de Seguridad for Madrid. They could also count on assistance from Contreras/Vidali and the Fifth Regiment and from Grigulevich and the *brigada especial*. However, they could do nothing against the will of the anarchist movement, which controlled the roads out of Madrid. Given that the anarchists had already seized and murdered prisoners, it was not likely that they would offer insuperable opposition to the Communists. Indeed, the formal agreement of senior elements of the CNT militias was soon forthcoming.

The inaugural session of the Junta began at 6.00 p.m. on 7 November.[93] Before the meeting, at around 5.30 p.m., Carrillo, coming out of Miaja's office in the Ministry of War, met a representative of the International Red Cross, Dr Georges Henny, with Felix Schlayer, the Norwegian Consul. Carrillo invited them to meet him in his office immediately after the plenary session. Before returning for that meeting, Schlayer and the Red Cross delegate went to the Cárcel Modelo where they learned that several hundred prisoners had been taken away earlier that day. On coming back to the Ministry of War, they were greeted amiably by Carrillo, who assured them of his determination to protect the prisoners and prevent any murders. When they told him what they had learned at the Cárcel Modelo, he denied knowledge of any evacuations. Schlayer reflected later that, even if this were true, it raises the question as to why Carrillo and Miaja, once having been informed by him of the evacuations, did nothing to prevent the others that continued that evening and on successive days.[94]

Later the same evening, a meeting took place between, on the one hand, two or three representatives of the JSU who controlled the newly created Public Order Council and members of the local federation of the CNT. They discussed what to do with the prisoners. Despite mutual hostility, liaison between both organizations was necessary, since the Communists held sway inside Madrid, controlling the police, the prisons and the files on prisoners, while the anarchists, through their militias, controlled the roads out of the city. The only record of the meeting is constituted by the minutes of a session of the CNT's National Committee held the next morning. Those minutes include a report by Amor Nuño Pérez, the Councillor for War Industries in the Junta de Defensa, who had been one of the CNT representatives at the previous evening's negotiation with the JSU. Amor Nuño's report outlined what had been agreed at that encounter with the JSU. The minutes did not include the names of the other participants at the CNT–JSU meeting. However, it is reasonable to suppose that the JSU representatives included at least two of the following: Carrillo, Cazorla and Serrano Poncela. The gravity of the matter under discussion and the practical agreements reached could hardly have permitted the Public Order Council to be represented by more junior members of the JSU. If Carrillo was not there, which is unlikely, it is inconceivable that he, as both Public Order Councillor and secretary general of the JSU, was not fully apprised of the meeting.

Nuño reported that the CNT and JSU representatives, on the evening of 7 November, had decided that the prisoners should be classified into three groups. The fate of the first, consisting of 'fascists and dangerous elements', was to be 'Immediate execution' 'with responsibility to be hidden' – the responsibility being that of those who took the decision and of those who implemented it. The second group, of prisoners considered to be supporters of the military uprising but, because of age or profession, less dangerous, were to be evacuated to Chinchilla, near Albacete. The third, those least politically committed, were to be released 'with all possible guarantees, as proof to the Embassies of our humanitarianism'. This last comment suggests that whoever represented the JSU at the meeting knew about and had mentioned the earlier encounter between Carrillo and Schlayer.[95]

The first consignment of prisoners had already left Madrid early in the morning of 7 November, presumably in accordance with the instructions for evacuation issued by Pedro Checa in response to Koltsov/Miguel Martínez. Thus some prisoners were removed and killed before the formal agreement with the CNT made later that evening. There is no record of there being any difficulty about their getting through the anarchist militias on the roads out of the capital. That is not surprising since there were CNT–FAI representatives on Serrano Poncela's Public Order Delegation. Nevertheless, the agreement guaranteed that further convoys would face no problems at the anarchist checkpoints and that they could also rely on substantial assistance in the gory business of executing the prisoners. The strongest CNT controls were posted on the roads out to Valencia and Aragon which the convoys would take. The necessary flotillas of double-decker buses and many smaller vehicles could not get out of Madrid without the approval, cooperation or connivance of the CNT patrols. Since Carrillo, Cazorla and Serrano Poncela knew this only too well, it is not plausible that they would have ordered evacuation convoys without first securing the agreement of the CNT–FAI. This undermines Carrillo's later assertions that the convoys were hijacked by anarchists. The grain of truth in those claims resides in the certainty that the anarchists took some part in the actual killing.

The first decisions taken by Carrillo and his collaborators had been the *saca* on the morning of 7 November at San Antón and, in the afternoon, the larger one at the Cárcel Modelo. The prisoners were loaded on to double-decker buses. Convoys consisting of the buses escorted by cars and trucks carrying militiamen shuttled back and forth over the next two days. Their official destinations were prisons well behind the lines, in Alcalá de Henares, Chinchilla and Valencia. However, of the more than 1,000 prisoners removed, only about 300 arrived there. Eleven miles from Madrid, on the road to Alcalá de Henares, at the small village of Paracuellos del Jarama, the first batch, from San Antón, were forced off the buses. At the base of the small hill on which the village stood, they were lined up by the militiamen, verbally abused and then shot. In the evening of the same day, the second batch, from the Cárcel Modelo, suffered the same fate.[96] A further consignment of prisoners arrived on the morning of 8 November. The mayor was forced to round up the able-bodied inhabitants of the village (there were only 1,600 in total) to dig huge ditches for the approximately 800 bodies which had been left to rot. When Paracuellos could cope with no more, subsequent convoys made for the nearby village of Torrejón de Ardoz, where a disused irrigation channel was used for the approximately 400 victims.[97] *Sacas* continued, with intervals, until 3 December. Some expeditions of prisoners arrived safely in Alcalá de Henares. The total numbers killed over the four weeks following the creation of the Junta de Defensa cannot be calculated with total precision, but there is little doubt that it was somewhere between 2,200 and 2,500.[98]

All these *sacas* were initiated with documentation on Dirección General de Seguridad notepaper indicating that the prisoners were either to be released or taken to Chinchilla or Alcalá de Henares. When the order was for them to go to Alcalá de Henares, they usually arrived safely. This suggests that 'to be released' (*libertad*) and 'Chinchilla' were codewords for elimination.[99] The specific orders for the evacuations of prisoners were not signed by Carrillo, nor by any member of the Junta de Defensa. Until 22 November, such orders were signed by Manuel Muñoz's second-in-command in the Dirección General de Seguridad, the head of the police Vicente Girauta Linares. Girauta was under the orders of Serrano Poncela, Muñoz's successor for Madrid. On 22 November, he followed Muñoz to Valencia. Thereafter, the orders were signed either by Serrano Poncela himself or by Girauta's successor as head of the Madrid police, Bruno Carreras Villanueva.[100] In the Causa General, there are several documents signed by Serrano Poncela. The anthology of this colossal archive, published in 1945, reproduces two. The one dated 26 November 1936 read, 'I request that you release the individuals listed on the back of this page,' and carried twenty-six names. The document dated 27 November read, 'Please release the prisoners mentioned on the two attached sheets,' which listed 106 names. All those on these two lists were assassinated.[101] Explicit orders for the execution, as opposed to the 'liberation' or 'transfer' of prisoners, have not been found.

While the *sacas* were taking place, Carrillo had started to issue a series of decrees that would ensure Communist control of the security forces within the capital and put an end to the myriad parallel police forces that had sprung up in the first weeks of the war. On 9 November, he issued two decrees that constituted a significant step towards the centralized control of the police and security forces. The first required the surrender of all arms not in authorized hands. The second stated that the internal security of the capital would be the exclusive responsibility of forces organized by the Council for Public Order. This signified the dissolution, on paper at least, of all *checas*.[102] Under the conditions of the siege, Carrillo was thus able to impose, by emergency decree, measures that had been beyond the government. Nevertheless, there was a considerable delay between the announcement of the decree and its successful implementation. The anarchists resisted as long as they could and the Communists never relinquished some of their own *checas*. Nevertheless, by his decree of 9 November, Carrillo returned the services of security and investigation to the now reformed police and suppressed all those groups run by political parties or trade unions, although many of their militants were given positions in Serrano Poncela's Public Order Delegation.[103]

Explicitly included within these reformed services was 'everything relative to the administration of the arrest and release of prisoners, as well as the movement, transfer etc of those under arrest'. They were under the control of the Public Order Delegation.[104] All functions of the Dirección General de Seguridad were controlled by Serrano Poncela. However, he followed the instructions of Carrillo or his deputy José Cazorla. Carrillo's measures constituted the institutionalization of the repression under the Public Order Delegation in the Dirección General de Seguridad.[105]

Within Serrano Poncela's Delegation, there were three sub-sections. The first dealt with investigation, interrogations and petitions for release. This was headed by Manuel Rascón Ramírez of the CNT. After interrogations had been carried out, this section made recommendations to the Delegation and final decisions were taken by Carrillo. This function was entirely compatible with the decisions taken at the meeting between JSU and CNT members on the evening of 7 November. The second sub-section, headed by Serrano Poncela himself, dealt with prisons, prisoners and prison transfers. It used small tribunals of militiamen set up in each prison to go through the file-cards of the prisoners. The third sub-section dealt with the personnel of the police and other more or less official armed groups in the rearguard.[106]

The procedures that would be applied to prisoners between 18 November and 6 December were established on 10 November at a meeting of the Public Order Delegation. Serrano Poncela laid down three categories: army officers with the rank of captain and above; Falangists; other rightists. This was roughly similar to what had been agreed at the meeting on 7 November between members of the CNT–FAI and representatives of the JSU, one of whom had almost certainly been Serrano Poncela himself. When lists of prisoners were compiled, they were passed to Serrano Poncela. He then signed orders for their 'release', which meant their execution. It seems that those expeditions of prisoners that arrived safely at their destination consisted of men not listed for execution by the prison tribunals. Serrano Poncela had to report every day to Carrillo in his office in the Junta de Defensa (in the Palace of Juan March in Calle Núñez de Balboa in the Barrio de

Salamanca). Carrillo also often visited the office of Serrano Poncela at Number 37 in nearby Calle Serrano.[107]

The procedure was that agents would arrive at each prison late at night with a general order signed by Serrano Poncela for the 'liberation' of the prisoners whose names were listed on the back or on separate sheets. The director of the prison would hand them over and they would then be taken to wherever Serrano Poncela had indicated orally to the agents. The subsequent phase of the process, the transportation and execution of the prisoners in the early hours of the following morning, was carried out each day by different groups of militiamen, sometimes anarchists, sometimes Communists and sometimes from the Fifth Regiment. The prisoners were obliged to leave all their belongings, and were then tied together in pairs and loaded on to buses.[108]

That Carrillo was fully aware of this is demonstrated by the minutes of the meeting of the Junta de Defensa on the night of 11 November 1936. One of the anarchist consejeros asked if the Cárcel Modelo had been evacuated. Carrillo responded by saying that the necessary measures had been taken to organize the evacuations of prisoners but that the operation had had to be suspended. At this, the Communist Isidoro Diéguez Dueñas, second-in-command to Antonio Mije at the War Council, declared that the evacuations had to continue, given the seriousness of the problem of the prisoners. Carrillo responded that the suspension had been necessary because of protests emanating from the diplomatic corps, presumably a reference to his meeting with Schlayer. Although the minutes are extremely brief, they make it indisputably clear that Carrillo knew what was happening to the prisoners if only as a result of the complaints by Schlayer.[109]

In fact, after the mass executions of 7–8 November, there were no more *sacas* until 18 November, after which they continued on a lesser scale until 6 December. The *sacas* and the executions have come to be known collectively as 'Paracuellos', the name of the village where a high proportion of the executions took place. Those executions constituted the greatest single atrocity perpetrated in Republican territory during the war. Its scale is explained but not justified as a response to the fear that rebel forces were about to take Madrid.

Whereas previous *sacas* had been triggered by spontaneous mass outrage provoked by bombing raids or by news brought by refugees of rebel atrocities, the extra-judicial murders carried out at Paracuellos were the result of political-military decisions. The evacuations and subsequent executions were organized by the Council for Public Order but could not have been implemented without help from other, largely anarchist elements in the rearguard militias.

The brief interlude after the mass *sacas* of 7 and 8 November was thanks to Mariano Sánchez Roca, the under-secretary at the Ministry of Justice who arranged for the anarchist Melchor Rodríguez to be named Special Inspector of Prisons.[110] The first initiative taken by Melchor Rodríguez on the night of 9 November was decisive. Hearing that a *saca* of 400 prisoners was planned, he went to the prison at midnight and ordered that all *sacas* cease and that the militiamen who had been freely moving within the prison remain outside. He forbade the release of any prisoners between 6 p.m. and 8 a.m., to prevent them being shot. He also insisted on accompanying any prisoners being transferred to other prisons. In consequence there were no *sacas* between 10 and 17 November, when Melchor Rodríguez was forced to resign his post by Juan García Oliver, the anarchist Minister of Justice. His offence was to have demanded that those responsible for the killings be punished.[111] After his resignation, the *sacas* started again.[112]

Manuel Azaña, who had succeeded Alcalá Zamora as President of the Republic, and at least two government ministers in Valencia (Manuel Irujo and José Giral) had learned about the *sacas*.[113] Indeed, a speech made on 12 November by Carrillo suggests that, at the time, secrecy was not a major priority. Speaking before the microphones of Unión Radio, he boasted about the measures being taken against the prisoners:

it is guaranteed that there will be no resistance to the Junta de Defensa from within. No such resistance will emerge because absolutely every possible measure has been taken to prevent any conflict or alteration of order in Madrid that could favour the enemy's plans. The 'Fifth Column' is on the way to being crushed. Its last remnants in the depths of Madrid are being hunted down and cornered according to the law, but above all with the energy necessary to ensure that this 'Fifth Column' cannot interfere with the plans of the legitimate government and the Junta de Defensa.[114]

On 1 December 1936, the Junta de Defensa was renamed the Junta Delegada de Defensa de Madrid by order of Largo Caballero. Having led the government to Valencia, the Prime Minister was deeply resentful of the aureole of heroism that had accumulated around Miaja as he led the capital's population in resisting Franco's siege. Thus Largo Caballero wished to restrain what he considered the Junta's excessive independence.[115] Serrano Poncela had already left the Public Order Delegation at some point in early December and his responsibilities were taken over by José Cazorla.

At the end of the war, Serrano Poncela gave an implausible account of why he had left the Public Order Delegation. He told the Basque politician Jesús de Galíndez that he did not know that the words 'transfer to Chinchilla' or 'release' on the orders that he signed were code that meant the prisoners in question were to be executed. The use of such code could have been the method by which those responsible covered their guilt – as suggested by the phrase 'with responsibility to be hidden' in the minutes of the meeting of the evening of 7 November. Serrano Poncela told Galíndez the orders were passed to him by Santiago Carrillo and that all he did was sign them. He told Galíndez that, as soon he realized what was happening, he resigned from his post and not long afterwards left the Communist Party.[116] This was not entirely true since he held the important post of JSU propaganda secretary until well into 1938. In an extraordinary letter to the Central Committee, written in March 1939, Serrano Poncela claimed that he had resigned from the Communist Party only after he had reached France the previous month, implying that previously he had feared for his life. He referred to the disgust he felt about his past in the Communist Party. He also claimed that the PCE had prevented his emigration to Mexico because he knew too much.[117] Indeed, he even went so far as to assert that he had joined the PCE on

6 November 1936 only because Carrillo had browbeaten him into doing so.[118]

Subsequently, and presumably in reprisal for Serrano Poncela's rejection of the Party, Carrillo denounced him. In a long interview given to Ian Gibson in September 1982, Carrillo claimed that he had had nothing to do with the activities of the Public Order Delegation and blamed everything on Serrano Poncela. He alleged that 'my only involvement was, after about a fortnight, I got the impression that Serrano Poncela was doing bad things and so I sacked him'. Allegedly, Carrillo had discovered in late November that 'outrages were being committed and this man was a thief'. He claimed that Serrano Poncela had in his possession jewels stolen from those arrested and that consideration had been given to having him shot.[119] Serrano Poncela's continued pre-eminence in the JSU belies this. Interestingly, neither in his memoirs of 1993 nor in *Los viejos camaradas*, a book published in 2010, does he repeat these detailed charges other than to say that it was during their time together in the Consejería de Orden Público that their differences began to emerge.[120]

The claim that he personally had nothing to do with the killings was repeated by Carrillo in his memoirs. He alleged that the classification and evacuation of prisoners was left entirely to the Public Order Delegation under Serrano Poncela. He went on to assert that the Delegation did not decide on death sentences but merely selected those who would be sent to Tribunales Populares (People's Courts) and those who would be freed. His account is brief, vague and misleading, making no mention of executions and implying that the worst that happened to those judged to be dangerous was to be sent to work battalions building fortifications. The only unequivocal statement in Carrillo's account is a declaration that he took part in none of the Public Order Delegation's meetings.[121] However, if Azaña, Irujo and Giral in Valencia knew about the killings and if, in Madrid, Melchor Rodríguez, the Ambassador of Chile, the Chargé d'Affaires of Argentina, the Chargé d'Affaires of the United Kingdom and Félix Schlayer knew about them, it is inconceivable that Carrillo, as the principal authority in the area of public order, could not know. After all, despite his later claims, he received daily reports from Serrano

Poncela.[122] Melchor Rodríguez's success in stopping *sacas* raises questions about Santiago Carrillo's inability to do the same.

Subsequently, Francoist propaganda built on the atrocity of Paracuellos to depict the Republic as a murderous Communist-dominated regime guilty of red barbarism. Despite the fact that Santiago Carrillo was just one of the key participants in the entire process, the Franco regime, and the Spanish right thereafter, never missed any opportunity to use Paracuellos to denigrate him during the years that he was secretary general of the Communist Party (1960–82) and especially in 1977 as part of the effort to prevent the legalization of the Communist Party. Carrillo himself inadvertently contributed to keeping himself in the spotlight by absurdly denying any knowledge of, let alone responsibility for, the killings. However, a weight of other evidence confirmed by some of his own partial revelations makes it clear that he was fully involved.[123]

For instance, in more than one interview in 1977, Carrillo claimed that, by the time he took over the Council for Public Order in the Junta de Defensa, the operation of transferring prisoners from Madrid to Valencia was 'coming to an end and all I did, with General Miaja, was order the transfer of the last prisoners'. It is certainly true that there had been *sacas* before 7 November, but the bulk of the killings took place after that date while Carrillo was Consejero de Orden Público. Carrillo's admission that he ordered the transfers of prisoners after 7 November clearly puts him in the frame.[124] Elsewhere, he claimed that, after he had ordered an evacuation, the vehicles were ambushed and the prisoners murdered by uncontrolled elements. He stated, 'I can take no responsibility other than having been unable to prevent it.'[125] This would have been hardly credible under any circumstances, but especially so after the discovery of documentary proof of the CNT–JSU meeting of the night of 7 November.

Moreover, Carrillo's post-1974 denials of knowledge of the Paracuellos killings were contradicted by the congratulations heaped on him at the time. Between 5 and 8 March 1937 the PCE celebrated an 'amplified' plenary meeting of its Central Committee in Valencia. Such a meeting, with additional invited participants, was midway between a normal meeting and a full Party congress. Francisco

Antón, a rising figure in the Party and known to be Pasionaria's lover, declared: 'It is difficult to say that the fifth column in Madrid has been annihilated but it certainly has suffered the hardest blows there. This, it must be proclaimed loudly, is thanks to the concern of the Party and the selfless, ceaseless effort of two new comrades, as beloved as if they were veteran militants of our Party, Comrade Carrillo when he was the Consejero de Orden Público and Comrade Cazorla who holds the post now.' When the applause that greeted these remarks had died down, Carrillo rose and spoke of the work done to ensure that the 60 per cent of the members of the JSU who were fighting at the front could do so 'in the certain knowledge that the rearguard is safe, cleansed and free of traitors. It is not a crime, it is not a manoeuvre, but a duty to demand such a purge.'[126]

Comments made both at the time and later by Spanish Communists such as Pasionaria and Francisco Antón, by Comintern agents, by Gorev and by others show that prisoners were assumed to be fifth columnists and that Carrillo was to be praised for eliminating them. On 30 July 1937, the Bulgarian Stoyán Mínev, alias 'Boris Stepanov', from April 1937 one of the Comintern's delegates in Spain, wrote indignantly to the head of the Comintern, Giorgi Dimitrov, of the 'Jesuit and fascist' Irujo that he had tried to arrest Carrillo simply because he had given 'the order to shoot several arrested officers of the fascists'.[127] In his final post-war report to Stalin, Stepanov wrote proudly that the Communists took note of the implications of Mola's statement about his five columns and 'in a couple of days carried out the operations necessary to cleanse Madrid of fifth columnists'. In this report, Stepanov explained how, in July 1937, shortly after becoming Minister of Justice, Manuel Irujo initiated investigations into what had happened at Paracuellos including a judicial inquiry into the role of Carrillo.[128] Unfortunately, no trace of this inquiry has survived and it is possible that any evidence was among the papers burned by the Communist-dominated security services before the end of the war.[129]

What Carrillo himself said in his broadcast on Unión Radio and what Stepanov wrote in his report to Stalin were echoed years later in the Spanish Communist Party's official history of its role in the Civil War. Published in Moscow, and commissioned by Carrillo when he became secretary general of the PCE, it declared proudly that 'Santiago Carrillo and his deputy Cazorla took the measures necessary to maintain order in the rearguard, which was every bit as important as the fighting at the front. In two or three days, a serious blow was delivered against the snipers and fifth columnists.'[130]

Rather unexpectedly, at the meeting of the Junta Delegada de Defensa on 25 December 1936, Carrillo resigned as Consejero de Orden Público and was replaced by his deputy, José Cazorla Maure. He announced that he was leaving to devote himself totally to preparing the forthcoming congress which was intended to seal the unification of the Socialist and Communist youth movements. It was certainly true that a JSU congress was to be held, for which he was preparing an immensely long speech. However, it is very likely that the precipitate timing of his departure was also connected with an incident two days earlier.[131] On 23 December, a Communist member of the Junta de Defensa, Pablo Yagüe, had been shot and seriously wounded at an anarchist control post when he was leaving the city on official business. The culprits then took refuge in the local anarchist headquarters, the Ateneo Libertario, of the Ventas district. Carrillo ordered their arrest, but the CNT Comité Regional refused to hand them over to the police. Carrillo then sent in a company of Assault Guards to seize them. At the meeting of the Junta at which this was discussed, he called for them to be shot.[132] It was the prelude to a spate of revenge attacks and counter-reprisals. Ultimately, Carrillo failed in his demand for the Junta de Defensa to condemn to death the anarchists responsible for the attack on Yagüe, something which was beyond its jurisdiction. He was furious when the case was put in the hands of a state tribunal where the prosecutor refused to ask for the death penalty on the grounds that Yagüe had not shown his credentials to the CNT militiamen at the checkpoint.[133]

Despite the Yagüe crisis, there can be little doubt that Carrillo needed to devote time to the JSU. The organization had expanded massively since July 1936 and its importance in every aspect of the war effort can scarcely be exaggerated. The PCE's determination to consolidate its control of the JSU could be seen in Carrillo's role in the national youth conference held in January 1937 in Valencia. It replaced the congress which had initially been scheduled to establish the structure and programme of the new organization. A congress had formal procedures that required the election of representative delegates, and wartime circumstances made that virtually impossible. A conference had the advantage of permitting Carrillo to choose the delegates himself. Thus he was able to pack the proceedings with hand-picked young Communists from the battle fronts and the factories. He then exploited that to perpetrate the sleight of hand whereby the conference made decisions corresponding to a congress. To the astonishment and chagrin of those FJS members who still harboured the illusion that the new organization was 'Socialist', the entire event was organized along totally Stalinist lines. All policy directives were pre-packaged, there was virtually no debate and there was no voting.[134]

One of the delegates from Alicante, Antonio Escribano, reflected later that 'Ninety percent of the young Socialists present did not know that Carrillo, Laín, Melchor, Cabello, Aurora Arnaiz, etc had gone over lock, stock and barrel to the Communist Party. We thought that they were still young Socialists and they were acting in agreement with Largo Caballero and the PSOE. If we had known that these deserters had betrayed us, something else would have happened.'[135] The impression that the proceedings were carried out under the auspices of Largo Caballero was shamelessly given by Carrillo, who declared, 'It is necessary to say that Comrade Largo Caballero has, as ever, or more than ever, the support of the Spanish youth fighting at the front and working in the factories. It is necessary to say here that Comrade Largo Caballero is for us the same as before: the man who helped our unification, the man from whom we expect much excellent advice so that, in defence of the common cause, the unity of Spanish youth may be a reality.'[136]

As newsreel footage revealed, apart from Julio Álvarez del Vayo and Antonio Machado, the poet and *alcalde* (mayor) of Valencia, the stage party was made up of Communists headed by Pasionaria, Dolores Ibárruri. Carrillo opened his long speech with thanks to the Communist Youth International, the KIM, for its support. He made especially fulsome reference to the KIM representative, Mihály

Farkas, introduced as 'Michael Wolf', with whom his relationship was growing closer. No longer the revolutionary firebrand of the Cárcel Modelo, Carrillo explained that, while the Socialist Youth, the FJS, had tried to undermine the government in 1934, now the JSU supported the Republican government's war effort. According to Carrillo's close collaborator Fernando Claudín, Farkas/Wolf had considerable input into Carrillo's speech. Thus the Comintern line was paramount in Carrillo's talk of broad national unity against a foreign invader. Central to his rhetoric was the defence of the small-holding peasants and the small businessmen with some bitter criticisms of anarchist collectives. There was also the ritual denunciation of the POUM (the Partido Obrero de Unificación Marxista) as a subversive Trotskyist outfit. With the guidance of Codovila and Farkas/Wolf, Carrillo had already started down the road of linking the POUM to the Francoists. The primary function of the JSU was no longer the fomenting of revolution but the education of the masses – the basic reformist aspiration of the Republican–Socialist coalition for which he had previously excoriated Prieto and the PSOE centrists. This was Comintern policy, although it also made perfect sense in the wartime context.[137]

Carrillo boasted that the new organization had had 40,000 members immediately after its creation but now had 250,000. He placed special emphasis on the fact that the JSU was a completely new organization entirely independent of both the PSOE and the PCE, in which neither component had the right to demand its leadership. This was a sophistry to neutralize Socialist annoyance about the fact that, since Carrillo, Cazorla and Serrano Poncela had formally joined the PCE, the JSU executive now had eleven Communists to four Socialists.[138] It was hardly surprising, given the primordial role of the Soviet Union in helping the Republic, that Carrillo should express such enthusiasm for the Communist Party. It would not be long before he would clinch his betrayal of his erstwhile patron.

In the light of Largo Caballero's incompetence as a war leader, the PCE was increasingly determined to see his removal as Prime Minister. Within barely a month of the JSU conference, the opportunity arose with the disastrous fall of Málaga to rebel forces on 8 February.

The disaster could be attributed to Largo Caballero's mistakes as Minister of War and those of his under-secretary, General José Asensio Torrado. By mid-May, mounting criticism had forced Largo Caballero to resign and he was replaced by the Treasury Minister, Dr Juan Negrín. An internationally renowned physiologist, the moderate Socialist Negrín shared the Communist view that priority should be given to the war effort rather than to revolutionary aspirations. An early contribution to the process of undermining Largo Caballero's reputation was made by Carrillo when, in early March 1937, he headed a delegation from the JSU to an amplified plenum of the Central Committee of the PCE. In his speech, he was especially savage in his criticism of the POUM. What entirely undermined his constant claims about the JSU's independence was his hymn of praise to the Communist Party. Moreover, the way he referred to his pride in leaving past mistakes behind must have galled Largo Caballero: 'Finally, we found this party and this revolutionary line for which we have fought all our life, our short life. We are not ashamed of our past, in our past there is nothing deserving of reproach, but we are proud to have overcome all the mistakes of the past and to be today militants of the glorious Communist Party of Spain.' His remarks on his reasons for joining the PCE were even more devastating for Largo Caballero. He referred to 'those who, when the rebels were nearing Madrid, set off for Valencia'. He went on to say that 'many of those who today are attacking the JSU were among those who fled'.[139]

Despite the prominence that came with his earlier position in the Junta de Defensa de Madrid and now as leader of the JSU, Carrillo's role within the Spanish Communist hierarchy was a subordinate one. He accepted this, doing as he was told with relish. At that March 1937 meeting, he was made a non-voting member of the PCE's politburo. He attended and listened but took little part in the discussions – being, as Claudín put it, 'simply the man whose job it was to make sure that the JSU implemented party policy. He did not belong in the inner circles where the important issues were discussed and debated by the delegates of the Comintern (Palmiro Togliatti, Boris Stepanov, Ernst Gerö, Vittorio Codovila), by the top Soviet diplomatic, military and security staff and by the most prominent leaders of the PCE (José

Díaz, Pasionaria, Pedro Checa, Jesús Hernández, Vicente Uribe and Antonio Mije). Carrillo himself believed at this stage that he was simply not trusted enough to be admitted to these top-secret meetings and was determined to achieve that trust. Accordingly, he was careful to maintain excellent relations with the Comintern representatives, especially with Togliatti and Codovila, the man he regarded as his mentor. Codovila was certainly satisfied with the progress made by his pupil.[140]

The extent to which Carrillo had transformed himself into 'his master's voice' was confirmed at the JSU National Committee meeting on 15–16 May 1937 – just as Largo Caballero was being removed from the government. Carrillo roundly criticized Largo Caballero's supporters within the organization and called for their expulsion. Indeed, throughout 1937 and 1938, together with Claudín, Carrillo presided over the systematic elimination of his erstwhile Caballerista allies from the JSU. Claudín's efforts earned him the nickname of 'the Jack the Ripper of the JSU' (*el destripador de las juventudes*). This process would return to haunt the PCE leadership at the end of the war.[141]

The importance of Carrillo's position derived from the fact that the mobilization of the male population, in which the PCE played a key role beginning with the creation of the Fifth Regiment, relied on the continued expansion of the JSU. Its members filled the ranks of the Fifth Regiment and then of the newly created Popular Army as well as those of the Republic's rearguard security forces. For most of the time during 1937 and 1938, Carrillo devoted himself to building up the PCE's most valuable asset. However, because he was of military age and should have been in a fighting unit, it was arranged for him to meet his obligations by spending brief periods attached to the General Staff of the commander of Fifth Army Corps, Lieutenant Colonel Juan Modesto. He claimed later to have witnessed parts of the battles of Brunete, Teruel and the Ebro. This later provoked outraged jibes by General Enrique Líster. It is almost certainly the case that any visits to the battle front were made in order to check on the JSU's many political commissars. However, Carrillo's subsequent attempts to fabricate an heroic military career in response to Líster's accusations of cowardice were perhaps unnecessary. He could legitimately have argued that he had made a substantial contribution to the Republican war effort through his work in terms of the political education of the great influx of new recruits.[142]

Indeed, he worked hard to bring both Republican and anarchist youth organizations under the umbrella of the JSU. At every turn, his loyalty to the Spanish Party and the Comintern was unquestionable, symbolized by the large portrait of Stalin that dominated his office. In April 1937, he drafted and presented in Paris an application for the entry of the JSU into the International Union of Socialist Youth, from which, three years earlier, he had removed the Spanish Socialist Youth (FJS). In Britain, France and other democratic countries, the Socialist youth organizations were putting pressure on their respective governments to support the Spanish Republic. It made perfect sense in terms of the Republican quest for international support for Carrillo to try to take JSU into the organization. He later claimed that the idea for this initiative was entirely his own. Since, as he later admitted, a key element of his initiative was to work towards the unity of the Socialist and Communist Youth Internationals, the idea received the approval of the KIM hierarchy. As the creation of the JSU showed, this would be the first step to a Communist take-over of the larger Socialist organization. The initiative led to the JSU being provisionally admitted to the International Union of Socialist Youth and generated the expected increase in support for the Republic.[143]

He was rewarded for his loyalty by being made the object of a carefully constructed personality cult. He was referred to as the 'undisputed leader of the youth of Spain' and as 'the rudder and great guide of our great Youth Federation'. On the first page of the JSU journal *Espartaco*, there was a photograph of Carrillo accompanied by a description of him as 'the leader beloved of all the young masses of Spain, the solid creator of, and the key to, the unity of the JSU. He, along with the executive committee, channels with a safe and steady hand the enormous strength of the young generation that is fighting for the independence of Spain.' In July 1938, the JSU newspaper *Ahora* carried a photograph under which the caption was 'Our secretary general ... beloved leader of Spanish youth, whose intelligent and selfless efforts have enabled him to lead the struggle and the labour of our country's youth in the fight for the independence of the motherland.' Not long afterwards, Claudín was to be found referring to Carrillo in identical terms. There was some ribaldry in other organizations about the interruptions to the war effort constituted by great public meetings in which it was not clear if the purpose was to raise the morale of the young militants or to massage Carrillo's ego.[144]

In April 1938, Franco's forces had reached the Mediterranean and split the Republican zone in two. By the summer, the Republic was edging to defeat, with Valencia under direct threat. The Prime Minister, Juan Negrín, decided to mount a spectacular counter-offensive to stem the continual erosion of territory. To restore contact between the central zone and Catalonia, an assault across the River Ebro was planned by his chief of staff General Vicente Rojo. In the most hard-fought battle of the entire war, Franco poured in massive reinforcements in reaction to the initial Republican success in advancing to Gandesa. For over three months, he pounded the Republicans with air and artillery attacks in an effort to turn Gandesa into the graveyard of the Republican army. Negrín hoped that the Western democracies would finally see the dangers facing them from the Axis. Before that could happen the Republic was virtually sentenced to death by the British reaction to the Czechoslovakian crisis. The Munich agreement destroyed the Republic's last hope of salvation in a European war. By mid-November, the decimated remnants of the Republican army, led by Manuel Tagüeña, abandoned the right bank of the Ebro. The Republic had lost the bulk of its army and would never recover.

In response to food shortages and conscription of ever younger recruits, demoralization was rife. The deteriorating conditions saw a growth of anti-communism. One symptom of this was the effort being made from the autumn of 1938 by the Socialist Party executive to re-establish a separate Socialist Youth. The JSU organizations of Valencia, Alicante, Albacete, Murcia, Jaen and Ciudad Real were in favour of returning to the old FJS model. Carrillo's knee-jerk, and futile, response was to denounce the dissidents as Trotskyists. His alarm was understandable since JSU members made up a high proportion of the Republican armed forces. The fact that Serrano

Poncela played a key role in this crisis, writing a critical report on the JSU passed to the PSOE executive in 1938, perhaps explains Carrillo's long-term resentment of him.[145] When the JSU headquarters in Alicante were taken over by supporters of Largo Caballero, the FJS was reconstituted. Busts of Lenin and large portraits of Carrillo were destroyed in an iconoclastic venting of rage.[146]

After the Ebro, and the end of any reasonable hope of victory, war-weariness overwhelmed the Republican zone. Hunger, privation and the scale of casualties took their toll and much of the frustration was visited on the PCE and the JSU. In October, Carrillo and Pedro Checa were sent to Madrid in an attempt to reverse the process whereby anti-communism was undermining what remained of a war effort. They found not only a generalized fatigue but the determined hostil-ity of the leadership of both the PSOE and the CNT. When the Francoists bombed Madrid with loaves of fresh white bread, JSU militants burned them in the streets. Given the scale of hunger suffered by the Madrileños, this was a less successful gesture than Carrillo later claimed. While in the capital, Santiago heard that his father was actively working with the anti-Negrín elements in the PSOE. They had a monumental row over Wenceslao's claim that the only solution was to seek an honourable surrender.[147]

Just before Christmas 1938, Franco launched a final offensive armed with new German equipment. His reserves were sufficient for his troops to be relieved every two days. Carrillo and others were sent to Barcelona in the vain hope that they might be able to organize the kind of popular resistance that had saved Madrid in November 1936. His days were spent commuting to the front trying to keep up morale, but the shattered Republican army of the Ebro could barely fight on. He also worked with militants of the Catalan JSU in an effort to organize popular resistance. Barcelona fell on 26 January 1939. Carrillo claimed later that he was still in the Catalan capital as the Francoists approached and did not leave until they were near the city centre. His own accounts are the only source for his claims that, as he headed north, he was nearly captured by Francoist troops in Girona on 4 February. Shortly afterwards, he crossed the French frontier.[148] The same is true of his assertion that he was anxious to return to

Madrid not only to continue the fight but to be reunited with his wife, Asunción 'Chon' Sánchez Tudela, and their one-year-old daughter, Aurora. They had married shortly before the outbreak of the Civil War. He was particularly anxious since Chon had heart problems and Aurora was weak as a result of consistently poor nutrition in the first year of her life.[149] Why Carrillo did not go back to Madrid and what happened to Chon and Aurora at the end of the war are issues clouded in mystery, as will be explained in the next chapter.

Hundreds of thousands of hungry and terrified refugees from all over Spain left the Catalan capital and began to trek towards France. A huge area of about 30 per cent of Spanish territory still remained to the Republic, but the population was afflicted with ever deepening war-weariness. Although further military resistance was virtually impossible, the Communists were determined to hold on to the bitter end. On the one hand, this was important to their Russian masters as a way of delaying inevitable fascist aggression against the Soviet Union.[150] It would also allow them to derive political capital out of the 'desertion' of their rivals. In fact, they were far from alone in the belief that, given the determination of Franco to carry out a savage repression, it was crucial to resist in the hope of the Western Powers waking up to the fascist threat. However, the Communists were seen as the main advocates of dogged resistance, and they thereby became the target of the popular resentment, frustration and war-weariness. In contrast, the determination of non-Communist elements to make peace on the best possible terms was immensely attractive to the starving populations of most cities in the Republican zone.

In France, Carrillo missed the coup launched on 5 March by Colonel Segismundo Casado, commander of the Republican Army of the Centre. Casado thought that he could put a stop to the increasingly senseless slaughter. Together with Wenceslao Carrillo and Julián Besteiro, and with anarchist leaders, Casado formed an anti-Communist National Defence Junta (Consejo Nacional de Defensa) under the presidency of General Miaja. Casado wrongly believed that this would facilitate negotiation with Franco, with whose representatives he had been in touch. In fact, he sparked off a disastrous civil war within the Republican zone, ensured the deaths of many Communists and undermined the evacuation plans for hundreds of thousands of Republicans. Wenceslao Carrillo was Councillor for the Interior in Casado's Junta and persecuted the Communists relentlessly until the last day of the war. His brutality was born of resentment of the way in which his friend Largo Caballero had been ousted from the government in May 1937. It also reflected virulent anger that the Communists had 'stolen' his son and that his son had betrayed him in letting it happen. In Paris on 7 March, a Party comrade, Luis Cabo Giorla, gave Carrillo two pieces of bad news. He told him about the coup and his father's role therein and also that his mother had died some weeks before. Carrillo's reaction, a virulent denunciation of his own father, would be among the most revealing episodes of his life.[151]

A Fully Formed Stalinist:
1939–1950

With the Civil War still raging, Carrillo remained in France along with other members of the politburo. The prominent Communist General Enrique Líster later claimed that his place should have been back in the central zone where the majority of the JSU's militants were to be found. However, Carrillo did not accompany Líster and some members of the politburo to Spain on the night of 13 February 1939. Interviewed in 1974, he claimed that he had wanted to return to Spain but had been prevented by a series of reasons. The most implausible of these was that the politburo wished to ensure that he would not find himself fighting against his own father. Carrillo had been in France for nearly six weeks when he learned of the coup carried out by Colonel Segismundo Casado on 5 March. Casado's anti-Communist Junta included Wenceslao Carrillo as Councillor for Public Order, an ironic echo of his son's role in 1936 – the irony being that it was Wenceslao's mission to hunt down Communists. Santiago claimed in 1974 that the news of his father's involvement with Casado had upset him more than did that of the death of his mother which he had received at the same time. News of the coup could hardly explain why Carrillo had not returned to Spain three weeks earlier. Hardly more plausible was his claim that he could not travel because there was no room on any aircraft flying to Alicante. Líster pointed out that the thirty-three-seat aircraft in which he travelled on 13 February had twenty empty seats. The head of the Republican air force, Ignacio Hidalgo de Cisneros, told Burnett Bolloten that the last six aircraft that flew from France to Republican Spain were 'nearly empty'. The most likely of Carrillo's three excuses, which did little for his attempts to construct an heroic past, was that he had been unable to travel because he had scabies. Since Manuel Tagüeña believed that Carrillo had just ignored orders to return, scabies may well have been the excuse that he gave to his superiors.[1]

The PCE's politburo met on 12 March to discuss the situation. This was followed by further meetings at which lists were drawn up of those cadres chosen to find refuge in the Soviet Union.[2] Santiago Carrillo's sentiments as he sat through these meetings may easily be imagined. Having nailed his colours so firmly to the PCE mast, he was at best deeply embarrassed, if not seriously frightened. He must have been extremely concerned that his father's participation in the Casado Junta might have undone at a stroke all his efforts to rise within the Party hierarchy. He needed to take drastic action to avoid being besmirched in the eyes of the PCE leadership. After all, the recent purges in the Soviet Union had demonstrated that the treachery of a militant's relative was believed to contaminate the blood of the entire family and so would have dire consequences for the Party member. Carrillo claims in his memoirs that he immediately locked himself in his hotel room and began to write an open letter denouncing his father. This is simply not true. His text is dated 15 May and opens by saying that it is a reply to a letter sent by his father from London. Since his father did not reach London until early April, that letter could not have arrived much before the end of the month. Moreover, there are ample signs in the letter that the two and half months' delay had permitted lengthy contemplation, if not consultation with others, in the drafting process. Moreover, the fact that Santiago's reply was very widely publicized suggested that his principal motivation was to prove his Stalinist orthodoxy by the ferocity of the attack on Wenceslao.

The letter was thus directed more to his superiors than to his father. Without the slightest hint of sadness or sorrow, its text was a mixture of understandable outrage about the consequences of the Casado coup and absurdly exaggerated Stalinist rhetoric. Santiago declared that he had decided to break off all relations with his father because of his participation in 'a counter-revolutionary coup and in the back-stabbing treachery that handed over the heroic Spanish people, bound hand and foot, to Franco, the OVRA [the Italian secret police] and the Gestapo'. He pointed out, rightly, that internationally the

Casado coup had tipped the balance of power in favour of Hitler and, within Spain, had opened the way to a brutal repression. In particular, he wrote with indignation of those Communists who had been imprisoned for the convenience of the Francoists.

Much of the rest of the extremely long text was a hymn of praise to those against whom the Casado coup had been directed: 'my Party and its most beloved leaders; you insulted Pasionaria, the woman all Spaniards consider a symbol of the struggle for freedom, you hunted her like wolves to hand her over to Franco'. He wrote in similar terms of the Casado Junta's denigration of, and determination to capture and execute, José Díaz, Jesús Hernández, Juan Modesto and Enrique Líster. He then moved on to insult his erstwhile idol, Largo Caballero, and his one-time fellow bolshevizers Luis Araquistáin, Carlos Baraibar and Carlos Hernández Zancajo, whom he now denounced as Trotskyists motivated by 'hatred of the great fatherland of social-ism, the Soviet Union, and the leader of the international working class, the great Stalin, because they are the vanguard and the faithful friend of all the peoples who fight for liberty, because they have consistently helped the Spanish people, and because they have been able with an iron hand to sweep aside your twin brothers, the Trotskyist, Zinovievist and Bukharinite traitors'.

The letter to his father ended with a final effort to convince the leadership of the PCE that he was a loyal element ready to sacrifice his family for the cause: 'I remind you that every day I feel more proud of my party which has been the example of self-sacrifice and heroism in the struggle against the invaders, the party that in these difficult times of illegality does not lower its flag but continues to fight fascism with determination and courage ... Every day I feel prouder of being a soldier in the ranks of the Great Communist International. Every day my love grows for the Soviet Union and the great Stalin.' He ended with the words, 'When you ask to be in touch with me, you forget that I am a Communist and you are a man who has betrayed his class and sold out his people. Between a Communist and a traitor there can be no relations of any kind.'[3]

The letter was published in early June in the mouthpieces of both the Comintern and the KIM, *La Correspondance Internationale* and

Jeunesses du Monde. Nevertheless, not everyone in the PCE believed in its sincerity. Manuel Tagüeña, who at the time was living in clandestinity in the same safe house as Carrillo near Paris, wrote later, 'Between Carrillo and me there was never much trust and certainly no friendship. I always believed that he would do anything to further his political ambitions. He had just publicly disowned his father Wenceslao for joining Casado's Junta. No matter how much it was made out to be the gesture of a heroic Spartan warrior, no one doubted that he had done it to show the PCE leadership that he was the complete militant, ready to sacrifice his family for the good of the cause.'[4]

When Wenceslao read the letter some weeks later, he refused to believe that it had been written by his son. Accordingly, his reply, on 2 July 1939, was directed not to Santiago but to the person he considered its real author, 'Señor Stalin'. Wenceslao suggested that the letter might have been dictated by Pasionaria and Jesús Hernández, but he believed it to have been inspired by Stalin. He acknowledged just how much 'this dagger in the heart' had hurt him. He ended with prophetic words: 'I, Señor Stalin, had always educated my son in the love of freedom, you have converted him to slavery. Since I still love him, despite such a monstrous letter, I will ensure by my example that he returns to the place that he should never have left.'[5]

It would be nearly five decades before Santiago Carrillo would return to the Socialist Party and nearly twenty years before he would see his father again. Then, the seriously ill Wenceslao Carrillo was living in Belgium with the support of the metalworkers' union. Artur Gallí, the union's secretary general, had brought Wenceslao to the clinic that he had founded in Charleroi and there he spent his last years. Santiago claimed that, after the PCE had developed its strategy of 'national reconciliation' in 1956, Pasionaria and others suggested that it would be politically useful if he were to be reconciled with his father. In this version, when they met, his father said, 'As far as I am concerned, you have always been my son.' Santiago introduced him to his wife and young sons and Wenceslao spent time with them at their home in Paris. According to an Asturian Socialist, Manuel Villa, when Wenceslao Carrillo died in 1963, Santiago appeared at the funeral. The many exiled Spanish Socialists who filed past the graveside gave their condolences to other members of the family but ostentatiously refused to shake hands with Santiago.[6] However, all that was still in the future.

In 1939, while in France, Carrillo was not part of the tortuous process whereby, since April, Comintern officials and the PCE leaders exiled in Moscow were engaged in the preparation of reports on the Party's role in the Republican war effort and on the reasons for defeat. There were various contributory drafts. From the Comintern officials who had been in Spain there were reports by the Bulgarian Stoyán Mínev (Stepanov) and Palmiro Togliatti (Alfredo). From the Spaniards, there were drafts from Jesús Hernández, Vicente Uribe and Antonio Cordón and testimony from many other witnesses to specific episodes. There was considerable disagreement as to whether the Party leadership was correct in assuming that the war had effectively been lost when Barcelona fell. Líster was convinced that greater foresight and resistance could have undermined the effects of the Casado coup.[7]

The final report was only for the eyes of Stalin, Dimitrov and the very top echelons of the PCE. The debate was not widened to the rank and file, on the plausible grounds that this could only cause scandal and demoralization among the militants at a time when the Party was scattered around the world and still suffering the trauma of defeat. The Russians wanted the Comintern to be cleared of any responsibility and Dolores Ibárruri exonerated, especially as she was being groomed to take over the Party leadership. Carrillo emerged unscathed. On the few occasions that he was mentioned, his work with the JSU was commended.[8] The way the process was managed ensured PCE loyalty to Moscow but left the Party committed to the unswerving defence of its own behaviour during the Civil War. It is difficult to see what else the exiled PCE leaders could have done in the context of the Soviet purges given their dependence on Russian charity. Nevertheless, the commitment to Stalinism deprived the Party of flexibility and credibility at a time when the unity of the entire anti-Francoist opposition was of the first importance.[9]

During the summer of 1939, Carrillo was occupied in a vain effort to prevent the expulsion of the JSU from the International Union of

Socialist Youth. In July, at the congress in Lille at which the issue was to be decided, his position was definitively undermined when the letter to his father was distributed to all the delegates.[10] This disappointment was followed by the news of the signing on 23 August of the Molotov–Ribbentrop pact, the Treaty of Non-Aggression between Nazi Germany and the Soviet Union. Such was the adherence of Carrillo to the Stalinist cause that it caused him no distress. His view of the consequences for the Western Powers, which he blamed for the defeat of the Spanish Republic, was: 'Those bastards have got exactly what they deserved.'[11]

Carrillo claimed that it was around this time that his wife Chon and their daughter Aurora arrived in Paris. He told María Eugenia Yagüe, with whom he prepared an authorized biography as part of his electoral campaign in 1977, that the Party leadership had not allowed him to risk going to get them out of Madrid. The dual implication was that he was far too valuable and that he put his loyalty to the Party above family considerations. The description that he gave Yagüe of their experiences in the ten months since he had last seen them is contradictory and also differs from that in his memoirs. Nevertheless, both versions recount intense suffering and hardship. He told Yagüe that Chon and Aurora had managed to get across the French border and, thanks to help from French Communists, had avoided internment in a concentration camp. In the same text, he also claimed that they *had* been held in a French concentration camp. Both in his conversations with Yagüe and in his memoirs, he asserted that Aurora had died later as a result of her privations in the French camp.[12] However, in those memoirs, in contrast, he claims that they had fled Madrid in the last days of the war and reached the port at Alicante where the expected evacuation failed to materialize thanks to the machinations of Casado. Like tens of thousands of others, he says, they were held for several months in the insanitary camp at Albatera where the lack of food severely worsened the already poor health of Aurora. Chon had not been recognized, and eventually they were released. At this point, Party comrades in Valencia managed to hide them and eventually get them across the Pyrenees and into the arms of Santiago Carrillo.

Apart from the contradictions between the two versions, there are other problems with Carrillo's accounts. In the first place, if Chon and Aurora had been in Alicante, they would certainly not have been in the camp at Albatera since there is no known record of any women being held there. When the Francoists entered the port, women and children were separated out, some put on a train to Madrid and others taken into the city of Alicante where they were held in the municipal prison, in a nearby barracks or in a cinema. Moreover, Líster claimed that Chon and Aurora had left Spain with Carrillo, evacuated by the Party on 8 February 1939 along with Antonio Mije, Luis Cabo Giorla and their wives. Líster asserted that he and the other three families had stayed together in a comfortable hotel in Toulouse three days later.[13]

The letter to Wenceslao had been essential to prove that Santiago was not contaminated by the Casado experience. Now, with that problem out of the way, Carrillo could derive benefit from the fact that, in the eyes of the Comintern leadership, he had a spectacular curriculum vitae. He had brought the hundreds of thousands of JSU members into the Communist orbit. This had given the PCE immense influence within the Republic's armed forces during the war. Until at least the mid-1960s, the wartime JSU recruits would form the bulk of the PCE's clandestine organization within Spain and were the nursery from which the future leadership would be selected. Carrillo had not wavered in his denunciations of Trotskyists, of his erstwhile Socialist comrades, nor even of his father.

Given the PCE's dependence on the goodwill of the Comintern, Carrillo and his comrades could hardly be anything other than the most hard-line orthodox Stalinists.[14] Nevertheless, there is no reason to doubt the sincerity of his faith in Stalin. This would be demonstrated by his lack of concern about the Molotov–Ribbentrop pact. Carrillo wrote articles in the PCE's theoretical journal *Nuestra Bandera* mocking the Spanish Socialists, including the PCE's erstwhile allies Julio Álvarez del Vayo and Juan Negrín, who supported the democratic powers. Since it was impossible for the PCE's publications to be smuggled into Spain, articles therein were aimed not so much at illuminating the rank and file of the Party as at demonstrating the author's loyalty to the Kremlin. When the Germans invaded the Soviet Union on 22 June 1941, Carrillo would happily change his position without acknowledgement of previous error.[15]

In early September 1939, the twenty-four-year-old Carrillo was ordered to go to Brussels where Vittorio Codovila ran the Western European headquarters of the Comintern. The idea was that he would join Fernando Claudín, Manuel Tagüeña, Antonio Mije and others who were being posted to Latin America. However, after a delay of several weeks, he was sent to Moscow where an important promotion awaited him. His denunciation of his father had borne fruit.[16] He was about to receive his reward in the Soviet Union with elevation to the highest echelons of the KIM, the Communist Youth International. With Chon and Aurora, he crossed Germany with a Chilean diplomatic passport provided by the poet Pablo Neruda, who was Special Consul for Spanish emigration in Paris. They reached Moscow on 26 December. On arrival, both Chon, who had long suffered serious heart problems, and the baby Aurora, who had failed to thrive after a difficult birth, were hospitalized. Despite better medical treatment and nutrition, Aurora would die within a year.

According to Carrillo himself, on the day after his arrival he was subjected to a rigorous vetting by what was called the Cadres Section of the Comintern, an internal security unit run by the NKVD. For several reasons, it may be wondered whether he was being investigated or trained. It is likely that Carrillo had been recruited by this section during his visit to Moscow in 1936. This suspicion is sustained by the fact that the NKVD assassination specialist Josif Grigulevich later described himself as 'the right hand of Carrillo' in the Consejería de Orden Público in the Junta de Defensa de Madrid. That would have been inconceivable unless Carrillo also had close links to the NKVD.[17] According to KGB records, Carrillo remained a close friend of Grigulevich.[18] Moreover, after a period in Mexico, Grigulevich arrived back in Moscow shortly before Carrillo and thus coincided with him. He remained there until February 1940 when he returned to Mexico to organize the first assassination attempt on Trotsky. Another reason to question what Carrillo learned in this period are the brutal interrogation skills that he was later to demonstrate against suspect Party comrades, which were reminiscent of Soviet police techniques. The military section of the Organization Department of the Comintern ran a special military-political school, recently relocated to Planernaya outside Moscow, that provided a three-month training course in tradecraft for secret work and interrogation techniques. Among its earlier graduates had been Palmiro Togliatti and the French Communist leader Maurice Thorez. Among its present officials were two of Carrillo's mentors, the secretary general of the KIM, Raymond Guyot, and his deputy, Mihály Farkas (Michael Wolf). Just as senior Spanish Communists with military experience were given further training (professional soldiers at the General Staff Academy and those from the militias at the Frunze Military Academy), there is reason to believe that Carrillo was selected for 'political' training at the Comintern school.[19]

He and Chon spent six months in the Soviet capital, living in the gloomy and cockroach-infested Hotel Lux, the home to most foreign Communists, although his work meant that he probably saw little of her. He was briefly attached to the secretariat of the KIM, attending meetings of the Comintern executive, which gave him frequent access to Dimitrov and Manuilsky. He was able to renew his friendship with Farkas/Wolf and to establish links with Dimitrov's secretary Boris Ponomarev, who years later would be in charge of the Kremlin's relations with foreign Communist parties. He later claimed, implausibly, 'If there was any fear of Stalin in the Soviet Union, I did not see it. For many years only a minority knew about the trials and the purges. Outside that circle, the families of the victims certainly knew about them, but I didn't meet any of them. I had entered a world that did not talk about such matters.' The only discomfort that he experienced in the Soviet Union was one night when he had left the Hotel Lux without his identity papers. When he returned, to his distress, the doorman refused to let him back in. One legacy of this period in the Soviet Union was an addiction to tobacco. Every day, he would find a packet of rough Russian cigarettes on his desk. This was long before there was widespread awareness of the link between smoking and lung cancer. Curiously, in the same period, he was advised to take a daily aspirin, advice which he followed religiously and which probably contributed to his longevity. He never managed to acquire a working knowledge of Russian.[20]

Dimitrov believed that Carrillo could be of more use in the field than in a bureaucratic position in Moscow. His first thought had been to send him to Switzerland to set up a centre for KIM operations throughout Europe. However, when the German occupation of ever more European territory made that impossible, Dimitrov decided to send Carrillo to New York to be part of a triumvirate controlling the Communist parties in the Americas. It consisted of Vittorio Codovila, who was now in Argentina, Earl Browder, who was secretary general of the Communist Party of the United States, and Carrillo. The choice of Carrillo rather than Farkas/Wolf, the obvious candidate, was the consequence of the Comintern hierarchy's belief that the best way to communicate with the clandestine Communist organization in Spain would be from posts in Latin America. Carrillo and Chon set off in June 1940, travelling eastwards from Moscow to Vladivostock, and then via Tokyo, Vancouver and Montreal.

In early July 1940, they arrived in New York, where preparations for a second attempt to murder Trotsky in Mexico were being made by Naum Isakovich Eitingon. Under the pseudonym 'Leonid Aleksandrovich Kotov', Eitingon had been the *rezident* in the NKVD sub-station in the Soviet Consulate in Barcelona during the Spanish Civil War. Carrillo coincided with both him and Grigulevich. They were working with a network of Spanish Communists recruited during the Civil War. According to the testimony of Enrique Líster to his son, Kotov/Eitingon was Carrillo's NKVD controller.[21]

Carrillo spent six months in New York, where he was deeply uncomfortable since his entire, and relatively limited, cultural baggage was Spanish. Unable to come to terms with the language and having been patronized and ignored by Browder, he was happy to be sent to Cuba. It was believed that he could fulfil his function better there and in Mexico where the bulk of exiled Spaniards were concentrated. The PCE organization in Latin America was under the leadership of Vicente Uribe and Antonio Mije. Carrillo continued to have responsibility for the JSU and recruited Fernando Claudín as his second-in-command.[22] Alternating between Mexico and Cuba, he chalked up few successes although, in Havana, he did consolidate his relationship with Julián Grimau García, a comrade who had worked in the Republican security forces during the Civil War and would later play a major role in the history of the PCE. Since Mexico recognized the Spanish Republican government-in-exile, it had virtually no contact with Franco's Spain, and Cuba had only a little more. The entry of the United States into the Second World War on 11 December 1941, followed by that of Cuba, cut off trade with Franco's Spain. Accordingly, Carrillo was eventually sent in early 1943 to Argentina, where there was still regular trade with Spain. Living as illegal immigrants, he and Claudín managed to recruit a number of Spanish and Portuguese Communist sailors to send propaganda, agents and messages to the clandestine organization in Spain.[23]

Claudín recalled that much of what they talked about centred on their female conquests. Chon had initially accompanied Santiago to New York and then on to Cuba. The baby had been left behind in the USSR where she had not responded to medical treatment and had died while they were in Cuba. However, in his interview with María Eugenia Yagüe in 1977 and also in a Spanish television programme in 2005, he implied that Aurora had died while still in France.[24] Whatever the truth of the child's death, it clearly had an impact on the marriage. At first, Chon had not accompanied him to Argentina and the consequent extended separation had not helped their relationship. Chon may well have perceived that, as was demonstrated by his treatment of his father, he had put his commitment to the Party above personal relationships. His various infidelities would also have taken their toll. When she finally decided to follow him to Buenos Aires, she found him in a relationship with an Argentinian girl named Lidia Márquez, the sister of Claudín's girlfriend, Ángela.[25]

In early 1944, he went to Montevideo as the first step towards returning to Europe. Chon accompanied him to Uruguay, where they remained for some months. What happened next is far from clear. In Carrillo's memoirs, there is no further mention of her. Years later, a story circulated within the Party that she had eventually remarried another PCE militant named Muñoz in Paris with whom she emigrated to Cuba, where she died in 1958. However, in 1961 in Prague, Vicente Uribe gave Enrique Líster an entirely different version. He told him that when Carrillo set off from Uruguay for Lisbon in June 1944 he had instructed Chon to remain in Montevideo. But some considerable time later Luis Cabo Giorla arranged a passage for her on a ship bound for France. Her appearance in late April 1946 in Toulouse was not welcomed by Carrillo. Apparently, he feared that his spurned wife might reveal secrets about his activities in New York and Latin America. In the hostile Cold War atmosphere in France, this would have been disastrous and so, according to Uribe, he had her murdered and then buried in the garden of a safe house used by the PCE. There is no way of verifying what Uribe told Líster since the safe house in question has long since been sold and an apartment block built on the site. However, it is certainly the case that this is what Uribe told Líster, who immediately told his son and included it in memoirs that he was writing. The story was soon widespread within Party circles in Paris and was believed by, among others, Jorge Semprún. In 1983, the allegation was removed from the draft of Líster's memoirs by the publisher because there was no verifiable proof. When Líster died in Madrid in 1994, Francisco Romero Marín, a former Soviet agent and intimate collaborator of Carrillo, appeared at the dead man's home and browbeat his widow into handing over his papers. This put paid to the plans of Líster's son to publish the papers which contained both the story about Chon and much other material that would have been damaging to Carrillo.[26]

Despite being far from Europe, Carrillo's articles endorsing the Soviet Union's vacillating position about the nature of the Second World War had underlined his unwavering loyalty to Moscow. They did him no harm at a time when the leadership of the PCE was in flux. José Díaz's stomach cancer was worsening despite three major operations, one in France and two in Russia. After the German invasion, he had been evacuated to Tblisi in Georgia. Deeply depressed by constant pain, his own isolation and the desperate military situation of the Soviet Union, he committed suicide on 24 March 1942 by throwing himself from a window of the sanatorium where he was being treated.[27]

This had opened a struggle for the succession in which there were three candidates, Dolores Ibárruri and Jesús Hernández in Russia and Vicente Uribe in Mexico. Hernández and his wife Pilar Boves were immensely popular among the Spanish exiles in the Soviet Union, who lived in appalling conditions. This was particularly true of the younger elements, the girls often forced into prostitution, the boys into theft. Hernández was always ready to help those in need – even those who wanted to leave Russia.[28] He was the PCE's representative in the Comintern leadership and was working with Dimitrov as a radio commentator in Kuiybyshev (Samara) where the Soviet government and foreign diplomats were evacuated in October 1941. He enjoyed the support of both Líster and Modesto. Pasionaria was with the rest of the Comintern leadership in Ufa in Bashkiria. She lived with a tightly knit clique of unconditional supporters including her lover Francisco Antón and her secretary Irene Falcón. They were regarded as insufferably arrogant and indifferent to the problems of the other exiles. Moreover, given the ostensibly puritanical Communist ethos, for the married Dolores Ibárruri to have a lover, let alone one fifteen years her junior, was regarded as scandalous. Dimitrov and Manuilsky initially supported Hernández, but other elements in the Soviet Party were suspicious of his popularity and his independent spirit. Eventually, the Soviet choice would be Pasionaria.[29]

There was an ironic contradiction for the Spanish Communists that real power within the Party lay in Russia but the only meaningful connection with Spain lay in Latin America. Both Carrillo and Pedro Checa were hostile to the deeply mediocre Vicente Uribe, known in the Party as 'Herod' for his abusive bullying. Because of failing health, Checa himself was not a viable candidate despite his links to the Soviet security services. He had serious lung problems related to the tuberculosis he had caught during the Civil War. He and Carrillo were determined that Uribe should not succeed Díaz as secretary general. They declared in favour of the candidacy of Dolores Ibárruri. It was a risky gamble but one that paid off in the long term. The death of her son Rúben, fighting in the defence of Stalingrad, inspired a wave of sympathy, and Dimitrov and Manuilsky finally threw their weight behind her. Her awareness of Carrillo's support would stand him in good stead over the next three decades. Shortly afterwards, on 6 August 1942, Pedro Checa himself died after an appendectomy with multiple complications.[30]

The final victory of Pasionaria would be clinched in the late summer of 1943, when Jesús Hernández was permitted to go to Mexico, which indicated that the Kremlin did not favour his candidacy. His vain hope was to muster support among the exiles in Latin America. He had secured the enmity of Uribe and Mije when he expressed his indignation at their indolence and irresponsibility and the luxury in which they lived on the basis of the Party subscriptions paid by rank-and-file militants. They countered by accusing him of trying to supplant Dolores Ibárruri. In May 1944, he was expelled from the Party in Mexico for 'sectarianism and factional activity'.[31]

Both Dimitrov and Pasionaria believed that Carrillo would be better employed working for the PCE rather than the KIM. Their view was reluctantly shared by Uribe. As incompetent as he was lazy, Uribe realized that an efficient workaholic like Carrillo was needed to redeem the Party from the organizational mess that he had let develop while Checa was ill. Accordingly, he swallowed his annoyance with him and suggested that he be incorporated into the politburo of the PCE as a full member. Carrillo had been a non-voting member since March 1937. Now he was one of the most important members of the Party hierarchy, after Pasionaria, Uribe and Mije.[32] The timing could not have been better since Stalin would dissolve the Comintern and the KIM in May 1943, partly as a gesture towards his wartime allies, Britain and the United States, but also as an element of his post-war project. After Stalingrad and with the battle of Kursk, Stalin foresaw the imminent recuperation of Russian territory to be quickly followed by the liberation of the countries of Eastern Europe. To help ensure that these countries should become solid allies of the USSR, it was necessary to give the impression that the local Communist parties should participate in national liberation fronts and committees as a prelude to participation in coalition governments, which, after the dissolution of the Comintern, would appear to be independent of Russian tutelage.

Carrillo's area of responsibility was Party organization, both in Latin America and in Spain. He had little solid information about Spain and immense suspicion about what was happening in the interior. The official Party line was that only slavish adherence to Moscow was acceptable. In the appalling conditions of the Francoist terror, this line was virtually impossible to follow, not least because of the difficulty within Spain of knowing what Moscow's position was. As he rose ever higher in the Party hierarchy, Carrillo demonstrated that he had entirely left behind the revolutionary firebrand that he had been before 1936. His incorporation into the politburo completed his transformation into a rigidly hard-line Stalinist. An understandable tendency to a mimetic loyalty to the Moscow line was exhibited by the politburo during and immediately after the period of the Ribbentrop–Molotov pact. This was demonstrated by the case of what came to be called 'Quiñonismo', a concept which requires some explanation. It shows how little empathy Carrillo and the rest of the exiled leadership had for the situation of the Communists left behind in Spain in 1939 as they tried to keep alive a primitive organization which could do little more than attempt to help prisoners, distribute propaganda and occasionally attack Falangist offices.

At the end of the Civil War, the Communist Party was virtually non-existent. Relatively little had been done to plan for its existence after the defeat, and the Casado coup meant that tens of thousands of Party cadres had been left on the docksides in Alicante and Valencia to be captured. One after another, attempts to build up clandestine networks had been dismantled by Franco's massive security apparatus. The efforts to build a network in Madrid were swiftly undermined when Matilde Landa, the senior PCE leader left in Spain, was arrested on 4 April 1939. Dozens of JSU militants were captured in the spring of 1939 because Casado's men had seized the JSU membership lists and then left them for the Francoists. Many were executed, including the thirteen young women known as the 'Trece Rosas'. José Cazorla and Ramón Torrecilla Guijarro who had worked with Carrillo in the Consejería de Orden Público of the Junta de Defensa de Madrid had remained in Spain to try to rebuild the Party. They were arrested on 9 August 1939 and interrogated under torture. They were tried on 16 January 1940 and sentenced to death. Cazorla was eventually executed on 8 April that year and Torrecilla on 2 July.[33]

Neither the signature of the pact on 23 August 1939 nor the Soviet invasion of Poland on 17 September caused the leadership of the PCE any visible embarrassment. In the official history of the PCE commissioned by Carrillo in the late 1950s, neither event was mentioned. The entire experience was abbreviated as follows: 'The conflict began as an imperialist war between France and England on one side and Germany on the other. But later its character changed. This change was originated, fundamentally, by the resistance of the peoples to Hitlerian aggression, by the entry of the Soviet Union into the conflict and the formation of a powerful anti-Hitlerian coalition made up of the USSR, England, the United States and other countries.'[34] In the mid-1970s, Carrillo was still claiming that, for the bulk of the rank and file, the Ribbentrop–Molotov pact had provoked no qualms of conscience. This, he asserted, was 'not only because of our unconditional confidence in Stalin, but above all because we had left Spain filled with hatred towards the so-called "democratic" European powers that had betrayed us, that had sold us out'. This might have been true for Carrillo, the rest of the leadership and the most hardheaded Stalinists but was far from the unanimous view within the Party.[35]

Indeed, for many militants who had shed blood in the struggle against Franco and his Axis accomplices, Russia's pact with the Third Reich was shocking. Manuel Tagüeña later alleged that the majority of exiled Spaniards in Russia had thought that it was shameful, although few would have dared say so openly.[36] Moreover, it would cause significant problems for the tens of thousands of Party members exiled in France. After the outbreak of war in September 1939, the pact meant that Communists were considered by the French government to be enemies of the state. Accordingly, the main preoccupation of the PCE leaders in France was to escape either to Latin America or to Russia. They departed without concern for those left behind in Spain or in France. Yet, against all the odds, the reconstruction of the Party in the interior was undertaken with remarkable, if short-lived, success by Heriberto Quiñones.

Born Yefim Granowsky in what is now Moldova, Quiñones was a Comintern agent who had been sent into Spain in 1930. He had first worked in Asturias and then settled in Mallorca, where in 1932 he married a prominent feminist and PCE militant named Aurora Picornell. He avoided death when the military rebels seized Mallorca only because, in July 1936, he was in a tuberculosis sanatorium in Madrid. Although he was already tough and determined, the news that his wife had been murdered by the Francoists in January 1937 further hardened his resolve. Thus, at the end of war, when Togliatti offered him the chance to be evacuated, he chose to stay in Spain – an implicit criticism of the leadership that went into exile. He was captured in Valencia but managed to pass for just another Republican soldier. He began to work to rebuild the Party in Valencia. Seriously ill with tuberculosis, he was arrested and severely tortured by agents of the Gestapo. He was returned moribund to the prison but, thanks to a venal priest who altered his records in return for a bribe, he was eventually released. He dragged himself to Madrid where, in April 1941, he began the mammoth task of setting up a new clandestine nationwide organization of the PCE. Astonishingly, in the eight months before his final arrest, he managed to complete this project. During that time, by dint of being always well dressed in public, he avoided the police attention that would have been attracted by a working-class man on the streets during the day – a feature which was later used against him by the Party.

The risks and hardships suffered by the seriously ill Quiñones and his comrades inclined him to be highly critical of those leaders who had not only fled into exile but had left without leaving adequate preparations for what would follow the inevitable defeat. Perhaps because he was a Soviet agent, Quiñones felt himself entitled to criticize the Party hierarchy. He was totally convinced, with every justification, that the exiled leadership, whether in Mexico or Moscow, could not understand the reality of the struggle in the interior. He had been outraged by the Hitler–Stalin pact and had made no secret of his belief that it was absurd for PCE members to have been ordered to have nothing to do with a reactionary, imperialist squabble. He believed that, as in the Civil War, it was necessary to forge links with

other elements of the anti-Franco opposition who supported the
Allied cause. In this, he was effectively anticipating the policy of
Unión Nacional that the leadership would adopt again in August
1941 after the German invasion of the Soviet Union the preceding
June.[37] His crimes, in the eyes of the exiled leadership, went further
than his theoretical 'deviations'. He had gone ahead and started to
reorganize the Party in the interior without awaiting instructions.
Even more outrageously, he had created what he named the 'Central
Politburo' as a substitute in the interior for the 'effective leadership
which is abroad'. He justified his strategy to the leadership in Mexico
in a lengthy document entitled 'Advance on Political Orientations' in
which he merely asked for their assistance in making contact with the
Comintern in Russia. The hostility of the leadership in Latin America
was guaranteed by his implication that the Party in the interior could
not be led from Mexico by people who knew nothing about the real
situation in Spain.

Thus, in the summer of 1941, Uribe sent militants via Lisbon into
Spain to take over from Quiñones. The most senior were Isidro
Diéguez and Jesús Larrañaga. Carrillo was consulted about the operation because others involved were JSU members. Their arrival was
probably betrayed by police informers in Lisbon which permitted
their nascent organization to be kept under close surveillance in
Madrid. They were detained by the Portuguese police, handed over
to the Spanish police and executed in January 1942. When Eleuterio
Lobo and 'Perpetua Rejas' (the pseudonym of Mari Ibarra), two
totally inexperienced JSU militants of their group, had contacted
Quiñones, he had imperiously informed the Mexican leadership of
his outrage at their inexperience and irresponsibility and broke off all
contact with them. Uribe sent another cadre, Jesús Carreras, to discipline Quiñones for this. In fact, Quiñones was right. When Lobo and
Ibarra were arrested and tortured, Lobo revealed to the police the
existence of Quiñones's organization. Before Jesús Carreras could
take action against him, Quiñones had been arrested on 5 December
1941. During months of torture in the cellars of the Dirección General
de Seguridad, which saw his spine and legs broken, Quiñones received
a letter informing him that he had been expelled from the PCE. When

he was executed on 2 October 1942 by firing squad, he had to be tied to a chair because he could not stand.[38]

It became the obsession of the exiled leadership to extirpate the crime of Quiñonismo, the sin of autonomy from central authority. Despite his heroic career, Quiñones was insulted for decades in articles, books and speeches by the leaders of his own Party, accused variously of betraying Diéguez to prevent his own substitution, of being an agent provocateur and an informer at the service of the Francoist police and of being an English spy. Carrillo led the charge then and subsequently, levelling accusations of Quiñonismo at successive elements that rejected the authority of the exiled leadership or when changes of the Stalinist line required sacrificial victims.[39] Until his death, Carrillo would never falter in his accusations against Quiñones. Nevertheless, other Party leaders, including Enrique Líster, Santiago Álvarez and Irene Falcón, eventually expressed their conviction that Quiñones had been unjustly treated by the PCE. As late as 2006, in the second edition of his memoirs, Carrillo was still insinuating that Quiñones was a British agent.[40] Quiñones was not vindicated by the PCE until after Carrillo's own expulsion in 1985.

That the crime of Quiñonismo would continue to surface was inevitable given the leadership's ignorance of the real conditions within Spain. After the police had dismantled Quiñones's organization, it took the PCE considerable time to rebuild in the interior. The exiled leadership, divided between Moscow and Mexico, still had virtually no control over developments either in Spain or in German-occupied France. Within France, the only person left with any authority in the PCE was an attractive young JSU militant, Carmen de Pedro. She had been a typist for the PCE Central Committee in Madrid and secretary to Togliatti. In 1939, she had been placed in the Chilean Embassy in Paris with the job of securing exit visas for the top leadership of the Party. After organizing the evacuation of the leaders, she was supposed to leave for Chile or Mexico, but she remained in effective charge of what remained of the Party organization in France. Her lack of experience hardly fitted her for such responsibility, but she was able to turn to a senior Party leader who was still in Paris, Jesús Monzón Repáraz. A trained lawyer from an aristocratic Navarrese family, he had been Civil Governor of Alicante from 31 July 1937 until late May 1938 and of Cuenca until the end of the year. He was then called to Madrid to work in the Central Committee. On 3 March 1939, two days before the Casado coup, he was appointed secretary general of the Ministry of Defence. On 6 March, he had left Spain in the same aircraft as Dolores Ibárruri.[41]

Given family wealth and connections, Monzón could easily have secured a comfortable exile. Yet, with remarkable courage, he remained in France and helped Carmen de Pedro in her efforts to secure the evacuation of less senior Communists. Following the German occupation of Paris on 14 June 1940, they headed for Bordeaux. After overseeing the departure of as many exiles as possible, they were able to establish a headquarters in Marseille in the zone ruled over by the Vichy administration. Although the Party leadership, true to the directives of Moscow, was opposed to any collaboration with the Allied war effort, Monzón recommended that militants joined work companies which would eventually be the basis of the Spanish units in the French resistance. Although the nominal leader was Carmen de Pedro, the day-to-day running of the interior was being overseen by the much more experienced and dynamic Monzón, who had become her lover. They were helped by the hardened militant Manuel Jimeno and Manuel Azcárate, the twenty-three-year-old son of Pablo de Azcárate who had been Republican Ambassador to London. Because of Monzón's social origins, elegant appearance and right-wing social connections in his native Navarra, he was the object of some suspicion within the PCE. Nevertheless, Azcárate found Monzón to be deeply intelligent, capable of listening and extremely open-minded, hardly qualities associated with Communist leaders in the Stalinist period.[42]

The entry of the USSR into the Second World War had an inevitable impact on PCE policy. The Russians were keen to reassure the Western Allies that they did not intend to spread revolution in Europe after a future victory. Specifically, with regard to Spain, they were desperate to ensure that Franco did not enter the war on the Axis side. Accordingly, Dimitrov ordered the PCE leadership to advocate the unity of all anti-Franco forces. In response, a declaration in favour of a coalition of all Republican forces was made in August 1941. On 16 September 1942, Dolores Ibárruri went much further with a Manifesto of Unión Nacional which embraced the idea of alliance with disgruntled monarchists and dissident Falangists. Since its ostensible ambition was merely 'a constitutional assembly without institutional prerequisites', it left open the possibility of the future return of the monarchy. The Communist radio stopped attacking members of the Francoist coalition except for the most pro-German Falangists and bellicose generals like Juan Yagüe and Agustín Muñoz Grandes.

There was even a programme each Sunday for Catholics in which Dolores Ibárruri spoke of the humanitarian spirit of Christianity. Spanish Socialists, anarchists and Republicans who had been following the Allied cause with the keenest interest were disgusted by the evident cynicism of this policy swerve. Already outraged by the official Communist policy that, in accordance with the recently signed pact, had execrated the Allies as just one side in an imperialist squabble, most Republicans saw Pasionaria's declaration of Unión Nacional as proof of the PCE's rigid dependence on Moscow. Moreover, the notion that the struggle against Spanish fascism could be undertaken by a broad coalition similar to those fighting Hitler elsewhere ignored the suffering inflicted on the Spanish left by those with whom Moscow now recommended friendship. It was basically a sound policy and was to remain at the centre of Party strategy until the transition to democracy in Spain. Nevertheless, the brusque and insensitive way in which it was launched merely discredited the Party in the eyes of both its own militants and other leftists.[43] Its inevitable failure in the short term would eventually be added to a list of 'crimes' laid at Monzón's door by Carrillo, who came to see him as a rival to be eliminated at all costs.

Monzón himself had already started advocating the policy of Unión Nacional through his astonishingly successful clandestine news-sheet *Reconquista de España*. This underlay his efforts with Azcárate to build a PCE organization in occupied France. By late 1942, this was bearing fruit and Monzón had also made major progress in creating Spanish guerrilla units within the French resistance. In this, he was assisted by Gabriel León Trilla, an important Party veteran. Trilla had been one of the founders of the PCE in the

1920s, had been expelled from the Party in 1932 after a policy swerve by the Kremlin and had returned to the ranks during the Civil War. In the spring of 1943, Monzón decided that it was time to go back to Spain to try to rebuild the Party. From Madrid in September, he announced the creation of a Junta Suprema de Unión Nacional. When the news reached Moscow, Pasionaria was overjoyed at what she perceived as the success of her policy announcement eighteen months earlier. The Junta Suprema was less impressive than it sounded, although it did have members from a wide spectrum of left-wing organizations as well as some disgruntled Francoists. Over the ensuing months, Monzón also managed to establish relations with Catholic groups in Seville. The millionaire Juan March, who had helped bankroll Franco's war effort, offered money, and Cardinal Segura of Seville, a fierce anti-Francoist, also expressed interest. Despite the fact that all this would later be used by Carrillo as proof that Monzón was a traitor, at the time it brought effusive praise from the leadership in Mexico as well as from Dolores Ibárruri in Russia (evacuated to Ufa).[44]

While he was in Spain, there was a development in Monzón's personal life that was to cause him immense future difficulties. He and Carmen de Pedro had selected an experienced Party militant from Valencia, the thirty-year-old Pilar Soler, to be his assistant in Madrid. She had been arrested and tortured in May 1939 and had only just been released from prison. Their cover was as a happily married couple but the pretence turned into a reality and they seem to have fallen in love. She later described how things developed: 'I acted as his wife. We lived in a pension; we slept in the same room and you can guess how that turned out because I really fancied him.' They later moved into a house on the outskirts of Madrid where the image of normality was enhanced by the presence of Monzón's 'mother-in-law', in reality Pilar's mother, Ángeles Soler, who was also a PCE militant. When Monzón wrote to tell Carmen of his relationship with Pilar, she was devastated, although as a loyal cadre she continued her work.[45] In Toulouse at some point in 1944, Carmen met and soon began a relationship with a close collaborator of Carrillo named Agustín Zoroa. They would eventually marry in 1945.

When Carrillo began the witch-hunt against Monzón in late 1944, Zoroa would be one of the most vicious accusers. His motives were not entirely political. Certainly, there was an element of jealousy of his wife's former lover. However, he may well have seen an attack on Monzón as a way of protecting her. In the event, Zoroa's execution by the Franco regime in December 1947 would leave Carmen at Carrillo's mercy. When she was ruthlessly questioned by Carrillo about her earlier collaboration with Monzón, she was still emotionally distressed by the news that her husband had been shot. According to Líster, the interrogation nearly drove her to suicide.[46]

In the meantime, in the spring of June 1944, the tide of the Second World War was turning and Carrillo was pushing to return to Europe. He managed to secure a Uruguayan passport in the name of Hipólito López de Asis and went to Lisbon. While he was on board ship, he learned of the Allied landings in Normandy. Passing himself off as a businessman hoping to learn the fish-canning trade, he became friendly with the Uruguayan Ambassador and his son, both named Carlos Gurméndez. During the day, he visited canning factories while at night he made contact with exiled PCE members and with the leader of the Portuguese Communist Party, Álvaro Cunhal. There was to be no meeting of minds with Cunhal. After a few weeks, Carrillo flew to Casablanca and from there went on to Oran in Algeria. He wrote to Dolores Ibárruri on 14 August explaining his plans for the reorganization of the Party within Spain.[47]

In Oran, chicanery by Spanish dockworkers and truck drivers saw weapons, food and medical supplies diverted from the deliveries to the Allied forces there. Motor launches were purchased in the hope of landing guerrilla groups in southern Spain to link up with those who had been fighting there since the end of the Civil War. These were the so-called *huídos*, Republicans separated from their units during the Civil War who took to the hills rather than surrender. According to Carrillo's memoirs, he planned to lead these groups himself. The implication is that, at the age of thirty, he had rediscovered the hot-headed temerity of his youth.[48]

His idea was totally unrealistic and typical of what was to be his hallmark, his triumphalist rhetoric. It is true that, within a few months of the end of the Civil War, there was a significant number of *guerrilleros* in rural, and especially mountainous, areas. There it was easier to hide, to avoid the patrols of the Civil Guard and even to find the wherewithal to live, if not with the help of sympathetic peasants, at least by means of hunting and collecting wild fruit. As in other twentieth-century guerrilla wars, the principal activity of the *huídos* was defensive, their initial objective simply survival. Unlike their Chinese and Cuban counterparts, the Spanish *guerrilleros* had little possibility of establishing liberated zones that might have served as bases for the future struggle against the regime. The only places sufficiently remote from the forces of repression to permit any possibility of establishing autonomous revolutionary communities were in the most inhospitable parts of the peninsula. Moreover, the depressed circumstances of the defeated Spanish left between 1939 and 1944 were hardly propitious for a revolutionary war. The repression, hunger, families destroyed by death and exile and, above all, the intense weariness left by the titanic struggles of the Civil War ensured that there would be no popular uprising in support of the *huídos*, who were condemned to a hard and solitary existence.

Occasionally they were able to emerge from their defensive positions. Attacks were carried out against Civil Guard barracks, local Falangist offices and Francoist town halls. It is absurd to suggest, as Enrique Líster did in 1948 and the official Party history was still doing in 1960, that the guerrilla occupied sufficient troops to prevent Franco entering the Second World War on the Axis side. Nevertheless, the activities of the *huídos* were a constant irritant for the regime.[49] In so far as the controlled press mentioned their activities, it was to denounce them as acts of banditry and looting. However, in some rural areas, the activities of the *guerrilleros* had the effect of briefly raising the morale of the defeated population until the savage reprisals of the forces of order took their toll on popular support.

Carrillo's euphoric idea of using units from North Africa to link up with the existing guerrilla groups and spark off a national uprising was utterly unrealistic. To go into Spain, he needed authorization and, initially, he was out of contact with the main PCE leadership centres in both Latin America and Moscow. However, via Russian representatives in Algeria, he managed to inform Dolores Ibárruri of his plan. She approved of the spirit behind it but was totally opposed to his participation in an incursion into southern Spain. Instead, since Paris had been liberated on 25 August 1944, she ordered him to go to France and establish links with the leadership of the PCE there.[50] He claims that he stowed away on a French warship in order to reach Toulon. He then took a train to Paris. The emaciated and unshaven creature that showed up at the headquarters of the French Communist Party was unrecognizable as the previously chubby Carrillo. He claimed that he had lost much weight as a result of poor nutrition in Algeria and the lack of food during the days hiding on board the warship and the fifteen-hour train ride to Paris. It is not known exactly when he arrived in the French capital but it was certainly well before the second week of October. In his memoirs, he asserted that, on arrival in Paris, he was told by the French leadership that an invasion of Spain had begun through the Val d'Aran in the Pyrenees. In fact, the invasion did not begin until 19 October and his claim makes no sense other than as part of a retrospective fabrication of an heroic role for himself in what was about to take place.[51]

It was understandable that thousands of Spanish *maquisards* who had been prominent in the French resistance had responded to progressive German collapse by moving towards the Spanish frontier, hopeful that Franco might be next. In his memoirs, Carrillo claimed that on his arrival at PCE headquarters in Toulouse he learned from Azcárate and Carmen de Pedro that the Agrupación de Guerrilleros Españoles had received orders for the attack through the Pyrenees from the Junta Suprema de Unión Nacional. Of the Junta, he would sneer fifty years later that it 'existed only in the imagination of Monzón'. He forgot that, at the time, it certainly existed in the imaginations of Pasionaria, Uribe and the rest of the PCE politburo, including himself. Indeed, his ostensibly cordial correspondence with Monzón both before and after the invasion suggested that he also believed firmly in the Junta Suprema. So warm was this correspondence that Monzón sent cigarettes to Carrillo when he was in Oran 'as a little sign of the great affection that Anita [Adela Collado] and I feel for you'.[52]

In his memoirs and in reports to Pasionaria in 1945, Carrillo alleged that the Junta Suprema's orders were the only basis for the over-optimistic and inadequately prepared operation. It is true that, in late August 1944, Monzón had sent the delegation in France an order for an invasion – albeit without specifying where it should take place. Flushed with the success of Spanish guerrillas against German units and underestimating the considerable social support enjoyed by Franco, the PCE both in France and in Moscow received the idea enthusiastically. On 20 September, Pasionaria herself had published a declaration hailing the guerrilla as the way to spark an uprising in Spain.[53] Given his own contact with her, it is impossible that Carrillo could have been unaware of her enthusiasm for the guerrilla which, in any case, coincided with his own. Unsurprisingly, when Carmen de Pedro and Manuel Azcárate went to Paris in early September to discuss Monzón's order with the leaders of the French Communist Party, André Marty and Jacques Duclos, no objections had been raised.[54]

Accordingly, Carrillo's later claim that he learned of the invasion only after it had started is false. Once Monzón's subordinates in France had decided on the venture, it was organized virtually as a conventional military operation with little by way of security. Its preparation was an open secret, with recruiting broadcasts by Radio Toulouse and Radio Pirenáica from Moscow. Before leaving for the south of France, some *guerrillero* units were the object of public tributes and large send-offs by the people of the French towns and cities where they had participated in the resistance. The PCE ordered its organizations in the interior of Spain to prepare for an immediate popular insurrection. The Franco regime was fully informed of what was imminent by its own agents as well as by the Communist press and broadcasts about 'the reconquest of Spain'.

Manuel Azcárate wrote later that, when Carrillo arrived in the south of France, 'his intentions towards Monzón were malicious. He wanted to ensure at all costs that Monzón's indisputable achievements should not receive the credit that they deserved.' In fact, far from opposing Monzón's illusion that an incursion of *guerrilleros* would trigger a popular insurrection against Franco, Carrillo shared it.

Indeed, he hoped to take some, if not all, of the credit. In March 1944, a cadre called Tomás Tortajada had been expelled from the Party for arguing against an invasion.[55] Monzón was far from alone in his readiness to risk the PCE's greatest asset, its thousands of battle-hardened *maquisards*, in a conventional military confrontation with Franco's forces. After all, with the Germans facing defeat, it was an attractive option. Carrillo, as his account of his preparations in Algeria suggested, may have also favoured a strategy of starting a guerrilla war by sending small groups into Spain over a long period. Nevertheless, his fictionalized account of the origins of the Val d'Aran operation dramatically exaggerates the differences between himself and a supposedly out-of-control Monzón. As Pasionaria's response to Carrillo's own plans for a smaller-scale invasion from the south had indicated, the idea of a guerrilla war was approved by the PCE leadership in Moscow as well as by the delegation in France, as indeed it had been earlier by Heriberto Quiñones. Carrillo's attitude towards Monzón can be understood only in terms of his own burning ambition.

The detailed military planning of the invasion was the work of the Spanish heroes of the French resistance, Luis Fernández and Vincente López Tovar. Beginning on 19 October 1944, approximately 5,000 men of the invading army began to enter Spanish territory through the Pyrenees with the principal attack focused on the Val d'Aran. Snow-covered for most of the year and sparsely populated, it was an area of shepherds and woodcutters, a place barely appropriate as the base or *foco* of a popular uprising. Despite the ostentatious military structure set up by the Communist leaders of the *maquis*, the invasion was essentially improvised. It disregarded the obvious fact that a conventional military incursion played into the hands of Franco's huge land forces. Nonetheless, over the next three weeks, the invaders chalked up a few successes, some units penetrating over 60 miles into the interior. In several individual actions, they roundly defeated units of the Spanish Army and held large numbers of prisoners for short periods. In the last resort, however, 40,000 Moroccan troops under the command of experienced Francoist generals, José Monasterio, Juan Yagüe, Rafael García Valiño and José Moscardó, were too much for the relatively small army of *guerrilleros*. Part of García Valiño's General Staff fell into the hands of the *guerrilleros* and Monasterio himself came near to being captured. However, these were isolated incidents. The invaders' hopes of triggering off an uprising were always tenuous. Deeply demoralized, the Spanish left inside Spain had still not recovered from the trauma of defeat, was ground down by fear of the daily repression and, finally and most importantly, was only distantly and vaguely aware of what was happening in France. The regime's iron control of the press and the minuscule circulation within Spain, at least, of Monzón's clandestine broadsheet *La Reconquista de España* ensured that the *guerrillero* invasion took place amid a deafening silence.

Carrillo claims that, when he heard of the operation in Toulouse, he drove frantically to the Val d'Aran to try to stop it but unfortunately found that the invasion had already started. He must have been one of the few people in France or indeed in the PCE leadership in Moscow not to have heard about it, all the more so since he had been in France for several weeks before the attack was launched. It is much more likely that he went to Aran with the intention of sharing the glory if the operation were a success or being in a position to blame Monzón if it were a failure. In his fanciful reconstruction, acting on his own initiative he was able to persuade the leaders that he had been sent by the PCE leadership in Moscow to convince them that the entire operation was madness. There is little doubt that he was acting on his own initiative, and there is reason to suspect that his intention was not so much to prevent a failure as to undermine the position of Monzón. The enthusiastic cooperation of the French resistance ensured that the invading forces were initially well equipped with supplies of food, fuel, light arms, ammunition and vehicles, most supplied by the Allies. However, they were massively outnumbered and outgunned, especially once their ammunition began to run out. The *guerrilleros* of the invading force were already on the point of retreat and needed no persuasion from Carrillo.

When Azcárate and Carrillo arrived at the border on 28 October, the *guerrilleros* had already been ordered to withdraw by Vicente López Tovar, the field commander. López Tovar stated later that

Carrillo did not order the retreat but rather had to be convinced to approve what had already been decided. In any case, the evacuation could certainly not have been organized overnight. Carrillo's claim that he personally had averted a disaster was an extreme fabrication. The number of casualties as a result of the fighting in the valley was relatively small, fewer than thirty.[56] Nevertheless, at the end of the month, Carrillo sent a telegram to Pasionaria in which he claimed to have prevented the capture of 1,500 *guerrilleros*, stated that the preparation of the invasion had been defective and added that he planned to investigate those responsible.[57]

Ever since his seduction by Moscow in 1936, Carrillo had always stood out for his strong sense of hierarchy and authority. His vertiginous rise within the PCE can be understood only in terms of his narrow loyalty to Moscow, symbolized both by his betrayal of the PSOE in 1936 when he took the FJS into the Communist orbit and by his denunciation of his own father in 1939. Another factor in Carrillo's success was always an exquisite sensitivity to the variations both of Soviet policy and of the power struggles within the PCE itself. This would be seen most starkly in an extremely long speech that he made in November 1944 at the headquarters of the Agrupación de Guerrilleros Españoles in Montrejeau in the Pyrenees south-west of Toulouse. Speaking to a group of the most prominent military and political cadres of the PCE in France, he praised the invasion of the Val d'Aran. His basic premise was that the strength of the Junta Suprema de Unión Nacional was such that the collapse of the Franco regime was imminent. Despite his later jibe that the Junta 'existed only in the imagination of Monzón', now he asserted that it was 'no phantom'. He claimed that the regime would be unable to withstand a national uprising. There followed slavish praise of Dolores Ibárruri. That, and the fact that he was still defending the Val d'Aran operation, demonstrated that his objective was not to expose an erroneous strategy but to remove Monzón from his own path to pre-eminence within the PCE.[58]

The rewriting of the Val d'Aran episode was the foundation stone of Carrillo's efforts to establish himself in the eyes of most militants in France and Spain as the real representative of the Party leadership.

Since Monzón had effectively rebuilt the PCE in both countries, with control of a substantial guerrilla force in France and with an enviable network of contacts with other groups inside Spain, this was no easy goal. Having ingratiated himself with the activists at Montrejeau, Carrillo now began the real witch-hunt against Monzón. Taking advantage of the absence of the senior exiled leaders, he seized the opportunity to replace Monzón's subordinates with his own loyal followers who had enjoyed a comfortable war in Latin America, such as Fernando Claudín and Ramón Ormazábal. The condemnation of Monzón, the only significant leader who had stayed behind, and the gradual elimination of the heroic militants who had kept the PCE alive in France helped mitigate their own discomfort about their own flight from Europe. In their eyes, those who had been in the German camps and in the guerrilla war were suspect. Among the first critical reports about Monzón used by Carrillo were those of Carmen de Pedro's new lover, and future husband, Agustín Zoroa.[59]

In early December 1944, Zoroa had delivered to Monzón in Madrid letters from Carrillo. Written in cordial terms, these consisted largely of warnings about police infiltration of the organization in the interior and instructions about how to deal with the problem. It was deeply patronizing of Carrillo, who had no experience of clandestine work, to send Monzón detailed security instructions about safe houses and contact points. Moreover, the letters contained a thinly concealed warning: 'It is necessary to deal with the question of correcting the political errors of the Party and the Junta Suprema ... This is the only way to shake off the negligence and lack of vigilance inside the Party.' Carrillo went on to say that Monzón should return to France to discuss all these questions.[60] Understandably, Monzón did not consider himself to be under the orders of Carrillo: he was responsible only to Dolores Ibárruri. Nevertheless, he replied in emollient terms, not mentioning a possible return other than in his flowery farewell: 'until we can properly renew our relations, which will be soon, we send you, dear Santi, a big hug'. It is not clear if this was meant to reassure Carrillo or was just sarcasm.[61]

On 6 February 1945, Carrillo despatched a report to Pasionaria in which malice and invention sat side by side. He described the PCE's situation in such wildly optimistic terms as to make it seem that the overthrow of the regime was imminent. By implication, if this had not happened, it was Monzón's fault for failing to link up the many groups all over Spain allegedly ready to rise up. He claimed that the Junta Suprema was 'continuing to grow in popularity and prestige'. He went on to give an entirely mendacious account of the Val d'Aran episode in which claimed that the guerrilla leaders had not wanted to take part and did so only out of reluctant obedience to Monzón. He praised himself for avoiding a bloodbath. Because of Monzón's poor preparation of the invasion, he claimed, three valuable months had been lost that could have been used to prepare a nationwide insurrection within Spain. He then accused Monzón of running the interior delegation in a tyrannical fashion in cahoots with Pilar Soler and Trilla and suggested that this group was close to acting against the Party.

Carrillo provided a long list of Monzón's faults, ranging from underestimation of the role of the masses via excessive links with the right-wing opposition to lack of vigilance regarding agents provocateurs. Carrillo said that he was sending Zoroa again to order Monzón to come to France. The clear implication was that, if Monzón did not obey, he would have to be liquidated: 'if he resists or produces excuses, I will tell him that this means confrontation with the Party leadership. In the event of him reaching such an extreme position, the comrades there will break off all contact with him and will leave him isolated. I hope that it will not be necessary to do this but we will not shy away from anything.'[62]

Having had no reply from Monzón, Carrillo sent a cable to Moscow, reiterating his criticisms. He complained that Monzón refused to obey his instructions and was obstructing the functioning of the Party in the interior. Accordingly, he repeated that, if Monzón declined to come to France, he would be separated from the organization and the necessary measures would be taken. Finally, Carrillo received authorization to expel Monzón and Trilla.[63] Zoroa had been sent to inform Monzón that this would happen if he did not return. Since his delegate in Catalonia, Pere Canals, had already been murdered en route back to PCE headquarters in Toulouse, Monzón rightly suspected a trap. That one had been set was subsequently confirmed by Vicente Uribe to Tagüeña. After receiving the threats from Zoroa, Monzón finally set off for France accompanied by Pilar Soler. En route, he was obliged by illness to delay in Barcelona, where he was arrested on 8 June 1945 by the Francoist police as part of an operation that had been long in the making. With characteristic malice, Carrillo later suggested that Monzón had engineered his own detention in order to avoid having to explain the invasion. This was nonsense but may have reflected Carrillo's concern that Monzón had turned himself in to avoid being murdered. Certainly, Líster claimed that the person who was sent to guide Monzón over the Pyrenees had been ordered by Carrillo to kill him. Francoist versions have suggested that he was betrayed by the Party itself, which is also possible. Given Monzón's record in Spain, once he was in custody the death sentence was hanging over him. It is thus significant that, despite his seniority in the PCE, the leadership failed to organize, as was normal in such cases, an international campaign of protest.[64]

Shortly after the arrest of Monzón, Carrillo sent a long report to Pasionaria, Uribe and Mije. His objective was to underline his own spectacular success in contrast to Monzón's failures, the consequence of treachery and sabotage. By lumping together, and exaggerating, every strike, demonstration and attack on policemen or Falangists, he gave the impression that the regime was reeling before the first stages of an imminent national uprising. Over many pages, he listed the triumphs of the guerrilla. In fact, even if everything he wrote were true, the list consisted of little beyond sporadic, random incidents. One of his wilder exaggerations inadvertently undermined his own triumphalism when he claimed that the regime had 500,000 troops near the French frontier. All of these successes he attributed to the fact that he had sent in a team of his most trusted cadres: 'Happily, the comrades currently running the delegation of the Central Committee in Madrid, the main centres of party activity and the guerrilla were sent in directly from Latin America or from the leadership here in France.'

All failures were blamed on Monzón, among whose crimes, Carrillo alleged, were having tried to subordinate the PCE to the right-wing

ABOVE: May Day demonstration in Madrid, 1936. *Left to right:* Santiago Carrillo (JSU), Francisco Largo Caballero (PSOE), Luis Araquistain (PSOE), José Díaz (PCE), Trifón Medrano (JSU).

RIGHT: At the tomb of Pablo Iglesias, founder of the Spanish Socialist Party, 17 August 1938, Carrillo (left) and Fernando Claudín (right) with young women of the JSU.

BELOW: Valencia, March 1937. At an amplified plenary meeting of the Communist Party's Central Committee, Carrillo boasts of his success in purging the Madrid fifth column in the previous November.

In the autumn of 1936 Dolores Ibárruri – seen here with a group of Republican soldiers on the Madrid front – began a long-term relationship with Francisco Antón (front right), a political commissar in the Fifth Regiment.

Madrid, 5 February 1937. *Left to right:* Maurice Thorez, secretary general of the French Communist Party, Antonio Mije and Francisco Antón.

Naum Isakovich Eitingon, the NKVD agent who prepared the murder of Trotsky. In Spain, he used the pseudonym 'Leonid Aleksandrovich Kotov'. Enrique Líster claimed that Eitingon/Kotov was Carrillo's NKVD controller.

Madrid, October 1936. *Left to right:* Josif Grigulevich (NKVD assassin, organizer of the Republic's crack security squads, the Brigadas Especiales, and almost certainly the murderer of Andreu Nin), the cameraman Roman Karmen, and two of the NKVD staff, Lev Vasilevsky and Grigory Sergeievich Syroyezhkin.

Moscow, May 1965. The twentieth anniversary of the defeat of fascism brought together a group of Spaniards who fought in the defence of the Soviet Union. *Back row:* Juan Modesto (second from left), Francisco Antón (third from left), Enrique Lister (fourth from left) and Fiodor Kravchenko (far right), the GRU agent who as 'Antonio Martínez Serrano' helped Carrillo run the post-1945 guerrilla in Spain.

Heriberto Quiñones, Comintern agent, rebuilt the PCE after the Civil War but clashed with the exiled leadership. He was expelled from the PCE and executed by the Franco regime in October 1942. He is seen here shortly after his arrest on 5 December 1941 and before the long period of torture at the hands of the Francoist secret police. Despite his heroic career, Quiñones was denounced for forty years by Carrillo as an agent provocateur guilty of 'Quiñonismo', the sin of autonomy from central authority.

A lawyer from a wealthy Navarrese family, Jesús Monzón Repáraz organized the PCE participation in the French resistance. He rebuilt the party after the death of Quiñones and was behind the failed invasion of the Val d'Aran in 1944. Carrillo set out to destroy him but he 'escaped' plans to murder him when he was arrested by the Francoist police. Monzón is seen here (above) in the prison at Teruel, though he often avoided capture by dint of his elegant appearance (below).

During the Civil War, Carmen de Pedro was Palmiro Togliatti's secretary. In 1939, despite her inexperience, she was left in formal charge of the PCE in France. To do her job, she had to turn to Jesús Monzón who became her lover. For her association with Monzón, she was later punished by Carrillo.

PCE safe house in Toulouse, 1949. *Back row:* Enrique Líster (far left, sitting on wall) and the guerrilla leader Luis Fernández (far right, sitting on wall). *Front row:* Santiago Carrillo (centre) and Carmen de Pedro (right).

Pilar Soler, a veteran Communist militant who was imprisoned after the Civil War and worked with Monzón in Spain from 1943 to 1945. They became lovers, and she was interrogated by Carrillo in an effort to make her denounce Monzón after his arrest.

Vicente Uribe, senior PCE leader with whom Carrillo clashed in the 1950s. Seen here in his pomp as politburo member and Minister of Agriculture in the government of Francisco Largo Caballero.

Meeting of PCE central committee in Toulouse, December 1945. *Foreground, left to right:* Enrique Líster, Francisco Antón, Santiago Carrillo, Dolores Ibárruri and Joan Comorera.

Politburo meeting in Toulouse, September 1945. *In front of wall, left to right:* Juan Rejano, Luis Fernández, Francisco Antón (sitting on wall), Santiago Carrillo, unknown (squatting), Fernando Claudín, Ignacio Gallego. *Behind wall:* Enrique Líster (third from left), Luis Cabo Giorla (fourth from left), Dolores Ibárruri (seventh from left), Juan Modesto (fourth from right), Julián Grimau (far right).

Carmen Menéndez and Carrillo's third son Jorge with Irène Romano, the wife of the guerrilla leader Luis Fernández, at the resort of Cayeux-sur-Mer in Northern France, summer 1955.

Prague, November 1954. The Fifth Congress of the PCE saw the first steps to post-Stalin liberalization of the PCE. *Front row, left to right:* Santiago Carrillo, Enrique Líster, Manuel Delicado, Simón Sánchez Montero, Ignacio Gallego, Jorge Semprún and Fernando Claudín. *Back row, left to right:* José Moix, Santiago Álvarez, Antonio Mije, Francisco Romero Marín, Sebastián Zapirain, Tomás García and Manuel Delicado.

In mid-July1956 a plenary meeting of the Central Committee held in Herman Göring's old hunting lodge near Berlin saw Carrillo's destruction of Uribe. *Standing, left to right:* Vicente Uribe, Simón Sánchez Montero, Tomás García, Manuel Delicado, Antonio Mije. *Seated:* Enrique Líster.

elements in the Unión Nacional and having passively done nothing to organize a national uprising. The reiterated accusation against Monzón and Trilla was of 'provocación' which implied that they were Francoist agents: 'As we told you in the previous report, they ordered the operations in the Val d'Aran, a real provocation that cost us many lives and much damage and would have caused much more if we had not intervened in time.' After this tribute to himself, he went on to lay out more clearly the accusations against Monzón: 'It is beyond doubt that Monzón was working against the party leadership for years. Taking advantage of the relative freedom in which he operated, he surrounded himself with elements that, like Trilla with his murky past, could bring his plans to fruition.' Finally, in distorting Monzón's arrest to suggest his complicity with the regime, Carrillo inadvertently exposed his own frustrated plans to eliminate him and indeed his determination to pursue both the imprisoned Monzón and the still-at-liberty Trilla: 'Significantly, Monzón has been arrested at the very moment that, in response to his refusal to come here, the party was about to take measures against him. It is clear that, either as prisoners or at liberty, these elements constitute a great danger.'[65]

An absurdly triumphalist open letter to PCE members and the entire anti-Franco resistance, written by Carrillo, had already been published in *Nuestra Bandera* at some point in the spring of 1945. As in the speech at Montrejeau, the invasion of the Val d'Aran was praised in ecstatic terms and guerrilla action within Spain was exaggerated as the great triumph of the Junta Suprema de Unión Nacional. It was contrasted with the alleged passivity, described in insulting terms, of those who placed their hopes on the Allies. The appeal to all anti-Francoists to join the Junta Suprema, combined with condemnation of anarchist, Socialist and Republican figures, was based on the belief that the rank and file of their organizations would flock to the PCE. However, quite early in the document, Carrillo claimed that there had been passivity within the PCE itself, grave failures in terms of organizing strikes and demonstrations prior to the hoped-for uprising and a lack of audacity in organizing the masses. This had all delayed the inevitable uprising and the defeat of Franco. The unnamed but unmistakable target of these accusations of passivity, elitism and lack of faith in the workers was Monzón. The idea that Madrid was a powder keg of revolutionary fervour and that Monzón had failed to light the touch-paper suggested either total ignorance of the real situation inside Spain or else a malicious determination to smear Monzón.

As well as attacking Monzón, the open letter appealed in violent language to every Spaniard who possessed a knife or a gun to assassinate those involved in the repression, from the torturers and executioners to the magistrates who signed death sentences. The violence was not to be exercised only against Francoists. There was an ambiguous passage in which Carrillo insisted, 'We must move to the physical liquidation of agents provocateurs. Every informer must pay for his treachery with his life. And in this task the *guerrilleros* must play the main role.' This call for the physical elimination of agents provocateurs was the beginning of the direct attacks on Monzón. The declaration that 'the remains of Quiñonismo must be extirpated by blood and fire' was a clear indication that Monzón would be next.[66]

If Monzón had seen a copy of *Nuestra Bandera* before leaving Madrid for France, it would surely have confirmed the suspicions already aroused by letters received from Carrillo. He almost certainly knew that Carrillo was already putting together a team of assassins exclusively at his service. For this, he selected from the many JSU militants who had gone to Russia after the Civil War, been trained at the Planernaya Academy and then, in 1941, been incorporated into NKVD guerrilla units.[67] Among the most trusted were Eduardo García López and José Gros. Gros, a Catalan from Tarragona, was in the NKVD guerrilla detachment created by the Administration for Special Tasks, responsible for kidnapping, assassination, sabotage and terror, now under the direction of Pavel Sudoplatov. Decorated for his bravery in the defence of Moscow, at the end of October 1944 Gros was invited to undergo special training at a secret school near Moscow together with his comrade-in-arms Ortuño Sebastián, and in early 1946 he left the USSR for France. On arrival, he put himself at the disposal of Carrillo.[68]

Carrillo's loyal team of hardened apparatchiks would play a key role in eliminating those who remained loyal to Monzón and those who questioned Carrillo's authority. One of the first victims was

Pascual Gimeno Rufino, alias 'el Commandant Royo'. After distinguished service in the French resistance, Royo had gone into Spain in
late September 1944 on the orders of Monzón as part of the invasion
plan. He was arrested in November and imprisoned in Barcelona. He
managed to persuade the police that he was simply returning to Spain
after having worked in Germany. In January 1945, he wrote to his
wife to say that he had been released and was under surveillance at
his sister's house in Valencia. He made contact with the PCE in the
city. After an internal Party investigation that dispelled suspicion that
he had been turned by the police, he was incorporated into the urban
guerrilla. On 23 July, he disappeared and, the next day, his disfigured
body was found near the railway station. He had been murdered, on
Carrillo's direct orders, by one of his team of assassins. He was suspect
because of his links with Monzón.[69]

Meanwhile, the assault on Monzón's reputation took another turn.
His partner Pilar Soler had eluded arrest in Barcelona. She managed
to get to France. In the words of the Party forger Domingo Malagón,
'she appeared in a black dress, like a reproduction of Dolores only
rather younger'.[70] She was detained for three months in solitary
confinement in a Party safe house. She was subjected to interrogation
by Carrillo, Claudín and Ormazábal and feared for her life. They
demanded that she write a report on Monzón's 'deviations'. In fact, for
security reasons, Monzón had told her little of his activities, and her
work for him had largely been as a messenger (*correo*). When none of
the versions that she produced met their needs, they forced her to
sign a text that they had drawn up.[71] Carmen de Pedro had already
been questioned and obliged to write an account of her work with
Monzón. These were the first of a series of interrogations of Monzón's
collaborators, including Azcárate and others. The information gathered was distorted and used to compile various reports accusing him
of maintaining friendships with reactionaries, womanizing, homo-
sexuality and sybaritic habits and alleging that, in prison, he was able
to pay for a life of bourgeois luxury. Some of these farcical accusations
were followed by faked signatures. They contained praise for Carrillo,
who was thanked for apparently opening the eyes of the denouncer
to Monzón's infamy.[72] While Monzón was in prison awaiting trial,

there was an attempt on his life by Communist prisoners. Shortly afterwards, he heard that he had been expelled from the PCE. After innumerable delays, he was tried on 16 July 1948 and sentenced to thirty years' imprisonment. He escaped execution thanks to testimonies on his behalf by the Carlist leader Antonio Lizarza, whose life he had saved during the Civil War, by the Bishop of Pamplona Marcelino Olaechea and by the Captain General of Barcelona, José Solchaga, a Carlist friend of his parents. These humanitarian efforts were the basis of Carrillo's venomous remarks about Monzón's friendships with generals and bishops in a 1948 *Nuestra Bandera* article and elsewhere. Monzón was released in January 1959 and died in October 1973.[73] According to Líster, Monzón's crime in the eyes of Carrillo was not just that he stood in his way but also that he had displayed bravery in both Spain and France during the Second World War while Carrillo was in comfortable exile.[74]

On 16 September 1945, Monzón's deputy, the veteran Gabriel León Trilla, was murdered by militants of the urban guerrilla group set up by Cristino García Granda. A miner from Asturias, Cristino García was a hero of the French resistance, who had been sent into Spain by Carrillo to reorganize the disparate guerrilla forces in the sierras of Gredos and Guadarrama to the north of Madrid. Those groups had been decimated by the Civil Guard, so García brought the remnants into the capital and tried to mount an urban guerrilla. Given the inexperience of his men, their bank robberies and attacks on Falangist offices provoked arrests on a scale which led to them being considered counter-productive. In his letter of 1 December 1944, Carrillo had told Monzón to isolate Trilla, but Monzón had ignored that instruction. Now, Carrillo's orders to murder Trilla were disobeyed by Cristino García, who declared that he was a revolutionary and not an assassin. However, he obediently delegated the execution to other members of his group. Trilla was stabbed to death in an abandoned cemetery known as the Field of Skulls (El Campo de las Calaveras). Although the excuse for Trilla's liquidation was the accusation that he was a thief and a police informer, his real crimes were his links with Monzón and his openly declared view that the exiles were out of touch with the situation in Spain.[75]

The fact that Trilla's right-hand man, Alberto Pérez Ayala, was assassinated shortly afterwards, on 15 October 1945, underlined Carrillo's determination to eliminate Monzón's team. Two years later in Prague, Vicente Uribe told Manuel Tagüeña that the assassination of Trilla had been carried out on the direct orders of Carrillo and Pasionaria. This was confirmed in 1978 by Líster, who revealed the name of the man who had taken to Madrid their orders to kill Trilla. Moreover, Carrillo himself inadvertently admitted this when he wrote in his memoirs: 'Líster accused Dolores and myself of ordering the execution of Trilla. At that time, it was not necessary to give such orders; whoever opposed the party when living in Spain was treated by the organization as a threat. I have already explained that the harshness of the struggle gave no margin for error.' Fifty years later, Carrillo had clearly forgotten that the organization in the interior to which he attributed the death of Trilla operated under his sole authority.[76]

Cristino García was captured on 20 October 1945, a few weeks after the murder of Trilla. He was tried on 22 January 1946. When the military lawyer defending him claimed that he had been tricked by the PCE into coming to Spain, García rose indignantly to contradict him, saying, 'We are convinced anti-Francoist patriots who have not abandoned the fight against the executioners who oppress our people. I have been wounded five times in the struggle against the Nazis and their Falangist lackeys. I know full well what awaits me, but I declare with pride that if I had a thousand lives I would put them at the service of my people and my country.' This outburst guaranteed a death sentence and he was executed on 21 February. After the squalid elimination of Trilla and the death of Cristino García, the PCE virtually abandoned the urban guerrilla which henceforth would be the exclusive terrain of anarchists of the Movimiento Libertario Español. It has been alleged that Cristino García was betrayed from within the Party because he had made no secret of his disgust at what he had been ordered to do to Trilla.[77]

At a plenary meeting of the Central Committee held in Toulouse between 5 and 8 December 1945, Carrillo had made a successful bid to take control of the guerrilla, repeating the view already expressed

by Dolores Ibárruri that it would be the catalyst for a popular uprising sufficiently broad-based to secure international support.[78] In his
euphoria, he had taken insufficient account of the overwhelming
repressive capacity of the regime. Moreover, it was soon clear that the
Allies had no intention of making a clean sweep of the Axis and
removing Franco. Remarks about the guerrilla in Carrillo's speech
were the prelude to a diatribe against the Alianza Nacional de Fuerzas
Democráticas, the rival front to the Junta Suprema de Unión Nacional
established by the rest of the anti-Franco forces. The ANFD had
grown out of the Junta Española de Liberación, initially founded in
Mexico in November 1943 by the Socialists and a variety of liberal
Republican groups and subsequently widened in Toulouse in August
1944 to include the CNT. This led in October 1944 to the creation
inside Spain of the ANFD. In contrast to the PCE policy of direct
action against the Franco regime, the ANFD was relying on Allied
armies removing the Caudillo. However, in the looming Cold War,
the Western Powers were coming to see Franco's authoritarianism as
a valuable asset. In his November 1944 speech to militants in
Toulouse, Carrillo had already made it clear that the Communist
objective was for the Junta Suprema to take over the rank and file of
the ANFD. Subsequently, in a 1948 article, Carrillo claimed that the
Junta Suprema de Unión Nacional had been immensely successful
and that the Socialist and anarchist rank and file had flocked to join.
Among other absurd lies in the article, he asserted that the British
Ambassador, Sir Victor Mallet, and London's Secret Intelligence
Service had set up the ANFD, using the collaborators of Casado, for
the sole purpose of undermining the Junta Suprema and the PCE.[79]

In 1945, Carrillo's rise to the highest echelons of the PCE was well
under way. He held the post of agitation and propaganda secretary on
the politburo and was in charge of the formation of cadres at Toulouse
and at other small indoctrination and training establishments. The
main guerrilla training school was at Gincla, a tiny village in the
Département de l'Aude, south of Lapradelle, at the foot of the
Pyrenees. Like Monzón before him, Carrillo and the remainder of the
PCE leadership were still convinced that a popular rising was feasible
if only the necessary spark could ignite it, but the objective of a full-

scale invasion was abandoned. It was now decided that a more feasible option than an invasion was the gradual infiltration of small groups of *guerrilleros* across the French frontier to link up with the existing groups of *huídos*.[80] This was a slightly more realistic strategy, but only for a brief period between mid-1945 and mid-1947. However, the training instituted by Carrillo had an additional agenda, as revealed by one of the graduates of the school, José Manuel Montorio Gonzalvo. Commenting on the indoctrination there, he wrote, 'There appeared a new word in the Communist lexicon: Monzonismo. Monzonismo was considered a deviation from Marxism-Leninism-Stalinism, a tool of imperialism that had to be unmasked and destroyed.' He claimed that his training demanded that he applied this 'lesson'. He found it difficult to accept that members of guerrilla groups previously organized by Monzón were agents provocateurs, but he acted on the basis of what he had been taught in Gincla: 'If luck, or misfortune, had led me to come face to face with Monzón, I wouldn't have hesitated a second before shooting him.'[81]

In the running of the guerrilla, Carrillo was assisted by the chief in southern France of Soviet military intelligence, the GRU, Colonel Fyodor Josevich Kravchenko. A totally fluent Spanish-speaker working under the name Antonio Martínez Serrano, Kravchenko had fought with distinction in the Spanish Civil War as the interpreter in a Russian tank unit. He and Carrillo had first met in March 1936 when he had been the young FJS secretary's interpreter during his visit to Moscow. They met again during the Civil War and on Carrillo's many subsequent visits to Russia. According to Carrillo, they became fast friends.[82] During the Second World War, Kravchenko fought with a guerrilla unit behind German lines and acquired considerable experience in sabotage. In May 1945, he was sent to France with the mission of setting up an intelligence network to report on the military capacity of Franco's Spain, which was seen by Moscow as an important bulwark of American geostrategic planning. Given the close relationship between the PCE and the Soviet military mission in Paris, agreement was quickly reached for Spanish *guerrilleros* to be part of this operation.[83] Established in Toulouse, Kravchenko not only set up his intelligence network but was able to bring his sabotage experience to the guerrilla training school. He was allegedly deputy chief of staff of the guerrilla movement from May 1945 to the second half of 1949. Ibárruri and Carrillo knew who he really was, as did several others, ex-combatants in the NKVD's wartime Spanish battalion.[84]

In addition to his links with Soviet military intelligence, in the months following the Second World War Carrillo demonstrated his outright Stalinism by slavish mimesis of the way in which the Russians were dealing with returning prisoners-of-war. The slogan 'revolutionary vigilance' was used to cover a paranoid, secret-police-style approach to internal issues. PCE members who returned from German concentration camps were not treated as heroes, as was the case with their French and Italian comrades, but were interrogated and then kept away from positions of responsibility in a kind of political quarantine.[85] In a speech made to an assembly of Party members in Toulouse on 14 May 1945, in the presence of Dolores Ibárruri who had arrived in France from Moscow three weeks earlier, he suggested that some of the returning Communists were agents of the Gestapo and the Falange. Despite the fact that Germany was defeated and Hitler dead, he proclaimed the need for 'Great vigilance, great attention, to prevent the infiltration of Francoist agents into the ranks of our Party and of the anti-fascist movement. Without distrusting our comrades, we need to know what they did, how they behaved, keep watch on those whose situation is doubtful and do so with the help of the comrades who have come from Germany who can help us implement the necessary control.'

Then, in his usual contribution to the cult of personality of Dolores Ibárruri, he went on to a sycophantic hymn of praise for 'this woman who is a true archetype of Spanish womankind as well as a great political leader ... our great and beloved comrade Pasionaria'.[86] When she spoke, she claimed that the survivors of Mauthausen must have collaborated with the SS. It was demoralizing for Communist militants to see their comrades and leaders in the anti-Franco struggle denounced by exiled leaders as traitors and provocateurs, as agents of the Gestapo and of American imperialism.[87] Even more serious was the effect on other groups who thus witnessed the perpetuation of the hated Communist methods of the Civil War period. Habitually referred to as traitors, Republicans and Socialists could only conclude that their treatment at the hands of the Communists, if they came to power, would be no better than that received by the PCE's own militants.

Carrillo was now *de facto* leader of the PCE in France, the most important section of the exiled Party after that in Moscow. This meant that he also controlled the Party within Spain. From 1945, he figured in the politburo as agitprop secretary and director of the Interior Commission which placed him in charge of the Party inside Spain and therefore of the guerrilla. Given his total inexperience of warfare of any kind, this was a disastrous appointment. Although Uribe and Mije were senior to him in the Party hierarchy, his power was considerably greater than theirs.[88] Once the effective direction of the Party had moved to Paris, Dolores Ibárruri had returned to Moscow and between 1947 and 1950 she suffered serious ill-health, which gave Carrillo considerable autonomy. Nevertheless, the Party was totally dependent on the Soviet Union for its finance, and Carrillo made every effort to demonstrate his identification with the needs of the Kremlin. In running guerrilla operations, he showed the same determination and self-confidence with which he had taken over the Socialist Youth. In doing so, he revealed the ruthlessness that was to be the hallmark of his future career. What he presented as ideological and tactical discrepancies with Monzón were simply a device to mask his own determination to assert total control. To this end, he sent into Spain a team of utterly loyal followers, most of whom had come through the ranks of the JSU during the Civil War and some of whom had been trained in Russia.[89]

Communist denunciations of the Alianza Nacional de Fuerzas Democráticas were unceremoniously stopped when it was decided that the PCE should seek to be represented in the Republican government in exile headed by the moderate Dr José Giral, which had been formed in August 1945. The PCE joined the ANFD and, in March 1946, Carrillo was named as Minister without Portfolio in Giral's cabinet, which would last only until January 1947. The nomination of Carrillo outraged the Socialists, who had never forgiven his 'theft' of the FJS or the letter to his father. More importantly, it severely diminished the already exiguous British and American sympathy for Giral. Carrillo's presence did lead to Giral's government being recognized by a number of Eastern-bloc countries, which merely intensified Anglo-American hostility. It was the view of Washington and London that the Republican forces should reach an agreement with the anti-Franco monarchists as a first step to re-establishing democracy in Spain. Carrillo, understandably, reinforced Giral's dogged refusal to compromise his commitment to the restoration of the Republic. Significantly, Stalin did not recognize the Giral government.

Giral was replaced by Rodolfo Llopis and, in his cabinet, Carrillo was replaced by Uribe, who had been a minister in Spain and who was hated less by the Socialists. Even so, the ferocious criticisms made by Llopis of the treatment received by Spanish exiles in the Soviet Union made it an uncomfortable collaboration. Between 19 and 22 March 1947, the Party held a plenum in the town hall of Montreuil in Paris under the presidency of Dolores Ibárruri. In her speech, clearly influenced by the reports of Carrillo, she spoke of the death agony of the Franco regime. She declared that the Spanish capitalists, financiers and senior army officers were uniting in opposition to the dictatorship, while important elements of the Catholic hierarchy were also distancing themselves from it. She expressed support for Llopis and the ANFD while calling for the alliance to be widened. When Carrillo spoke, he referred in sycophantic terms to the call made by Pasionaria in December 1945 for Spain to be washed over by 'a wave of protests, strikes and demonstrations'. Thanks to her inspired guidance, he said, a resurgent working class was on the march, threatening the dictatorship. He was adamant that the industrial workers had to boycott the 'vertical syndicates', the regime's official corporative trade unions. He also claimed that there existed a mass peasant resistance – awareness of which was confined to himself – which he linked to the guerrilla.[90] The Llopis government was even more short-lived than that of Giral. In August 1947, the PSOE decided to negotiate with the monarchists and Llopis resigned, to be replaced by an entirely Republican cabinet presided over by Álvaro de Albornoz. By then, utterly alone, out of both the Republican government and the ANFD, the PCE was reduced to hurling unrestrained insults at its erstwhile allies.[91]

Not surprisingly, given his obsessive dedication to the Party and his own rise therein, Carrillo's marriage to Chon had come to an end. While in exile in Latin America, before he returned to Europe in 1944, they had separated. From 1947, he was working with a young woman in his team called Carmen Menéndez, who was in charge of correspondence and the Party archives. He married her (or openly acknowledged her as his partner) in 1949. She was to be his faithful – and equal – partner until his death. In France, they lived as Monsieur and Madame Giscard, and had three sons, Santiago (b. 1950), José (b. 1951) and Jorge (b. 1952).[92]

Carrillo's leadership team made desperate attempts to justify its own existence by endlessly propounding the absurdly triumphalist line that the fall of the Franco regime was imminent.[93] They seemed utterly unaware that Franco enjoyed considerable social support. Certainly, the Great Powers had called for Franco voluntarily to cede power to a representative provisional government. In response, his cabinet had started to organize a massive propaganda campaign to give the impression that the nation was united around the Caudillo. It was to conclude with a carefully staged rally of 'workers' acclaiming him 'the first worker of Spain' in the Plaza de Oriente.[94] The Spanish question was discussed at the Political and Security Committee of the General Assembly of the United Nations between 2 and 4 December 1946 at Lake Success in New York State. Despite much empty rhetoric critical of Franco, the American and British representatives argued against foreign interference lest it provoke civil war in Spain. Eventually, a sub-committee was named to draft a resolution to be put to the General Assembly. It was to be based on a proposal from the United States that consisted of a denunciation of Franco's Axis links and another invitation for him to 'surrender the powers of Government'.[95]

The huge demonstration in the Plaza de Oriente in front of the Palacio Real on 9 December 1946 demonstrated that the overthrow of Franco was not imminent. It was, of course, a choreographed affair with shops ordered to close for the day and the Falangist syndicates, the Youth Front (Frente de Juventudes) and Civil War veterans' organizations fully mobilized. The Francoist police claimed unconvincingly that 700,000 people had attended. Nevertheless, contemporary photographs show the square and surrounding streets packed to overflowing. Hundreds of banners carried slogans attacking the Russians, the French and foreigners in general. There were insistent and deafening chants of '¡Franco sí, comunismo no!'[96] The final agreed resolution on Spain was adopted by a plenary session of the General Assembly on 12 December 1946.

Essentially toothless, it excluded Spain from all the UN's dependent bodies, called upon the Security Council to study measures to be adopted if, within a reasonable time, Spain still had a government lacking popular consent, and urged all member nations to withdraw their ambassadors. The resolution was passed by thirty-four votes, including France, Britain, the Soviet Union and the United States, to six, all Latin American countries, with thirteen abstentions.[97] It was increasingly obvious that the Allies were not going to do anything to remove the dictator. Their statements that it was up to the Spaniards to do it themselves tallied with PCE declarations, but unfortunately it was a more difficult task than optimistic propaganda suggested.

Even if this development did not dent the confidence of the Carrillo leadership, developments within the Party apparatus in Russia surely did. In the aftermath of the Second World War, a number of the Spaniards who were exiled in the Soviet Union expressed a desire to return to Spain or to join relatives in Latin America. Of the exiles, many had been killed fighting for the Soviet Union during the Second World War and others were entirely integrated into Soviet life. However, there were others who were deeply unhappy. Their requests were automatically regarded as proof of 'mentalidad anti-soviética'. It was feared that, if they were allowed to leave, their testimony about life in the Soviet Union would be used by the Franco regime. Accordingly, such suspect persons would have to be 're-educated'. Between 4 August 1945 and 1 January 1947, of the 1,763 exiles permitted to leave the USSR only 41 were Spaniards. Thereafter, that trickle dried up altogether.

During these years in the late 1940s, there were purges within the PCE in Russia and an ongoing campaign against the alleged 'enemies' and 'traitors' among the exiles. Completely cut off from the other anti-Francoist organizations, the PCE took refuge in a rigid Stalinism. Worsening conditions within the Soviet Union had seen many Spanish exiles seeking visas from the embassies of Mexico, France, Argentina and Chile. Fearing that any exiles who were allowed to leave would defame the USSR, in the spring of 1947 the politburo called for Carrillo to come to Moscow to deal with the problem. It is not clear if this was in response to a complaint by the Russian authorities or a reflection of Dolores Ibárruri's concern about the repercussions for the PCE if Spanish Communists expressed a desire to leave.[98] On arrival, Carrillo created a committee to interrogate those who wished to leave. He, Fernando Claudín and Vicente Uribe prepared the cases against them or those suspected of helping them. He presided over several meetings with the militants who had secured visas in which they were accused of anti-Sovietism. He assured them that 'our comrades are dying of hunger in France, England and Mexico.'[99] They were browbeaten into giving up the idea of leaving and tearing up their visas in order to demonstrate their love of the USSR and their fidelity to the Party. The more intense the pressure, the greater the credit accumulated by the interrogators. A few of the exiles held on, but the majority capitulated, after being told that a desire to leave constituted treachery because 'the true Communist' would always prefer to stay in the USSR. They were obliged to sign a document saying that 'the undersigned has decided voluntarily to reside in the USSR and therefore rejects any appeal by his family or by any foreign government for him to leave the country. From this moment, he has decided not to leave the USSR other than if he were to be sent abroad on special service by the Soviet government.' However, only two signed, most hoping to keep open the possibility of leaving at some point in the future.

One night in July 1947, Spanish émigrés were called to a meeting to debate the 'treachery' of those who wanted to leave. When Carrillo ranted against the 'traitors who leave the country of socialism to go and live among the capitalists', he was greeted with an ovation in the midst of which someone was heard to shout, 'They should be shot in the back.' This provoked more applause. Shortly afterwards, on his return to France, Carrillo made a grovelling speech about the love of the exiles for Dolores Ibárruri. As well as denouncing life in capitalist countries, he waxed lyrical about the Soviet Union: 'Our people shout "Thank you, Stalin! For having made men of our sons. And thank you, Dolores Ibárruri who lavished your affection on them".' Meanwhile, in Russia, the apparatus left by Carrillo under the command of Claudín sent the would-be exiles to camps in Siberia or Central Asia. The more senior cadres, accused of 'softness' with them, were condemned to work in Soviet factories.[100] The choice of punishment was an ironic commentary on the workers' paradise.

Having gone to Moscow to put a stop to the 'shame' of the returning émigrés, and before he returned to Paris, Carrillo had choreographed a full-scale piece of Stalinist theatre. This took the form of an alleged plot to murder Dolores Ibárruri and Francisco Antón in the Hotel Lux. It was supposed to have been hatched by Jesús Hernández and Enrique Castro Delgado with the help of Líster and Modesto. This nonsensical farrago was easier to sell because Hernández and Castro were not around to dispute it, having long since been expelled from the PCE. According to Líster it was:

> entirely invented by Carrillo, but, killing two birds with one stone, it let him appear as the heroic defender of the secretary general of the PCE while smearing the image of the exiles in the Soviet Union, slandering and striking down a group of comrades who had stood with honour alongside the Soviet people, sharing with them all the tremendous difficulties of the war while Carrillo and the other party leaders who were now their accusers had lived high on the hog on the other side of the pond.[101]

The 'plot' was alleged to have taken place in Jesús Hernández's room on the sixth floor of the Hotel Lux. The case for the prosecution was drawn up by Fernando Claudín and Vicente Uribe, who opened the 'trial' on 25 November 1947 before a mass meeting of Spanish residents in Moscow, not all of whom were Party members. Before this assembly, five prominent leaders were lined up for ritual humiliation. Their crimes were collusion in the discontent of the 'anti-Soviet émigrés' and more seriously their failure to unmask the 'plot' by

Hernández and Castro to assassinate Pasionaria and Francisco Antón. The five were banned from positions of responsibility within the Party. Only by confessing their 'errors' and accepting blame did they avoid being despatched to the camps, being condemned instead to work in the Stalin Automobile Factory in Moscow. Even though the inquisition was carried out by Claudín and Uribe, the brains behind the 'plot in the Hotel Lux' was Carrillo. In some twisted logic, the five men considered responsible for failing to control the émigrés who wanted to leave were made accomplices of the plot. The consequences of these 'show trials' were not death, torture or the labour camps, as they were for members of Communist parties from the Soviet bloc. Nevertheless, the victims were subjected to serious psychological torture and ritual humiliation.[102]

While this pantomime was going ahead, Franco's situation was improving steadily. In the wake of the popular support manifested in the Plaza de Oriente, plans were being drawn up by Franco's adviser Luis Carrero Blanco to institutionalize the regime as a monarchy and give it a veneer of 'democratic' legitimacy with a referendum. Moreover, help from the Argentinian populist dictator Juan Perón was crucial in bridging the time gap between the exclusion of Spain from the United Nations and the hoped-for change in Washington's attitude. Wheat was already being delivered on credit. Argentina had defended Spain in the United Nations General Assembly in December 1946 and, in contravention of the UN resolution, had sent a new ambassador in January 1947. The envoy's arrival was greeted by orchestrated demonstrations and euphoric press coverage.[103] Even more spectacular propaganda was made out of the visit to Spain by the glamorous María Eva Duarte de Perón (Evita) in the summer of 1947.[104] The visit coincided with the referendum being organized to ratify the so-called Ley de Sucesión which declared the regime to be a monarchy under the regency of Franco, who would eventually name his own successor. On the eve of the referendum, appearances along-side the beautiful Evita, the rallies and the publicity were extremely useful for Franco. Calls for a 'yes' vote appeared opposite coverage of the Señora Perón tour. Her speeches contained lavish praise of the Caudillo.[105] While she was in Spain, on 5 June, General George C.

Marshall, the US Secretary of State, announced his ambitious plan for the economic recovery of Western Europe. The Marshall Plan to build up European economies to combat the spread of Soviet communism excluded Franco's Spain. In response to this snub, the Franco–Perón Protocol was signed by which further credit was granted to Spain and wheat deliveries guaranteed until 1951.

On the eve of the referendum, pro-Franco propaganda grew more frenetic. Spaniards were told to vote 'yes' if they were Catholics and if they did not want to see their fatherland in the hands of Communists and to vote 'no' if they wanted to abandon Catholicism, to betray those who died on the Nationalist side in the Civil War and to help international Marxism destroy Spain's prosperity.[106] With the full power of the Church mobilized and Falangist officials stating that ration cards would not be valid unless stamped at the polling booths, a large turnout was inevitable. According to the official figures, for which there was no independent scrutiny, in the referendum held on Monday 6 July 1947, as many as 89 per cent of the 17,178,812 qualified electors voted. Of the 15,219,565 votes cast, 93 per cent were 'yes' votes. The remaining 7 per cent was made up of 4.7 per cent (722,656) 'no' votes and 2.3 per cent (351,746) blank or spoiled ballot papers. For all of the pressure, intimidation and falsification, the results showed that Franco now enjoyed considerable social backing.

Moreover, things were not going well with the guerrilla war. At first, arriving with small supplies of food and arms, the ex-*maquisards* had been able to organize relatively efficacious guerrilla units. Given the lack of any other leadership initiatives from anarchists or Socialists, the PCE filled the gap, acting as the coordinator of these groups and sending in militants hardened in the French resistance or in guerrilla units in the defence of the Soviet Union. Civil Guard barracks were attacked, trains were blown up and electrical power lines were brought down. The reaction of the peasantry appeared, at first, to be passively sympathetic, especially when the *guerrilleros* undertook specific actions by request, such as the burning of municipal archives to impede the collection of taxes. In general, the Spanish *maquis* were never able to establish any impregnable safe territories or indeed sink roots among the local peasantry. The *guerrilleros* saw themselves as the vanguard of a future invading army. However, after three years of civil war and five more of state terror and near famine, the rural population could barely survive, let alone take part in any kind of uprising.

Although doomed to ultimate failure, for a few years, from 1945 to 1948, the guerrilla was a considerable irritant to the regime. Part of the Communist tactic was to inflate the importance of the guerrilla by inventing a national structure of 'guerrilla armies' for each region of the country. It was thereby hoped both to allay the fears of the civilian population and to undermine the belief of the repressive forces in the stability of the regime. It was intended to give the forces deployed in the anti-guerrilla struggle, primarily the Civil Guard but also regular units of the army, of the Spanish Foreign Legion and of the Spanish native police, the Regulares Indígenas, the impression that they were fighting tens of thousands of *guerrilleros*. It is difficult, given the exaggerations of both sides, to calculate the exact numbers of men and women who participated in the guerrilla. Though it was once thought to be about 15,000, Francisco Moreno Gómez has argued plausibly that it was nearer to 7,000. The impression that they were more numerous was created by the technique of striking in successive days in places 25 or 30 miles apart.

However, given the impossibility of establishing *focos* or liberated zones, it was not surprising that the peasantry began slowly to reject the *maquis*. When, as occasionally happened, the *guerrilleros* were able to capture a village and fly the Republican flag from the town hall, they invariably had to withdraw when Civil Guard reinforcements arrived. At that point, violent reprisals would be taken against villagers accused of giving succour to the *guerrilleros*. The brutality of the reprisals was linked to what amounted to a deliberate scorched-earth policy with entire villages put to the torch. The process of peasant rejection of the guerrilla was accelerated by another tactic used by the Civil Guard. It consisted of the creation of special units of agents provocateurs, known as *contra-partidas* (counter-guerrilla bands). They would imitate the routine of the authentic *guerrilleros*, enter a village and, by asking for food and shelter, encourage sympathizers to come forward. Once support networks had been revealed, they would be dismantled with brutality. At other times, these fake or counter-*guerrilleros* would simply rampage through villages, raping and plundering. The combined effect of these special operations gradually made it impossible for the *guerrilleros* to return to villages where they had once been welcome. When they could no longer count on peasant sympathy, which was the case by the late 1940s, they were obliged to steal simply to survive. That gave substance to the regime claim that they were never more than bandits. Both suspected *guerrilleros* and mere sympathizers were frequently arrested and murdered without trial by the application of the so-called *ley de fugas* (prisoners shot in the back 'while trying to escape').[107]

Ignoring the difficulties faced by the guerrilla, in early 1947 the PCE was still propounding a fiercely triumphalist line. Despite the wild optimism of Carrillo's speech to the March 1947 plenum in Montreuil, it was already obvious that the uprising that he announced was not going to take place. In May 1947, the French and Italian Communist parties had been forced out of government. With the French frontier subjected to military vigilance, it became ever harder to get supplies of food, weapons and ammunition. Conditions within Spain had deteriorated to the point where many *guerrilleros* were ready to lay down their arms. To prevent further useless losses of hardened militants, an evacuation should probably have begun in 1947, but Carrillo remained committed to the belief that the guerrilla was on the verge of overthrowing Franco. The few *guerrilleros* who did manage to get out of Spain on their own initiative were denounced as 'traitors' and 'deserters'.[108]

Worsening conditions combined with wider Soviet interests indicated the need for withdrawal of the guerrilla. It has been suggested that the first step on the road to withdrawal was initiated in Moscow by Stalin himself. In February 1945, when Pasionaria was preparing to leave Moscow to go to France, Stalin had given her his approval for the guerrilla.[109] As late as February 1948, Carrillo went to Belgrade with Líster to seek support for the guerrilla operations. In a long conversation with the Yugoslav leaders Milovan Djilas and Marshal Tito himself, he demonstrated both extreme irresponsibility and culpable ignorance by asking for guerrilla units to be parachuted into the Levante on Spain's eastern Mediterranean coast. At the time, the guerrilla had already been defeated in Toledo, Cáceres and La Mancha, and the remaining units in Galicia, León and Asturias, as well as in Córdoba, Jaén, Granada and Ciudad Real, were deeply demoralized. Carrillo was clearly out of touch not only with the reality of the situation inside Spain but also with the various momentous changes in the international context.

The French and Italian Communist parties were excluded from participation in coalition governments. After four years of an increasingly tense relationship, Moscow was already on the verge of splitting with Tito. If the request for air support for the beleaguered guerrilla had been granted, Tito might easily have had to declare war on Spain, the consequences of which, in the Cold War, would have been catastrophic. Understandably bemused, Tito responded by asking Carrillo if he had consulted 'our Soviet comrades' and, instead of granting his request, gave him 30,000 dollars in consolation. He made it clear that the money was not to be used for the guerrilla but to help with the bureaucratic costs of running the PCE in France. It is reasonable to suppose that Tito's question was a disturbing wake-up call. The Yugoslav leaders had prevented a monumental faux pas by a man usually so sensitive to Soviet needs. This uncharacteristic error had its origins both in Carrillo's own hubris and in the fact that he, like most of the rest of the Spanish leadership, had limited foreign-language skills. The only politburo member with good Russian was Líster, who had worked as a labourer in the building of the Moscow metro system, had studied at the Frunze Academy and had been briefly married to a Russian woman. Pasionaria had the most halting command of Russian and relied on her daughter Amaya for translations of the press and documents. Carrillo, Uribe and Mije had no Russian whatsoever and only adequate French. In 2000, Carrillo made the astonishing claim that, in the late 1940s, the PCE was not in the habit of consulting with the Soviets about policy changes.[110]

Stalin finally broke off relations with Tito in June 1948. Four months later, Dolores Ibárruri, Carrillo and Antón were received in the Kremlin by Stalin, Molotov, Voroshilov and Suslov. Such an audience was unprecedented. Even during the Spanish Civil War, the

Great Helmsman had not had direct contact with the PCE leadership. The invitation now was almost certainly related to his awareness of Carrillo's meeting with Tito and to his desire, given his need for a free hand in the Balkans, not to provoke difficulties with the Western Powers over Spain. According to Pasionaria's eyewitness account, over tea, cakes and chocolates Stalin did not insist on the abandonment of the guerrilla. Instead, quoting Lenin, he advocated the need for the PCE to place greater emphasis on other forms of struggle, particularly the infiltration of the regime's own mass organizations, and to be patient. That Stalin's principal objective was to ensure the docility of the Spanish leadership was indicated by Suslov's visit the next day to the offices of the Spanish Party. He brought a gift from Stalin – a small suitcase containing 500,000 US dollars.[111]

Despite, perhaps even because of, such generosity, Carrillo, as the advocate of a total boycott of the Francoist vertical syndicates, must have been concerned for his own future. He made the incredible claim in his memoirs that he had stood up to Stalin and had argued strenuously in favour of continuing the guerrilla. More credibly, he admitted that he had prudently made no mention of his earlier request to Tito. Of course, it was utterly inconceivable that Stalin did not know all about it. Carrillo had already begun to expiate his sins by becoming the most ferocious anti-Titoist in the Spanish Party. His stress level may be deduced from the fact that, at this time, he began to suffer from stomach ulcers. The Franco regime's campaign against the guerrilla was being stepped up. In the light of both regime successes and Stalin's suggestions, the PCE politburo in France called an urgent meeting with guerrilla leaders at which a major strategic change was decided. Falangist syndicates would be infiltrated and the guerrilla wound down. Henceforth, guerrilla units were to cease offensive actions and concentrate on protecting PCE committees in the interior. This strategy opened the way to disaster, partly because many fighters were reluctant to abandon the struggle but largely because Carrillo vacillated and did nothing about organizing an evacuation. Interestingly, at this time, to disguise the failure of the guerrilla in Aragón the Party changed the name of the more successful Agrupación Guerrillera de Levante to Agrupación Guerrillera de

Levante y Aragón. A typical case of the fate of the last *guerrilleros* was that of the few from Granada who managed to reach France. They did so, with no help from the PCE, by dint of a forced march of more than 600 miles. After crossing the border, they were subjected to hostile questioning by Carrillo's apparatus.[112]

Nevertheless, Carrillo acknowledged the change in an article notable for a significantly less triumphalist tone than had been evident in his previous efforts. Indeed, it contained an auto-critique of the Party's 'failure to understand the need to use legal forms and its resistance to entrench itself in legal organizations'. There was hardly any mention of the guerrilla, nor of the immediate fall of Francoism, only of the need for patience since the dictatorship enjoyed the support of British and American imperialism. Quoting the same texts of Lenin that Stalin had used, Carrillo now declared that to advocate illegal trade unions was to isolate the workers and that the correct road was to enter the regime's organizations.[113]

Carrillo's ostensible renunciation of the guerrilla struggle was evidently influenced by what Stalin had said. The deterioration of the USSR's relations with the United States was sufficient to incline Stalin to remove a gratuitous irritant in the form of the ever more unsustainable conflict in Spain. Stalin's recommendation of infiltration of the unions had been no more than the pretext for the meeting, suggested to him by one of his functionaries. However, such was the loyalty to Stalin professed by the Spanish leadership that his sacred words provoked Carrillo's half-hearted U-turn. Nevertheless, 'news of the so-called decision to put an end to the guerrilla', according to the principal expert on the subject, Francisco Moreno Gómez, 'certainly did not reach the sierras of central and southern Spain'.[114] In 1950, the Party was still issuing statements that the guerrilla was ongoing and that the work of propaganda, agitation and organization within the rural population was being actively pursued.

Carrillo always tried to maintain rigid control over the militants in the interior of Spain. Líster claimed that Carrillo exercised 'a real terror' and that even the most heroic Party members were likely to be accused of being agents provocateurs if they questioned his views.[115] In making such accusations, Líster was not alone. The family of one of his victims, Juan Ramón Delicado, spoke of a reign of terror imposed by Carrillo on the guerrilla in the Levante, alleging that he had assembled an assassination squad from hardened *guerrilleros*. 'Carrillo, a pathetic general and a feeble strategist, was a sorcerer's apprentice who used the suffering of the Spanish people to hoist himself to power. During this new desperate and cruel war which sputtered over Spain's countryside, numerous Spanish leaders and guerrilla fighters who had been outstanding in the French resistance were sacrificed.'[116] It is certainly the case that clashes between Carrillo and those in the interior were frequent, and Líster alleged that recalcitrant militants were simply denounced to the Francoists. Obviously, Carrillo's actions were not simply capricious. It suited Líster not to mention the remorseless efficacy of the police operation being run by Roberto Conesa, who during the Civil War had been an agent provocateur in the PCE's own ranks. When militants in the interior were captured, they were subjected to sadistic torture, and inevitably some were broken and revealed key information. Seen from France, the only safe method of dealing with this was to eliminate those who came under suspicion. Carrillo's view was revealed in a letter to Monzón about how to combat possible police infiltration: 'Forget your feelings and don't be afraid to commit injustices. They can be dealt with later.'[117]

Of course, it is impossible to distinguish between those killed for real or suspected collaboration with the authorities and those who met their fate because, for whatever reasons, they had disobeyed Carrillo's instructions. Trilla and Alberto Pérez Ayala were far from being his only victims in the interior. Carrillo himself wrote of the condemnation and execution of a party activist. His deliberately vague account does not make clear whether the offence of the unnamed man was to have set up a regional committee without Carrillo's permission or to have acted as a double agent. In fact, the man in question was José Tomás Planas, known as 'el Peque' (the Kid). In his memoirs, Carrillo was at pains to obscure the fact that Planas was one of his most valued protégés, trained in the guerrilla school at Gincla and sent into Spain to replace Zoroa. He was arrested by Roberto Conesa at the beginning of 1947 and quickly agreed to become a double agent. Thanks to his cooperation, many party cadres sent into Spain were captured, an entire guerrilla group from Toledo killed and the party apparatus in Spain destroyed. With the cooperation of Planas, Conesa was able to edit and print a fake *Mundo Obrero* in the Dirección General de Seguridad. Carrillo ordered Planas to come to France where he was interrogated, confessed and was ostensibly pardoned, then sent back to Spain to expiate his sins as a triple agent. In fact, his passage across the frontier was arranged with a guerrilla group that had orders to liquidate him. Carrillo's failure to name Planas reflected his desire to obscure the extent of his own responsibility in the case.[118] There exist numerous cases of militants in the interior sentenced to death by Carrillo and eliminated either by the teams in charge of frontier crossings or by *guerrilleros*.[119]

Cadres were punished for their refusal to renounce Monzón, for excessive independence or on suspicion of being Civil Guard agents. One of the most striking examples was the fate of Delicado, a veteran of the Civil War and French resistance. A trusted collaborator of Monzón, he had been sent into Spain shortly before the Val d'Aran episode. He had reached Tarragona where he successfully linked up numerous disparate groups of *huídos* from various parties, the first step towards the creation of the Agrupación Guerrillera de Levante. His links with Monzón and his readiness to collaborate with a broad range of anti-Francoists, including anarchists and Socialists, made him the object of some suspicion in Carrillo's guerrilla training school at Gincla. In May 1946, Delicado established himself in Valencia in order to run the AGL. However, on 8 July, he was recognized in the street and arrested by a pair of Civil Guards whom he knew, like himself natives of Albacete. Since his group was desperately short of ammunition, he had been en route to buy some from CNT contacts in the city. He convinced the police that he had just returned from France and was looking for work. Failing to recognize him as a guerrilla leader, they released him.

Delicado then followed the security rules that he had himself established within the AGL. The first was to inform the group of an arrest. To do this, he let himself be seen in bars with his Civil Guard friends. The second was to break contact with the rest of the group in case he was being followed. To do this, he went to Elda to be with his sister, who was ill. He returned to the mountains in late August and reported on what had happened. Command of the group had been taken over by Carrillo's emissary, Doroteo Ibáñez Alconchel 'Maño', who had been sent to root out devotees of Monzón. Ibáñez and his team, which included José Manuel Montorio Gonzalvo, assumed that Delicado's release without visible signs of having been tortured and his subsequent absence meant that he had become an agent of the Civil Guard. He was subjected to relentless interrogation, tortured and then kept under observation. Since his record was spotless and the interrogation proved nothing, his links with the CNT were used to justify his elimination. At the beginning of November 1946, he and a long-time collaborator, Valentín Pérez, were executed by Doroteo Ibáñez.[120] They were only the first of several executions carried out by Ibáñez on Carrillo's orders. At the end of October 1952, Ibáñez himself would be betrayed by the PCE. Seriously ill, he had annoyed Carrillo by requesting his withdrawal from Spain. He was arrested by the Civil Guard after a tip-off and later executed.[121]

In Galicia, the local leader, Víctor García Estanillo 'O Brasileño', was regarded as having been too close to Monzón. In January 1946, falsely accused of being an agent provocateur and a bandit, his death, and that of his deputy Teófilo Fernández, was arranged by José Gómez Gayoso, the replacement sent from France. Similarly, another leader in Galicia, Manuel Fernández Soto 'O Coronel Benito', was condemned by Carrillo as a traitor; but, before the sentence could be carried out, he was killed by the Civil Guard in April 1948.[122] Typical of the clashes between Carrillo's emissaries and those whom they were sent to replace was that involving Baldomero Fernández Ladreda 'Ferla' in Asturias. After violent confrontations in which guns were brandished, he declared that he was not 'prepared to put up with any pedant who had not lived the reality of the Francoist terror because it is they who must listen to us, not us who have to listen to them, who have been many kilometres distant from the situation in which they abandoned us'. 'Ferla' was denounced to the Civil Guard from within the Party and executed.[123]

As the guerrilla failed to produce his own loudly trumpeted predictions of overthrowing the regime, Carrillo had become ever more paranoid, always assuming treachery rather than the efficacy of the Civil Guard. Antonio Beltrán 'El Esquinazao' was a veteran militant who, after attaining prominence in the Civil War, was selected for training at the Frunze Military Academy and played a part in the defence of the Soviet Union in the Second World War. In 1948, already under suspicion for his frequent outspoken criticisms of Carrillo's policies and for his links with the Socialists, he made the mistake in a Party meeting of saying that the foreign policy of the USSR was every bit as imperialist as that of the USA. Two assassins were sent to kill him in Bayonne, but he was well armed and scared them off. He escaped to Mexico, and his wife was then held in Russia to ensure his silence.[124]

Another case was that of Luis Montero Álvarez 'Sabugo', who was executed on the French border, according to Líster, by a squad led by one of Carrillo's most loyal cronies, Eduardo García. According to a member of the Party apparatus, Mariano Peña Hernando, the actual assassin was José Gros. Luis Montero was an Asturian railwayman who had fought in the Civil War and played a prominent role in the French resistance before being captured by the Gestapo on 30 November 1942. He was severely tortured but revealed no names of comrades. He was sent to the German concentration camp at Mauthausen in March 1943. There he led the Spanish Communist resistance against the camp authorities. He survived Mauthausen, although his health was shattered. On his return to France, like other survivors of the camps, Montero was subjected to interrogation by Carrillo's team. He was present in Toulouse on 14 May 1945 when Carrillo made the speech suggesting that some of the survivors were agents of the Gestapo and the Falange. He courageously made an indignant defence of his comrades.[125]

Despite Montero's precarious health, Carrillo insisted on using him for actions with the guerrilla in Asturias. Carillo frequently ordered suicide missions to rid himself of those he wanted out of the way. Those who refused the order were simply expelled from the Party. In late 1949, Montero requested permission on health grounds to return to France, but Carrillo refused. Shortly afterwards, at the end of January 1950, he was captured by the Civil Guard. Despite his precarious health, he resisted torture involving beatings and injections of sodium pentothal long enough, he hoped, for his comrades to escape, although he eventually revealed where they had been hiding. To his horror, he learned that they had remained in their refuge and were killed by the Civil Guard.[126] Released by the Civil Guard, Montero made the decision to return to France and report to the Party on what had happened. He was taken across the frontier by José Gros and then interrogated at length in a Party safe house in Perpignan by Eduardo García. Denounced by Carrillo as a 'Monzonist agent provocateur' and spy for the Civil Guard, he was executed in March 1950. Carrillo subsequently justified the execution but denied any knowledge of his executioners.[127]

Líster claimed that, in 1948, he had produced a report on mysterious deaths in which he suggested that the only explanation was that the Party apparatus must have been infiltrated by the Spanish police. However, in the 1970s, Líster published accusations that *guerrilleros* and other militants had actually been murdered on Carrillo's orders by José Gros, who was in charge of frontier crossings, and other staunch collaborators. Years later, Gros became head of security for the PCE. These allegations replicated more detailed ones made earlier in a long report to the politburo drawn up by Francisco Abad Soriano, at the time a member of the Paris leadership team. Prompted by suspicions that there were double agents inside the apparatus, Abad's investigation led him to the conclusion that some deaths had been the result of deliberate assassinations and that others had occurred at the hands of the police after denunciations emanating from inside the Party. The report was apparently suppressed by Pasionaria and Claudín, who managed to get Abad detained in a Soviet psychiatric hospital. It is clearly to this episode that Carrillo referred in his memoirs when he wrote of being the object of a denunciation by someone who 'had a brain tumour and was not in his right mind'. He made this oblique reference to the report and the fate of its author safe in the knowledge that, having died in 1979, Abad could not contradict him. In fact, there was nothing wrong with Abad and, when he managed to get a copy of the report to the KGB, he was released from the hospital. He had left a résumé of the report with his daughter and, after his death, she confirmed the initial comments by Líster. When confronted with this in 2008, Carrillo made the absurd claim that Abad's report was an attempt by Soviet security services to discredit him for his anti-Soviet views. In fact, it would be many years after this incident before Carrillo would make any criticism of the Russians.[128]

By the end of the decade, the guerrilla was limping to its end, but Carrillo refused to recognize the success of the regime's forces and the desperate conditions in which the remaining activists were surviving. It was the opinion of Montorio Gonzalvo that he thereby uselessly sacrificed many lives of hardened militants.[129] Carrillo sent two of the most experienced veterans, José Gros and 'Teo' (Adelino Perez Salvat), into Spain in August 1950. 'Teo' had been advocating an evacuation since 1949. Now, he and Gros found that the main preoccupation of the *guerrilleros* was simply to feed themselves. When they came out with a group of *guerrilleros* in June of the following year, Carrillo chaired a meeting with them and members of Agrupación Guerrillera del Levante y Aragón, 'Galán' and 'Jacinto'. The proceedings of the meeting on 6 June made it clear that Carrillo's intention was to blame the *guerrilleros* and absolve himself of all responsibility for failure. He dismissed excuses about the lack of sympathy from the local peasantry and the existence within the ranks of anarchists and others who rejected Communist discipline. He patronizingly explained the mistakes that had been made, particularly in terms of a failure to identify and eliminate suspect elements, as well as making accusations of cowardice and bourgeois tendencies. Most shocking was his callous dismissal of the guerrilla as no more than a spontaneous movement that the PCE had tried to help by giving it a political content, rather than (as it had been) the Party's central policy.

The only possible mistakes that he acknowledged were that he had attributed too much importance to the guerrilla, thereby wasting valuable energy. All the errors of the AGLA were bizarrely attributed to the fighters in the interior. He denounced them for having 'an anarchist and adventurist line and failing to organize the working class and the peasantry, for denying the leading role of the Party and for thinking that a group of heroes in the hills could overthrow the regime'.[130]

Having delivered this utterly cynical verdict, in the autumn of 1950 Carrillo sent Gros back into the Levante with a group that had served in NKVD guerrilla units in Russia. Their objective was to reorganize the guerrilla, but the situation was beyond repair. The sheer unreality of what they proposed and the rigidity of their methods provoked the opposition of the leaders that they had been sent to replace. At the end of 1950, Gros invited the two principal objectors, Francisco Corredor Serrano 'Pepito el Gafas' and Francisco Bas Aguado 'Pedro', to go to France to discuss their objections with Carrillo. They were murdered en route by Doroteo Ibáñez. Unable to revitalize the guerrilla, Gros was obliged to return to France in March 1951. There was no organized withdrawal. Instead, there was a long forced march of individual groups, not because of any evacuation order from Carrillo but in response to impossible conditions within Spain. The last units did not leave Spain until well into 1952.[131] Gros would subsequently remain with Carrillo into the 1980s as his bodyguard and security chief.

Even before the meeting with Stalin, ample evidence of the PCE's slavish dependence on the Kremlin had been revealed in the PCE politburo's response to the Soviet attack on Tito. On 16 June 1948, a communiqué was issued by the Cominform (Communist Information Bureau), the successor to the Comintern, from its headquarters in Bucharest denouncing the anti-Soviet and 'liquidationist' policies of the Yugoslav Communist Party. The PCE's politburo immediately endorsed the expulsion of the Yugoslavs and particularly praised the 'far-sightedness, firmness and vigilance' of the Communist Party of the Soviet Union (CPSU). Over the next year, more than 200 PCE members would be expelled and a smaller number liquidated for questioning the attack on Tito. Presumably, their puzzlement was aroused by the knowledge that, in its eulogies of Tito, until recently the Spanish leadership had outdone most other parties.[132]

Carrillo was understandably anxious to dissociate himself from Tito and to reassert his loyalty to Moscow. His first response was to associate the 'crimes' of Tito with those of Monzón. He accused Monzón of plotting to destroy the PCE, something which was explained by Monzón's being 'an intellectual of bourgeois education, full of personal ambition, with family ties to reactionary elements'. To carry out his nefarious plans, Monzón had surrounded himself with a group of 'deeply resentful, embittered, ambitious adventurers'. Prominent among them was Trilla: 'this veteran provocateur had returned to the Party, faking a Jesuitical repentance for his past conduct, and waiting for the chance that Monzón gave him to do damage to the Party'. Monzón and Trilla were accused of being adventurers and enemy agents who had organized the invasion of the Val d'Aran in order to bring about 'the physical annihilation of our militants'. In an amazing act of hypocrisy, Carrillo also denounced as traitors those comrades who, in North Africa, had advocated sending guerrilla groups into Spain, a policy that he himself had pushed.[133]

The vehement enthusiasm with which Carrillo repeated his vicious attacks on Quiñones and Monzón suggested something more than just his own ambition. The vendetta that he had pursued since late 1944 against those who had carried on the struggle inside Spain was a reflection of something that also occurred in the Communist parties of Eastern Europe. The bulk of the Spanish Communist leadership replicated the experience of their counterparts from most countries of Eastern Europe. With the exceptions of the Albanians and Yugoslavs, they had gone into exile, usually to Moscow. Inevitably, proximity to, and dependence on, the Kremlin led those Party functionaries to believe that they were the bearers of the sacred flame of Communist orthodoxy. No less inevitably, their slavishly Stalinist notions increasingly diverged from the perceptions of those who remained in the interior to carry on the anti-fascist struggle. In a process exemplified for the Spanish Party by the activities of Carrillo since late 1944, the bureaucrats of the East German, Polish, Hungarian, Romanian, Czechoslovak and Bulgarian parties returned to purge those who had fought fascism but had lost touch with Stalinist orthodoxy. Since Tito did not face this problem, he had been able to pursue an independent line in defiance of Moscow.

Other Communist leaders were to be executed after carefully rehearsed show trials at which, after months of torture and sensory deprivation, they made scripted confessions of crimes they had not committed. The process began with the former Internal Affairs Minister in Albania, the pro-Tito Koçi Xoxe (executed in June 1949), followed by those of the former Internal Affairs Minister in Hungary, László Rajk (executed on 16 October 1949), of the former Prime Minister of Bulgaria, Traicho Kostov (executed on 16 December 1949), of the former secretary general of the Czechoslovak Communist Party, Rudolf Slansky (hanged on 4 December 1952), and of the former Minister of Justice in Romania, Lucreţiu Pătrăşcanu (shot on 17 April 1954). The chosen victims were all accused of treachery as agents of a foreign power. The 'proof' was that they had had contact with Noel Field, director of the American Unitarian relief organization which operated in Eastern Europe after the war. Field himself was accused of being an American spy. In fact, as a committed anti-fascist, he had worked for both the Soviets and the Americans. He had supported the Republican side in the Spanish Civil War. Working for the League of Nations in Spain between 1938 and 1939, he had helped to repatriate International Brigaders. In occupied France and in Switzerland, he had worked selflessly on behalf of refugees, particularly Jewish ones. Many of those whom he helped had reached positions of prominence in the Soviet bloc, and contact with him was a convenient accusation of treachery.

Within the Spanish Party, those who had had contact with Noel Field included Monzón, Carmen de Pedro and Azcárate. In late 1942, Monzón had sent the other two to Geneva in order to establish a base from which it would be possible to communicate with the PCE in Moscow and Latin America. While there they had met Field, from whom they had received funds to help Spanish refugees in France. When news began to spread about the trials in the Soviet bloc, Azcárate informed Carrillo about his own innocuous connection to Field. Carrillo immediately ordered him to cease all work for the PCE and to present himself at a flat in Paris which belonged to the Party. There, over many days from mid-January to early February 1950, he and Carmen were subjected to ferocious interrogation by Carrillo. With great skill, almost as if he were following an NKVD manual, Carrillo used each revelation by one of them to push the other into revealing more information in self-defence.

Carrillo asserted that they had been sent to Geneva by Monzón specifically to make contact with Field. Every attempt on Azcárate's part to defend Monzón was thrown back at him as proof that they were the accomplices of Field. So ruthless was the interrogation that Azcárate was left half believing that he was in fact a capitalist spy. Carmen de Pedro was nearly driven to a nervous breakdown by the pressure to which Carrillo subjected her. The fact that she and Monzón lived well, in fact on the basis of money sent to him by his wealthy mother, was taken as proof that he was in the pay of Field. In hour after hour of psychological torture, Carrillo accused her of treachery for not exposing the crimes of Monzón. He threatened her with expulsion from the Party, pointing out that she had already lost everything and that outside the Party she was nothing. She was so disorientated by the experience at his hands that she accepted that Monzón was a traitor who should be liquidated and signed a humiliating confession.

The document that she signed is a revealing testament to the nature of the interrogation carried out by Carrillo. She stated that her declaration was 'a reflection of the current mind-set of a petite bourgeoise, full of serious defects, morally, physically and politically annihilated by the weight of the grave errors she has committed'. The degree to which she was humiliated may be measured by her statement that she was returning to the Party the photograph that Dolores Ibárruri had affectionately dedicated to her, because she no longer felt herself worthy to keep it. She reiterated throughout that, thanks to the explanations given her by Carrillo, she had been able to see both the full horror of the crimes committed by Monzón and her own guilt as his accomplice. Thus she admitted that because of the inferiority complex which underlay her devotion to Monzón, 'I have been the instrument of the treachery of the foreign imperialists who aimed to liquidate the Party as the vanguard of the working class and deprive it of its character as the Marxist-Leninist-Stalinist revolutionary party of the proletariat'. She wrote that she had acted in concert with Monzón on the Val d'Aran operation out of 'my vanity, ambition, moral decay and political deformity'. She described the invasion as 'the work of the enemy with enormous repercussions that have signified incalculable delays in the liberation of our Fatherland'.

The utter desperation and disorientation to which she had been driven by Carrillo is illustrated by her statement that 'I am over-whelmed and, if it were not for the fact that I know that the Party would not wish it, I would confess even to things that I have no memory of having done, because I am convinced that I do not deserve to be a member of the Party.' Having virtually destroyed her, Carrillo then had her expelled from the Party. Not content with that, when she applied in the 1970s to the French government for the war pension to which she was entitled for her work in the resistance, he refused the necessary letter of support. Only the intervention of Luis Fernández, who had been one of the leaders of the invasion of the Val d'Aran and an acclaimed hero of the resistance, enabled her to claim the pension.

In contrast, Azcárate, having protected himself by more readily endorsing Carrillo's accusations against Monzón, was merely removed from his positions of responsibility. Nevertheless, he kept his salary as a Party functionary and would be eventually 'recuperated' as one of Carrillo's closest assistants. The information extracted from both Azcárate and Carmen de Pedro was distorted by Carrillo to substanti-ate his accusations that Monzón was a spy recruited by Noel Field for the Americans as well as a Francoist agent provocateur.[134]

According to a grotesque diatribe that Carrillo wrote in 1950, 'Quiñones was a daring and unscrupulous adventurer, clearly an agent of the English Intelligence Service' who was guilty of denounc-ing Diéguez, Larrañaga and others. Carrillo accused Quiñones of sectarianism and indiscipline with regard to the Party leadership and of the crime of criticizing the Hitler–Stalin pact. As well as accusing him of being a British agent, he also alleged that he was working for the Francoist police. Carrillo bizarrely claimed that Monzón's entire activity in France and Spain had been directed by Noel Field. 'This', he proclaimed, 'explains the close resemblance between Monzón's policy and that of the Titoist bandits.'[135] In the same issue of the PCE's journal, there was an hysterical article by Ignacio Gallego denouncing 'Titoism'. Gallego accused Tito of being a fascist murderer and claimed that Titoist spies had hidden among the International Brigades in order to aid Franco. Those indicated by Gallego as guilty of Titoism included Trilla, Monzón, Jesús Hernández and Enrique Castro Delgado.[136]

Carrillo's nauseating lies about Monzón and Quiñones and his treatment of Carmen de Pedro were not just manifestations of the central plank of his ambition, his rigid commitment to the Moscow line. The savagery of his language reflected two other things. On the one hand, there was the need to cover up his own failure to denounce Tito in time. On the other, the defeat of the guerrilla represented the collapse of a policy to which he had committed much of his own credibility.

A commitment to Stalin's advice that the dictatorship could be overthrown only by a broad alliance of opposition forces faced two obstacles. The first was the sheer difficulty of infiltrating the Falangist vertical syndicates. The second was the extent to which the rest of the Spanish democratic forces breathed the Cold War atmosphere of anti-communism and still felt smouldering resentment of PCE high-handedness over the previous decade. Accordingly, the creation of a broad front would oblige the Communist leadership to mount a show of credible moderation. And that would involve a degree of de-Stalinization. Carrillo would eventually undertake that task but only once there had been the appropriate changes in the Kremlin. He was always ready to recreate himself in the Soviet image. Thus any de-Stalinization would be in terms of policy directives, not of the Party's internal structure. As the purges associated with Quiñones and Monzón had demonstrated, the preservation of the exiled leadership's power would always have the first priority. Moreover, the anti-Titoist campaign was far from over.

4

The Elimination of the Old Guard: 1950–1960

At the end of the Civil War, defeated, in exile and utterly dependent on Russian assistance, the leadership of the PCE had understandably given greater priority to their role as the frontier guards of the Soviet Union than to the struggle against Franco. Meanwhile, inside Spain, rank-and-file Communists had faced the horrors of the Francoist repression and were pre-eminent in the guerrilla campaign against the dictatorship. Inevitably, this had led to conflict with the leadership in Moscow or in Mexico. Separated by immense distance from the day-to-day reality of Franco's Spain, the exiles reacted with incomprehension to those who questioned the Nazi–Soviet pact and with hostility to the independent thinking of the likes of Quiñones or Monzón. Even after 1945, the leadership remained isolated from Spanish realities. The expulsions of Jesús Hernández and Enrique Castro Delgado, the vilification of Quiñones and Monzón and the purges of the exiled militants in the USSR had nothing to do with the struggle against the dictatorship in Spain and everything to do with the need for ingratiation with the Kremlin. Dependence on Moscow had a corrupting effect on many exiled leaders, although it was probably the case that, for some at least, defence of the stronghold of world communism seemed a worthy end in itself.

There were reasons in 1950 to think that nothing had changed. The trials in Eastern Europe were going ahead in an atmosphere of deepening paranoia and intensifying material hardship. There were more purges to come inside the PCE, yet there were the faintest glimmers of change. In the late 1940s, the Spanish Party was showing signs of renewal in physical, if not ideological, terms. As militants began to emerge from prison, the Party began slowly to rebuild its cells inside

Spain. However, neither the new cadres in the interior nor the exiled leadership fully realized that Franco's improving relations with the United States presaged economic development in Spain that would strengthen the dictatorship. At the beginning of the 1950s, despite Stalin's 1948 recommendation of patience, PCE propaganda still pushed an aggressively optimistic line which, in the long term, as hopeful predictions were continually proved wrong, would damage its credibility. Dolores Ibárruri in Moscow and Carrillo, Antón and Uribe in Paris all failed to see that economic growth was possible and that prosperity would create a wider loyalty to the regime than had existed in the 1940s.

The PCE line was that a small Francoist clique was exploiting the rest of the country and leading it to ruin. Accordingly, it was argued that a broad front would be all that was necessary to overthrow the regime. The recognition of the need for a broad coalition was a not inconsiderable insight and it put the Communists in advance of other sectors of the opposition, although the failure to realize the time-scale involved was to prove a major handicap. For the moment, the priority was not so much the long-term undermining of the Franco regime as the immediate and never ending quest for the approval of the Kremlin. Quiñones and Monzón had been convenient targets, but their offences were in the past. An even more convenient victim was now selected by Carrillo in the person of Joan Comorera, the head of the Partit Socialista Unificat de Catalunya, the Catalan Communist Party. He had been a loyal, not to say brutal, Stalinist. In November 1944, Carrillo himself had praised the way in which Comorera had cleared the PSUC of 'Trotskyist scum'.[1] Those past services would count for nothing. Now, as a sacrificial victim, Comorera offered two advantages – first of all his 'crimes' were ongoing and, secondly, he was head of a party whose nationalist tendencies flouted the authority of the PCE. Thus his position was presented as analogous to the Yugoslav Communists' relationship to Moscow.

Comorera had been invited to join the PCE politburo in October 1948, but his presence there had been rather conflictive. His advocacy of the continued separate existence of the PSUC encountered opposition not only within the PCE but also within the more Stalinist elements of the PSUC itself. The argument used in favour of a single centralized Party apparatus was that, since there was only one working class in Spain, there should be only one Communist Party. This thesis was applied ruthlessly and unilaterally in the wake of the anti-Tito campaign. In July 1949, Comorera was outraged to learn that a consignment of Catalan-language copies of *The Communist Manifesto* destined for the interior had been burned by the PCE. Shortly afterwards, he was removed from the politburo. He was even more distressed when he discovered that, behind his back, a public meeting had been arranged for 28 August in Paris to announce the incorporation of the PSUC into the PCE. This provoked a vicious confrontation between Comorera and those within the PSUC who favoured absorption – Josep Moix, Rafael Vidiella, Josep Serradell, Margarida Abril and Pere Ardiaca. Comorera seized the funds of the PSUC on 2 September, only to be removed as secretary general of the PSUC and, within a week, expelled from the PCE. His efforts to garner support in both France and Catalonia were taken as proof that he was a Titoist bent on undermining the unity of the PCE.[2]

Absurd accusations followed of unbridled personal ambition and megalomania. His earlier attacks on the CNT, made in accordance with Party policy, were now denounced as undermining the recruitment of the masses. The authorship of Carrillo could be seen in the statement that Comorera had been ungrateful for the PCE's efforts 'to re-educate him'.[3] That the entire process was driven by obedience to Soviet directives was shown by Carrillo's explicit references to the trials of the Hungarian László Rajk and the Bulgarian Traicho Kostov and his statement that 'the Party is strengthened when it purges itself'.[4] Carrillo's mentor from the KIM, Mihály Farkas (Michael Wolf), who was now Minister of Defence in the Stalinist dictatorship of Mátyás Rákosi in Sofia, played a vicious role in building the case against Rajk. Farkas/Wolf had written scripts for Carrillo in the past. There was reason to suppose that he provided advice during the campaign against Comorera.[5] In an extraordinary echo of Carrillo's letter to his father, Comorera's daughter Núria was obliged in March 1950 to write a similar letter denouncing her own father. She was married to Wenceslao Colomer, Comorera's one-time ally who, in the

PCE–PSUC power struggle, had aligned himself with Carrillo. In it, she declared her loyalty to the PCE and to 'the beloved Comrade Dolores' and called any effort to divide the Party 'a miserable treachery'. She announced that she understood why the PCE had been obliged to unmask her father as 'an anti-Communist and anti-Soviet mad dog ... an agent of reaction and of imperialism'. She expressed her repugnance and holy hatred and declared that 'on the day Comorera the traitor was born, my father died'.[6]

According to Enrique Líster, on the basis of information given him by Vicente Uribe, Carrillo and Francisco Antón had already pronounced a death sentence on Comorera. On the last day of 1951, he left France and went into Spain. Líster later spoke to five members of the six-man assassination squad sent to the place where Comorera was expected to cross the frontier. By changing his planned route, Comorera avoided them and managed to go underground in Barcelona.[7] Accompanied by his wife, Rosa Santacana, he lived in clandestinity for three years while, allegedly, refusing offers of financial help from Tito. Soon after his arrival, through the PCE's press and its radio station, Radio España Independiente (otherwise known as La Pirenaica), Carrillo orchestrated a smear campaign against him. It was claimed that he had been sent to Barcelona by his American paymasters. He was vilified as a 'Titoist reptile', a 'Titoist dog', a Francoist agent and the traitor at the head of 'a gang of poisonous agents of imperialism'. In *Mundo Obrero*, in the unmistakable prose of Carrillo, Comorera and his followers were denounced as a gang of 'evildoers' and Catalan Party militants were urged to 'isolate and surround him', a covert invitation to them to kill him: 'Comorera and his gang play the role of police lackeys and agents of imperialism and of Francoism, the same role played in Yugoslavia by the Judas Tito and other "teachers" of Comorera.' Although the intention was to inform the police of his presence in Barcelona, the articles and broadcasts were not believed. Nevertheless, the campaign ensured that he would receive no help from most Party militants.[8]

In March 1953, in the rival version of the PSUC newspaper *Treball* that he managed to publish in Barcelona, Comorera alleged that a hit squad had been sent to Barcelona to get him. In a denunciation of the politburo, he wrote,

> Without scruple, you have exhausted the supply of insults and calumnies. You have twisted the poisoned knife in the incurable wound of the deepest and most intimate family feelings. You have tried everything. What is left for you to do? An 'M' protocol? That is possible, since the necessary technical elements are easy enough to find. The intentions of the Politburo may be guessed. Locate the secretary general, assassinate him if you can or, if not, have him eliminated by the police.

An 'M' protocol was the code used by Soviet security agencies for the assassination of recalcitrant militants within the international Communist movement. The arrest of Comorera on 9 June 1954 was described by the PCE as a charade choreographed by the police to hide the fact that he was their agent provocateur. When he was finally tried three years later, Comorera was sentenced to thirty years in prison. After a lengthy illness, he died in the infirmary of Burgos prison in May 1958.[9]

Carrillo later lamented that the Spaniards had acted 'like a herd of sheep' in mounting the vituperative attacks on the Yugoslavs and in seeking sacrificial victims like Comorera.[10] Ironically, Comorera's track record since 1936 suggested that he was every bit as much a Stalinist as Carrillo. However, his defeat, like that of Monzón before him, was yet another triumph for the central bureaucracy of the PCE. The downside was that, yet again, the assertion of the politburo's control was a reaction, not just to Muscovite directives, but also to fear of the autonomy of local activists. In consequence, the leadership in Paris was left ever further removed from the realities and political necessities of opposition to the Franco regime. The problems of distance became more acute when, on 7 September 1950, the French government outlawed the Spanish Communist Party. In what was called 'Opération Bolero-Paprika', gendarmes with little warning entered PCE headquarters near the Arc de Triomphe and seized large quantities of documents. Not only were the PCE's newspapers and journals closed down, but many cadres were arrested and deported to Tunisia, Algeria or Corsica. Many of those were later able to reach Eastern Europe. Those not arrested and deported began to operate clandestinely within France. Thanks to a tip-off from comrades in the French Communist Party, Carrillo and Antón had managed to go into hiding and so avoid arrest. On the same day as the police crackdown, Carmen Menéndez gave birth to Carrillo's first son, Santiago.[11]

The immediate consequence of the crackdown was that the most senior elements of the Party hierarchy who had been in Moscow and therefore not suffered arrest in Paris set up a new headquarters in Prague. With Vicente Uribe, Antonio Mije and Enrique Líster in Czechoslovakia and Pasionaria in Moscow, Carrillo and Francisco Antón were left in charge of the organization in Paris. Leading a semi-clandestine existence, Carrillo controlled the underground apparatus within Spain itself while Antón ran the Party in France. With three centres, Paris, Prague and Moscow, the command structure was unwieldy. The distances involved severely complicated the existing divisions, some personal, some ideological, within the leading group. Even before the French police operation, the ill-tempered bullying and disorganization of Vicente Uribe had provoked the hostility of Carrillo and Antón. Things had remained manageable while Dolores Ibárruri was still in France to keep Uribe in check, but after she had returned to Moscow they became impossible, all the more so when she fell seriously ill. Moreover, there was another issue in that, although they seemed to function well as a team, Carrillo was not entirely happy that Antón considered himself the senior partner in Paris. This was reflected in the arrogant and dictatorial manner in which he treated other members of the hierarchy. For the moment, however, Carrillo held fire.

Both he and Antón were committed to modernizing the Party by marginalizing the often inebriated Uribe. Dolores Ibárruri agreed with them but was reluctant to risk division in the Party at such a high level. Uribe, despite his frequent alcoholic stupors, was cunning. As they had done in Mexico to deflect similar accusations of incompetence and indolence made by Jesús Hernández, he and Mije fought back by blaming Carrillo and Antón for failing to foresee the French crackdown and prepare for the Party to go underground. These personal and generational differences would intensify over the next few years. From 1953, after the abandonment of the guerrilla, from the PCE HQ in Paris Carrillo ran a number of agents who went in and out of Spain. These included Francisco Romero Marín, a hardened militant who during his exile in Russia had held the rank of colonel in the Red Army, and Jorge Semprún, a young intellectual who had fought in the French resistance and had been captured by the Germans, tortured and sent to the camp at Buchenwald. Liaising mainly with working-class groups, Romero Marín used the simple pseudonym of 'Aurelio', although he was often referred to as 'El Tanque' (the tank), a nickname deriving partly from his brusque no-nonsense style and partly from his service in a tank regiment in the defence of Leningrad. Since Semprún's job was liaison with the intelligentsia and university students, he had to change his nom de guerre frequently. He was known variously as Jacques Grador, Federico Artigas, Rafael Bustamante, Federico Sánchez and Agustín Larrea, although Federico Sánchez was the name by which he came to be known within the PCE. Semprún would play a key role within the PCE over the next decade and a half. The passage of agents in and out of Spain was organized by José Gros and Julián Grimau with the aid of false documentation prepared by the Party forger, the extraordinary artist Domingo Malagón. Thanks to these agents, and despite the limitations of his own perceptions of Spanish reality, Carrillo had more contact with what was happening in Spain than the old guard behind the Iron Curtain.[12]

Carrillo was shrewd enough to deflect the attacks from Prague. Francisco Antón was not so fortunate. It will be recalled that in 1937 Dolores Ibárruri had begun a love affair with the then twenty-seven-year-old Antón, fifteen years her junior. The relationship with the slightly built, darkly handsome Antón had lasted a surprisingly long time, but it frequently provoked criticism from other members of the PCE leadership. In 1940, Antón had been captured by the Gestapo in France after the German invasion. Ibárruri was devastated by the news, spending hours locked in her office, neither speaking nor smiling. According to various renegade Communists, she finally asked

Dimitrov to intervene. Enrique Líster claimed many years later that Stalin had commented, 'Well if Juliet can't live without her Romeo, we'll get him for her, since we're bound to have a German spy we can swap for Antón.' Whether Pasionaria made the request or not, it is the case that, in this period, the Soviet Embassy in Paris made many deals with Otto Abetz, Hitler's Ambassador to France. In one of them, Antón was released from the concentration camp at Le Vernet, provided with a Soviet passport and escorted through Germany by a Soviet diplomat.[13]

In the vicious power struggle within the PCE leadership which had followed the death of José Díaz in 1942, Pasionaria's relationship with Antón was used as ammunition against her by her principal rival Jesús Hernández and his allies, Enrique Líster, Juan Modesto and Enrique Castro Delgado. Antón had effectively acted as campaign manager for Ibárruri and helped defeat Jesús Hernández in Mexico. Carrillo had also thrown his weight behind her candidacy and had subsequently missed no opportunity to fuel the personality cult that surrounded her. In consequence, he and Antón were frequent and apparently cordial collaborators. After the abuse to which she was subjected by the Hernández–Castro alliance, Ibárruri had made an effort to be more discreet about her romantic link with Antón. Nonetheless, they remained close and, when they coincided again in Paris in 1945, their relationship had been resumed until she returned to Moscow for medical treatment in 1948. What Dolores Ibárruri did not know was that Antón, since October 1947, had been involved in a love affair with a beautiful twenty-five-year-old Party militant, Carmen Rodríguez.[14]

In late 1948, Pasionaria contracted a severe lung infection after an operation in Moscow to remove her gallbladder. She nearly died, spending six months in hospital. Her convalescence was long and slow and marked the beginning of the end of her effective leadership of the Party. Both Carrillo and Antón were terrified that, if she died, the Party would be left in the hands of Vicente Uribe, who was no friend of the one-time JSU leaders. Although she would gradually resume her activities from the end of 1949, Pasionaria would never recover the driving energy that had previously been her hallmark.

Moreover, because of the ban on the Spanish Communist Party in France, she would remain in her gilded exile in Moscow until well into the 1960s. Nevertheless, despite her physical weakness, she was soon obliged to deal with the intensifying divisions within the Party. In the short term, the sacrificial victim would be Francisco Antón. Carrillo, who was 'guilty' of the same crimes of which Antón was about to be accused, visited her in December 1948 and clinched his relationship with her during frequent visits to her bedside.[15]

Initially, after the witch-hunt against Comorera, the PCE needed another victim in order to show a readiness to emulate the continuing Soviet purges within the East European parties. Pasionaria, Claudín and Ignacio Gallego in Moscow and Uribe, Mije and Líster in Prague accused Carrillo and Antón of not providing adequate reports on their activities. The accusation was carried to Paris by Gallego, and Carrillo and Antón composed a reply in June 1951, pointing out the physical difficulties of getting information for such reports and then transmitting them to Prague and Moscow.[16] This was deemed to be unsatisfactory. Accordingly, Antón went to Moscow to put their case to Pasionaria. To his utter surprise, she was cold and hostile, attacking him violently and accusing him of wanting to replace Uribe. His self-confidence was such that it had not occurred to him that she might have reacted badly to hearing the news that, since they had last met, he had married Carmen Rodríguez, who had given birth to their first daughter in June 1949. He was a nervous wreck when he returned to Paris and said to Carrillo, 'Antón is finished.'[17]

Shortly afterwards, Uribe was sent to Paris to pursue the matter. In June 1952, Carrillo wrote an extensive seventy-five-page auto-critique. In it, he recognized his failures in terms of the organization of the guerrilla. He accepted that there should have been an earlier transition to the infiltration of the legal syndicates in Spain. Implicitly, part of the blame had to fall on the rest of the politburo, but he made great play of his own inexperience and of the fact that he had learned much from the help given by Dolores Ibárruri and from the writings of Stalin.[18] Most remarkably, he recognized that his greatest fault was impatience, 'confusing our good intentions with the real state of the consciousness of the masses'. In a similar auto-critique, Antón accepted that his behaviour had been high-handed, but Pasionaria rejected this document while accepting the one written by Carrillo. She wrote to the other members of the politburo on 28 June 1952, saying that Antón's behaviour went beyond 'the vice of *caciquismo*' and was the worst kind of factionalism – the crime of splitting the Party. She even accused him of being a police agent.[19]

Antón was subjected for a period of nearly two years – from mid-1952 to mid-1954 – to a wave of relentless accusations and interrogations in Paris. At several meetings of the politburo, with the approval of Pasionaria, who did not attend, Antón was put on trial, accused by Uribe of factional activity and authoritarian methods. At the session on 2 August 1952, Antón praised Dolores Ibárruri's exceptional leadership qualities while confessing errors that derived from his own 'idiotic pride and arrogance'. Carrillo was sufficiently shocked by Antón's self-flagellation to state: 'I am convinced that, in personal terms, Antón is an honest comrade.' He thus managed to avoid having to explain how he and Pasionaria herself had managed years of collaboration with someone dishonest. On 8 August, Carrillo dropped his half-hearted efforts to defend Antón and turned on his erstwhile ally, accusing him of vanity, egoism and attacks on Pasionaria: 'I believe that the factional activity of Antón derives from the fact that, carried away by his vanity, his egomania, and the practice of personal methods that in the politburo must necessarily lead to the division of the leadership, Antón fought against the comrades of the party leadership who were abroad, resisting and demonstrating hostility to all of their opinions.'[20]

Antón confessed his factionalist activity and was instructed to write a detailed account of his offences. In it, he abased himself further by confessing that his bourgeois past had led him to try to destroy the PCE. Required to reveal the number of activists he had expelled from the Party, he produced a year-by-year table with a total of 1,320. It was still not enough for Pasionaria, who delayed several months before issuing her verdict. She decreed that more investigation was needed, which meant more interrogation at the hands of Carrillo in much the same way as he had questioned Azcárate and Carmen de Pedro. Antón was ordered once more to appear before the politburo on 24 March 1953. Some of the accusations against Antón – factionalism and ignoring the authority of the politburo – were comprehensible. Others – undermining the revolutionary struggle of the masses and flouting internal democracy – bordered on the comical. Antón was accused of activities for which Carrillo was equally guilty: the use of terror to expel or 'sanction' (a word which included the liquidation of inconvenient militants) behind the excuse of internal security. He was instructed to draft a third auto-critique in which he was required to explain why he had previously hidden the fact that his father had worked in the Dirección General de Seguridad. He was also required to answer a series of absurd and unanswerable questions such as 'what influences had led him to plan the destruction of the PCE?' and 'how far was he aware of the criminal policy implemented by him?'[21] Carrillo stated that the vanity and egoism that he had first seen in Antón was merely a façade to hide his determination to destroy the Communist Party. In view of the alleged crimes, he suggested that the appropriate punishment would be for Antón to be removed from the elevated functions that he had hitherto fulfilled and begin a process of re-education at a more modest level of the Party.[22]

Still in Moscow at the time, Fernando Claudín suspected that behind Pasionaria's extreme hostility was her awareness of the relationship between Antón and Carmen Rodríguez. Santiago Carrillo, however, claimed later that, in the murderous atmosphere of suspicion which was beginning to take hold in Moscow, Ibárruri was merely protecting herself and others. Antón was the most suitable target for attack precisely because her earlier relationship with him could be seen as a dangerous debility. Moreover, she was concerned about the implications of the Slansky trial in Czechoslovakia. If the secretary general of an important Communist Party could become an object of the purges, the worrying implication was that no one was safe. Moreover, in 1951 Pasionaria had established closer relations with the Czechoslovak Party in order to get an operational base in Prague after the French crackdown on the PCE. The successful negotiations with Slansky's deputy Biedrich Geminder had been carried out by Antonio Mije and Ibárruri's close friend and assistant Irene

Falcón. Falcón had been chosen because she was Geminder's partner. Now, in November 1952, the trial began in Prague of both Rudolf Slansky and Biedrich Geminder. It was therefore unsurprising that the accusations that Pasionaria made against Antón should replicate those being made against Slansky.

Antón meekly submitted to the accusations and the relentless interrogations. He could simply have walked away from the Party, but it never occurred to him to do so. This was because, according to Carrillo, the PCE was Antón's whole world. However, it is also possible that he feared either being sent back to Spain to the mercy of the Francoist authorities or being targeted by the assassination squads that had liquidated Trillo and tried to kill Comorera. At the end of the long process, the politburo met again in July 1953 and delivered its verdict that Antón was guilty of factionalism and trying to destroy the Party, for which he was to be removed from the politburo and the Central Committee.[23] After a delay occasioned by ill-health, on 13 November 1953 Dolores Ibárruri responded with a fiercely vengeful judgement stating that the problem with Antón was not his personal political degeneration but his unbridled ambition. It favoured, she said, 'the most rabid enemies of the party, the enemies of the working class, the enemies of democracy, the police services of who knows which imperialist power'. 'Proof' of this was that he had been sent to the Soviet Union in 1940 by the Germans – an operation that the PCE itself had initiated at her behest.[24] The other members of the politburo refrained from pointing out that this meant that she had been sleeping with the enemy for at least ten years. Psychologically destroyed, Antón was ordered to leave his wife, Carmen Rodríguez, and his children in Paris and go to Warsaw, where he was to live and work in isolation, even prohibited from making contact with PCE exiles. Only the death of Stalin in March 1953 protected him from worse punishment. He was offered comfortable work by the Polish authorities in the state publishing house. He chose instead martyrdom and redemption through poorly paid piecework on the assembly line in a motorcycle factory. Eventually joined by his wife and two daughters, the younger of whom had serious health problems, he lived in abject poverty in Warsaw.[25]

Carrillo later claimed that Antón's docile acceptance of his fate was not unusual – 'at that time, we were like crusaders in a medieval military order'. He wrote in his memoirs that what had been done was 'a shameful exercise of self-flagellation and moral torture of Antón for which, deep down, I have never forgiven myself'. Nevertheless, despite this self-criticism, in three pages of his memoirs he skimmed over an issue which, at the time, generated copious documentation.[26] In 1964, an extremely discreet rehabilitation began at the hands of a somewhat regretful Carrillo, who invited Antón to a plenum of the Central Committee. That Carrillo's relationship with Antón had not been as straightforward as he implies in his memoirs was made obvious by his role in the denunciation and subsequent interrogation of Pasionaria's ex-lover. Indeed, it has been alleged that, in private, Carrillo used to refer to Pasionaria herself as 'the old whore' and to Antón as 'her pimp Paco'. The witness was Jorge Semprún's brother Carlos, who was thrown together with Carrillo after the French crackdown. The Semprún family home in Paris was used for clandestine meetings of the PCE and was probably where the interrogation of Antón took place.[27]

Antón was replaced in the Paris headquarters by Ignacio Gallego who, according to Claudín, 'tended to look on Carrillo as his boss'.[28] Carrillo had survived, in part by betraying his friend, but also because his knowledge of the apparatus in Spain combined with his astonishing capacity for hard work made him indispensable. Nevertheless, the generational conflict that had led both him and Antón to oppose Uribe still simmered below the surface. In fact, Uribe was the immediate beneficiary of the destruction of Antón. Having survived the storm himself, Carrillo would next seek the elimination of Uribe. A powerful ally in what was about to happen would be Fernando Claudín, whose role in that process would earn him a reputation as a liberal. However, the harsh rigidity with which he had fulfilled his duties as head of the Spanish exile community in Russia marked him out as anything but. According to Carrillo, in the 1950s Claudín was an orthodox hard-line Stalinist. This description was deserved not, as Carrillo suggested, because Claudín had studied Marxism in the Leninist University in Moscow but rather because of the high-handed brutality with which he had treated the exiled militants. Nevertheless, it is certainly the case that, by dint of determined study, and with the help of many young Spanish intellectuals who had trained in Moscow, Claudín had turned himself into the nearest that the PCE had to a Marxist theorist. Other, more pragmatic leaders like Carrillo and Dolores Ibárruri therefore thought of him as a useful asset. What neither Carrillo nor Pasionaria realized was that the application of his theoretical musings would take him in directions that would ultimately be damaging to both.[29]

The year 1951 had seen the beginning of a serious bid for economic expansion in Franco's Spain. The immediate result of huge investments was galloping inflation without corresponding wage increases. Just to stay at subsistence level, workers had to increase their working hours. The first consequence of this worsening of conditions was a major strike in Barcelona followed by others in Madrid and Asturias.[30] These strikes owed far more to the changing economic situation than to Communist influence. However, working-class militancy seemed to suggest that Party predictions of mass opposition to the regime were valid. To take advantage of the changing situation would require alliances with other opposition forces. To secure them, internal reform of the PCE would be necessary and that would be a long and painful process.

With its leadership dependent for funds and hospitality on the Soviet Union and with its rank and file involved in a clandestine struggle with a fiercely reactionary dictatorship, it is hardly surprising that the PCE would remain firmly Stalinist in both its thinking and its organizational methods in the fifteen years following the Spanish Civil War. It was not until after the death of Stalin that a slow and grudging effort would be made to de-Stalinize. In the early 1950s, things looked bleak for the PCE. Its organization had been largely dismantled by the French security forces. Within a month of the Party being banned in France, the United Nations had decided to permit its members to return their ambassadors to Madrid. It was the beginning of a process that would see the Franco regime find ever greater acceptance in the Western world. The reaction of the PCE was to emulate its Soviet masters and withdraw into ever greater isolation.

Any criticism by other Spanish Republican forces of the USSR or its policy was denounced as collaboration with American imperialism and with the Franco dictatorship. The Republican government-in-exile was denounced as 'the accomplice of Tito's fascist gang'. The PCE leadership saw the changing diplomatic situation as proof that American imperialism planned to use Franco's Spain as a base for future attacks on the Soviet Union.[31]

Things changed somewhat with the great public transport strike in Barcelona in 1951. Although the PCE was quick to claim credit, the cause was the deteriorating economic situation inside Spain. Food shortages and inflation, rather than Communist activity, lay behind the revival of labour militancy despite the brutal machinery of repression. Per-capita bread consumption in Spain in 1950 was only half of what it had been in 1936 and meat consumption only half of what it had been in 1926. Prices had outstripped working-class wages since 1939 by more than 200 per cent. Moreover, strict rationing meant that much food was available only on the black market, where prices were more than double the official rate.[32] Spain's inefficient agriculture left the country dependent on food imports at a time of dwindling foreign currency reserves. The prices of raw materials were rocketing in the context of the Korean War, which had broken out in 1950, and energy was also in short supply. Power cuts were leaving factories idle and workers were being laid off or put on short time.

In March 1951, plummeting working-class living standards saw social tensions in Barcelona finally boil over. Franco's cabinet, oblivious to the deterioration, had authorized the previous December a 40 per cent increase in the fares on Barcelona's decrepit trams. There was outrage that the new average fare of 80 cents was double that imposed in Madrid. Accordingly, by late February, there was a boycott of public transport and cases of trams being stoned.[33] By 12 March, the city was at a standstill, with more than 300,000 workers taking part in a general strike. Despite the PCE's attempts to claim the strike as its own, it involved broad sectors of the population. There was participation by local Falangists along with activists of the Catholic workers' organization, HOAC – the Hermandad Obrera de Acción Católica (the Workers' Fraternity of Catholic Action) – and members of the middle class. The regime's reaction was typically exaggerated. Franco insisted that 'public order must be maintained' and sent three destroyers and a minesweeper to the port of Barcelona. Marines marched through the streets. However, the Captain General of Barcelona, the austere monarchist General Juan Bautista Sánchez, refused to deploy the army to repress disorder provoked by the Civil Governor's short-sightedness. He prevented large-scale bloodshed by calmly confining the garrison to barracks. In fact, within two or three days, fearing for their jobs and the sustenance of their families, most workers were drifting back. Nevertheless, there were nearly a thousand arrests. Among them, in apparent justification of the regime's claim that the strike was the work of Communist agitators, were thirty-four members of the PSUC.[34]

There can be little doubt that PSUC militants were active participants in the events of 12–14 March in Barcelona, but they were not alone. Although delighted by news of the strike, Carrillo was distressed that the French press did not even mention the PSUC. He was claiming that the strikes were entirely the work of the PCE and the PSUC. One of those arrested in its aftermath was Gregorio López Raimundo, who had been sent into Catalonia by Carrillo as a more pliant replacement for Comorera. However, López Raimundo had not been involved in the strike, since he had been in France at the time receiving medical treatment. Carrillo had doubts about López Raimundo, who had questioned his instruction to impose centralized control over the activities of militants on the grounds that the repressive capacity of the regime made it virtually impossible. Even when López Raimundo explained that the only way to take advantage of the spontaneous militancy of the rank and file was by infiltrating the Francoist vertical syndicates, Carrillo insisted on the maintenance of the strict rules of a clandestine resistance group.

López Raimundo did not leave for Barcelona until 24 March, ten days after the strike had ended. After a complicated journey via the Basque Country, Navarre and Aragon, he arrived in early April. He was arrested on 9 July, badly beaten and then put on trial in June 1952, accused of organizing the tram strike. The prosecutor demanded a sentence of twenty years in prison. After a huge international campaign choreographed by the PCE, he was sentenced to four years and finally exiled to Latin America. The Party accused Comorera of responsibility for the arrest of López Raimundo, which was absurd. If the responsibility lay anywhere it was with Carrillo. Indeed, in his auto-critique of June 1952, when he was trying to avoid sharing the fate of Antón, Carrillo confessed to his own over-optimistic impetuousness in sending activists into dangerous situations in the vain hope that they could undermine the regime by organizing strikes.[35]

The Barcelona tramway stoppage saw solidarity strikes by students in Granada and Madrid. The textile industry in Manresa was still closed when, on 23 April 1951, some 250,000 men began a forty-eight-hour strike in the shipyards, steelworks and mines of the Basque Country. Again, Falangists and members of HOAC joined in alongside leftists and Basque nationalists. The regime denounced the strike as the work of foreign agitators. The employers, aware of the problem of the cost of living and not prepared to lose skilled labour, ignored the regime's orders for mass sackings. Despite savage police beatings of strike leaders, many of whom were rounded up and taken to a concentration camp near Vitoria, industrial action continued sporadically for several weeks. In the third week of May, there was another transport strike in Madrid. The initial reaction of the regime was to blame Moscow, a claim which the PCE was delighted to endorse.[36] In fact, the strike wave would lead only to the smallest token steps towards liberation by the dictatorship. American aid, clinched by the Treaty of Washington, and the Concordat with the Vatican, saw the regime stronger than ever. Nevertheless, the strikes, and particularly the transport boycott in Barcelona, were what finally persuaded Carrillo to drop the guerrilla and push for the infiltration of the regime's vertical syndicates. In his report to Pasionaria, Carrillo claimed that the events in Barcelona were the fruit of the PCE having adopted Stalin's 1948 advice. The highly questionable attribution of credit to the PCE and to Stalin made the change of policy more palatable to her.[37]

The speech made by Dolores Ibárruri on 25 October 1951 to a group of Party leaders in Moscow, in which she claimed for the PCE credit for the 1951 strikes, was to have far greater significance than seemed likely at the time. The main burden of her speech was the usual triumphalist prophecy of the imminent collapse of the Franco regime couched in hard-line Stalinist terms. She called for continued 'revolutionary vigilance' in the struggle against the 'the gang of Titoist spies and provocateurs working for the imperialist security services'. She was really talking about Antón, just as she was when she denounced sectarianism and authoritarianism.[38] However, this speech would later be used with immense cunning by Carrillo at the Fifth Congress. He would repeatedly cite her as the authority for what were essentially his own ambitions. The most important and immediate practical implication of the speech was that the combination of the strike waves and recognition of the end of the guerrilla imposed the inevitable decision to work within legal organizations.

Still using the vitriolic language of the purges to denounce internal enemies and 'Titoists', the Party leadership was devastated by the death of Stalin on 5 March 1953. In Moscow, the man whom Stalin had called 'Our Himmler', his security chief Lavrenty Beria, seized the initiative. Other senior figures were briefly satisfied with key positions. Klim Voroshilov became titular head of state, Nikita Khrushchev head of the CPSU, Viacheslav Molotov Minister of Foreign Affairs, Georgi Malenkov Prime Minister. Astonishingly, given his bloodstained track record as Stalin's right-hand man, from his position in the Interior Ministry Beria began a process of liberalization. To the alarm of his rivals, this led to unrest all over Eastern Europe, and there was an uprising in Berlin in June. His rivals were even more distressed when he halted ongoing purges and suggested that Stalin's crimes be exposed. Fearful that their own part in collective decisions would be revealed, they arranged for the arrest and execution of Beria, who was accused of being an American agent. The next stage would be to exonerate themselves by blaming all past crimes and errors on Beria and Stalin. By 1955, there would be reconciliation with Tito and, by 1956, an attack on the record of Stalin himself.[39]

Despite much lamentation at the death of Stalin, the leadership of the PCE could not remain unmoved before these seismic shifts at the heart of the Kremlin. As rhetoric about the need for collective leadership filtered out, the possibilities were not lost on Carrillo. He sensed that a move to collective leadership could be favourable ground on which to fight the battle against the old guard for control of the Party. He proposed, and then undertook the organization of, a congress. This would be, eighteen months later, the Fifth Congress of the PCE, which took place at Lake Máchovo near the town of Doksy to the north of Prague from 12 to 21 September 1954. For security reasons, PCE publications gave the dates as 1–5 November. It was more than twenty-two years since the Fourth Congress held between 17 and 23 March 1932 in Seville. Understandably, during the Civil War and the Second World War, there had been no further congresses. Such a gathering would have been possible during the years of legal existence in France but hardly welcome to the leadership when their principal concern was to maintain central control through purges that replicated what was happening in Russia. The last time that there had been an election for the Central Committee was the plenum of March 1937, at which Carrillo had been elevated to the politburo. Of the sixty-five members elected then, only nineteen remained in the Party. A further nineteen were dead and twenty-seven had been expelled.[40]

Even in 1954, in the void left by Stalin's absence, there would be little de-Stalinization in a PCE devoid of internal democracy. The selection of delegates was symptomatic of the spirit in which the congress would be held. Manuel Azcárate commented later, 'To call a meeting like the one in 1954 a "Congress" is an exaggerated euphemism. The "delegates" were the people picked by Carrillo and Uribe. Not even in France, where it would have been possible, was there anything resembling an election of delegates.' Security reasons inevitably ensured that there could be no open elections, even in France. Nevertheless, Carrillo ensured that only the most loyal and least critical militants were chosen.[41]

The proceedings at the Fifth Congress hinted at a willingness to change but also indicated how painfully gradual de-Stalinization was likely to be. Relative to earlier assemblies, a slightly more critical tone could be noted about some of the speeches, and there would be a degree of rehabilitation of some of the lesser figures who had suffered during the anti-Tito purges. The proceedings were opened at 4.20 on the afternoon of 12 September 1954 by Vicente Uribe, who presided over the congress. His ninety-minute speech was mainly a hymn of praise to Stalin and made a very poor impression on the assembled delegates. At 6.00 p.m., the PCE secretary general, Dolores Ibárruri, began to read out her report. She roundly denounced Franco's alliance with the United States as damaging to Spanish interests and excoriated the leaders of the PSOE for criticizing the USSR and for praising American initiatives such as the Marshall Plan, NATO and German rearmament. Her report was interrupted at 8.00 p.m. and Carrillo announced that she would continue the next day.[42]

Ibárruri's main theme was the need for democratic unity against the Francoist clique. She even offered an olive branch to Indalecio Prieto, but there were several aspects of her report that were unlikely to seduce the Socialists, Republicans and anarchists with whom unity was proposed. Only three years earlier, she had denounced all these groups for 'their dirty game on behalf of reactionary and fascist forces'.[43] Now, in her lengthy analysis of Spanish history from 1931 to 1939, she effectively accused them of responsibility for Franco's Civil War victory and stated that it was difficult for the PCE to contemplate alliance with them. She also implied that their anti-Soviet attitudes showed that they were lackeys of American imperialism. She further blamed their lack of cooperation for the failure of the guerrilla. Asserting that the PCE led the anti-Francoist opposition, she simply called for the rank and file of other groups to follow the Communist lead. The most notable previous attempt at unity, the Alianza Nacional de Fuerzas Democráticas, sponsored by these groups in 1944, was declared to be a police montage.[44] If such references preoccupied Socialists, Republicans and anarchists, their effect was hardly minimized by reiterated praise for Eastern-bloc countries and declarations of the PCE's determination to follow the example of the Soviet Communist Party.[45]

Pasionaria's report scarcely concealed her conviction that the leaders of the other left-wing groups could be bypassed and their rank-and-file members simply absorbed into the PCE.[46] On the other hand, by comparison with the virulence which had characterized the Communist attitude to Socialists and anarchists since the departure of the PCE from the Republican government-in-exile in August 1947, one or two of the things that Dolores Ibárruri said signified some effort at moderation. Thus she recognized as an error the failure to infiltrate the regime's vertical syndicates. Indeed, she spoke at length of the need to eliminate sectarian attitudes within the Party, the responsibility for which was nevertheless blamed on middle-rank cadres or elements already disgraced, such as Quiñones, Monzón, Trilla, Hernández and Comorera.

However, the language used by Ibárruri to justify the expulsion of such 'traitors' can hardly have been enticing to those she was trying to attract into the fold:

the Party has faced the perfidy of a group of murky elements, of political degenerates that had hidden their real face as enemy agents whose mission was to castrate the Party. We have unmasked and expelled from our ranks the likes of Hernández, Comorera and Del Barrio, whose conscience was rotten and whose rat-like teeth had bitten into the steely muscular tissue of the Party ... and there they are, like force-fed capons, reciting the glories of the imperialism on whose scraps they depend ... We have had to deal with the desertions of the weak, of those most influenced by enemy propaganda, with the moral collapse that defeats always produce and also with the betrayal of the people who accidentally came into our ranks in the hope of making their career and who after seeing their hopes evaporate, impotent and crippled, became rabid dogs that spat their contagious saliva over the party.[47]

It should be explained that José del Barrio, who left the Party in 1939 in protest against the Nazi–Soviet pact, was one of the few real 'Titoists' in the PCE. He had set up a rival group with finance from Belgrade.[48]

Given the virulence of Ibárruri's language, it was not difficult for her tentative steps towards liberalization to be surpassed by those of Carrillo. He was concerned that the rigidity of the aged Party leadership in exile diminished the ability of the militants within Spain to react to economic and political changes and also stood in the way of his own ambitions. As PCE organization secretary, he was a powerful figure in the Party hierarchy, with responsibility for the interior apparatus. His spectacular rise to prominence in the PCE between 1936 and 1954 had been marked by ostensibly slavish loyalty to the Party leadership and strict adherence to Moscow. However, by 1954, both his own personal experience and his links with cadres inside Spain had convinced him that the loutish and alcoholic Stalinist Vicente Uribe was out of touch with the interior and incapable of running the PCE's operational centre in Paris. The Civil War leadership of the PCE – Pasionaria, Uribe, Mije and Líster – tended to think in terms of re-establishing the Republic and creating a broad front of left-wing forces to do so. Carrillo felt that the PCE should cast its net even wider in search of democratic partners against Franco and should accept that there could be no return to 1936. He had allies on the politburo, in the persons of Ignacio Gallego and Fernando Claudín, but they were of secondary status by comparison with Uribe, Mije and Líster. Carrillo was thus faced with a delicate problem. Dolores Ibárruri remained the grand arbiter and was likely to favour the old guard.

Accordingly, when Carrillo rose to address the Fifth Congress in the late afternoon of 18 September, his report on Party statutes and internal organization was cautious and technical. In guarded language, he called for the renovation of the apparatus within Spain. However, by advocating collective responsibility as the key to leadership, he sidestepped potential criticism by seeming merely to be advocating what was happening in Moscow. That, together with a push for the introduction into the Central Committee of younger militants from the interior, would both enhance his own position in a future power struggle and prepare the Party for a search for a politically broader alliance against the dictatorship.[49] His praise for democratic centralism, with rank-and-file militants electing the committees which would elect the Central Committee which would, in turn, elect the politburo, was risible in its hypocrisy. Although he explained plausibly why such procedures were impossible inside Spain, he continued to imply that elsewhere, in Latin America, in France and in Russia, democratic centralism was the order of the day. In a theatrical display of auto-critique, he expressed regret for the arbitrary authoritarianism of which the Party leadership had 'occasionally' been guilty but clearly, without naming him, blamed this on Antón.

Moreover, the new statutes that he had drafted – and circulated before the congress – tended to give more initiative to the militants within Spain and undermine the power of the old guard in Moscow. In his speech, and in supportive ones by Fernando Claudín and Ignacio Gallego, there were repeated claims that his proposals simply implemented what Dolores Ibárruri had suggested in her speech of October 1951. This was nonsense of course since her denunciation of sectarianism and authoritarianism in the Party had come from the most extreme Stalinist motives – the desire to eliminate Antón and Comorera in emulation of the trials taking place in Eastern Europe. In the minutes of the congress, there are manuscript notes by Carrillo indicating which parts of his speech should not subsequently be published. The censoring of some remarks relative to activities in factories within Spain might be justified in terms of security. Others, however, either redolent of Stalinist attitudes within the Party or insulting to Socialists, were clearly omitted because of their probable negative impact on would-be allies.[50]

Other speeches to the congress reflected the persistence of hard-line Stalinist and also triumphalist attitudes. For instance, 'Román' (Josep Serradell) of the PSUC denounced Quiñones and Monzón as degenerate terrorists and declared that the success of the 1951 strikes was the consequence of the expulsion of Comorera. Carrillo also denounced Quiñones and Monzón, albeit in slightly less vehement terms, and made implicit criticisms of Antón without naming him.[51] Nevertheless, his speech did carry a muted call for a renovation of Party structures. His intervention was preceded on 14 September by others from cadres from the underground, including 'Federico Sánchez' (Jorge Semprún) and 'Vicente Sainz' (Simón Sánchez Montero).[52] What they had to say had considerable impact, and both were elected to the Central Committee, although not to the politburo. Other loyal followers of Carrillo, such as Víctor Velasco, Julián Grimau and Tomás García, also became members of the Central Committee. As Azcárate complained, 'a Central Committee was appointed but it never met more than once or twice a year and then only to listen to and endorse what the politburo said'.[53] Thus the Party would continue to be ruled by the politburo, but Carrillo's reforms were not entirely superficial. The renovation of the Central Committee, which included forty-five new members, among whom were several from inside Spain, would improve the Party's ability to react to the situation in the interior. It was hardly surprising that most of the new members had once been in the JSU and were followers of Carrillo. This significantly strengthened his position in the latent power struggle. Although the changes implied a democratization of the inner workings of the PCE, it was Carrillo's firm intention to maintain tight control.

Carrillo's meteoric rise had been postulated on his identification with Pasionaria and the old guard. The Fifth Congress was the beginning of a new phase in which his subsequent promotion would be in opposition to them. He based his position on identification with a new generation of younger militants able to operate inside Spain. Jorge Semprún (Federico Sánchez) was assuming considerable importance as his liaison with an influential group of intellectuals and students inside Spain. Simón Sánchez Montero was fulfilling a similar role with workers' groups. The next stage would be for Carrillo, with the enthusiastic assistance of Claudín and Gallego, to eliminate Uribe. Success in that endeavour would inevitably open the way to a clash with Dolores Ibárruri. The leadership's decision to end Claudín's stint in Moscow and send him to Paris in January 1955 would be a crucial element in this process. Claudín himself believed that the initiative derived from a suggestion by Carrillo to Pasionaria. Nevertheless, the decision was hers, taken with confidence in his reliability and perhaps a belief that the Paris operational centre required the ideological reinforcement that only he could bring. Carrillo was delighted both on a personal level – their friendship went back a long way, with shared experiences in Mexico and Buenos Aires, where, it will be recalled, they had relationships with two Argentinian sisters, Santiago with Lidia, Claudín with Ángela. In political terms, their alliance was a powerful one. Claudín was the back-room strategist, the deep thinker. Carrillo remained the quick-witted, daring cynic, endlessly flexible and with the congeniality necessary to mask his ambition. Yet within this apparently perfect team there was the potential for conflict between Claudín's strategizing based on Marxist theory in the long-term interests of the Party and Carrillo's short-term tactical improvisations based on his own ambition.[54]

For the moment, however, Claudín became Carrillo's indispensable right-hand man. After the gloom and remoteness of Moscow, Claudín was delighted to be in Paris and involved in the organization of the struggle within Spain. Initially, he shared and even exceeded Carrillo's triumphalist conviction that the fall of Franco was imminent. This exacerbated the tension with the old guard led by Uribe, whose scepticism and indolence they perceived as a defeatist obstacle to their revolutionary hopes.[55] They both felt that they were closer to Spain than the rest of the politburo, who visited Paris only for meetings. Uribe, Mije and Líster all lived in Prague and Dolores Ibárruri was temporarily established in Bucharest. The inevitable clash would come, however, not because of discrepancies over the situation in Spain but as a result of dramatic changes in the international situation. Carrillo had been shocked by the Kremlin's reconciliation with Tito and Khrushchev's visit to Belgrade at the end of May 1955. Having been the most vehement anti-Titoist in the PCE, he was determined not to be wrongfooted again. A showdown was to come within twelve months, probably sooner than Carrillo had anticipated. Towards the end of 1955, the bulk of the Party leadership was about to go to Bucharest to celebrate Pasionaria's sixtieth birthday on 9 December, and the Paris operational centre was being run by Carrillo, Claudín and Gallego. News came in that the United Nations, including the Soviet Union, had voted in favour of the entry of sixteen new members, including Spain.

The reaction of the PCE's Paris group was positive. The principal objective of Russia's vote had been to secure the addition of Hungary, Bulgaria, Romania and Albania to the United Nations. Spain's inclusion was seen as a Soviet gesture to the West as part of the post-Stalin quest for peaceful coexistence; only coincidentally was Moscow recognizing the reality of the Franco regime's stability. In addition, there was a feeling among the PCE's 'young lions', or rather slightly younger lions, that the end of international isolation would contribute to political liberalization in Spain by increasing cultural, commercial and political relations with democratic countries. This impression was confirmed by Jorge Semprún, who returned from a mission in the interior to report on the growing anti-regime feeling among university students, dissident Falangists and Catholics.[56]

Carrillo quickly produced an enthusiastic article on the United Nations vote in *Mundo Obrero* and a lengthier version for the journal *Nuestra Bandera*. Hailing it as a victory for the USSR's peaceful policy, he claimed that it prevented the Francoists depicting the regime's international isolation as the result of a Communist conspiracy. Carrillo hoped that it would lead to the Spanish bourgeoisie moving on from the false dilemma of 'Francoism or Communism' to the true one: 'Francoism or democracy'.[57] His view was not shared by the old guard in the politburo. In contrast, the knee-jerk response of Dolores Ibárruri, Uribe, Mije and Líster was to denounce Spain's inclusion in the UN as evidence of yet another betrayal by Anglo-American imperialism. Without criticizing the Soviet Union, they drafted a savage attack on the UN admission of Francoist Spain that was broadcast on 30 December 1955 on the Party's radio station, Radio España Independiente. Their affront at the betrayal of 'Republican legality' revealed a rigid exile mentality in contrast to the notably more flexible and realistic stance of the somewhat younger group.

When he wrote the articles, Carrillo was not initially planning to launch a factionalist initiative and thus provoke a conflict. After all, his argument was supportive of the line being taken by Khrushchev, who was emerging as the probable winner in the Soviet power struggle. He tried to retrieve his text from the printers and only when it turned out to be impossible did he decide to take up the cudgels in earnest. Carrillo chose to send Jorge Semprún eastwards to put the Paris group's case. Semprún was an attractive option, young, brilliant and with the indisputable merit of his unique knowledge of the PCE's organization in the Spanish interior. When he reached Prague, he was told that Pasionaria was at a congress of the East German Communist Party in Berlin and would be returning with the Romanian delegation in a special closed train. He was received by Uribe and Líster in the latter's study. In Semprún's version, they were shocked by what they regarded as the rebellious provocation implicit in Carrillo's article, the text of which Semprún had brought with him. Even more so, they were infuriated when Semprún cited his own experiences as 'Federico Sánchez' to criticize the rigidity of Party policies and explain their utter irrelevance to the reality of Franco's Spain. They were particularly outraged that a recently nominated Central Committee member should have the temerity to criticize the politburo. Líster threatened Semprún and, when Semprún stuck to his guns, Uribe said that he would have to discuss the matter with Pasionaria.[58]

When Pasionaria's train reached Prague, Semprún was told to accompany her on what he later recalled as the forty-eight-hour onward trip to Bucharest. He was astonished by the opulence in which senior Party officials lived, first on the luxuriously appointed train and later in Romania. He was impressed that Ibárruri, when presented with a cornucopia of delicacies by the white-gloved waiters, took only a glass of mineral water. He found her ready to listen but hostile when she realized that what he was telling her implied a major strategic shift in favour of Carrillo and the Paris group. Anxious not to precipitate a major split in the Party, she said that the politburo's declaration against Spanish entry into the UN would be withdrawn and that the views expressed in Carrillo's articles would be considered at a forthcoming meeting of the politburo.[59] When she discussed the matter with the rest of the politburo, it was decided that the threat could best be met by skilfully stage-managing the promised meeting which would take place in Moscow. Accordingly, in the hope of dividing the Paris group, Claudín was included, with Uribe, Mije, Líster and Pasionaria, in the PCE delegation to the Twentieth Congress of the CPSU in February 1956. Carrillo was ordered to stay in France to run the Paris organization.

Pasionaria was confident that it would be easy to 'recuperate' Claudín. Then, with him on board, Carrillo would be denounced as a social democratic reformist and opportunist, citing both his past in the PSOE and his 'factionalist' stance. Before leaving Paris for Moscow, however, Claudín had agreed with Carrillo that he would not give in to the old guard. If defeated, they would both go down in the fight to renovate the Party. The politburo meeting was held both before and in the intervals between sessions of the Moscow congress. In the harshest language, Pasionaria denounced the way that Carrillo, using the network that he had built as leader of the JSU, had created his own parallel apparatus within the Party. She and Mije made every effort to show Claudín that they did not hold him responsible for the crimes of Carrillo. However, Claudín courageously resisted the blandishments of the old guard and forcibly put his group's view to Ibárruri. The old guard and the Parisian *jóvenes* differed not only on the international situation. The old guard were outraged when Claudín reiterated what Semprún had already told Ibárruri – that the failures of the PCE in the interior should be attributed to the rigid policies emanating from the leadership in Prague and Moscow.

At first, Pasionaria sided with Uribe, and things looked bleak for the liberalizers. Then, having had a preview of Khrushchev's secret report denouncing Stalinism and the cult of personality, she decided that the views of Claudín and Carrillo were in line with the new currents of liberalism emanating from the Kremlin. What gave urgency to her deliberations was the realization that she herself could be in danger. She was pushed in this direction by the intervention on 12 March of Claudín who, while directing his main attack against Uribe, made a cunning aside: 'Among us too, the leaders of the PCE, the cult of personality has weighed heavily ... If it stood in the way of us being able to criticize Comrade Uribe, who among us in previous years would have been capable of seriously criticizing Comrade Dolores Ibárruri?' If the Soviet leadership had decided that the personality cult of Stalin could be blamed for all ills in the Communist system, the 'little Stalins' of the various national parties were in trouble. It suited her that the 'little Stalin' in the PCE should be Uribe and not herself.

Accordingly, Pasionaria agreed when Claudín argued that the issue could not be decided without the presence of Carrillo. A meeting was set up for some weeks later in Bucharest and Carrillo was summoned. When he reached the airport in the Romanian capital, there was no car awaiting him, which suggested that, facing an accusation of 'factionalism', he had already been condemned. On the eve of the meeting, Carrillo had a long private conversation with Pasionaria, during which he made an extremely revealing remark: 'I have come here to discuss the unavoidable changes in the party line and in the functioning of the leadership. All I ask is that I get a hearing. Then you can decide to do whatever you want. If I'm wrong, the solution is easy; you leave me here or in Central Asia.' The mention of Central Asia was a reference to the concentration camp of Karaganda in Kazakhstan where Spanish Communist dissidents were held – clear evidence that Carrillo was fully aware of its existence.

In the course of the conversation, in which he launched a fierce attack on Uribe, he demonstrated to Pasionaria that his position was in tune with new currents in Khrushchev's Kremlin. Moreover, Vitorio Codovila, who had been in Moscow for the Twentieth Congress of the CPSU, advised her to support Carrillo. She had lived too long in the USSR not to realize that her own position might be threatened if she found herself in conflict with the new line. In any case, she no longer had the same combative spirit that had character-ized her before her illness. In the course of the sessions of the Twentieth Congress, the Italian Communist Vittorio Vidali, who had known her in Spain during the Civil War when he used the pseudo-nym 'Carlos Contreras', met Ibárruri in the corridors of the Kremlin. He was struck by how much she had been affected by her illness:

> How she had changed! I had always remembered her as she was when I knew her during the period of illegality when she had helped me in aiding the political prisoners and their families after the rising in Asturias, and during the Spanish Civil War: beautiful, majestic, now joyous, now sad; intelligent and a splen-did impromptu speaker; her beautiful face had been marked by illness and her glance was less bright, but her voice was still the same and rang like a silver bell.

For Vidali, she was 'the most tragic figure at the congress', worn down by seventeen years of exile. Khrushchev's report had come as a bitter shock. She revered Stalin and the Soviet system. They had been central to her political activities for nearly thirty years. Khrushchev's demolition of all her certainties in some way diminished her will to fight on.

Now, in the course of her conversations with Carrillo, Pasionaria saw that to maintain her alliance with Uribe would be suicidal. Accordingly, at what had originally been intended to be the trial of Carrillo, Uribe was to be the sacrificial victim, the one guilty of the crimes that Khrushchev had denounced in his secret report. At a series of politburo meetings held in Moscow from 5 April to 12 May, the PCE's mini-replica of the Twentieth Congress of the CPSU, it was clear where Dolores Ibárruri stood. Mije and Líster were not slow to see what was happening and immediately changed sides. Of the 169 pages of the minutes of the meeting, fifty-nine record Carrillo's speech on 2 May – and thirty of those consist of a long diatribe against Uribe, who according to Vidali seemed 'to be living in another world'.

Carrillo cleverly managed to give the impression that his attack on Uribe was actually a defence of Pasionaria, accusing him of self-worship, of an exaggerated cult of personality and therefore of diminishing her prestige:

> Comrade Uribe, especially in recent years, infatuated with himself, has consistently demonstrated an egotism that has led him to build a real cult of his own personality. He misses no chance to spotlight his own role, the decisive importance of his activities and the significance of his ideas in the running of the party. This is how he behaves with us at every meeting, with a really lamentable lack of modesty or sense of his own ridiculousness. When Uribe exaggerates his own role, he diminishes that of the Politburo and that of the Secretary General of the party without any respect for either of them.

Uribe was stunned by the cunning barrage of accusations that could equally well have been applied to Dolores Ibárruri or to Carrillo himself. What Carrillo was doing with Uribe was what Khrushchev had done with Stalin, masking his own, and Pasionaria's, complicity in past crimes by loading all the blame on to another – in this case, Uribe. In doing so, he was seconded by Claudín, who spoke of his shame at having collaborated with Uribe in Moscow in 1947 in mounting the trials of the comrades accused of anti-Soviet activities. His regret may have been sincere, but he failed to mention that those episodes had been choreographed by Carrillo. Claudín went so far as to criticize the politburo for its failure to explain the actions taken against Jesús Hernández, Enrique Castro Delgado and even Antón, all matters in which both Ibárruri and Carrillo were every bit as much to blame as Uribe.

Carrillo categorically denied that he had created his own Party apparatus from loyal cadres from the wartime JSU. In fact, this is precisely what he had done. He cleverly anticipated possible attacks by stating that he had had to use one-time JSU cadres because the Party could hardly survive in Spain if the risks could be taken only by sixty-year-old militants. He reminded the meeting that of the sixty-one-member Central Committee 'elected' at the Fifth Congress, nineteen had been members of the JSU and a further sixteen had joined the PCE during the war – thereby revealing the very basis of his own strength. Then he declared, 'If someday I were to become a lunatic or a swine, something which I am confident will not happen, and I tried to implement a scheme in my own interests, those comrades would be the first to denounce me to the party ... I might be incompetent, I might one day commit errors but of one thing I am confident, I will never be a danger to the party.'[60] Dolores Ibárruri effectively admitted that the crown was passing to another when she declared at the end of the cycle of meetings that, on the issue of the Russian vote on Spanish entry into the United Nations, 'I must state that Comrade Carrillo was right and I was wrong,' in that his article had appreciated the significance of the Soviet Union's vote in favour of Spanish entry into the UN.[61]

Thus, in both the provocation and the resolution of the conflict, the de-Stalinizers found their aspirations paralleled by those of the Russian leadership. Totally isolated, Uribe was replaced shortly afterwards as director of the Paris centre by Carrillo, who was now virtually acting secretary general. Uribe was allowed to remain a member of the politburo, but he was a broken reed. In 1958, he was struck by the illness that would take his life three years later. Before their victory over him, the group led by Carrillo had been reluctant to undermine the leadership of Pasionaria lest it favour the ambitions of Uribe. Now, with Uribe out of the way, they could support Carrillo in his bid for power. Dolores Ibárruri was fully aware that her days as secretary general were numbered. For the moment, Carrillo was satisfied with playing the role of the respectful second-in-command. He went through the motions of seeming to keep her informed about every-thing, although in reality he told her only what he wanted her to know. Khrushchev's denunciation of the Stalinist cult of personality, and Carrillo's assault on Uribe, had tarnished Pasionaria's halo of saintliness and infallibility. Isolated in Bucharest, she was ever more depressed and aware that she was being deprived of news by Carrillo and the Paris group. Her sense of impending defeat was intensified when Carrillo suggested that she devote herself to chairing a com-mittee to write the official history of the PCE during the Civil War.[62]

Carrillo had every reason to be delighted by Khrushchev's policies, which seemed to coincide with his own desires to renovate the PCE. The revelations of the Twentieth Congress were satisfactory evidence for him that the USSR was on the road to democratization. In contrast, for Claudín, the recital of the crimes of Stalin was profoundly disturbing and set him off on a long intellectual pilgrimage to under-stand how the socialist ideal had been deformed by the Stalinist ex-perience. The Soviet invasion of Hungary in October 1956 would exacerbate Claudín's doubts even further, while Carrillo would simply accept that Khrushchev was in the right.[63] These divergences were eventually to lead to a traumatic crisis within the PCE in 1964. In the meantime, however, Carrillo was pressing home his victory over the Party's Stalinists. To an extent, he did represent a spirit of reform within the Party but he would never apply it to himself. Indeed, his inability to accept critical discussion would perpetuate Stalinist atti-tudes in the PCE.[64] In the past, he had accepted the contrary positions either of those who had authority over him or of potential allies.

The first fruit of the apparently new flexibility in the politburo was the elaboration of the policy of national reconciliation. Free of the Stalinist stranglehold, the Paris centre could now allow the militants in the interior of Spain to seek common ground with the new opposition to Franco emerging among students and Catholics. In the first week of February 1956, major student disturbances had broken out in Madrid. Students, even left-wing and liberal ones, were almost exclusively from comfortable middle-class families and could not simply be subjected to the savage repression casually dispensed against working-class strikers. Semprún had carried news of the changing situation to the Paris operational group. In response, Carrillo, on his return from Bucharest, had published a document entitled 'For the National Reconciliation of all Spaniards and for a Democratic and Peaceful Solution to the Spanish Problem'. He argued that the cliché of 'the two Spains' divided between the victors and vanquished of the Civil War was no longer valid. Instead, he asserted that the real division was between the minority that benefited from the dictatorship and the majority damaged by it. In fact, *reconciliación nacional* was simply a new name for a policy that the PCE had been pushing sporadically since 1941. Nevertheless, when the document was taken to Madrid by Semprún, it was received with enthusiasm by the Communist underground apparatus.[65]

After lengthy discussions in the course of a plenary meeting of the Central Committee held in Hermann Göring's old hunting lodge near Berlin from 15 July to 4 August 1956, Carrillo went further with a declaration in favour of burying the wartime hatreds fostered by the dictatorship. The new policy not only expressed Communist readiness to join with monarchists and Catholics in a future parliamentary regime but also indicated a commitment to peaceful change.[66] The Berlin plenum was to witness a dramatic extension of the process of liberalization tentatively begun at the PCE's Fifth Congress, although important Stalinist habits survived.

The two principal reports were presented by Dolores Ibárruri and Santiago Carrillo. They both reflected a desire to emulate the example of the CPSU, a further indication of the influence of Moscow over the PCE's 'democratization'. Nevertheless, the two reports also heralded important changes in the Party's methods. Pasionaria paid tribute to the CPSU for its courage in publicly recognizing its errors and for pointing the way to different roads to socialism. She spoke of the growing importance of the student opposition within Spain and went on to speak of the need for alliances with conservative and liberal forces inside Spain in order to secure a pacific transition to democracy.[67] This clearly represented a new departure from past sectarianism, but it was mild by comparison with what Carrillo had to say. His three-hour report was an intensely critical survey of the defects of the Party leadership. Virtually no member of the politburo, with the exception of Carrillo himself, was immune from his pungent and lucid criticisms of the exiled leadership for preventing internal democracy, for dogmatism, for subjectivism, for sectarianism and for isolation from the realities of the interior.

Crucially, he produced a devastating demolition of the cult of personality of the secretary general of the PCE, albeit diluting it with a flowery tribute seeming superficially to absolve Dolores Ibárruri of complicity:

> The external signs of the personality cult stand out in our Party. These external signs have existed with regard to both Comrade José Díaz, when he was alive, and Comrade Dolores Ibárruri. They have presented these two comrades as the sole architects of everything that was actually done by the Party, depicting them as little less than miracle-workers, from whose brain and activity has sprung everything produced by the thinking and activities of thousands of Communists. In these signs of the personality cult, we have reached levels that strictly speaking can be considered truly infantile.

Although he went on to say that Dolores Ibárruri had always opposed this practice, he was effectively dismantling her legendary status. In the later view of Semprún, this speech was to be the apogee of Carrillo's readiness to liberalize the Party. He could thus criticize the role of secretary general because he was not yet secretary general himself. He argued that the leaders identified their personal interests with those of the Party and punished criticism of themselves by treating them as attacks on the Party. These would be precisely the criticisms that would one day see Carrillo himself expelled from the Communist Party.[68]

When Carrillo spoke of the narrow authoritarianism of the politburo, he specifically blamed Uribe for being an obstacle to collective leadership and self-criticism. Both Uribe and Mije were to be sacrificial victims, making public confessions of their errors to the plenum. The two main reports were unanimously approved by the Central Committee. The slavish auto-critiques and the unanimity suggested that little had changed. There was nothing about the plenum that might indicate a sudden adoption of democratic procedures. The agenda and the conclusions had been decided beforehand by Carrillo and the new politburo. According to Líster, Carrillo ensured that the members of the Central Committee were given no details of the power struggle that had taken place in Bucharest. Their presence was simply to endorse the conclusions presented in the two main reports. There was no serious discussion. All that was known of Uribe's fall from grace was his humiliating auto-critique and not the demolition that had been carried out in Bucharest by Carrillo. There was no analysis of the fact that Ibárruri and Carrillo were equally guilty of the crimes to which Uribe had 'confessed'. The Party's errors, in which Carrillo had been an active accomplice, were thus expunged at no cost to himself. Stalinist methods and thinking would remain an intrinsic part of his repertoire. All the guilt for past sins – the persecution of Quiñones, Monzón, Comorera and Antón, among so many others – was piled on Uribe. As Jorge Semprún commented: 'after 1956, the leadership of the PCE refused to indulge in any public self-criticism, confining itself to sweeping Stalinist rubbish under someone else's carpet, rejecting any objective historical analysis of its own past'.[69]

Similarly, the leadership's renewed commitment to the rules of democratic centralism was somewhat devalued by the fact that Central Committee members were still co-opted by the politburo. However, this time there was a difference. Hitherto, it had been the secretary general who suggested the names of new members to be co-opted. On 1 August, to the stupefaction of Pasionaria, a proposal was made that the recently deceased Víctor Velasco be replaced by one of Carrillo's protégés, Luis Zapirain. She complained about this breach of procedure, but the meeting went ahead and voted unanimously to incorporate Zapirain into the Central Committee. She was mortified by this and protested vehemently. It was to no avail. It is not known how she felt about the successful proposal by Claudín that the sanctions against Francisco Antón be lifted. That, together with the election of Zapirain, meant that effectively Pasionaria had ceased to be the most important person in the PCE.[70]

The airing of a critical spirit and the broadening of the politburo and Central Committee promised, in theory at least, some progress towards democratization. This was particularly true of the move to incorporate into the politburo senior militants working in the interior, such as Semprún, Simón Sánchez Montero and Francisco Romero Marín. However, despite their ability to report on the growing opposition to the Franco regime, their views, and particularly those of the intellectuals recruited by Semprún such as Javier Pradera, would often be ignored by Carrillo. When they challenged his ideas, as would happen in the early 1960s, he would react by resorting to the Stalinist habits of the previous twenty years. Thus, in its achievements and its limitations, the Berlin plenum of the summer of 1956 was the PCE's equivalent of the Twentieth Congress of the Soviet Party with Carrillo playing the role of Khrushchev.[71]

In the summer of 1956, Carrillo and his family took a holiday in Bulgaria and coincided there with the Czechoslovak Communist Artur London and his French wife Lise Ricole. Carrillo had known them since the Civil War, when London had been a member of the International Brigades. After the Spanish war, London had fought in the French resistance, had been captured by the Gestapo and had survived the concentration camp at Mauthausen. Subsequently, he had returned to Czechoslovakia where, in 1948, he became deputy Minister of Foreign Affairs. In 1951, he was one of those arrested during the Slansky purges. He had been horribly tortured and forced to confess to imaginary Zionist, Trotskyist and Titoist activities. He was then sentenced to life imprisonment. When Carrillo met him in Bulgaria, London had recently been released as a consequence of Khrushchev's revelations to the Twentieth Congress. Carrillo claimed in his memoirs to have been profoundly shocked by London's account of what had happened to him, which was subsequently enshrined in his book *L'Aveu* (1968) and in the film version (1970) by the Greek director Costa-Gavras with a script by Jorge Semprún. That in 1956 Carrillo, who had earlier applauded the Rajk, Kostov and Slansky trials, should have been distressed by London's remarks is impossible to believe. His own treatment of Carmen de Pedro and Francisco Antón, to name only two, suggested that he had little to learn about the extraction of false confessions. About them, in his memoirs, he said only that they had been 'relegated' and that 'they didn't deserve to be treated like that'. Regarding his encounter with Artur London, Carrillo stated that 'I swore that I would never again believe anything that I had not seen with my own eyes and touched with my own hands, no matter who said it.'[72]

How seriously he took this good resolution may be assessed by his reaction to the Soviet invasion of Hungary on 4 November 1956. Russian forces brutally crushed the reformist movement under Imre Nagy which had been inspired by the apparent liberalization initiated by Khrushchev at the Twentieth Congress. The PCE, like the rest of the international Communist moment, was concerned with possible threats from the Western Powers, particularly as a result of the Suez Canal crisis at the end of October. Carrillo commented in his memoirs that Suez 'helped us conclude that any weakening of the Soviet bloc would increase the danger of the imperialist powers launching dangerous adventures that would threaten the peace and independence of other countries'.[73] In the later analysis of Manuel Azcárate: 'The invasion of Hungary was perhaps the moment when the Western Communist parties hit their lowest point: our strategy was simply one of blind support for the interests of the Soviet state.' Paradoxically, during the Suez crisis the imperialist interests of both the USA and the USSR coincided in their desire to put an end to Anglo-French colonialism. The Russians backed Egypt and the Americans withdrew support for Britain, France and Israel.[74] It was revealing that Carrillo saw no contradiction between Soviet action to protect the freedom and peace enjoyed by the Egyptian people and the intervention to crush the freedom and peace enjoyed by the Hungarian people.

Despite his later claims that he had concerns about the invasion of Hungary, at the time Carrillo was entirely in agreement with the official Kremlin line that it had been necessary to crush a counter-revolution organized by an alliance of imperialist agents and Hungarian reactionaries. It will be recalled that he had a close relationship with the Hungarian Stalinist Mihály Farkas (Michael Wolf). In contrast, Claudín had argued that the detonating factor in the revolution was the rigid policy of the Hungarian Communist Party. An acrimonious discussion in the politburo terminated with Claudín in a minority of one. Carrillo sent a telegram to the Kremlin expressing the PCE's support for the Russian intervention. He also wrote an article justifying the Soviet invasion as a necessary response to fascist and imperialist machinations. It was the beginning of a cooling in the hitherto close collaboration between Carrillo and Claudín.[75] Carrillo's new line was entirely in accord with the position adopted by Khrushchev, but he claimed later that it had provoked criticism elsewhere in the Communist world. When the secretary general of the Portuguese sister party, Alvaro Cunhal, came out of prison in the late 1950s, he initiated a purge of the Communist leadership in Portugal. Their crime, according to Carrillo, was called *españolismo* – that is to say, sympathy with the policy of 'national reconciliation' recently adopted by the PCE.[76] Carrillo seemed to see no contradiction in his advocacy of national reconciliation in Spain and support for the Soviet repression of the opposition in Budapest. Indeed, not long afterwards, he issued a declaration in which it was stated that 'the CPSU is the authoritative guide of world communism'.[77]

The year 1956 was to be the culmination of Carrillo's efforts to liberalize the Party, at least until the Soviet invasion of Czechoslovakia in 1968 obliged him to initiate further progress towards internal democracy. It would be wrong to underestimate the changes which took place between 1954 and 1956. By comparison with other opposition forces, and in particular with the Socialists and anarchists, the PCE was relatively strong and united, and could boast meaningful links between its exiled leadership and militants in the interior. However, the hard-won flexibility of 1954 and 1956 was soon stultified by Carrillo's rigid reaction when the national reconciliation policy failed to achieve the immediate overthrow of the dictatorship. The PCE had always been blessed by a generous component of subjective optimism. This was especially true of Carrillo; indeed, it was one of his greatest strengths. When the dictatorship did not totter before a nationwide opposition, he would react by exhibiting intensified optimism and hostility towards those cadres who had the temerity to point out the unreality of the Party line.

Carrillo owed his rise in the Party to, among other things, his capacity for hard work and his strength of personality. After 1956, he began to concentrate power in his hands in an unprecedented way. He was now head of the Paris operational centre and also organization secretary. This involved working days of fourteen to sixteen hours which meant that he had virtually no family life other than during holidays at Eastern European resorts. He moved around Paris thanks to a car and driver supplied by the French Communist Party. Claudín was later to comment that, after 1945, Carrillo never went anywhere other than in a chauffeur-driven car.[78] Between meetings of the politburo, the writing and receiving of reports and briefing cadres who were to go into Spain, virtually every aspect of Party life was in Carrillo's hands. However, it left him with little time to study the real situation in Spain. Members of the Central Committee tended to produce reports which conformed to the Party line rather than to concrete reality. The conditions of clandestinity exacerbated this problem in the interior. PCE agents entered Spain with instructions from the Paris centre and handed them on to their contacts on a kind of chain basis. Inevitably, the creativity of the rank and file was stifled by the simple transmission of abstract orientations or slogans. Reports from cells in the interior tended to aim at proving the validity of the Party line. Carrillo's main preoccupation was the maintenance of his own position. It was rarely challenged. When Claudín commented in a meeting that, between 1956 and 1964, the Central Committee had never opposed Carrillo's wishes, Mije objected that it had happened once, albeit to deny him permission to risk his person on a clandestine mission to Spain.[79]

The problem was highlighted by the practical difficulties of applying the policy of national reconciliation. Although superficially events seemed to vindicate the new line, it was premature. In 1957, in response to the harsh conditions created by the incoming government's devaluation of the peseta as well as other stabilization measures, a major wave of strikes started in Catalonia and then spread to Madrid, Asturias and the Basque Country. The first action was in Barcelona in mid-January. In response to another increase in tram fares, Miguel Núñez of the PSUC together with other opposition groups had successfully organized a massive two-week boycott of public transport. It was linked with anti-regime demonstrations in the university organized on the pretext of solidarity with the uprising in Hungary. The Civil Governor, General Felipe Acedo Colunga, used considerable violence in evacuating the university and stopping demonstrations in favour of the strikers. The Captain General of the Barcelona military region, the monarchist Juan Bautista Sánchez, was critical of Acedo Colunga's harsh methods and counselled caution, and was therefore considered in some circles to have given moral support to the strikers. Rumours flew around Madrid, apparently believed by Franco himself, that Bautista Sánchez was planning a coup in favour of the monarchy. Although the General would die shortly afterwards, speculation about monarchist opposition to the regime seemed to the PCE organization in Paris to suggest that the idea of national reconciliation had a real basis.[80]

Inspired by what had happened in Barcelona, the senior PCE cadres in Madrid, Simón Sánchez Montero, Luis Lucio Lobato and Juan Soler, decided to call for a two-day boycott of public transport in Madrid to take place on 7–8 February. Sánchez Montero wrote a strike appeal, with no mention of the PCE, to be read out on the Party's radio station, Radio España Independiente. He sent his text to the Paris operational centre. When he made contact with Semprún, who was accompanied by Francisco Romero Marín, they expressed doubts about the wisdom of his initiative. Nevertheless, they did not try to stop him. Equally sceptical but reluctant to miss a chance to prove the validity of his policy of national reconciliation, Carrillo authorized the broadcast, and the Madrid organization laboriously printed strike leaflets on a primitive home-made mimeograph machine which were distributed around the working-class districts. To the surprise of the Parisian leadership, the boycott was total.[81]

Blinded by his own optimism, Carrillo was quick to claim the credit for the PCE, hailing the events in Barcelona, Asturias and Madrid as the fruit of his new policy and evidence of working-class endorsement of the Party line. Pointing out that Socialists, anarchists, Catholics and unaffiliated liberals had been involved, the PCE eagerly announced its readiness to make pacts and alliances with them.[82] Carrillo's commitment to the policy was consolidated by Franco's cabinet reshuffle of 22 February which he saw as a reflection of the dictatorship's growing weakness. Certainly, at the beginning of 1957, the regime faced political and economic bankruptcy. However, the incorporation of Opus Dei technocrats into the reshuffled cabinet would eventually lead to huge foreign investment, massive industrialization, population migration, urbanization and educational expansion. In the long run, there would be enormous economic change whose social consequences would not only turn Franco and Falangism into historical anachronisms but also render irrelevant Carrillo's triumphalist predictions of the regime's imminent downfall. Within five years, those changes and their implications would lead to bitter conflict within the PCE.

Now, however, interpreting the cabinet changes as a symptom of the regime's decadence, Carrillo thought that a broad alliance against the regime was feasible. He announced to the politburo that 'the working class of Madrid responded en bloc to the guidance of the Communist Party based on its correct analysis of the situation'. Simón Sánchez Montero reported to a plenum of the Central Committee in May 1957 that the wide social participation in peaceful actions in Madrid and Barcelona 'has converted the boycotts into real plebiscites against the dictatorship, living examples of national reconciliation among Spaniards, and has shown that the non-violent overthrow of the dictatorship is a real possibility'. Sánchez Montero's optimism was not entirely subjective since he had been greatly impressed by the streams of people walking to work during the public transport boycott in Madrid.[83]

In fact, what neither Sánchez Montero nor Carrillo had perceived was that the militancy behind the transport strikes was nothing to do with the directives of the PCE and everything to do with the soaring inflation and plummeting living standards that were the first fruits of the economic liberalization imposed by the new technocratic cabinet. A prodigious devaluation had been the first phase of a harsh monetary stabilization programme. Carrillo failed to see the extent to which the strikes had been a non-political reaction to the consequent economic conditions. At the same time as Sánchez Montero was making his report, the dictatorship of General Gustavo Rojas Pinilla fell in Colombia as a result of a day of national protest on 10 May known as the 'coup d'état of public opinion'. Convinced by the transport strikes, Carrillo persuaded himself that something similar was on the horizon in Spain. In September 1957, at a plenary meeting of the Central Committee, he announced an action day of 'national reconciliation' (Jornada de Reconciliación Nacional) for 5 May 1958. Such was Carrillo's confidence in his own misplaced assumptions about the weakness of the regime that he blithely assumed that an action whose success was owed to specific social discontent in Madrid and Barcelona could be repeated on a national scale.

Militants in Barcelona were astonished by the initiative. The up-and-coming cadre Jordi Solé Tura called it 'a leap in the dark'. Despite pessimistic feedback from the interior, Carrillo insisted that it would be a decisive step towards the fall of Franco. His wildly over-optimistic manifesto called for a twenty-four-hour strike, for students and professors not to go to the universities, for shopkeepers to close their establishments, for peasants not to go into the fields, for a boycott of transport in major cities, even for industrialists to collaborate in shutting down factories. The effects of the one-day action were minimal, yet Carrillo, as the prime mover behind the idea, claimed that millions of Spaniards had participated in a successful rehearsal for a great national movement against the dictatorship: 'with this day of action a new stage has begun in the Spanish people's struggle for freedom, with the overthrow of the dictatorship now on the agenda in an urgent and concrete way ... Let us march united towards new actions, towards a great national mass movement that will put an end to the hated dictatorship and bring the triumph of liberty and democracy.'[84]

Jordi Solé Tura went to Paris to report on the total failure of the Jornada. He was sent on to Prague where he met most of the PCE leadership, including Dolores Ibárruri. His eyewitness account of the lack of strike action on 5 May was simply ignored and he was told that it had been a tremendous success involving millions of workers. It is likely, however, that Pasionaria remembered Solé Tura's long conversation with her when she heard about Carrillo's next, and bigger, scheme.[85] Back in Paris, declaring that the dictatorship was on the ropes and that the high command of the army was turning against Franco, Carrillo planned a mass movement, called the Huelga Nacional Pacífica (National Peaceful Strike), or HNP, for 18 June 1959. To some extent, his initiative was related to the sensation created in Madrid by a political dinner held five months earlier on 29 January in the Hotel Menfis. A group of influential monarchists led by the lawyer Joaquín Satrústegui had created the Unión Española. The dinner, at which the social democrat Enrique Tierno Galván was present, saw discussions about the creation of a non-Communist democratic front. Carrillo wrote to Pasionaria that there was a monarchist–Socialist plot afoot to exclude the PCE from the future democracy. It was a real fear. On the one hand, the Communist Party was the most effective anti-Franco force within Spain but, on the other, there was a danger that the growing anti-Communist opposition might achieve some limited democratic reform from which the PCE would be excluded. Accordingly, to clinch the support of other groups, as was made clear in a long report by Tomás García to Pasionaria, it was decided to publish editorials in *Mundo Obrero* developing the idea of the great national action which would be the twenty-four-hour strike. Carrillo wanted to mount a show of strength to demonstrate that nothing could be done without the PCE.[86]

The timing was disastrous. As the stabilization plan was biting, workers were understandably reluctant to risk their jobs, knowing as they did that industrialists would welcome the opportunity provided by a strike to reduce their labour force. One of the great achievements of the dictatorship was the de-politicization of the masses. Thus strikes based on real local issues were one thing, great national demonstrations based on theoretical notions altogether another. Moreover, the chances of securing a broad opposition front were extremely slim. Within Spain, the HNP was organized, with considerable trepidation, by Sánchez Montero, Grimau, Semprún and Romero Marín 'el Tanque'. Attempts by Carrillo in Paris to secure cooperation from the Socialist Party had been firmly rebuffed, serving only to remind him of the depth of anti-Communism that drove Rodolfo Llopis, faithful follower of Indalecio Prieto.

In fact, Llopis would go so far as to denounce the strike in his editorials in *El Socialista*. In Madrid, a series of university groups pulled out, repelled by what they saw as the Communists' patronizing arrogance. Semprún met the repentant Falangist Dionisio Ridruejo, who expressed sympathy but confessed that his Partido Social de Acción Democrática was tiny and unlikely to add anything. The only group that showed solidarity with the PCE was the recently created Frente de Liberación Popular (FLP), a revolutionary amalgam of progressive Catholics and students enthused by the Cuban revolution. It was led by the Catholic diplomat Julio Cerón and the lawyer Ignacio Fernández de Castro.

After weeks of preparation, Sánchez Montero went to Paris and told Carrillo that he doubted that the strike would spread because of the strength of the regime's repressive apparatus. In Barcelona, Solé Tura and his comrades were sceptical about the chances of success, not least because they knew that there was no broad alliance of forces. Claudín and Ignacio Gallego made clandestine visits to take part in the preparations. Claudín interviewed Ridruejo and Cerón. Ridruejo told him that the regime was getting stronger rather than weaker. He also reiterated that his own group was tiny and commented that the negative attitude of the Socialists would prevent success. Claudín dismissed this as an excuse. Cerón was equally negative. Although he shared the fears of Sánchez Montero that the overthrow of the regime was not as imminent as Carrillo regularly declared, Claudín dutifully transmitted the Party line. When he returned to Paris, he downplayed the doubts and reservations of the militants in the interior as simply a natural response to the sheer difficulty of mounting such a wide-ranging action. Carrillo was determined that the strike should go ahead, despite receiving letters from Dolores Ibárruri, now back in Moscow, questioning the idea. She was irritated that he had decided on the HNP without fulfilling his duty to consult her, but she was also worried about the risks of the Party's clandestine apparatus being destroyed in such an outright challenge to the regime. Santiago Álvarez, who acted as Carrillo's liaison with her, had considerable difficulty in persuading her of the wisdom of the proposed action, which, she commented acidly, was 'as useless as parading statues of saints to make it rain'.[87]

The strike declaration called for workers, peasants, students, civil servants, shopworkers and artists to stop work and for Catholics to pray for freedom. In the event, the Huelga Nacional Pacífica was even more of a failure than the previous year's Jornada de Reconciliación Nacional had been. Not a single major factory stopped work and there was only random participation by isolated individuals from some other parties. The Socialist Party officially condemned the initiative. In its optimistic eagerness to clinch deals with other social sectors, the PCE was trying to use the working class for public mobilizations so as to prove its own weight as an ally. This involved considerable self-deception about the current level of working-class politicization and about the PCE's influence among the masses. It was a subjectivist approach which could only undermine the Party's credibility among those it should have been most concerned to impress – the workers themselves. With unemployment increasing and workers fearful of losing their jobs, the failures were hardly surprising. Moreover, the fanfare about the strike from the PCE press and radio gave the security forces ample time to prepare. In consequence, there were widespread arrests of leading figures, including, on the very eve of the strike, Julio Cerón and the two key elements in the PCE's working-class organization, Sánchez Montero and his right-hand man Lobato.[88]

What was more unexpected was the way in which Carrillo asserted his authority and imposed his view that the strike had been a major propaganda triumph. It was an indication of one of his obsessions – the maintenance of optimism within the Party. At the first meeting of the politburo after the event, Carrillo presented the HNP as a success, claiming vaguely that it had inspired the sympathy of the masses and provoked panic in the Francoist authorities. Claudín opposed this interpretation with the tepid support of Ignacio Gallego, who had been in Asturias, and Santiago Álvarez, who reported Pasionaria's misgivings. Although they all accepted their collective responsibility in authorizing the strike, Carrillo, no doubt fearing for his own position, chose to see as a personal attack what had been Claudín's critique of the entire politburo, including himself. He accused Claudín of wanting to demoralize the masses and declared that a successful national strike was just around the corner. When it came to a vote, Gallego and Álvarez sided with Carrillo, and Claudín was once more left in a minority of one. Carrillo went on to publish a pamphlet about the strike which presented it as a massive victory over the regime.[89]

In an equally outrageous distortion of the truth two decades later, while finally accepting that the Huelga Nacional Pacífica had been a failure, he blamed the entire operation on Claudín:

> It must be said, in order to re-establish the historical truth, that the Party leadership agreed to issue the call for the national strike for a specific date after Claudín went to Madrid to ascertain if the conditions were ripe for it and returned to Paris saying that yes they were. And so we decided to declare the strike. Then it turned out that the conditions were not propitious and Claudín, perhaps feeling the weight of his responsibility for playing a key role in the declaration of the strike, adopted more radical positions. But the truth is that we declared the strike call fundamentally because Claudín told us that the conditions were right.[90]

Nevertheless, he was concerned that, because he had overcome the doubts expressed by Dolores Ibárruri about the HNP by dint of exaggerated predictions of its inevitable success, she might blame him for its failure. To put his case to her, at the end of July 1959 he led a delegation to Russia consisting of Líster, Gallego, Álvarez, Tomás García and Semprún. Before leaving, Carrillo told Semprún about the proceedings at the politburo. He said that Claudín's stance had not surprised him but made a comment about Ignacio Gallego's brief dissidence that revealed much about himself: 'it is very unusual for Gallego to oppose the real power'. The group met Pasionaria at her dacha in Uspenskoie, near Moscow. Hardly had Carrillo started to justify the HNP than Dolores Ibárruri dropped a bombshell by announcing her resignation as secretary general. She had been fully aware, since the humiliations visited upon her at the August 1956 plenum and again in 1957, when Carrillo tried to persuade her to write a history of the PCE during the Civil War, that he aspired to replace her. Then, to his chagrin, she had suggested the creation for him of the post of vice-secretary general. The fact that he rarely consulted her on important Party business and particularly his failure to heed her advice not to launch the HNP convinced her to put an end to a false situation in which she was secretary general in name only. It was a dignified gesture. As always judging others by his own standards, Carrillo's immediate reaction was to snap at Semprún: 'What sneaky trick has she got up her sleeve?' After the customary protests and feeble efforts to get her to change her mind, Líster proposed that Carrillo become secretary general and someone else that Pasionaria become president of the Party.[91]

Carrillo's reaction to the disaster of the Huelga Nacional Pacífica confirmed that 1956 had been the high point of any inclination on his part to de-Stalinize the PCE. Indeed, it suggested that such readiness had been largely the instrument of his ambition to supplant the leadership group of Pasionaria, Uribe and Mije. There would be no more liberalization until the events of 1968. Indeed, when the new line of national reconciliation did not immediately secure the overthrow of Franco by a broad coalition of democratic forces, Carrillo reacted with Stalinist rigidity and extreme subjectivism. His dogged determination to see a confirmation of the correctness of the new line in every event inside Spain was already leading him into conflict with his erstwhile ally, Fernando Claudín. Unable to tolerate any dissent, he was furious when Claudín contradicted his interpretation of the HNP and called for greater sensitivity to the changing situation in the interior.

Carrillo's suppression of the debacle was to have far-reaching consequences within the PCE. Both Claudín and Semprún had started to reflect on the inadequacies of the PCE's analysis of Spain's social and political development as the key to the inefficacy of the official line. When Carrillo deployed his considerable authority to impose a mendacious interpretation of what had really happened, they were impelled to examine the question of internal democracy in the PCE. However, there was a difference between them in that Semprún believed that outright criticism of Carrillo would lead nowhere and that it would be better to try to persuade him gradually of the defects of Party policy.[92] The consequences of their reflections were not to hit the Party for another four years. In the meantime, Carrillo remained fully committed to the idea of a national general strike and reacted to the failure of 1959 with measures aimed at ensuring success next time. Changes intended to give the PCE's interior apparatus more flexibility were introduced at the Sixth Congress.

On 24 December 1959, without having been told the purpose, Central Committee members were convened for a meeting in a large school building on the outskirts of Prague. Only after their arrival were they informed that the Sixth Congress would begin the next day and continue until 1 January. The agenda of the Sixth Congress had been decided by the politburo well in advance and not distributed for security reasons. In a flimsy measure to protect members coming from the interior, the date had been selected to make it appear as if they were going to France for Christmas. To this end, postcards were left in Paris and posted to their families in Spain. Similarly, subsequent statements about the congress announced that it had been held from 28 to 31 January 1960. None of these measures protected those who had to return to Spain, not least because it was easy enough for the Spanish police to discover who had taken the sparsely occupied pre-Christmas flights from Zurich to Prague. After the congress, the arrests of many of the delegates triggered a domino effect that decimated the interior organization. The cause was almost certainly that one of the delegates, an unknown individual from Pamplona, was a police informer. There were, however, other security lapses. Many group photographs were taken, and Santiago Álvarez held gatherings in his house at which real names were used.[93]

What there was in terms of discussion did not go beyond the mildest criticism and consisted mainly of enthusiastic endorsements of the speeches of the politburo members.[94] Carrillo opened the proceedings at 9.15 on Christmas morning and finished reading his ninety-five-page speech at 4.15 in the afternoon. In his triumphalist tone, Carrillo surpassed his own previous track record. Before sixty delegates from inside Spain, men who knew that the Huelga Nacional Pacífica had been a non-starter, his fiery oratory convinced them that it had been a resounding triumph. He announced that the defeat of the Franco regime was imminent, even claiming that the army was deeply divided. Still more astonishing was his statement that elements of the Civil Guard and the police had helped in the preparation of both the 1958 Jornada de Reconciliación Nacional and the Huelga Nacional Pacífica. He asserted that 'millions of men and women had peacefully demonstrated their opposition to the dictatorship by not shopping, not using public transport and by going on strike'. Saying that details were unnecessary since the delegates themselves had taken part in the HNP, he asked if it had been justified. He admitted that the strike had not reached the scale foreseen but claimed that the Party had been reinforced because of what it had taught the masses. He even alleged that the Party had been hardened by the arrests of key militants such as Simón Sánchez Montero. He went on to assert that the failure of the HNP had been the fault of sabotage by Rodolfo Llopis's PSOE and Satrústegui's Unión Española. Even more bare-faced was his claim that both had explicitly recognized their dreadful error in not supporting the PCE's initiative.[95] Most of the next two days consisted of interventions by delegates from all over Spain who unanimously confirmed Carrillo's view that the HNP had been amply justified.[96]

The announcement of changes to the Central Committee was made by Ignacio Gallego who, on the afternoon of 30 December, read out a script prepared in collaboration with Carrillo. Its theme was the need for a new generation to take over the work of the Party. However, according to Solé Tura, Gallego's speech took the form of a settling of accounts with the old leadership. Solé Tura found its tone and arguments, in the style of old Stalinist denunciations, chilling. Certainly, Gallego went into specific detail as to why particular comrades were being removed from the Central Committee – the names were revealed of those excluded for alcoholism, incompetence, laziness, sexual indiscretion or breaking down under torture.[97]

Carrillo was formally confirmed as secretary general and Dolores Ibárruri 'promoted' to the newly created post of Party president. In her address, a review of the PCE's history in its fortieth year of existence, Pasionaria made no reference to Carrillo's elevation. Her main theme was the importance of the PCE's commitment to the defence of the USSR.[98] As part of the apparent modernization of the Party, the politburo was renamed the executive committee and increased to fifteen members. The Central Committee was also increased in size. This formal democratization was nullified by the creation of a five-man Party secretariat, consisting of the secretary general, Fernando Claudín, Ignacio Gallego, Antonio Mije and Eduardo García, the KGB agent who ran Carrillo's personal apparatus. Since the last three were unconditional Carrillo supporters, the secretariat was considerably narrower than the politburo had been.[99]

Claudín's role was to present the Party programme which necessarily involved a survey of the socio-economic changes to justify its updating. Essentially, he argued that the development of capitalism under the Franco regime suggested that the next stage would be a bourgeois democratic one and that, to help bring this about, the policy of *reconciliación nacional* was correct. Solé Tura noted that, in the subsequent discussion, Claudín's tone suggested that 'he was not sure about some of the things he himself said, and above all, about the things being said by other members of the leadership'.[100]

Carrillo's commitment to the Huelga Nacional Pacífica was confirmed by the congress and changes were to be made to ensure its success. The nearest that the congress came to admitting the failure of the 1959 strike was a report, distributed but not read out, by Semprún as 'Federico Sánchez'. He delivered what was tacitly an inquest into the 1959 disaster, which, in so far as failure was admitted, was attributed to organizational deficiencies. An expurgated version was published later in *Nuestra Bandera*. Semprún highlighted the rigidities of the clandestine 'system of contacts', whereby the Party leaders had to meet activists in Spain on a one-to-one basis on street corners, outside factories, in 'casual' encounters on trains or buses.

This chain permitted only the transmission of instructions from above. It was both laborious and dangerous as well as limiting possibilities for new recruitment. To remedy these limitations, Semprún called for a more democratic committee structure, suggesting that these committees should be able to continue to function even if contact with the leadership was broken off. In a party that had condemned so many previous activists for their initiatives when isolated from the centre, this was a dramatic recommendation.

Semprún also made a comment that should perhaps have set off alarm bells for Carrillo: 'A Communist leader must not only be able to explain our policy, he must also know how to listen. And to know how to listen is not as easy as it seems: to know how to listen to comrades, to know how to listen to the masses, to know how to listen to the voices and rumours that emanate from the social reality of our country.' If Carrillo thought that these remarks contained any hint about his own style, he did not react at the time.[101]

The congress recognized that the policies of reconciliation and the national strike would involve opening up the PCE to the middle and professional classes. PCE statutes were modified to admit looser conditions of membership and a decision was taken to intensify recruiting efforts. Carrillo made a revealing statement of his ambitions, predicting that the PCE would be the most important party in a future democracy, with a third or a quarter of the votes cast. The sessions were closed by a short speech by Carrillo. He reiterated the need to advance towards the definitive Huelga Nacional Pacífica. He also stressed the need for security, explaining why the PCE would announce that the congress had taken place at the end of January 1960. His warnings would be in vain.[102]

The consequent transition from a party of cadres to a mass party, along with national reconciliation and the pacific strike, was a substantially correct, but premature, concept which would finally come to fruition between 1975 and 1977.[103] The resolutions of the Sixth Congress put the PCE firmly in the vanguard of the anti-Franco struggle and also signified irreversible progress towards the liberalization of the Party. In the short term, however, discrepancies were emerging between rhetorical liberalization and the real lack of internal democracy. Not only was the practical application of the new line inside Spain difficult, but its theoretical formulation also caused some doubt among its potential followers. Many of the radical students formed in the university struggles of the mid-1950s had serious doubts about the Communist Party's new moderate policy. National reconciliation seemed to them to be a denial of class realities and, in any case, the PCE overture seemed to be falling on stony ground among the middle classes. Some considered that the PCE had played a reactionary role during the Civil War. Accordingly, many young leftists, rather than join the PCE, began to seek a non-orthodox Communist revolutionary alternative. The first of these groups which emerged in the late 1950s was the Frente de Liberación Popular (FLP), which had, however, been weakened by the repression after the HNP. It would eventually be destroyed by police persecution, but it represented the beginning of an anti-Communist tendency on the left that would be a seedbed for many other organizations. The noisiest manifestations of dissidence came from a number of pro-Chinese ultra-leftist groups that denounced Carrillo as a bourgeois revisionist. If anything, they wished to turn the clock back on the organizational and tactical reforms made in the PCE since 1945.[104] The Marxist-Leninist factions deprived the Party of some revolutionary students but probably contributed to the PCE's growing image as a serious and moderate party. For Carrillo, these were just noises off-stage. He had attained his goal of becoming the secretary general of the Communist Party and he was convinced that he possessed the key to the next stage of his unstoppable ascent.

The Solitary Hero:
1960–1970

Carrillo had declared in his report to the Sixth Congress that 'the historical failure of the Franco regime is an established fact' and asserted that the various components of the repressive apparatus of the state had collaborated in making the Huelga Nacional Pacífica a success on 18 June 1959. Accordingly, the major police crackdown that followed and that decimated the Party was a bitter blow and should have been perceived as such. Nevertheless, in response, Carrillo simply intensified the optimistic tone of his rhetoric. He wrote to Dolores Ibárruri a fanciful letter in which he claimed that the rest of the anti-Franco opposition was ashamed of not joining with the Communists in the HNP. He assured her that its impact had been such as to provoke major changes in these other groups, as a result of which they were eager to take part in the next general strike.[1]

While he might have been able to get away with sending a fictitious interpretation of the situation to Moscow, Carrillo still had to face those within the PCE inside Spain who knew what had really happened. In May 1960, the Paris organization received a devastatingly pessimistic report on the HNP sent by Javier Pradera, one of the most valuable of the student activists at the University of Madrid recruited by Jorge Semprún. The scion of a famous Carlist family, whose father and grandfather had died in the Civil War, Pradera had uniquely good contacts on the right. He had been heavily involved in the organization of the HNP, had witnessed its failure and knew that the various declarations by Carrillo bore little relation to what had really taken place.[2] Carrillo could not have anticipated the extent to which Pradera, albeit in cautious language, would dismantle his own optimistic rewriting of the failure of the HNP. Pradera's essential point was that the entire operation had been premature, not to say irresponsible. He reported, not without a degree of irony, that one of those right-wing groups of whose collaboration Carrillo had been certain had pointed out that 'it had no wish to collaborate in establishing the dictatorship of the proletariat in Spain'.

As well as demonstrating that the middle classes had no interest in participating in Communist-sponsored strikes, Pradera pointed out that, in the provinces, the workers existed in a different historical time-frame from those in the principal industrial centres. Most shockingly, he argued that PCE activists in the underground were more demoralized by the Party's prior optimistic predictions and subsequent distortion of what had happened than by the failure itself. Dismissing Carrillo's claim that the HNP had been a massively successful propaganda operation, Pradera stated that both over-optimism beforehand and exaggeration afterwards had repelled many potential allies. Moreover, he made the perceptive point that economic development in Spain was raising the possibility of entry into the European Common Market, something which the Party opposed. He argued that this required a rethink of Party strategy. Carrillo was furious at what he perceived as an act of indiscipline and, since it had been committed by someone recruited by Semprún, leaped on the opportunity to drive a wedge between them. He thus obliged a reluctant Semprún to reply.[3]

Since Pradera's report made, albeit more strongly, the same points as those made by Claudín at the first meeting of the politburo after the HNP, Carrillo wanted to use Semprún's indisputable prestige among the militants in the interior to silence this outbreak of revisionism. Claudín believed that Carrillo's motive was to cut off support from inside Spain for his dissent and also to get Semprún to distance himself, in writing, from both Pradera and Claudín. Hence, in June 1960, with little conviction, Semprún wrote as instructed a sarcastically patronizing letter. It was rambling and twice as long as Pradera's original. Semprún accused his friend of being abstract and unrealistic. Picking on Pradera's own admission of a lack of a detailed overview of the HNP, he described his points as having an 'abstract, hardly dialectical, not to say frankly metaphysical character'. This he attributed to Pradera's university education, his isolation from real problems intensified by the fact that he had been in prison, and his 'excessively bookish' theoretical approach. The central accusation, which reeked of dictation by Carrillo, was that Pradera was guilty of a lack of confidence in the power of the masses and therefore of the ultimate success of the HNP policy.

In his intelligently sardonic reply, Pradera made it quite clear that he suspected that this letter had been written under duress. Nor did he conceal his dismay at what he felt was a betrayal by a friend. The long and detailed letter, despite its ironic tone, registered his astonishment at Semprún's mixture of 'patronizing benevolence and thunderbolts from Jupiter'. Pradera noted that the fireworks of Semprún's letter were utterly contrary to his normal style. 'In my judgement, you have chosen a bad way to convince me. I believed that dialogue with a friend was one thing and polemic with the enemy another; that debate was one thing and impertinence another.' The last paragraph of the letter reflects his personal distress: 'I really don't like this tone for debating with friends. Since you are doubly a friend, a "friend" and a personal friend (to whom I owe a lot in every way), it upsets me even more. As in urchins' squabbles, I will say "I didn't start it". If "I let myself get involved", it is because when things are not brought out into the open, they end up festering and eating away inside you.'[4]

Pradera was excluded from his position in the Madrid organization and then, two years later, summoned to Paris where he was subjected to interrogation by Carrillo in the presence of Semprún and Claudín. They did nothing to defend their friend, who was nauseated by the entire process – indeed, he vomited in the street after the first session. Carrillo loathed him instinctively as a privileged posh boy and, until Pradera drifted out of the Party, saw him as the fount of all dissent emanating from Madrid. Nevertheless, he was happy to boast to Pasionaria about Pradera's presence in the Party as proof that the policy of national reconciliation was working.[5]

The humiliation of Pradera seems to have had an impact on Semprún's attitude to Carrillo. Moreover, he had begun to recall his experience in Buchenwald, an experience he had hitherto repressed. Already, during his periods of inactivity in Madrid, he had started to write his first novel, *Le Long Voyage*.[6] It was the beginning of a process which would culminate in his departure from the PCE. Another important figure of the Communist intelligentsia in Madrid about to leave the Party was the film producer Ricardo Muñoz Suay, a friend of both Semprún and Pradera. A member of the JSU since the Civil War, he had been instrumental in helping Semprún build contacts among the intelligentsia when he first entered Spain clandestinely in 1953. Muñoz Suay was a key figure in the production company UNINCI (Unión Industrial Cinematográfica SA), a powerful cultural instrument heavily influenced by the PCE. Among its triumphs were *Bienvenido Mr Marshall* by Luis García Berlanga. Muñoz Suay had also persuaded the great film director Luis Buñuel to return to Spain to make the film *Viridiana* which won the Palme d'Or at Cannes in March 1961.

The Franco regime had initially supported the making of *Viridiana*, believing it to be a wholesome story about a nun when in fact it was about her moral disintegration. When the film was denounced by the Vatican, the regime took punitive measures against the production company. In extremely complex circumstances, facing financial disaster, Muñoz Suay decided to sell his shares in the company. The other shareholders were in no position to buy him out and, if he sold the shares on the open market, the PCE's influence over UNINCI would have been at an end. Muñoz Suay made vague threats that, if he wasn't paid, he would denounce the company's relations with the PCE. A furious Carrillo authorized payment from Party funds. He commented to the film director Juan Antonio Bardem, 'Once upon a time, this traitor would have been found dead in a ditch.' Semprún, who was present, confirmed later that Carrillo had made this nostalgic remark. Carrillo himself, while not admitting that he had spoken those exact words, commented that, had this been the 1940s, it would have been dealt with by *guerrilleros* on his orders. As it was, the Party's revenge was limited to spreading rumours that Muñoz Suay was a police informer.[7]

Carrillo's first major public speech after the Sixth Congress was made to a plenary meeting of the Central Committee held in Paris between 10 and 12 October 1961 at the height of the crisis over the erection of the Berlin Wall. In mid-August, work had started on the wall and two weeks later President John F. Kennedy had ordered an increase of American military strength in Europe. With Washington and Moscow at loggerheads, Carrillo presented a firmly pro-Soviet line. He made much of the existence of American bases in Spain as part of an overall Western threat to the USSR. The KGB was mounting a deception campaign to give the impression that the Soviet Union had more sophisticated and ample weaponry than previously believed, and was prepared to launch a nuclear attack in response to Western armed provocations over West Berlin. In Carrillo's interpretation, the Soviet action was an heroic effort to defend the world from American aggression. Denouncing the Western presence in Berlin, he presented the entire crisis in terms of an imperialist scheme to provoke a war against the USSR.

Asserting that the Spanish people felt a special sympathy for the Soviet Union and its commitment to world peace, he called on Communists and Catholics to unite in mobilizing against the Franco regime to prevent American bases being used against the USSR. He then progressed to a hymn of praise for the abundance that the citizens in the Soviet bloc would soon enjoy thanks to the 600 per cent increase in industrial production and a 350 per cent increase in agricultural output planned by the CPSU. His confidence that this would happen and that every Russian family would have a modern, comfortable home was boosted by the achievements of the astronaut Yuri Gagarin who, in the spacecraft *Vostok 3KA-3*, had become the first man to orbit the earth. 'These plans,' he declared, 'like all those drawn up by the Soviet Union, have a strict scientific basis and will lead to the complete and absolute disappearance of differences between classes, between town and country, between manual and intellectual labour, and to the ever wider fulfilment of the material and spiritual needs of society.'

Repeating his stock assertions about the imminent collapse of the dictatorships and the success of the policy of *reconciliación nacional*, he then moved on to an empty threat that, if the rest of the anti-Franco forces did not join in a great anti-regime front, the PCE would go it alone, lead the urban and rural proletariat to victory and therefore head the subsequent regime. The strategy adopted in order to guarantee this success would be the HNP, albeit with the possibility of 'armed clashes between the masses and the recalcitrant defenders of the regime'. He did not discount the possibility of armed struggle in the event either of social conditions worsening or of Spain siding with the USA in a war against the USSR. In fact, Carrillo had been examining proposals made by Líster, and supported by Romero Marín, for an attack on the American base at Morón de la Frontera. The idea was given serious consideration, despite its obvious contradiction of the policy of national reconciliation. It was eventually abandoned.[8]

The implied threats to the rest of the opposition reflected Carrillo's concern, not to say desperation, about the growth of the non-Communist opposition. In the report to the Sixth Congress, he had exposed his fear that the emergence of the monarchist Unión Española and the hostility of the PSOE would lead to the exclusion of the PCE from a post-Franco democratic monarchy. He had perhaps revealed more than he had meant to do about the motives behind the HNP when he said, 'the Party leadership had to find a way of combating those schemes'.[9] The continuing failure of Carrillo's determination to prove the PCE's moderation before a middle-class audience was underlined at the historic meeting of interior and exiled opposition figures at the Hotel Regina Palace in Munich on 5 and 6 June 1962. The event was organized by Salvador de Madariaga, the president of the Liberal International, and his opposite number in the Socialist International, Alsing Andersen. The intention was to bring together representatives of the democratic anti-Franco opposition from both inside and outside Spain. By collecting such an 'assembly of notables', seventy figures from the interior and fifty from exile, Madariaga hoped to belie the regime's propaganda that the only choice was between Francoism and communism. The notion quickly gained adherents and was picked up and developed within Spain by the Asociación Española de Cooperación Europea, whose president was the conservative Christian Democrat and monarchist José María Gil Robles. The scheme eventually came to fruition with the two-day meeting devoted to discussion of the Spanish situation under the heading 'Europe and Spain' within the wider proceedings of the Fourth Congress of the European Movement held in Munich from 5 to 8 June 1962.

Preparations for the meeting coincided with a wave of industrial unrest in northern Spain. Both the meeting and the strikes would have an important impact on the PCE. A series of factors combined in the first years of the decade to sharpen the basic contradictions implicit in the efforts by a Communist Party to woo bourgeois allies. On the one hand, the death of Stalin, the revelations at the Twentieth Congress of the CPSU and the declarations of Carrillo all seemed to mark a certain liberalization of the PCE. On the other, the relaxation was more apparent than real since Carrillo, despite his carefully maintained liberal façade, would never tolerate dissidence within the Party. Nor was he open to rethinking his own positions. The early 1960s also saw the beginning of a spectacular economic growth in Spain that would strengthen the regime while at the same time increasing the self-confidence and level of mobilization of the working class. The immediate consequence of the latter was the series of strikes which swept Spain in 1962. Beginning in Asturias, they quickly spread to the Basque Country, Catalonia and Madrid despite the efforts of the forces of repression. These spring strikes effectively ended in victory for the workers, and Carrillo jubilantly saw them as the beginning of the national general strike to overthrow the regime. In fact, he failed to realize the extent to which the strikes were economic in motivation and based on the simple fact that the workers saw the possibility of pay rises. His optimistic view that the end of the dictatorship was nigh was founded on the assumption that a narrow Francoist clique ruled over a backward economy on the point of social explosion. He therefore did not see that the seeming capitulation of the industrialists owed more to growing prosperity and a determination not to disrupt production than to any retreat by the Franco regime.[10]

The tactical reconsiderations necessary for Carrillo to be persuaded that the predicted economic disaster was not imminent would create serious divisions within the PCE. For the moment, through the Party press, he continued to talk as if the regime faced impending doom. He seized on every strike as incontrovertible evidence that his view was correct when in fact evidence was growing to the contrary. In a long speech to PCE militants in Paris in June, he congratulated himself that the 1962 strikes constituted proof of his thesis that a broad alliance of social forces was coming together to overthrow the backward Francoist clique, proof that his policy of national reconciliation was paving the way to a national pacific strike: 'the analysis that the Party leadership made last October has been brilliantly confirmed by reality. But, in a wider sense, the strikes of April and May have corroborated the entire political and tactical line of the Party.' He declared that 'what in other countries might have been just another more or less serious labour conflict gravely undermined the entire regime in Spain, revealing its impotence and senility and shaking society to its very foundations'. Applauding his own insight, he declared that, 'in a brilliant way, the Party's entire concept, its tactical approach, has been confirmed'.[11]

Five months later, Carrillo published a book in Paris about the strikes with a text that reiterated his triumphalist interpretation. It celebrated an unbroken line of correct prophecies, starting with the declaration of national reconciliation in August 1956, via the Jornada de Reconciliación Nacional in 1958, the HNP in 1959 and Carrillo's report to the Sixth Congress, and culminating in his speech to the October 1961 plenary meeting of the Central Committee. With an arrogance more breathtaking than that expressed in his Paris speech, Carrillo now claimed that he had accurately predicted the strikes: 'With its political efforts, the Party prepared the strikes of April and May and was the very soul of their organization and leadership.' According to this document, the strikes began when a number of Party militants decided in March that the time had come to deliver the decisive blow against the dictatorship. Once they began, the strikes responded to PCE policy as expressed through the broadcasts of Pasionaria and Carrillo on Radio España Independiente throughout May. On 5 May, the executive committee had drafted a call for all of the forces of the opposition to unite behind what was presented as a great general strike to overthrow the dictatorship. It was broadcast by Carrillo the following day. The book recognized the economic basis of the strikes but still interpreted them in terms of the inevitable

HNP. Thus, although it was notorious that the repression against the miners in Asturias had been ferocious, Carrillo argued nonsensically, as he had at the Sixth Congress and in his Paris speech, that the majority of the forces of order sympathized with the strategy of HNP.[12]

Linking the strikes and Madariaga's planned Munich meeting, the Francoist press announced that, in order to deal with unrest provoked from abroad, martial law would be declared. Inadvertently, the regime was recognizing both the symbolic significance of Munich and the economic changes revealed by the strikes. The exiled opposition was coming to terms both with conservative anti-Francoists and with the new opposition which had grown up in the 1950s. Were it not for the exclusion of the Communists, the meeting at Munich of monarchists, Catholics and renegade Falangists with Socialists and Basque and Catalan nationalists could be seen in many ways to have prefigured the great movement of democratic consensus which was to bear fruit in the 1970s.

Not all those who attended had approved of the exclusion of the Communists. Some of those organizing the meeting felt that the entire anti-Franco opposition should be present. However, both Gil Robles and Enrique Adroher 'Gironella', once of the quasi-Trotskyist POUM, were fiercely hostile to the idea of inviting Carrillo to Munich. Beyond their visceral opposition, there was the practical problem that the Munich meeting aimed to secure a place for a future democratic Spain in a future united Europe. The inclusion in the project of what was still perceived as a Stalinist party would not help achieve that goal. All of the participant groups had expressed a commitment to the Common Market while the PCE had declared its rejection thereof. It was feared that the presence of Carrillo or one of his subordinates would impel other groups to stay away. In the event, there was a fleeting and virtually unnoticed attendance by 'Juan Gómez' (Tomás García) and Francesc Vicens of the PSUC, both of whom were present in the hotel but did not attend the official sessions.[13]

The Assembly of the European Movement was closed on 8 June by a moving speech by Madariaga. He ended with the words: 'the civil war which began in Spain on 18 July 1936, and which the Regime has maintained artificially through censorship, the monopoly of the Press and the Radio and its victory parades, that civil war ended in Munich the day before yesterday on 6 June 1962'. Nearly a thousand delegates of the European Movement applauded and approved by acclamation the conclusions of the Spaniards and the five conditions which the EEC should demand for Spanish entry: the establishment of democratic representative institutions, the effective guarantee of human rights including freedom of expression, the recognition of Spain's regional communities, the guarantee of trade union rights, particularly the right to strike, and the possibility of organizing political parties.[14]

The joint document produced by the interior and exterior delegations denounced the dictatorial power of Franco and the abuse of human rights in Spain and concluded that 'Either Spain evolves or she will be excluded from European integration.' Desperate not to be left behind, Carrillo quickly declared his agreement with the five conditions for Spanish entry into the Common Market. Franco was furious at what he saw as a plot to torpedo his regime's efforts to secure an association with the European Economic Community. Many of the Spanish delegates were subjected to police harassment on their return for their part in what was denounced as the 'filthy Munich cohabitation' (*contubernio*). All were detained on their return to Spain. Some, such as the law professor Vicente Piniés and the influential Christian Democrat from Seville Manuel Giménez Fernández, were released after interrogation. Other, more prominent ones were given the choice of immediate exile or internal exile in the Canary Islands. Dionisio Ridruejo chose exile in France and José María Gil Robles in Switzerland. Among the majority who chose the Canary Islands were Joaquín Satrústegui and two who would reach prominence in the post-Franco political establishment, Fernando Álvarez de Miranda, who would become president of the first democratic Cortes in 1977, and Iñigo Cavero Lataillade, who would be successively Minister of Education and of Justice in the governments of Adolfo Suárez.[15]

In his Paris speech, Carrillo expressed solidarity with the broad spectrum of groups represented at Munich and offered to collaborate with them as fellow combatants for democracy in the fight to overthrow the dictatorship. He lamented that there were obstacles to cooperation with the PCE coming from the Socialist Party led by Rodolfo Llopis and what he called 'the extreme anti-Francoist right' – an unmistakable reference to Gil Robles. He declared plausibly that a broad front extending from the right to the Socialists but excluding the Communists could not guarantee an orderly and peaceful transition to democracy.

There was more than an element of menace about his point that a peaceful transition to democracy required the removal of the repressive armoury of the dictatorship and that the consequent democratic regime would require the cooperation and not the enmity of the Communist masses: 'In the situation that is approaching in Spain, anyone who knows the reality, any intelligently conservative individual must recognize that the only guarantee of a transition without violence lies first of all in an agreement with the Communist Party.' Having declared earlier in his speech that the PCE would not renounce its role and its mission as a Marxist-Leninist party and as the representative of the working class, the rural proletariat and the progressive intelligentsia, the hints of threat were unmistakable. It was clear that he was expecting the other anti-Francoist forces simply to fall in line with the idea of a Huelga Nacional Pacífica. What was striking was his confident assertion of his conviction that many bourgeois elements including bishops and army generals would soon understand that he was right. Having admitted that the PCE would collaborate in the establishment of democracy only in order to facilitate its long-term goal of the establishment of socialism, he was not exactly offering an enticing prospect to groups that associated communism with Soviet dictatorship.[16]

Moreover, Carrillo's certainty that the dictatorship would soon fall and the PCE dominate the subsequent regime was about to suffer a major blow. Quite separately, two members of the executive committee, 'Federico Sánchez' (Jorge Semprún) and Fernando Claudín, were coming to feel ever stronger doubts about Carrillo's stance. A significant element in their growing disillusionment with Carrillo was provoked by the capture, torture and execution in

Madrid of a fifty-two-year-old Central Committee member, Julián Grimau García, who had been working in the interior since 1957. He had been arrested in Madrid on 7 November 1962. Horribly beaten and tortured, he was thrown out of a window of the Dirección General de Seguridad by interrogators attempting to conceal what they had done. Despite his appalling injuries, he was then tried on 18 April 1963 by court martial charged with 'military rebellion', an indictment which covered crimes allegedly committed during the Civil War. No witnesses for the defence were permitted and the evidence for the prosecution was exclusively based on hearsay. Among numerous irregularities in the proceedings, it later emerged that the military prosecutor, Comandante Manuel Fernández Martín, had falsified his legal qualifications. Grimau was found guilty, condemned to death and shot by firing squad two days later.[17]

Grimau had been sent by Carrillo into Spain in 1957 first to Andalusia and then to Barcelona. As a dedicated and fearless militant, he had gone willingly. After Simón Sánchez Montero had been arrested on the eve of the HNP in 1959, Grimau had replaced him at the head of the PCE's Madrid workers' networks. The international scandal caused by his execution did immense damage to the efforts of the Franco regime to normalize its relations with Europe. The consequences within the PCE were also dramatic. Semprún saw Carrillo's decision to send Grimau into the interior as utterly irresponsible. Given his Civil War record, he should never have been used in this capacity.

Grimau's father Enrique had been a police inspector in Barcelona in the 1920s. However, because of disquiet at the brutal methods advocated by the Civil Governor, General Severiano Martínez Anido, he had left the police and gone into publishing. Julián Grimau had worked in the same publishing house, then at the beginning of the Civil War he joined the newly restructured Republican police force. After taking the entrance examination he had become a detective in the Brigada de Investigación Criminal. He joined the PCE in October 1936. This made him just the kind of man to be useful to Santiago Carrillo when he became Consejero de Orden Público in the Junta de Defensa de Madrid in November that year. Carrillo put Grimau in charge of one of the units working to control the fifth column. Thereafter, he played a similar role as Secretario General de Investigación Criminal in Valencia and later was extremely active in Barcelona hunting down and interrogating Trotskyists and fifth columnists.[18]

The effect of the execution of Grimau on the attitudes to Carrillo of Semprún and Claudín is related to the fact that concerns had already been raised about Grimau's position in Madrid. In the summer of 1962, Semprún had informed the executive committee about the careless and impulsive way in which Grimau worked with little concern for his own security. Indeed, his awareness of the long hours that Grimau spent on the street going from contact to contact lay behind Semprún's report to the Sixth Congress on the dangers of the system of individual contacts on a chain basis. Semprún argued that he should not have been posted there in the first place and that now he should certainly be recalled to France. There could be no doubt that, if caught by the Francoist police, Grimau's Civil War record would ensure the death sentence. That equally senior Party cadres such as López Raimundo in 1951 and Sánchez Montero in 1959 faced only long prison sentences underlined the difference. Carrillo, who was on holiday when Semprún delivered his comments, had taken the decision to send Grimau into Spain in 1957 without discussion with the executive committee. Now, in his absence, the other members of the executive decided to send a letter containing Semprún's criticisms to Grimau and Francisco Romero Marín, who were running the PCE in Madrid. They rejected its content out of hand. However, when Carrillo returned from holiday, he told Semprún that he intended to get Grimau out. Nothing was done. Semprún recalled later that he had often been struck by the arrogant contempt with which Carrillo always treated Grimau. Others have commented on the way Carrillo's sarcastic barbs may have been intended to push Grimau into volunteering to go into Spain.[19]

Claudín later lamented that he and Carrillo shared the responsibility for sending Grimau into Spain but claimed that neither he nor Carrillo had had any idea of Grimau's activities during the Civil War. While that might have been true in his own case, it cannot have been true of Carrillo. In his memoirs, Carrillo makes no mention of Grimau's wartime record and, both there and in another of his books, he claimed to have met him for the first time in Havana in 1941.[20] Apart from having had Grimau under his orders in 1936, Carrillo would also have had access to Party records which gave full details of his background.[21] Certainly, the Francoist authorities had no difficulty in uncovering Grimau's past. The new Minister of Information, Manuel Fraga, seized the opportunity in interviews, in newspaper articles and in a book written by the Civil Guard Ángel Ruiz de Ayúcar to claim that the current PCE was the same Party of the wartime *checas*. Franco was underlining the fact that his Spain was still a country of victors and vanquished. It was equally true that the affair, especially given the dignity and integrity with which Grimau had comported himself, enabled the PCE to proclaim that the regime's pretensions to liberalization were false and that the dictatorship was as brutally repressive as ever.[22] Whatever irresponsibility there may have been in sending Grimau into Spain, Claudín had no doubt that there was irresponsibility in not getting him out in time. Moreover, he concluded that Carrillo's misplaced confidence in the imminent collapse of the dictatorship had led to risks being taken.[23] It all contributed to eroding his faith in the secretary general.

Years later, Carrillo was to blame the fate of Grimau on Claudín and Semprún. In 1978, forgetting his own connections with Grimau in Spain, in Cuba and in France, and obscuring the reasons why Grimau, as an ex-Republican policeman, should not have been sent into Spain, he told the journalist Rosa Montero that 'the person who knew Grimau most was Claudín who had even lived with him. He was the one who knew his record. Why does Semprún make me responsible for Grimau coming to Spain? Why doesn't he blame himself and his friend Claudín since they were both party leaders at the time? And above all, why does Semprún think that the fact that Grimau had fought for the Republic was a reason for not coming to Spain?'[24]

Two decades later, Carrillo had refined his story further with a much more malicious fabrication. In an interview with the journalist José Luis Losa, he set about dismantling Jorge Semprún's well-earned reputation as a courageous militant, as the principal liaison between the Paris centre and the clandestine organization in Madrid. Rather, he described to Losa 'a man who was liable to panic attacks born of his time as a prisoner in the concentration camp at Buchenwald; a Semprún who was rattled, without the strength to return to Spain', and claimed to recall an episode in Paris 'when Semprún's wife Colette Leloup begged Carrillo not to let Jorge return to Madrid'. And according to Carrillo, Semprún's alleged refusal to go to Madrid led to the secret police being able to capture Grimau, whose cover was already blown and who should have been substituted by Semprún and thus enabled to leave Spain.[25] Needless to say, even if Carrillo's character assassination were a faithful account of a real failure of nerve on Semprún's part, that would hardly account for the fate of Grimau. Semprún was already under suspicion as far as Carrillo was concerned and was being used ever more sparingly for missions into Spain. As will be seen later, when discussing Semprún's role with his deputy Claudín, Carrillo made no mention of any such personal crisis.

In 1985, Francisco Romero Marín wrote that Semprún's last mission had ended several months before the arrest of Grimau when he returned to Paris to deal with some family problems. Moreover, since Semprún's role had been as the liaison with the intelligentsia, he would hardly have been sent into Spain to replace Grimau as the liaison with the working-class movement. In any case, there was no reason why Grimau could not have been pulled out of Spain irrespective of the attitude of Semprún. There were numerous other candidates to take his place. It is worth noting that the views of Grimau's daughter Carmen regarding her father's death coincided with those of Semprún. Once the propaganda value of the Grimau case had faded, his wife Ángela Martínez Campillo was forgotten by the Party. She was even removed from her job in a Paris pharmacy to make room for Carrillo's wife Carmen. Even after the re-establishment of democracy, Ángela's later efforts to clear her husband's name received no support from Carrillo. By then, as a parliamentary deputy, he was not prepared to endanger his now cordial relations with Manuel Fraga.[26]

Despite the implications of the capture of Grimau, at the beginning of 1963 Carrillo had reiterated his view that the HNP was about to overthrow the dictatorship, stating that this was to be the critical year that would see the end of Franco. Then in the PCE's May Day declaration he announced that 'a great general strike' could set off 'a huge civic uprising' that would finish off the regime. He called on 'all workers to accelerate preparations to bring about, as soon as possible, the political general strike'. There were strikes in Asturias between May and September but, despite being proclaimed by Carrillo to be precursors of the political general strike, they sparked off no action elsewhere. This was explained by Carrillo as a consequence of their having taken place in the summer when political action was difficult. Nevertheless, even though the next strikes in Asturias were in the spring of 1964 rather than the summer, the national general movement still did not materialize.[27]

In fact, the strikes of 1962 had marked a major turning point in the evolution of both the dictatorship and the opposition. They were a response to the birth-pangs of an important industrialization process. The specifically economic nature of the subsequent actions in Asturias in 1963 and 1964 was not understood by Carrillo, deeply wedded as he was to the notion of a general strike overthrowing a decrepit regime. In contrast, it was perceived by many militants inside Spain and by both the Party's most sophisticated theorist, Fernando Claudín, and the man who, until December 1962, had been the principal liaison between Paris and the interior organization, Jorge Semprún. The PCE within Spain now had a number of highly intelligent intellectuals in its ranks as a result of the university expansion that had taken place since 1956. Men like Javier Pradera, Ramón Tamames, Luis Goytisolo, Fernando Sánchez Dragó and Enrique Múgica were perfectly capable of seeing the absurdities of the Party line which they were expected to implement obediently. They wanted their perception of Spanish realities to play a part in the elaboration of a more realistic PCE strategy.[28] Their discontent had, to a certain extent, been tempered by Semprún, whom they liked and considered their intellectual equal.

However, after the arrest of Grimau, Semprún had been replaced as the leadership's liaison with Spain. Carrillo claimed that, after ten years of clandestine work, this decision had to be taken for his own safety. However, Semprún had considerable doubt about Carrillo's motives. He reflected that no such security concerns had applied to Grimau or to Romero Marín, who lived in equal or greater peril. Semprún's last trip into Spain was to accompany and introduce his replacement, José Sandoval, who was far from suitable. Sandoval had been in Russia since 1939, apart from two years in Romania from 1954 to 1956, and was likely to be a fish out of water in Madrid. The way he carried himself, the way he lit his cigarettes, his lack of knowledge of Spanish football or bullfighting, made him stand out. Within twelve months, he had been captured and with him collapsed a large part of the PCE intellectual organization in Madrid. Inevitably, after the Pradera controversy, Semprún began to wonder if Carrillo had not taken a decision that was profoundly dangerous to the Party simply in order to limit the possible criticism of his own position.[29]

In the meantime, the arrival of Sandoval had done little to improve relations with the young intellectuals in Madrid. Nevertheless, he tried to be conciliatory and suggested that representatives of the Madrid organization meet the Paris leadership. This encounter took place in the course of a two-week seminar held in the last week of July and the first week of August 1963 at a chateau outside Arras in northern France. The idea was that around 100 militants from inside Spain would meet the leadership and Carrillo would bring the potential rebels under control. However, the result was that the potential divisions in the Party were brought out into the open. The detonator was José Ruibal, a thirty-seven-year-old dramatist who had already written four plays. Unaware of the deference required in dealing with the secretary general, Ruibal irritated Carrillo by the forthright manner in which he set about criticizing what he denounced as 'the worn-out methods of work used by the leadership that put a brake on recruitment, political efficacy and ideological creativity'. He demanded doctrinal materials 'with fewer exclamation marks and more ideas'. By quoting Pradera in support of these statements and remarking that the situation had been intolerable since the removal of 'Federico Sánchez', Ruibal inadvertently intensified Carrillo's suspicions of Semprún. A suggestion by Claudín that Pradera be brought into a new committee of intellectuals had a similar effect. Carrillo infuriated Claudín by suddenly interrupting a speech by Francesc Vicens in order to make a crude intervention denouncing the intellectuals. Before Claudín could respond, he brusquely announced that he was short of time and left. Claudín then broke Party protocol by speaking out against dogmatism and conformism in the Party. He did not specifically name Carrillo, but when the secretary general heard what had been said he was deeply irritated. Claudín's intervention had exposed publicly the growing divisions in the leadership.[30]

The Arras meeting opened two crises for Carrillo. The more serious derived from the emergence of figures like Ruibal, and Pradera before him, who both criticized the authoritarian internal structure of the Party and disputed Carrillo's line. They argued that the end of the dictatorship was still years away and required further economic development before it would come to pass. These were the positions to which Claudín and Semprún had arrived separately. The gravity of their dissent was that, involving as it did two highly prestigious members of the executive, it affected the Party at its very core. In contrast, the other problem could be dismissed simply as an irritant. It largely involved students who, inspired by Mao Zedong and Fidel Castro, advocated a return to more orthodox Marxist-Leninist positions.

In the summer of 1963, shortly after the Arras seminars, these young revolutionaries started to publish an alternative Party newspaper called *Mundo Obrero Revolucionario*. Under the leadership of an ex-PCE veteran, Paulino García Moya, in late 1963 or early 1964 they created a new party called the PCE-Marxista-Leninista. This group were known initially as *chinos* since it was alleged that they received funding from the Chinese Embassy in Paris. Moreover, in the wake of the Sino-Soviet conflict, which had begun in 1959 when Mao accused Khrushchev of being a revisionist traitor, they regarded Carrillo as equally revisionist because of his pro-Soviet position.[31] Carrillo never engaged fully with the *chinos* other than to accuse them of being guilty of an 'infantile leftist disorder'. To a certain extent, the existence of extremist groups that accused the PCE of moderation had some advantages in terms of the Party's credibility in the eyes of the middle classes. However, it has been alleged that Carrillo resorted to the tactic of having its militants denounced to the Francoist police.[32] The 'Chinese' schism would never be numerically large and would also be riven by factional disputes. Nevertheless, its very existence raised the levels of paranoia during the debates that culminated in the expulsions of Claudín and Semprún.[33]

After the clashes at Arras, Semprún and Claudín began to argue ever more openly that the fundamental changes which Spanish capitalism was undergoing required a major rethink of Party strategy. If they were right, and events were to show that they were, then national reconciliation would materialize only at the point of future economic development when the industrial bourgeoisie began to find the Franco regime an impediment to its continuing prosperity. However, at the time, given the exploitation being suffered by the Spanish working class and the acute shortages of housing and schools, it was understandable that Carrillo should remain convinced that the regime's days were numbered. Even radical leftist groups, such as the FLP, which disagreed with the Communist quest for alliance with the bourgeoisie, were equally convinced that economic development, foreign capitalization and the integration of the workers were unlikely. In fact, a process of economic expansion was under way which was to change the nature of working-class discontent and consolidate the tendency towards *obrerismo*, or straight non-political wage claims.

In addition, the incipient tourist boom and the export of labour were beginning to solve some of the worst structural problems of the Spanish economy, thus undermining Carrillo's prediction of impending doom. Yet, throughout most of the 1960s, Carrillo would continue to act on the premise of the certain success of the strategy that he now called the Huelga Nacional Política. He thereby squandered much of the PCE's influence in the growing working-class movement. The Party's clandestine union organization, the Workers' Commissions (Comisiones Obreras), would grow throughout the second half of the decade. Nevertheless, it would be damaged by Carrillo's calls for street demonstrations as shows of strength, which simply facilitated repression. Communist prestige too was lost by dramatic appeals for 'days of national action', such as those on 27 October 1967 and 14 May

1968, that were ignored by the rank and file.[34] That was still in the future.

Now, in the autumn of 1963, the next step on 'the revisionist slope down to the cesspool of treachery' for Claudín and Semprún took the form of two articles in the PCE's new theoretical journal *Realidad*. Its creation was the executive committee's response to the complaints of the Madrid intellectuals about the poor intellectual quality of the materials being sent in by the Paris leadership. In its first issue, Claudín and Semprún each had an article. Despite their moderate tone, Carrillo chose to see both as evidence of outright rebellion. He was furious not to have been consulted before they went into print. He had been en route to Moscow when they appeared and was embarrassed to have had to fend off questions there about articles implicitly critical of the Soviets.[35] Claudín's ostensibly innocuous article was a criticism of the dogmatic implications of the Marxist concept of 'socialist realism' in art. Claudín himself later described his defence of freedom in artistic creation as 'timid, moderate but unacceptable to the dominant philo-Sovietism in the executive committee'.

Semprún's article was less abstract and more relevant to the current situation. It dealt with the Chinese Communists' denunciation of the alleged revisionism of the Italian Communist Party, the PCI, and defended the ideas of Togliatti about the need for the various Communist parties to elaborate their own policies independently of the CPSU. In a footnote, he suggested that the evolution of the Communist movement since 1956 needed to be analysed and implicitly criticized the guerrilla policy of the 1940s – something which Carrillo saw as a personal attack. In consequence, Semprún's article was subjected to virulent criticism by Carrillo's most loyal acolytes on the executive committee. In retrospect, like Claudín, Semprún was struck by 'the extreme prudence – not to say timidity – of its arguments'. Carrillo was deeply irritated by Semprún's defence of Togliatti, having himself recently denounced the positions of the Italian Party as dangerous in the same way that those of the Hungarian Party had been in 1956. The immediate consequence was that the editorship of the journal was immediately assigned to the stolidly loyal Manuel Azcárate.[36]

Not long after the offending issue of *Realidad* had been circulated, in November 1963, Carrillo called a plenary meeting of the Central Committee. Semprún was not present and Claudín did not intervene, although he was fully aware that Carrillo was setting out his strategy for the now inevitable conflict. That was obvious from the way in which he used the excuse of the Sino-Soviet clash to warn that revision of policy was not on the agenda. This was an implicit criticism of Semprún's article. Carrillo delegated to one of his closest allies, Horacio Fernández Inguanzo from Asturias, an analysis of the strikes as the decisive step towards the major general strike now known as the Huelga Nacional Política. Claudín said nothing because "To say what I really thought about the Spanish situation would have meant moving towards a split; to say what I didn't think was no longer possible." Claudín believed that there was nothing cynical or opportunistic about Carrillo's position. The secretary general certainly genuinely believed that the HNP was possible. Whether he feared that the arguments of Claudín and Semprún really constituted a threat to Party unity is another question. More probably, he believed that any criticism of the Party line was an attack on himself. Since he identified himself with the Party, he could presume that it was therefore also an attack on the Party itself. However, the vehemence of his response suggested real insecurity. If he had not realized the validity of the Claudín–Semprún theses, he would not have felt the need to annihilate them.

In his report to the plenum, Carrillo's criticism of the Chinese Communists confirmed his own commitment to Moscow. His key remarks regarding the situation inside the PCE came near the end of his lengthy intervention. In a fine display of hypocrisy, he declared that the days of personality cult were over: 'It is necessary to explain, to persuade, to convince. The masses and the militants of the Party also deserve, without demagogy on the part of the leadership, great respect. They are not just soldiers who obey orders and even less are they "robots".' Then came the central point: 'It would be another matter altogether to want to turn the leadership committees into an academy and the rank-and-file organisms into a debating society where there is nothing but interminable talk.' He made it clear that consideration of reality was not part of his decision-making process: 'A political initiative just had to be taken and implemented immediately; not on the basis of practical experimentation, but because of a prior calculation and decision.'[37]

A final effort to avoid a split was made on 8 January 1964 when Carrillo suggested that Claudín come to talk to him in private. Both later published broadly similar accounts of the encounter. According to Claudín, the meeting was superficially cordial and Carrillo was conciliatory. Carrillo listened while Claudín explained that there was no proper debate in the executive committee because the secretary general's authority, explicitly or implicitly, always saw his opinion prevail. Giving Ignacio Gallego as an example, Claudín pointed out that even those who started out with different points of view would change tack rather than end up disagreeing with him, doing so not from conviction but out of deference. Carrillo apologized for the fact that, since he regarded Claudín as 'my other self' (in his own words) or 'his double' (in those of Claudín), he had not fully felt the need to discuss things with him. Nevertheless, when Claudín spoke approvingly of the Italian Communists, Carrillo stated that he regarded them as right-wingers and dismissed the idea of emulating their more open style because the PCE as a clandestine party could not permit itself the luxuries enjoyed by the PCI, which was legal.

Carrillo maintained his views on Pradera as a troublemaker in Madrid but conceded that perhaps Claudín had been right in 1956 in calling for an examination of the contradictions of the Soviet position. However, he did not agree with Claudín's comments about his subjective evaluation of the internal situation in Spain. Furthermore, when Claudín questioned his decision to terminate Semprún's work as the liaison with the interior in his guise as 'Federico Sánchez', Carrillo responded with comments that were as manipulative as they were mendacious: 'it has been necessary to criticize him for the lack of follow-through in his work … Fede is not a man for a specific political or organizational task; for that you need to be dedicated and organized.' It is notable that, in this discussion of Semprún's role in the Party, he made no mention of the alleged nervous crisis that he later blamed for the death of Grimau. It is inconceivable that, if such a crisis really had occurred, it would not have been raised with Claudín.

Carrillo did make complaints about Claudín's behaviour. He was deeply irritated when he heard about Claudín's speech made after he had left the Arras seminar. He was mortified to be accused of dogmatism: 'talking with people, I noticed something weird but I could not believe that you had made a speech like that ... You presented me, in fact, as being hostile to a critical spirit, as a champion of dogmatism, in opposition to the new generations.' The way Claudín's speech had been reported back to him had clearly touched a raw nerve. He vehemently described his own entry into the Party as the action of a non-conformist firebrand: 'I came to the Party by dint of a fierce struggle, showing absolute disagreement with the leaders and the policy of the PSOE. I came because of my refusal to conform.' Claudín denied that his remarks about dogmatism and conformity were aimed at Carrillo, who replied that what mattered was that the audience had taken them in that sense. He then showed that he was equally affronted by the two articles in *Realidad*. His main complaint was less about the content than about the fact that the articles were published without his prior permission, when he was on his way to Moscow. He was deeply embarrassed there to be asked about them by Pasionaria and Santiago Álvarez. Carrillo talked of his hope that they might resume their previous collaboration and tried to blame any discord on Semprún. However, his reiterated references to the unfairness of Claudín's intervention in Arras suggested that agreement would be virtually impossible despite the apparently optimistic note on which they took their leave. As Claudín recalled, 'We parted without the dying embers of our old friendship showing any glimmers of revival.'[38]

The Stalinist rigidity with which Carrillo reacted to criticisms of his misinterpretation of Spanish reality would convert a potentially creative debate into a debilitating internal crisis. In a pattern that he would also follow in the case of the rebellion of the hard-line Stalinists under Enrique Líster in 1969–70, Carrillo's response would be to stifle internal debate, expel the offenders and then claim that the numbers involved were negligible. His leadership style was starkly revealed by the conflict with Claudín and Semprún. Between late 1963 and the end of 1964, his two leading critics would argue ever more openly and with greater conviction that changes were taking place in Spanish capitalism that would alter the nature of working-class discontent and ultimately of the regime itself. They had been disturbed for some time by the gulf between the real situation in the country and Carrillo's complacent predictions about the regime's weakness and the readiness of the working class to overthrow it.

Claudín was a man essentially driven by Marxist theory. Now he was increasingly disillusioned by Carrillo's reluctance to analyse the 1962 strikes in the light of the economic boom and not as the confirmation of his predictions. The major theoretical issue in the debate between them was over the level of development reached by Spanish capitalism. Carrillo's position was based on the premise that Spain had the same structural problems as in 1931 – backward, fragmented industry and semi-feudal agriculture. In that sense, he was still drawing on ideas that he had picked up in the 1930s while a disciple of Largo Caballero. The obstacles to growth created by the Franco regime's sheer technical incompetence throughout the 1940s and 1950s had given considerable plausibility to Carrillo's analysis that its collapse was imminent. However, American aid, international investment, the tourist boom and the technocrats' stabilization plans had kick-started economic development. Trapped in his belief that the regime remained in the hands of a reactionary clique, Carrillo was sure that it would be easy to find bourgeois allies. In contrast, what Claudín and Semprún perceived was that the industrial and banking bourgeoisie was, for the moment, satisfied. They saw that it would not be until the regime became a major obstacle to further growth, by for instance impeding membership of the Common Market, that there would be any chance of a broad front against the dictatorship. One major difference between them was Carrillo's enthusiasm for the slogan 'land for those who work it'. To Claudín, this was a revolutionary throwback to the 1930s which he now felt could only alienate the bourgeois allies that the PCE needed. Economic development was changing Spain and Carrillo remained in the mental world of the Second Republic.

Three weeks after his meeting with Claudín, on 29 January 1964, Carrillo summoned the executive committee. The purpose was to discuss a draft document on the Spanish situation to be sent to Dolores Ibárruri and later presented at a conference of the four Western European Communist parties that formed the Spain Solidarity Committee. The meeting went on intermittently over several days well into February. Carrillo opened the proceedings with a characteristically upbeat speech arguing that Spain was on the verge of catastrophe, and that the bourgeoisie would eagerly join the working class in overthrowing the regime. His view was approved by all present except Claudín and Semprún, who tried gently to push him towards a more realistic assessment of developments in Spain. Claudín pointed out that 'the improvement of the economic situation of the masses is the result of their own struggle but also of the practical possibility that the bourgeoisie has had to make concessions'. He and Semprún were vainly trying to convince the executive committee that the success of the technocrats' development plan (Plan de Desarrollo) would give the bourgeoisie a wider margin for manoeuvre. Claudín went further, talking about the effects on working-class militancy of wage rises since 1962 and of the labour shortages consequent on mass emigration to northern Europe.

Initially, Carrillo pretended to find what Claudín was saying interesting and worthy of further discussion. When he summarized Claudín's views, implying that they reflected what he had been saying all along, the rest of the executive fell into line in an exact confirmation of what Claudín had predicted in his conversation with Carrillo. José Sandoval commented that Carrillo 'has powerfully and bravely underlined a series of new elements'. Similarly, Ignacio Gallego now piped up and said, 'Santiago has summed up the concerns and worries that we all have about the situation and the prospects for the future.' However, it soon became clear that Carrillo's intentions were not to seek compromise.

His second-in-command, the organization secretary and Soviet agent Eduardo García, now said what Carrillo had preferred not to say himself. In what may well have been a pre-scripted intervention, García declared that what was going on was a dialogue of the deaf, pointing out that what Claudín and Semprún were saying contradicted the Party line as expounded by the secretary general. The man Semprún considered to be Carrillo's 'lapdog with a bite' referred to Claudín's speech at Arras, the two dissidents' links with Pradera and the *Realidad* articles as evidence that they were trying to split the Party. That there had been prior collusion with Carrillo was revealed by a blustering speech from Enrique Líster. He gave the game away by declaring that, when the agenda for the meeting had been drawn up, 'I understood that this question of Party unity was part of item one.' Carrillo then spoke again and showed that he was still seething over Claudín's speech at Arras and the *Realidad* articles. Putting great emphasis on the lack of respect shown to the secretary general, he revealed the extent of his own resentment, mocking Semprún as pretentious and Claudín as indolent. He then said that, although he had chosen not to raise the issue of unity, he was glad that García and Líster had done so. By mentioning the 'dialogue of the deaf', he said, García had done a great service to the executive committee.

Recognizing that, as a minority in the executive, they had little chance of being heard, Claudín and Semprún suggested that a congress or a plenary meeting of the Central Committee be called where a full discussion could take place. Inevitably, the proposal was rejected since it was likely to provide substantial support for the dissidents. Líster said that what was needed was a full meeting of the executive, including Pasionaria and other members resident in the Soviet bloc who had not been able to attend these Paris meetings. Since Claudín and Semprún would be even more outnumbered in such a meeting, the proposal was approved. There was a clear Soviet rationale behind all this. Moscow was facing dissidence from the Chinese and the Italians, and Claudín and Semprún made no secret of their attachment to the PCI. García's intervention had revealed where Soviet interests lay and Carrillo, who remained a fervent admirer of Khrushchev, had no wish to be seen as a revisionist. So Claudín and Semprún had to be eliminated. In the course of the meeting, Carrillo stated that, if the situation were not resolved satisfactorily, he would be obliged to resign. This empty threat was no more than an act of blackmail to clinch the support of the entire committee against Claudín and Semprún.[39]

That full meeting took place from 27 March to 2 April 1964 near Prague in a gloomy castle once occupied by the kings of Bohemia. Having decided that he was not prepared to stay in the Party at the cost of surrendering his intellectual liberty, Claudín went on to the attack with a long and detailed analysis of the economic situation in Spain. For five hours, he argued lucidly that, despite the view of Carrillo and the majority of the executive, democracy would not come about as a result of a revolutionary overthrow of the system. With neo-capitalism well on the road to expansion, he demonstrated that the bourgeoisie had no motive to take part in any risky confrontation. In fact, Carrillo had conflated a real crisis of the regime, deriving from the obsolescence of its semi-fascist forms of authoritarian domination, particularly its commitment to autarky, with a non-existent crisis of Spanish capitalism. Yet, as Claudín understood, there was benefit to be gained from the situation, since many bourgeois sectors shared with the working class a desire for political liberalization. Carrillo's search for compromise with the bourgeoisie did make sense, but not his extreme over-optimism. Claudín agreed with Carrillo that the Party had to push for a peaceful road to socialism. However, while opting for alliance with the bourgeoisie, Claudín warned of the need for awareness of the severe limits of that alliance. Given Spain's integration into international capitalism, it was the only option open, but the Party had to try to avoid playing the game of the haute bourgeoisie.

Without engaging in any consideration of whether this analysis might be correct, Carrillo unleashed his allies before speaking himself. One after another, they laid into Claudín and Semprún. Santiago Álvarez accused Claudín of 'objectivism'. Líster denounced him as a revisionist traitor. For Manuel Delicado, the problem was his total lack of faith in the Party and the working class. José Moix denounced both Claudín and Semprún for their 'subjectivism' and their right-wing revisionist ideas and bourgeois opportunism. Dolores Ibárruri spoke most powerfully of all. Her infallible oratory played successfully on the emotions of those present, but her rejection of Claudín's analysis engaged neither with its content nor with its call for the PCE to modify its line. Instead, with evident contempt, she dismissed his analysis of Spanish development as merely the treachery consequent upon his loss of faith. Like Carrillo, who spoke next, she couched everything in personal terms and implied manipulatively that Claudín was advocating defeatism.

She started gently enough but soon built up to a ringing denunciation:

> I now see Fernando in a new light, as a pessimistic sceptic, without beliefs, who doubts everything, who doubts the capacity for struggle of the working class, who doubts the political capacity of the party, who doubts Marxism-Leninism, who doubts his comrades in the struggle and in the leadership of the party, he treats them in a manner unbefitting a comrade ... He is impressed only by the supposed power of the oligarchy, attributing to it the power, something Marxism rejects, to decide for itself the historical development of our country. His conclusions, more than those of a Marxist-Leninist, are those of a bourgeois sociologist or a Social Democrat ... His analytical method is not that of a Marxist, but rather that of a petit-bourgeois reformist who refuses to see reality because he is scared of the difficulties of the fight.

This supposed degeneration on the part of her one-time protégé she attributed to the attrition of age, exile and family commitments.

Resurrecting her characteristic oratorical power, she then stirred the emotions of the rest of the executive by skilful reference to the Civil War: 'Did we really go through the war, fighting to stop the triumph of fascism, so that, after twenty-eight years of struggle against the oligarchies that brought Franco to power, we have reached the moment to renounce that struggle, to chant *mea culpa* and beg those oligarchies for a place in the sun?' She then asked Claudín rhetorically if he would dare present his analysis to the workers of Asturias, the Basque Country, Madrid or Catalonia or to the peasants of Andalusia, Extremadura or Castile rather than in the safer environment of a closed meeting. Without the approval of the masses, his analyses were simply 'the idle ravings of bird-brained intellectuals'. Rhetorically effective though it was, her speech was similarly manipulative. Where else could major adjustments of Party policy be discussed other than in such meetings? When a new line had been elaborated in tune with the changing reality in Spain, then it would be up to the Party to adjust its propaganda.

Carrillo spoke next. He began with a crude summary of Claudín's position: 'For Fernando, the issue is as follows: power will remain in the hands of the oligarchy. We are moving towards a more or less democratic change in power which will open a new and relatively long period of capitalist development in Spain. A long period of stability and development. Therefore, he concludes, we must adapt to this process and renounce until some distant date confronting the problems of the revolution in our country.' He went on to condemn Claudín's analysis as 'bookish and abstract', identical words to those used in Semprún's letter to Pradera. Revealing the rigidity of his own thinking, he declared that Claudín's analysis was not scientific, 'in the sense in which we understand a scientific analysis, that is to say in the revolutionary, Marxist-Leninist, class sense which our analyses have to have'. Recalling the accusation made at Arras that he was dogmatic, he repeated several times that it was Claudín who was rigid and dogmatic. In Claudín's later judgement, 'it was clear that he just could not handle the reproach of being dogmatic and he reacted, as in children's squabbles, by saying, "well you're worse than me"'.

It is difficult to avoid the conclusion that Carrillo's deep hostility to the position taken by Claudín and Semprún derived from his resentment of criticism of any kind. As his remark to Semprún about Ignacio Gallego revealed, he considered himself to be the supreme arbiter in the Party, 'the power'. Another issue, and the one that he would subsequently use to justify his behaviour, was that, if they were right, it meant that the policy of national reconciliation would be a long time, possibly decades, in maturing. With economic development on the horizon, the bourgeoisie was hardly likely to join with the PCE against Franco. As Claudín implied, and as events were to show, the Party's policy would become relevant only at the point when a new bourgeoning industrial bourgeoisie found the political mechanisms of Francoism to be a hindrance to their prosperity. Unable to countenance the possibility of having to tell the Party rank and file that, after twenty-five years of struggle against Franco, the dictatorship could well last as long again, Carrillo used his control of the PCE apparatus, rather than intellectual arguments, to silence Claudín and Semprún. His reiterated statements in Prague that the ruling classes were in a state of panic and that the Party could prepare an armed uprising within three or four months were laughably unrealistic.

He ridiculed Semprún and Claudín as snooty intellectuals who were sarcastically presenting both himself and his fellow members of the executive as ignoramuses. He also made a theatrical auto-critique, confessing 'sins' such as not realizing sooner what Claudín and Semprún were up to and not removing Semprún sooner from his role in the clandestine organization. They were guilty, he declared, of 'going little by little, step by step towards a modification of the Party line'. Because of this, he thanked Eduardo García for raising the issue at the Paris meeting in February: 'he lifted the lid' on these heinous crimes. Having accused Claudín of being more right-wing than the Socialists or even the Christian Democrats, he stated that he still thought that the PCE was the best place for both him and Semprún. All they had to do was 'rectify their mistakes, correct their erroneous positions'.[40]

Claudín and Semprún both declared that they had no intention of changing their position. At the conclusion of the meeting, they were suspended from the executive until all the documents in the case had been put before the Central Committee. By agreeing to this, they were giving up any chance of having a serious discussion within the Central Committee. As might have been expected, far from putting the case honestly, Carrillo circularized Party leaders inside Spain with a highly tendentious account of the debate which accused Claudín and Semprún of being revisionists and defeatists. They were excluded from meetings and given no chance to reply to the smear campaign directed against them. For denying the imminent collapse of the regime and pointing out the high level of capitalist development in

Spain, they were accused of defeatism and revisionism. Then Carrillo took the astonishing decision to organize a mass meeting in Paris. Since the PCE was still illegal and in clandestinity, he was taking a serious risk but he did so out of a desire to build up hatred against the two dissidents within the Party.

On 19 April, Carrillo chose the deeply emotional occasion of the first anniversary of Grimau's execution to make a savagely dema-gogic speech to Party militants in Paris. In opting to speak that day he ensured that his words would be received uncritically. In highly charged language, he denounced as revisionist social democrats and Mensheviks those who believed that the transition to democracy would be a gradual process without the need for revolutionary confrontations. In contrast to these pariahs, he declared that the PCE was ready to smash the Franco regime by violence. Ironically, he reflected the views of Claudín and Semprún when he acknowledged that the HNP would take time to prepare and that it would be neces-sary to wait for a propitious moment. However, he also aimed both to justify his own triumphalism and to discredit the dissidents when he asked the absurd rhetorical question, 'what would the Party members have said in 1939 if they had been told that Franco would still be in power in 1964?' Ostensibly called to commemorate Grimau, the assembly mainly heard Carrillo chillingly denouncing traitors who he said were in the pay of Manuel Fraga, the minister who had mounted the propaganda campaign against Grimau. Not having been invited, Semprún and Claudín were the only members of the executive not present on the platform. Carrillo did not mention them by name, although that job was done by Party cadres planted in the crowd. The speech was replete with denials of any dogmatism on his own part – a reflection of his own obsession with Claudín's accusation. A somewhat more moderate version was later published as a pamphlet. Carried away by his own pro-Soviet rhetoric, he made the ludicrous statement that 'the Soviet Union will not establish relations with Spain unless it is approved by the Central Committee of the PCE', while the more discreet printed version read 'the Soviet Union will take no step unless it is of assistance to the Spanish people in its fight for democracy'. Jordi Solé Tura, who was in the crowd, recalled that he and many around him found Carrillo's tone alarming.[41]

This theatrical event, together with the documents now distributed, secured knee-jerk support from Central Committee members. Only those in exile received the full minutes of the meeting – those in the interior were sent a distorted résumé. Among the few exceptions was Jordi Solé Tura, who felt impelled by the sinister spectacle of Carrillo's performance on 19 April to join the dissidents: 'it seemed as if, all of a sudden, he was bringing back the macabre rituals of that Stalinism that I had not known but which frightened me'. Puzzled by the savagery of Carrillo's speech, the young Catalan intellectual felt that there was something personal behind it. Certainly, that was what he perceived in Carrillo's repeated rebuttals of what he insisted was Claudín's accusation of his dogmatism. Used to the daily adulation served up by the majority of the executive committee, Carrillo could not bear to be challenged or criticized.[42]

Claudín and Semprún protested to Carrillo about the distortion of their views, but they were simply ignored. Far from arranging the creative debate that they had sought, Carrillo had set up a Manichean situation in which he portrayed any serious consideration of their views as treachery to the PCE. On 3 September 1964, the executive informed Claudín and Semprún of the reaction of the Central Committee's members to the tendentious documents distributed by Carrillo. They pointed out that Party statutes had been flouted by the circulation of distorted versions of their opinions without their having any opportunity to reply. The meeting ratified the earlier decision to suspend them from the executive and effectively excluded them from the Party.[43] Claudín and Semprún rejected the resolution and demanded the right to appeal against it at the next congress. When this was refused, Claudín prepared a lengthy statement of his position in the hope of reopening the debate.

In the meantime, the smear campaign was intensified. At another assembly of 600 cadres held in Paris on 13 September, to which Claudín and Semprún were not invited, Santiago Álvarez made a venomous speech. Having applauded a young militant who, on the basis of the documents distributed by Carrillo, had declared that

Claudín and 'Federico Sánchez' denied the class struggle, he referred to Party militants captured by the Francoist police. Calculatingly, he said, 'I don't know whether the lives and the blood of these comrades matter to Claudín,' and went on to repeat his insinuation that both were in the pay of Manuel Fraga. More directly, he stated that they were objectively helping the enemy despite collecting their wages from the PCE. Since the success in 1963 of his novel *Le Long Voyage*, Semprún was in fact living off his literary earnings, and Claudín immediately renounced his salary and returned the balance of his last pay packet. This was the beginning of an attempt to destroy both men socially and economically. They and their families were shunned by their erstwhile comrades. It was easier for Semprún, given his burgeoning success and celebrity. However, for Claudín, his wife Carmen and their two daughters, Carmen and Tania, the difficulties were immense, and Carrillo soon began to tighten the screws to make it even more difficult.[44]

Carrillo's determination to crush Claudín and Semprún totally was reinforced by the fall of Nikita Khrushchev on 14 October 1964. Regarding himself as the Khrushchev of the PCE, he was stricken with fear that now he might himself fall foul of Moscow's return to Stalinist orthodoxy. He thus produced an article praising the Soviet Union and sought reassurance from Pasionaria, concerned that she might take advantage of the change to reassert her own position. In their exchange of letters, he expressed his total commitment to the Soviet Union and condemned the increasingly independent line of the Italian Party. Once reassured about his own position, he sought, and received, her approval for firm action to extirpate the 'revisionist' threat of Claudín and Semprún.[45]

Presumably unaware of this, Claudín delivered his document to the executive on 8 December 1964 with a letter stating that, since the Party had published a deliberately inaccurate version of what he and Semprún had been arguing, he felt justified in distributing his statement among Party members to rectify the untruths circulated. Helped by Semprún, Solé Tura and Francesc Vicens, and using up his exiguous savings, Claudín published the text as a book in Paris in January 1965. In response, the PCE journal *Nuestra Bandera* reprinted carefully chosen extracts from Claudín's text with a tendentious commentary (in much larger print) under the heading 'Document – Factional Platform of Fernando Claudín'. Claudín was accused of 'wallowing in the opportunist swamp'. There was no debate. In April 1965, Claudín and Semprún were expelled from the Party, a decision about which they learned only when they read the news in *Mundo Obrero*.[46]

The viciousness of the efforts to destroy the lives of Claudín and Semprún revealed the hand of Carrillo even when the immediate instruments were his faithful acolytes Santiago Álvarez and Ignacio Gallego. The speeches and the publications had decimated their social networks among fellow Communists. Now efforts were made to ensure that Claudín could not work. The only documentation that gave him a 'legal' existence in France was a Cuban passport held by the PCE. It was not returned to him. His family lived in a house rented by the PCE. The rent was not paid. Gallego wrote to Carrillo on 17 November 1965:

> We'll show that bastard Claudín what's what, clearly and strongly. We haven't done so yet. But I think that individual won't leave the house. That's my impression. In which case, I think we should not pay a cent. But if he pays the rent himself, it won't be so easy to get him out unless we lean on him, using the landlord, who is French and may not be up for the fight. The first thing to do is lay out the situation clearly and of course not pay the rent for the swine.[47]

In response, Carrillo sent a militant named Pepe to tell Claudín to leave the house. Pepe threatened that, if he did not do so, the PCE would not pay the arrears of rent which went back to long before the expulsion. When Claudín pointed out that he had no money, Pepe told him that he shouldn't therefore have spent what he had to pay for a book attacking the Party.[48]

The Claudín schism left Carrillo with absolute power in the PCE. There was no one left to question him. By depriving the Party of its most creative thinkers, he ensured its impoverishment. He also revealed the extent to which he was skilled in the Stalinist arts of party manipulation. Francesc Vicens, the Catalan Communist leader who was expelled for siding with them, claimed that, given Carrillo's grip on the Party, it was tactical lunacy for Claudín to have raised the issue at executive committee level. In his view, the tactic which should have been applied was for Claudín and Semprún to persuade Carrillo privately that the official line was in error and that he should push the new orientation as his own. That would hardly have favoured the creation of a more flexible and democratic structure which was largely the point of the exercise.[49] In his reply to the Central Committee, Claudín quoted a similar expression of disbelief made by an anonymous fellow member of the executive committee (whom he revealed in 1977 to have been Gregorio López Raimundo): 'Even though you're right, you should submit; you've eaten so much shit in your life, why not continue? I replied: there are limits to everything, even the consumption of shit. And the fact is that I believe that the time has come for the Party to abandon this horrible and indigestible diet. I think it's time that in the Party we debate with arguments, with reasons, with data, with facts and not with shit.'[50]

Carrillo subsequently argued that his actions had been motivated by concern that the Claudín–Semprún interpretation of the situation would demoralize the rank and file. He was worried that they would reject the Party line, saying, 'leave us in peace to earn our living, don't ask us to sacrifice our lives and our freedom, leave us alone until there is actually some point to taking part in the struggle'. In arguing thus, Carrillo obscured the personal resentment that motivated the fury with which he set out to crush Claudín and Semprún. He also expressed a fear that their interpretation implied that a situation might develop in which democracy could be achieved without the PCE, revealing thereby that his Party organization was much more important to him than the cause of democracy to which he claimed to be devoted. He was effectively saying that he thought he could get away with lying to the Party membership for many years to come.[51] In any case, what Claudín and Semprún were arguing was not nearly as negative as Carrillo chose to make it seem. Rather, a recognition of a changing society opened many more possibilities of alliances against the regime.[52]

Carrillo would continue to throw doubt on the analysis of Claudín and Semprún even after he had started to incorporate it into his own writings.[53] Indeed, he insinuated in his famous conversations with Max Gallo and Régis Debray that they had been deceived by the boasts of the Opus Dei technocrats who were overseeing economic development within the regime. Playing on the saying that 'se tromper, c'est avoir raison trop tôt', he also claimed, mendaciously, that he had bent over backwards to avoid a rupture. What he meant, of course, was that they had failed to take the opportunity to submit humbly to his line. That could be seen in his claim that, by carrying the polemic into the wider arena of the Party, they were creating a faction that would paralyse the PCE's freedom of action. He asserted that the publication of their views within the Party – and therefore questioning his authority – was 'a far too expensive luxury for a clandestine party'. Nevertheless, he also claimed that the entire affair had been extremely painful because he and Claudín had worked together since their time in the leadership of the JSU in the 1930s. In fact, opening a debate was a far cry from the conspiratorial activity of factionalism. Moreover, the viciousness with which Carrillo had spread a distorted version of the Claudín–Semprún thesis in order to generate support for their expulsion did not suggest that he was inhibited by regret.

In his numerous later accounts of the crisis, vibrating with barely concealed malice, Carrillo tried to divert attention from the discrepancies between his analysis and that of Claudín and Semprún by implying that they had simply wanted to give up the struggle for personal reasons. In his memoirs, Carrillo went further, alleging that both Claudín and Semprún had already decided to leave the PCE and therefore choreographed their own expulsion. He claimed that Semprún wanted to pursue his vocation as a writer and was just looking for an excuse to leave his arduous work as the coordinator of the Party's clandestine work in the interior. Similarly, on numerous later occasions, he quoted Claudín saying to him in the midst of the conflict: 'Santiago, I'm fifty-two years old and still have done nothing in my life. I can't face any more leadership meetings.' From this, he claimed, it could be deduced that, if Claudín believed that his contribution to keeping the PCE alive during the long years of dictatorship did not constitute a satisfactory outcome of his life so far, it meant that he was determined to leave. Claudín himself put a different gloss on this. He admitted that he was weary of the meetings in which conformity mattered more than truth. This, he was sure, was something that Carrillo could never understand since, for him, such meetings 'were like oxygen. I've often thought that he enjoyed those meetings more than sex.'[54]

The reduction of the conflict to alleged personal crises in the lives of Claudín and Semprún was Carrillo's way of obscuring his own aggression throughout the affair and of masking the importance of the issues raised. In 1983, he published his transcript of the conversation with Claudín on 8 January 1964, discussed earlier. It is certainly true that Claudín stated then that he did not enjoy Party work and that he had long wanted to be able to devote himself to theoretical research. However, at no point did he say that he wanted to give up a leading role in the PCE. His most repeated point is that the overwhelming authority enjoyed by Carrillo was the principal obstacle to creative discussion.[55] Moreover, Carrillo's claim to Debray and Gallo that Claudín and Semprún were always welcome in his home in Paris hardly chimed with the efforts made to evict Claudín from his home or with the obstacles put in the way of him finding work once his meagre salary as a Party functionary was withdrawn. This was less of a problem for Semprún who, since the publication of Le Long Voyage, was already on the verge of international celebrity as a novelist and scriptwriter. That Carrillo resented the success of someone whom he had considered to be his protégé was revealed in a letter to Pasionaria written shortly after the April 1964 meeting in Paris. He referred to Semprún as 'a lying posh boy' (señorito mentiroso). The crime of Claudín and Semprún had been to keep arguing when they were in a minority, and now the principal task was 'to neutralize their right-wing positions'.[56] Carrillo's claim that he maintained cordial relations with both is belied by the malice of his later attacks on them.

Carrillo's Stalinist approach to the Claudín–Semprún crisis could be seen also in the way that, shortly after publicly trashing their ideas, he quickly set about incorporating those same ideas into the Party line. That he should do so showed that his brutal efforts to silence them had little justification other than his personal resentments. This became clear at the PCE's Seventh Congress held in a school at Choisy-le-Roi near Paris from 6 to 11 August 1965. The congress was prepared in great haste because its primary objective was to wrap up the loose ends of the Claudín expulsion. It was held in near secrecy even within the usual norms of clandestinity. Indeed, at various points, the delegates were asked not to applaud lest they be heard outside. This was in large measure because, after the relatively well-publicized Sixth Congress, so many delegates had been arrested on their return to Spain. It also reflected a desire for a discreet resolution to the expulsion. There were no references to it in PCE periodical publications, and none of the reports was published as such.

Carrillo's boastful and self-satisfied report to the congress, which took him a day and a half to deliver, denounced Claudín, Semprún and Vicens, and hypocritically praised the 'democratic' manner in which their arguments had been dismantled: 'the Party has faced a right-wing and liquidationist attack, all the more serious because it was mounted by two Party leaders who were isolated in the executive committee and the Central Committee and then in all our wider organizations, after a process of discussion that was the widest and most democratic possible in a Party that has to function in the conditions of fascist illegality'. He then reaffirmed his view that a broad front of forces could rapidly overthrow the isolated Francoist clique of landowners and financiers. Nevertheless, there were indications within it that he was already on the way to adopting the positions for which Claudín and Semprún had been vilified, in the form of references to the long-term decomposition of the Franco regime.[57]

There was an endless procession of militants from the interior who ratified the correctness of Carrillo's commitment to the national political strike. Then Eduardo García, as organization secretary, made a report in which he stressed the importance of a strong executive.[58] In his closing speech, Carrillo himself claimed proudly that the PCE had been involved in 'a great debate' which, with equal self-satisfaction, he declared to be over. He suggested that 'without impatience, without hurry' the Party had to undertake the important task of organization and preparation needed to take advantage of changing circumstance. It was an implicit acknowledgement of the validity of the theses of Claudín and Semprún and also demonstrated the absurdity of his catastrophist arguments that to adopt those theses would destroy the Party.[59]

In fact, the choreography was not quite as trouble free as it might have been. Among the Central Committee members who had received a distorted version of what Claudín and Semprún had argued were several who were in Burgos jail. These included Miguel Núñez and Pere Ardiaca of the PSUC and Ramón Ormazábal of the Basque Communist Party. On the basis of their own experiences in clandestinity, they believed that Carrillo had underestimated the extent of social and economic change in Spain and therefore concluded that the PCE's alliance strategy was insufficiently daring. That part of their analysis had similarities with the Claudín–Semprún analysis, but it was dramatically different in that they still retained their faith in the efficacy of the HNP if only it could be organized rapidly and energetically. They managed to get an eighty-page document expounding their rather contradictory views transmitted to Carrillo. In it, they accused him of being over-cautious, virtually of being a Claudinista. Needless to say, the document was not made available to those attending the congress on the grounds that there were insufficient copying facilities available and that its contents would shock those present.

Nevertheless, their views were subjected to a fierce attack delivered by León Lorenzo, a Central Committee member from Madrid. It is reasonable to suppose that his intervention had been scripted, or at least edited, by Carrillo, who thereby reacted to what he again chose to interpret as a challenge to his authority. The Burgos trio were denounced, as the recently expelled Claudín and Semprún had been, for their audacity in criticizing Carrillo and the executive committee. They were subjected to a lesson in the need for democratic centralism. That was all to be expected. However, what was really surprising was that they were also censured for not accepting that the HNP was still far in the future. In terms that could have been formulated by Claudín, Lorenzo castigated them for suggesting, as Carrillo used to do, that the HNP was just around the corner: 'these comrades do not understand, or they have forgotten, that every general strike always has been, is and always will be the fruit of long, laborious, uneven preparation, not of declarations in meetings, above all the result of the patient organization and building up of the working masses'.[60]

Immediately after the congress ended, a plenary meeting of the Central Committee was held. Now Carrillo himself denounced the Burgos document as negative and made a comment that exposed his rejection of any criticism no matter how constructive: 'if each group of Central Committee members thinks of itself as a Party leadership centre, there will be no leadership nor indeed will there be any Party at all'. He declared benevolently that he accused the three men not of being 'enemy agents' but of unreliability. After receiving a fierce letter from the executive, they all dropped their criticisms, made an auto-critique and accepted Party discipline.[61]

The interventions at the Seventh Congress demonstrated that, in his fiftieth year, his control over the PCE undisputed, his willpower undiminished, Carrillo had the confidence now to start altering the Party line in accordance with the arguments mobilized by Claudín. The specific points made by Claudín and Semprún about the PCE had been taken up on a European scale by Palmiro Togliatti in the document known as the *Promemoria di Yalta*. This memorandum had been written in Yalta on the Black Sea where Togliatti was waiting for a meeting with Khrushchev. It was basically a call for Khrushchev to go further with the liberalization announced in 1956. Togliatti died before the scheduled meeting and the document was published shortly afterwards by his successor in the PCI, Luigi Longo.[62] At first, Carrillo, who had started to see one of his old Comintern mentors as an anti-Soviet revisionist, was unmoved by Togliatti's appeal in favour of more internal discussion and democracy. However, his stance would soon change.

The revelations of the Twentieth Congress of the CPSU had convinced Carrillo that the USSR was on the road to democratiz-ation. One of his initial differences with Claudín and Semprún was what he saw as their dangerous and gratuitous efforts to examine the nature of Soviet socialism. Indeed, in the course of his attacks on them, he declared that the PCE would never adopt anti-Soviet positions merely to facilitate an alliance with bourgeois elements.[63] Having based his own form of disciplined and limited change on the model of Khrushchev, Carrillo had been confused by the manner of his mentor's fall from grace in October 1964. Nevertheless, throughout the 1960s, despite persisting with the idea of the national general strike criticized by Claudín and Semprún, he made increasing theoretical concessions to them without, of course, admitting the fact. From 1965 to 1970, the only public acknowledgement of debate within the PCE came in the form of Carrillo's speeches and writings published as books and articles. In this format, they had far greater impact than as internal Party reports, and they had the advantage of spreading the idea that the Spanish Communist Party was Santiago Carrillo. Bit by bit, he was adopting positions similar to those for which Claudín and Semprún had been expelled. Contrary to his predictions that to do so would destroy the morale of Party members, his calls for patience had no negative effects, as surely he knew all along. Nevertheless, without ever renouncing his commitment to the national political strike, many of his declarations were still characterized precisely by the complacent over-optimism or 'triumphalism' criticized by his erstwhile comrades.[64]

His acceptance that the development of neo-capitalism was gradually producing a dissident bourgeoisie, his most explicit recognition of the validity of Claudín's analysis, came in the form of his adoption of the mantra of 'the alliance of the forces of labour and of culture', which replaced the old revolutionary slogan 'the alliance of workers and peasants'.[65] This also reflected an awareness that, along with economic development, there was a massive expansion of Spanish universities. In consequence, many students were joining the PCE as the most serious opposition to the dictatorship. Industrial development was also fomenting a considerable growth of the clandestine Communist unions, the Comisiones Obreras. Ever more confident, Carrillo made overtures to the bourgeoisie so exaggerated as to damage his credibility among many Party militants. His offers to both the army and the Church, while unlikely to convince either generals or bishops, could only disillusion the more committed Party cadres. It is difficult to know whether he actually believed his optimistic predictions about the readiness of Catholics and military officers to embrace the PCE's plans for a future democratic Spain or was simply endeavouring to keep up the spirits of the militants.

In the case of the Church, Carrillo was perhaps carried away by a number of signs whose impact he overestimated. Since the 1950s, there had been Catholic groups such as the Hermandad Obrera de Acción Católica (the Workers' Fraternity of Catholic Action, HOAC) and its youth branch the Juventud Obrera Católica (the Catholic Workers' Youth Movement, JOC), both of which were increasingly committed to social justice. From them, there had emerged, in response to the beginnings of industrial development, the phenomenon of worker-priests who collaborated with the clandestine Communist unions. Then there was Pope John XXIII's Second Vatican Council which had begun its work in October 1962 and the consequent surge of activities within Spain by Christian Democrat groups. The Pope's encyclical of 1961 *Mater et Magistra* had talked of just wages and humane conditions for industrial and agricultural labourers, redistributive taxes and trade union rights. At the Munich congress, Catholics and monarchists had consorted with exiled democrats, and groups sponsored by the Church were at the heart of the reviving internal opposition. Within Spain, there had emerged the influential and tentatively liberal Catholic journal *Cuadernos para el Diálogo*, and the Church's own semi-official weekly *Ecclesia* showed increasing concern for social issues. Carrillo derived hope from the activities of the one-time Francoist Minister of Education Joaquín Ruiz Giménez, who had lost his job because of his liberal initiatives in support of students. Similarly, he applauded the work in Seville of the Christian Democrat Manuel Giménez Fernández, who was to be a great inspiration to the future PSOE leader Felipe González.[66]

However, despite Carrillo's optimism, the attitude of Gil Robles at Munich showed that the Christian Democrats were still far from ready to receive overtures from the Communist Party. Moreover, although there was a liberal wing within the Church, especially in Catalonia and the Basque Country, and even a left wing within HOAC and JOC, there was not the remotest chance of the deeply reactionary ecclesiastical hierarchy in Spain being open to any project for the future that involved the Communist Party.[67] In the case of the military, Carrillo was much influenced by a book published in 1967 by one of the most liberal officers therein, Captain Julio Busquets, future founder of the Unión Militar Democrática. He latched on to the points made by Busquets to the effect that the officer corps had changed since the 1940s and that the domination of the sons of the landed oligarchy was no longer apparent. Nevertheless, he was wildly over-optimistic in his conviction that, since sociologically the army of the mid-1960s was no longer the army of the Civil War, it was therefore ripe for alliance with the PCE.[68]

Carrillo chose to ignore the fact that a generation of ultra hard-line generals dominated Franco's high command. Most had joined the army as volunteers during the Civil War, becoming acting second lieutenants or *alféreces provisionales*, and by the mid-1960s were reaching posts of crucial importance in the military hierarchy. Even those not actively linked to the Falange had passed through the deeply reactionary Academia General Militar where they had been indoctrinated with a fierce anti-communism and the belief that the army was the supreme arbiter of the nation's political destiny.[69] As Carrillo and indeed the entire democratic spectrum in Spain would discover in the 1970s, iron loyalty to Franco ensured that the one-time *alféreces provisionales* would be the fiercest defenders of the regime in its dying agony. By the late 1960s, the so-called 'blue [Falangist] generals', such as Alfonso Pérez Viñeta, Tomás García Rebull, Carlos Iniesta Cano and Ángel Campano López, were reaching key operational positions. They and other hard-line Francoists were known as the 'bunker', a reference to the last days of Hitler when he and his followers retreated into the cellars of the Reich Chancellery. In collaboration with their civilian counterparts, they would use their political influence to block reform from within the system and their repressive apparatus to smash opposition from outside.[70]

Fierce criticism of Carrillo's olive branches to the military and ecclesiastical pillars of the Franco regime was aroused among both young leftists and the older Stalinists within the Party. The theoretical concessions that Carrillo had to make in order to construct an appeal to the bourgeois groups simply guaranteed that the PCE would be subject to accusations of treachery and opportunism from leftist youth.[71] There was a widespread belief among younger militants that the representatives of the oligarchy, the Church and the army would negotiate with the Communists only if they could guarantee to control the revolutionary impulses of the working class. Many Party members were convinced that Carrillo was either indulging in self-deception or else was sufficiently ambitious for power to accept what they perceived as such a reactionary role.[72] The first visible sign of that kind of opposition had been the splitting off from the Party of the pro-Chinese youth. They denounced Carrillo's alleged revision-ism and demanded an insurrectionary tactic of armed violence against the regime. Thereafter there was a complex proliferation of Maoist and Trotskyist factions of which the most significant were probably the PCE-ML (Marxista-Leninista), the PCE-Internacional, Bandera Roja, the Organización Revolucionaria de los Trabajadores and the Liga Comunista Revolucionaria.[73]

The existence of these myriad factions committed to revolutionary violence created serious difficulties for Carrillo's attempts to fashion a moderate image for the Party. Sporadic acts of violence merely confirmed for many of the middle classes the regime's denunciation of communism as violent and anarchic. Public opinion in general did not follow the doctrinal twists and turns of these groups and simply saw them all as 'Communists'. Violent actions against the regime also led to indiscriminate reprisals. The most notorious of the activist groups grew out of the PCE-ML. Known as FRAP, the Frente Revolucionario Anti-fascista y Patriota, it was created in January 1971 by Julio Álvarez del Vayo in a Paris flat belonging to Arthur Miller, the playwright who had been married to Marilyn Monroe.[74] The FRAP aimed at creating a broad front of groups dedicated to the violent overthrow of Francoism. Their ambitions never got beyond the PCE- ML and its student group FUDE (Federation of Democratic University Students). The most significant FRAP action would be the assassination of a secret policeman on May Day 1973 which, as even the FRAP's own bulletin admitted, provoked a tremendous wave of arrests and the torture of leftists not connected with the incident.[75] The killing also led to the establishment of Admiral Carrero Blanco's dour cabinet and thus to suspicions that the FRAP had been infiltrated by agents provocateurs.

All of this was in the future. In the second half of the 1960s, Carrillo found himself having to consider whether his fervently pro-Soviet line was an obstacle to his desire to forge alliances with bourgeois forces in Spain. Some of the most venomous criticisms directed at Semprún and Claudín in the 1964 conflict had focused on their attempts to question the socialist nature of the Soviet regime. At that time, Carrillo still had faith in Khrushchev's ability to correct the bureaucratic degeneration of Stalinism. Having based his own brand of tightly controlled and limited reform on that of Khrushchev, he had been seriously disorientated by the unexpected disgrace of the Russian leader in 1964.[76] Thereafter, and until 1968, a certain ambiguity came to be increasingly discernible in his many references to the Soviet Union. On the one hand, the habits of thirty years of unqualified support for Moscow prevailed, most notably in his vituperative attacks on the Chinese.[77] On the other, there began to emerge glimmers of independent thinking which derived partly from his unease with the dour leadership of Leonid Brezhnev. He was also coming to recognize that national reconciliation required that the PCE convince potential allies that it was untainted by the dictatorial habits of the Russians.[78]

With the PCE still in clandestinity and persecuted by the Francoist police, with its leadership in exile and dependent on international, and particularly Russian, solidarity, Carrillo's early efforts in this regard were tentative and ambiguous. As late as 1967, ritual sycophantic articles about the Soviet leadership and the achievements of the Russian revolution abounded in the PCE press. However, despite his declarations that the Soviet Union would never establish relations with Franco without his approval, he cannot have been unaware of the growing warmth of relations between Moscow and Madrid. In 1966, he cautiously criticized the trial in Moscow of the satirists Andrei Sinyavsky and Yuli Daniel which signalled the end of the liberalization process opened in 1956. However, at the same time, on his orders Manuel Azcárate undermined an attempt to assemble a petition of protest by Spanish writers. In November 1967, Carrillo, along with

Pasionaria and others, was received in the Kremlin by Brezhnev and Boris Ponomarev, now head of the International Department of the CPSU. Carrillo was seriously nonplussed when they argued that it was time for the PCE to advocate a monarchist succession to Franco. He was even more distressed when an article signed by 'Ardatovski' appeared in *Izvestiya*, the official mouthpiece of the Soviet government. Carrillo arranged for the PCE to reply with an article in *Mundo Obrero*, entitled 'No camarada Ardatovski'. It was couched in deeply respectful terms towards the Kremlin and it brought forth an apology.[79] Carrillo later made a revealing remark about this incident in his interviews with Debray and Gallo. He told them that when the Soviet leadership reproached him for wishing to be independent, he said, 'It's not what we want; it's what our policy needs.'[80]

Before this, in a report to the Central Committee in early 1967, published as *Nuevos enfoques a problemas de hoy*, Carrillo had tentatively confronted the issue of the lack of democracy in Eastern Europe, albeit trying feebly to explain it away in terms of the exigencies of the Cold War. He admitted that a fervently pro-Soviet Communist Party committed to the dictatorship of the proletariat was unlikely to attract bourgeois allies.[81] At the same time, references to the narrow Francoist clique started to disappear from his writings. Instead there emerged a more realistic assessment of the fact that the bourgeoisie was benefiting from economic growth under the new technocratic policies but might well come to resent the regime's archaic political machinery. Committed as he was to his new slogan of 'the alliance of the forces of labour and culture', Carrillo had come out in favour of the student movement in France in May 1968.[82] Similarly, his combination of a critical approach to the Soviet bloc with a more flexible line regarding relations with other groups inside Spain was clinched by the developments in Czechoslovakia after the fall of President Novotny. Carrillo had seized on these developments as proof that socialism and liberty were compatible. Enthusiasm for the Prague Spring and Alexander Dubček's advocacy of socialism with a human face was combined with praise for the tolerance of the USSR.[83]

Carrillo's optimism was initially fed by reports from Francisco Antón, who was now in Prague. It was short lived. He was about to face what he later called 'one of the bitterest moments of my life as a Communist'. In July 1968, he had been informed by the Russian Ambassador in Paris that the Soviet Union intended to put a stop to the Czech experiment. He thus had three weeks in August to reflect on how to react when the inevitable blow fell. He informed the Russians that, if an invasion took place, the PCE would condemn it publicly. Initially, he decided to cancel his holidays in the Crimea as the guest of the CPSU. However, at a conference in Bratislava attended by representatives of the East German, Hungarian, Polish, Bulgarian, Czech and Russian leaderships, it looked as if the crisis had been averted. In a declaration on 14 August, the PCE announced its delight at this apparent resolution of the crisis. Reassured, Carrillo and his family went to Russia accompanied by Francisco Romero Marín and Simón Sánchez Montero. On the morning of 21 August, he was awoken with the news that Russian troops were in Prague. After the great enthusiasm that he had expressed for the Prague Spring, he was placed in an extremely awkward position by the Soviet action.

The censorious publicity given in Spain to the invasion was seriously damaging to the PCE's national reconciliation strategy. Nevertheless, it seemed inconceivable that the PCE would make a stand against Moscow since it had traditionally been regarded as one of the most loyally subordinate of the national parties. Just a year before, Carrillo had authorized a virulent campaign against Mao Zedong during the Sino-Soviet dispute, which had intensified in 1966 with the launch of the Chinese Cultural Revolution and which by 1967 had degenerated into border disputes. With the PCE's exiled leadership dependent on Soviet funding, Carrillo was hardly in a position to condemn the Russian action in Czechoslovakia. Yet to maintain the PCE's credibility as a moderate democratic segment of the anti-Franco opposition, he had to condemn the Soviet intervention and risk open conflict with the CPSU and accusations of anti-Sovietism, nationalism and revisionism.

Thus he left his dacha and went to Moscow where he and Dolores Ibárruri had a very tense meeting with Brezhnev's second-in-command, Mikhail Suslov, and Ponomarev on 24 August. Carrillo announced that he would have to criticize the invasion. He disputed the absurd official line that Soviet intervention had been requested by the Czech leadership. In front of Luigi Longo and Gian Carlo Pajetta of the PCI, Suslov brutally reminded Pasionaria and Carrillo of the PCE's dependent position. Suslov's tone can hardly have come as a surprise to Carrillo, who had known him since Stalin's meeting with the Spanish Communist delegation in 1948 and was probably aware that he had played a key role in the purges of Russians who had fought for the Republic during the Spanish Civil War. Certainly, the insulting reminder that his was a small party made him more determined to stick to his guns. He left for Bucharest in order to use Radio España Independiente to broadcast his denunciation of the Russians. In Bucharest, he held discussions with the Romanian Communist Party and then, in Rome, with the PCI. Both shared his opposition to the Czech invasion.[84]

On the eve of Carrillo's return to Paris, Agustín Gómez Pagola, since 1960 effective head of the Basque Communist Party, wrote an emotive letter to Dolores Ibárruri. Hitherto, Gómez had been a loyal component of Carrillo's team. Born in Rentería in 1924, he had been evacuated to Russia in 1937 and educated there. Now, as well as declaring his support for the Soviet action 'to suppress counter-revolution', he expressed his concern about attempts by Carrillo and others 'for some time now to spread doubts and undermine confidence in the CPSU'.[85] Gómez was not the only executive member to think along those lines. Nevertheless, the following day Carrillo was able to convince the PCE executive committee to issue a statement that was far from being a condemnation. There was only one dissident voice, that of Eduardo García, the Party's organization secretary, and a KGB agent. The declaration began with an assertion of loyalty to the USSR: 'We proclaim and we will always proclaim with pride our commitment to the glorious Socialist Revolution of October 1917, our solidarity with the achievements of the Soviet people and of the CPSU and our intimate friendship with the Soviet Union. We condemn with the greatest energy any attempt to use the tragic error committed in Czechoslovakia to denigrate the glorious history of the CPSU and of the Soviet people.'

However, having noted the 'tragic error', the declaration went on to justify Dubček's daring in terms that inadvertently offended the Soviet leadership even more. Carrillo was effectively embracing Togliatti's 'polycentrism', the notion that divergence should be possible within the Communist world.

> In the international Communist movement there is no longer a party that is the single guide or leader! All parties are equally responsible for the orientation of their own movement ... We are no longer, and we never accepted such a role, simple groups of propagandists of the achievements of socialism in one country or in several. Our aim is to make our own revolution ... the fulfilment of that task necessarily demands that our line takes into account the reality and the peculiarities of our country.

He described this as simply the logical conclusion of Khrushchev's speech to the Twentieth Congress of the CPSU. Nevertheless, with an eye on his potential audience in Spain, he made the extraordinary statement that 'when [not if] the PCE attains power, it will mount fierce resistance to any similar intervention by a socialist country'.[86]

On 15 September, Carrillo spoke to an assembly of militants. He had to be careful since he had hitherto put so much effort into maintaining the PCE's pro-Soviet line and there was considerable rank-and-file sympathy for the invasion, both inside Spain and among the exiles. Accordingly, his speech was full of praise for the Soviet Union and included a defence of the invasions of Hungary and Poland in 1956 which were not to be confused with the error committed in Czechoslovakia. On 18 September, the Central Committee met in Paris to discuss the executive's action. In his report, Carrillo argued that the problem was that the Soviets had let their state interests override their socialist ideals. At one level, this was another step in the direction of adopting the positions of Claudín and Semprún. It was not, however, a very big step. He did not engage in any analysis of the fact that the CPSU leadership had become a sclerotic oligarchy but rather limited himself to declaring that Khrushchev's lead had not been followed by his successors. His essential point, however, aimed at bringing around a Central Committee whose majority was fiercely pro-Soviet, was that the difference with the Russians went no further than this one issue of Czechoslovakia: 'We might disagree with the Soviet Union on one question, but this in no way affects our affection, our devotion, nor our sense of what the Soviet Union represents, nor our readiness to defend the Soviet Union if the Soviet Union were at any time to find itself threatened as it was in 1941.' Although there were numerous speeches in support of the Soviet action, the committee voted by 66 to 5 to accept Carrillo's report. That Dolores Ibárruri did not speak against him certainly worked greatly in his favour.[87]

The scale of Carrillo's effort in this speech suggests that he was far from fully perceiving the real extent of the changes that he had just inaugurated. In fact, in many respects, it would be the Russians rather than Carrillo who would push this dispute to its logical conclusion. The eventual consequence would be his international celebrity as a result of becoming the champion of what came to known as Euro-communism.

The two most notable members of the five who voted against Carrillo in the Central Committee meeting were Eduardo García López and Agustín Gómez Pagola. Born in 1918, García had joined the JSU, fought in the Spanish Civil War and participated in the Second World War in a guerrilla detachment of the NKVD. Agustín Gómez Pagola, who had also fought in the world war, was celebrated in Russia for having played football as centre-half and captain for Moscow Torpedo and had been picked for the Russian Olympic team in 1952. Since 1960, he had been in the Basque Country. On agreeing to abide by the rules of democratic centralism, they were both allowed to keep their posts.[88] In April 1969, Carrillo convened the executive committee to examine their dissidence. He ensured that the dissidents would be given no official opportunity to air their views or rally support.

Although denied access to *Mundo Obrero* and *Nuestra Bandera*, García and Gómez managed to circulate their views among Party militants. They were relatively well received among PCE members resident in the Eastern bloc and among older militants who recalled Russian aid to Spain during the Civil War. Carrillo was furious at what was clearly Soviet-sponsored factionalism. He hardened his position. After the ritual suicide of the student Jan Pallach in Prague on 16 January 1969, he wrote to the CPSU denouncing the situation in Czechoslovakia.[89] Since Gómez and García had some backing within the Party, Carrillo used his control of the internal organization to silence them. On 22 May 1969, a meeting of twenty-seven Central Committee members, out of a total of eighty-nine, voted to exclude Gómez. In July, Carrillo forced García to resign from the secretariat and the executive by threatening him with expulsion from the Party.[90] The pro-Soviet dissidents responded by stepping up their activities, sending a number of documents to Central Committee members accusing Carrillo of being anti-Soviet, a revisionist, a liquidationist, an opportunist and an anti-Marxist. Carrillo responded by asserting that their activities were financed by the Soviet security services. According to Líster, he also spread rumours that they were being paid by the CIA.[91]

At the same time, more direct pressure was brought to bear on Carrillo himself by the Russians. In July, he was to lead a PCE delegation to Moscow to participate in an international conference of Communist parties called in the wake of the Czech crisis. He would be accompanied by Pasionaria, Azcárate and Líster. In fact, Azcárate had tried to persuade Carrillo to withdraw from the conference on the grounds that the Party's credibility demanded a total break with the Russians. Carrillo refused, citing the PCE's economic dependence on Moscow and his conviction that the CPSU would evolve.[92] The text of the PCE intervention had been prepared by Azcárate then submitted for translation into Russian and, from Russian, into other languages. This process offered endless possibilities for the Soviets to put their own spin on what finally appeared. Nevertheless, in tense confrontations during the preparatory meetings, Azcárate managed to save much of a speech that was based on Carrillo's report to the Central Committee in September 1968, with its criticisms of the Czech intervention and its assertions of the right to autonomy of individual Communist parties.

When Carrillo arrived in Moscow, the Spanish delegation was given lavish treatment. This was a softening-up process prior to them being asked to remove the offending points of the PCE intervention. When they refused, they were invited to a meeting with Brezhnev (secretary general of the CPSU), Alexei Kosygin (the Soviet Prime Minister), Nicolai Podgorny (the Soviet President) and Suslov. It began cordially enough, with ample supplies of vodka and caviar. However, Carrillo and Pasionaria were subjected to intense pressure to change their position. When Carrillo held his ground, Brezhnev barked threateningly, 'Think about what you are doing. With this attitude of yours, you are risking a break with a Party with fourteen million members and a country with 250 million inhabitants.' Accordingly, Carrillo's speech to the conference ended with a declaration of faith in the Bolshevik revolution. More importantly, he signed the final communiqué of the conference, something that Enrico Berlinguer, on behalf of the Italian delegation, refused to do. The declaration of approval contradicted his criticisms of the Czech invasion: 'we want to reiterate our friendship with the CPSU and our recognition of the aid that it gives to the peoples who are fighting for their freedom'.[93]

Brezhnev's threat was implemented in renewed Soviet encouragement to Gómez and García, though it is unlikely that a rapprochement between the Kremlin and the Franco regime which allowed the delivery of Polish coal to Spain during the December 1969 Asturian miners' strike was related to the dispute with Carrillo. In response to the Soviet stance, Carrillo took up the challenge and, at a Central Committee meeting held between 27 and 31 December 1969, Gómez and García were expelled from the PCE, despite the resolute opposition of Enrique Líster, who was flattered by the Kremlin into taking up the pro-Soviet banner.[94] At the time, the imminent departure of the Stalinists under Líster seemed even more serious for the PCE than the schism of the Maoists, although in retrospect it turned out to be a blessing in disguise. In Líster's favour, he had the support of the Kremlin and of the substantial group of PCE members resident in Russia – who almost certainly had little choice other than to support the Soviet line. He campaigned actively, through a stream of letters, to have the García–Gómez expulsions revoked and to have Carrillo's stewardship of the Party examined. Several things ensured his defeat: his own chaotic approach, Carrillo's control of the apparatus and the attitude of Pasionaria.

There were various pleas from Líster and others for Dolores Ibárruri to denounce Carrillo. However, she threw her weight behind the secretary general. Despite her own pro-Soviet sympathies, she was presumably reluctant to preside over the disintegration of the PCE. Moreover, she was fully aware that the Party's long-term survival in Spain depended on the more modern positions associated with Carrillo. The secretary general himself took no chances. Líster was simply not informed of the times or places of executive and Central Committee meetings. Finally, in September 1970, a meeting of the Central Committee was convened to resolve the question of Líster's dissidence, which had grown more openly anti-Carrillo. Líster made ever more bitter personal attacks on Carrillo for supposed Stalinist crimes, the guilt for which was to some extent shared by Líster himself as well as, of course, by Claudín and most of the Party leadership. To ensure a majority in his favour, Carrillo co-opted twenty-nine new members on to the Central Committee. Yet again Líster's supporters were not told when or where the session was to be held, and Líster himself was informed at such short notice as hardly to be able to prepare his case. He alleged later that two of his supporters were prevented from entering the plenum and that he himself was physically threatened. The meeting ended with the expulsion from the Party of Líster and four other pro-Soviet dissidents, Celestino Uriarte, Jesús Sáiz, José Bárzana and Luis Balaguer, all one-time residents of the USSR, members of the CPSU and prominent figures in the Russian section of the PCE.[95]

Prevented from presenting their views to the Party, Líster and a considerable number of followers set up a rival PCE. With exiguous funding, Líster, Gómez and García formed their own PCE with its own *Mundo Obrero* and *Nuestra Bandera*, produced in parlous conditions. Consisting of veteran members, it had little long-term future. Nevertheless, the seriousness of the schism was diminished only when Líster's PCE itself became subject to internal divisions, eventually breaking up into fragments led by himself and García. Líster formed yet another party, known as the Partido Comunista Obrero

Español (PCOE). Carrillo had kept the central apparatus of the PCE and therefore had won the day. Even as Russian attacks on him continued, he reacted by gradually using his control of the Party machinery to eliminate not just senior Stalinist elements from his own Party, like García and Gómez, but militants at all levels, and thereby accelerating the process of modernization. Hard-line veterans of the Civil War resident in the East were replaced at all levels of the Party apparatus by working-class militants from within Spain. The Russians were gradually to realize this and to come to terms with the PCE. In any case, while financing the various splinters, they had at no point stopped their economic support for the PCE itself. They now ceased to finance Líster, who survived economically thanks to the support of his family.[96]

This renovation of cadres accelerated the process of modernization and intensified the PCE's sensitivity to developments within Spain.[97] There was an underlying contradiction in this renovation in terms of the entirely Stalinist manner of Carrillo's unilateral co-option of these new cadres. As organization secretary, Carrillo had used his accumulated bureaucratic wisdom as a Stalinist apparatchik to prepare the ground for the renovation of 1954–6. Now, during 1969 and 1970, impelled on the one hand by Russian hostility and on the other by the need to respond to the changing situation inside Spain, he resorted to the same trusted and efficacious methods to give the PCE the image he believed to be essential to its survival. Despite his Stalinist methods, the changes imposed did open up the PCE, made it more attractive to intellectuals and students and ultimately reduced the average age of militants.

The PCE's original criticism of the invasion of Czechoslovakia had not been intended to provoke an all-out confrontation with the CPSU. However, it was the crudity of the Russian response, especially in challenging Carrillo's internal authority in the PCE, that pushed him ever more to outright independence. Forced away from the CPSU, the PCE moved correspondingly nearer to the Italian Communists, another development which was to have a liberalizing effect on the Spanish Party. The reforms begun by Carrillo in the early 1950s in response to developments within the CPSU were thus consolidated nearly twenty years later by the same methods but in reaction against the Russians.

Carrillo's victory was based not least on his iron grip on the apparatus. That was made clear by the report to the amplified plenum of September 1970 made by his now closest collaborator, Ignacio Gallego, who replaced García as organization secretary. Like García and Gómez, the sinuous Gallego had hitherto been notable for his pro-Soviet convictions. Indeed, he remained a recipient of Soviet funds. Recognizing the failures of Líster and García, the Kremlin was now relying on Gallego as its man within the PCE. Like Carrillo before him in relation to Uribe and Pasionaria, Gallego knew how to ingratiate himself with the secretary general. In the face of the evident unease of some Central Committee members regarding the expulsions, Gallego denounced the factional work of Gómez and García, and even more vehemently that of Líster. He contrasted what he described as their calumnies against Carrillo and the leadership with the theoretical stance of Claudín and Semprún.[98] In defence of their expulsion, he declared:

> Each one of us has the right to express and defend his opinion on any problem but here we are not concerned with that right. What we are concerned with is the unity of the party, of its principles of organization, of the attitudes that a militant, and particularly that a member of the central committee, should have towards an attempt to divide the party. In a clandestine party, it is impossible to accept ambiguity regarding a question of this kind. Anyone who fails to condemn and combat the faction is in fact helping it, an attitude incompatible with their presence in the central committee … In these conditions, we cannot allow ourselves to be carried away by an absurd liberalism which would only make us lose time and energy that we need to push forward the efforts of the party on so many fronts to accelerate the fall of the dictatorship.[99]

Gallego's use of the phrase 'un liberalismo absurdo' reinforced the message that there could be no toleration of any deviation from

Carrillo's line. In 1970, Claudín pointed out that the pro-Soviets could have been defeated in open debate and the PCE would have been healthier for the experience:

> The fact that, in the PCE's variant of democratic centralism, centralism has always weighed more than democracy, or to be precise has wiped out democracy, is not the result of clandestinity but rather of Stalinism and the same thing is happening today, as is shown by the way that the leadership has dealt with the conflict with the CPSU and the internal struggle against its own pro-Soviet elements. Why were Eduardo García, Agustín Gómez and the other pro-Soviet elements not allowed to express their points of view freely in *Mundo Obrero* and *Nuestra Bandera*, opening a debate in which, to demolish their positions, it would have been necessary to get to the bottom of the real nature of the Soviet system and of a Stalinist Party, and so on? Why was a similar debate not begun about the Party's problems of strategy and tactics?

Claudín went on to suggest that for the PCE to play its role in the future, a wide-ranging debate was needed, both within the Party and with other left-wing groups, about the nature of the anti-Franco struggle and about the nature of Spanish capitalism. This clearly was not something likely to appeal to Carrillo.[100]

Yet even leaving aside the possibility that the number of veteran Stalinists still in the PCE in the late 1960s obliged Carrillo to act as he did, the fact remains that the Party came out of the crisis of 1968–70 considerably changed in its rank and file if not in its secretary general. Behind his rhetoric of moderation and openness could be discerned Carrillo's reliance on authoritarian methods of Party management. Nevertheless, the effect of the Claudín–Semprún crisis had been, at enormous cost to the Party, to make him more aware of the need to respond to Spanish realities. Now, at greater numerical cost, albeit at lower intellectual and moral cost, the Czechoslovak crisis left the PCE less rigid. Throughout the 1960s, in response to the reforms introduced at the Sixth Congress, the PCE extended its membership in the universities and the factories of a rapidly modernizing Spain. When Carrillo rebranded the strategy of national reconciliation as 'the Pact for Liberty' in 1969, the PCE had become altogether more modern, more moderate and more responsive than it had been ten years earlier. In responding to the challenge sponsored by the Russians in a party with a high proportion of Stalinist veterans he risked Party unity in order to strengthen his own credibility within Spain. His gamble paid off, and it left him and the Party in a strong position to take advantage of the death throes of the regime.

From Public Enemy No. 1 to National Treasure: 1970–2012

Despite his victory over the Stalinists, the García–Gómez–Líster split had been a significant blow to Carrillo, in terms both of morale and of prestige vis-à-vis the non-Communist opposition. It was thus in a mood somewhat less than buoyant that the PCE entered the 1970s. In any case, Stalinist methods or not, the PCE was changing in such a way as to make a return to the past difficult. The removal of the Stalinists obviously made the Party less rigid, a development ostensibly symbolized by Carrillo's choice of the urbane Ignacio Gallego to replace the rather sinister Eduardo García. In fact, Gallego's loyalty to Moscow was hardly less than that of the expelled trio. Nonetheless, there were several other more significant changes in the nature of the PCE. Throughout the 1960s, the Party was extending its membership in the universities and the factories. The presence of students and the growth of the Workers' Commissions imposed upon the rank and file and the middle cadres a need for flexibility in relation to the realities of Spanish society. This was a result both of the reforms introduced at the Sixth Congress and of lessons taught by Claudín which had been gradually assimilated by Carrillo in what Javier Pradera was to call a 'plagiaristic plundering'. In fact, Claudín and others thought that Carrillo went too far in his search for alliances to overthrow the dictatorship.[1] However, the fact remains that the reconciliation strategy, renamed in 1969 the Pact for Liberty, was now being pushed by a Party far more modern, moderate and responsive to social change than the narrow Stalinist organization of the early 1950s.

The growth of highly politicized student movements and powerful semi-clandestine unions was largely a reflection of the vertiginous economic growth of Spain in the 1960s. Yet no other opposition group reacted to the changes as effectively as the PCE. As the Communists became increasingly involved in the mass struggle against the regime, Carrillo began to talk of conquering 'zones of liberty' and 'bases for democratic struggle'. By 1968, such 'zones' were to be found in the growing frequency of strikes, demonstrations and meetings held in the face of police repression. At the same September 1970 session of the PCE Central Committee which saw the expulsion of the Stalinists, Carrillo reported on the Party's 'salida a la superficie', or return to the surface from the catacombs. Although he spoke of collaboration with other liberal and leftist groups, he insisted on what he called the 'leading role' to be played by the PCE. He mocked the pretensions of extremist revolutionary factions to overthrow the dictatorship by armed action – pretensions that he had harboured himself barely six years earlier and which would re-emerge from time to time.

His emphasis on the need for mass action by student, worker and neighbourhood groups was valid evidence that he was adjusting Party policy to the economic and social realities of a rapidly developing Spain. Nevertheless, in an astonishing display of short-sighted egoism, he attributed to his Party – and therefore to himself – the entire credit for the emergence of the new forms of mass opposition to the regime: 'This entire process is not a casual chain of events but rather the fruit of a conscious political strategy. There can be seen clearly the leading role of the Party.' He acknowledged that other groups might be making a contribution to the process and even to be reaching an awareness of the social and political mechanisms at work. However, in an exhibition of self-satisfied triumphalism, he went on to say that 'From the very first, the credit for the idea, the credit for opening up this road when things were very different from now when they are beginning to be clear, a time when many thought that there was no way out; the credit for the initiative belongs to the ability of our Party to apply the Marxist-Leninist method to the specific historical situation.'[2]

To facilitate the 'capture of democracy', in 1970 Carrillo launched a massive recruiting drive called the Promoción Lenin which he hoped would provide mass support for the national general strike. It saw the Party swell not only in the big industrial areas but also in the countryside.[3] Simultaneously, PCE members became more involved in legal associations of housewives, consumers, residents, parents and teachers while Party lawyers were prominent in the defence of trade unionists on trial. All of this constituted, within the limits of the dictatorship, an attempt to emulate the successes of the Italian Communists in municipal governments such as in Bologna, a demonstration that Spanish Communists too were efficient, reliable and helpful.

As a result of the various expulsions throughout the 1960s, Carrillo's authority in the PCE was absolute. Because of the gradual absorption of the ideas of Claudín and the changes imposed by Moscow's brutal reaction to criticism, both the PCE and Carrillo were more ideologically flexible. That, together with the organizational expansion fostered by economic development, masked Carrillo's Stalinist habits when it came to internal Party management. There is little doubt that Communists enjoyed considerable prestige within Spain among non-partisan opponents of the Franco regime. Moreover, the strength of the Workers' Commissions ensured that key figures in the economic elite had little choice but to take the Communists into account when they elaborated their own strategy for survival after Franco. Already in the late 1960s, negotiations had taken place between a few top industrialists and leaders of the Workers' Commissions to bypass the regime's antiquated vertical syndicates. Contacts between Marcelino Camacho and these businessmen were arranged by the wealthy lawyer Antonio García Trevijano.[4]

This tendency increased in the 1970s. Carrillo exploited the foundation of the Assemblea de Catalunya in November 1971 by announcing that the Pact for Liberty was gaining wider relevance than ever before. The Assembly movement included a diverse range of left-wing parties, of which the most important were the Catalan Communist Party, the Partit Socialista Unificat de Catalunya; a number of working-class organizations, of which the dominant one was the Workers' Commissions; and a broad span of legal associations. The Assembly was represented all over Catalonia and, apart from its wide spectrum of popular support, included bankers among its leaders. It soon revealed a capacity for mass mobilization in the form of amnesty demonstrations which were to reach their apogee in 1976. Carrillo began to claim that similar organizations, known as 'democratic platforms', were starting to appear in Andalusia, Aragon, Valencia and Asturias. However, these tended to be exclusively Communist initiatives rather than the broad-based entities that he hailed. In an echo of his optimism for the HNP, his anxiety to evangelize the Pact for Liberty saw him exaggerating the strength of these platforms.[5]

Theoretical and organizational preparations for the future inside Spain were made at the very brief Eighth Congress held in the PCF's chateau near Arras in the late summer of 1972. Carrillo dismissed the hopes nurtured by some moderate opposition groups that it would be possible to negotiate a future transition to democracy when Prince Juan Carlos succeeded Franco, thus bypassing the Prince's father Don Juan de Borbón, the legitimate pretender to the Spanish throne: 'Juan Carlos is Franco's creature, educated under his control. He has sworn to implement fascist principles, the Principios del Movimiento [the Francoist laws].' Confident that the Assemblea de Catalunya was a first step to the Pact for Liberty, he began to talk of it as an instrument for a 'democratic break' (*ruptura democrática*): 'Who could realistically imagine the passage from a fascist dictatorship to a democracy without a true political revolution?' This would require force, and that meant a mass movement along the lines of the Huelga Nacional Pacífica. Clearly, he was still some way from adopting the positions for which Claudín had been expelled. Indeed, as Claudín later commented, the *ruptura* outlined at the Eighth Congress was very like the revolution of February 1917, the prelude to the Bolshevik revolution of October. It was difficult to see why bourgeois forces would prefer the *ruptura* with its prospect of a subsequent revolution to some kind of negotiated transition.

A substantial number of young militants from inside Spain were incorporated into the Central Committee. These included some, like Nicolás Sartorius and Carlos Alonso Zaldívar, who in the mid-1970s would be his allies in an apparent liberalization of the Party, only to become his enemies in the 1980s when it grew clear that the changes were cosmetic. Among them was the head of the PCE's university section, the attractive twenty-nine-year-old Pilar Brabo. She became Carrillo's confidante, and perhaps something more as she accompanied him on foreign trips. Her devotion remained total until, concerned that she was becoming too ready to criticize him, he increasingly distanced himself from her from 1978 onwards.[6]

While the opposition was growing more daring and coming out on to the streets, the regime was enjoying continued economic expansion and had its arrangements for the future well prepared. The hope that this process would continue and lead to a bloodless overthrow of the dictatorship received a heavy blow when violence by militants of the FRAP (Frente Revolucionario Anti-fascista y Patriota) was instrumental in provoking the formation of the hard-line government of Admiral Luis Carrero Blanco in June 1973. Constituted to carry out a holding operation to cover the transition from Franco to his designated successor, Prince Juan Carlos, it was a cabinet that not only augured a return to 1940s-style Francoism but also had every indication of longevity.[7] Two of the three major divisions which had sundered the PCE in the 1960s, those of the pro-*chinos* and the pro-*soviéticos*, had been provoked by Carrillo's need to maintain the credibility of his moderate policies. It now began to look as if the sacrifice had been in vain. A broad coalition with bourgeois forces seemed as far off as ever and the regime looked as strong as it had ever been.

However, in late 1973, the final crisis of the Franco regime began. The prosperity which was the dictatorship's main claim to the loyalty of industrialists and bankers was undermined by soaring energy prices. This was the consequence of an oil embargo imposed by the Organization of Arab Petroleum Exporting Countries in retaliation for American support of Israel during the Yom Kippur War in October. The prospect of future labour discontent as prosperity diminished was a considerable stimulus to capitalists in Spain to contemplate negotiation with the Workers' Commissions if not actually with the PCE. They realized that the antiquated and semi-fascist structures of the dictatorship would be incapable of resolving the forthcoming economic crisis without damaging confrontations. Accordingly, their readiness to accept some kind of political reform began to coincide with popular pressure for change. This convergence of interests gave the Pact for Liberty an apparent relevance and thus enabled the PCE to play a crucial role in the events of 1975–7, if hardly the one predicted by Carrillo at the Eighth Congress. Nevertheless, the Franco regime was far from helpless. The armed forces and the police were intact and Franco's plans for the succession of Juan Carlos under the tutelage of Admiral Carrero Blanco were well laid. In an outright conflict between the forces of reaction and those advocating change, the odds lay with the dictatorship.

Nevertheless, as economic problems pushed the working class towards the kind of mass action long predicted by Carrillo, the Francoist elite was seriously undermined by the assassination of Admiral Carrero Blanco on Thursday 20 December 1973. On that day, the show trial (Proceso 1.001) of ten leaders of the PCE's underground trade union, Comisiones Obreras, was due to commence, as a demonstration of the regime's determination to crush the clandestine unions. Shortly before 9.30 a.m., a squad of ETA activists detonated an explosive charge in the street under Carrero Blanco's car as he returned from daily mass. Carrillo himself was seriously alarmed by the news of the assassination. He feared that it would lead to a night of the long knives against the left and was desperate to show that the PCE had had nothing to do with the action. Subsequently he claimed that the Basque separatists of ETA had chosen the day of the 1.001 trial specifically in order to damage the PCE. His perverse logic perhaps derived from the fact that the ETA commando had had contact with two renegade Communists, Eva Forest and Alfonso Sastre.[8]

On the day, he received a reassuring phone call from a Madrid lawyer, Antonio García López, a Social Democrat close to Dionisio Ridruejo. García López transmitted a message from an unnamed senior member of the General Staff reassuring him that there would be no bloodshed. Carrillo believed, erroneously, that the message came directly from the Chief of the General Staff, General Manuel Díez Alegría. Nevertheless, it did come from someone who reflected the Chief's views. Carrillo knew that the Director General of the Civil Guard, the extreme rightist Carlos Iniesta, had drafted an order for his men to repress leftists and demonstrators energetically, using firearms if they felt it necessary. Iniesta was abusing his authority by ordering the Civil Guard to go beyond its rural jurisdiction and act in the towns. On the advice of Díez Alegría, within less than an hour a triumvirate consisting of the Deputy Prime Minister Torcuato Fernández Miranda, the Minister of the Interior Carlos Arias Navarro and the senior military minister Admiral Gabriel Pita da Veiga had ordered Iniesta to withdraw his telegram before it reached the local garrisons.[9] In fact, what Iniesta did not know was that his chief of staff, Colonel José Antonio Sáenz de Santa María, had deliberately refrained from sending the telegram.[10] In consequence, Carrillo would tell the Central Committee four months later that senior officers, by preventing a bloodbath, had shown that everything was possible.[11]

In the meantime, seeing the Assemblea de Catalunya as just the sort of vehicle required for the conquest of 'zones of liberty', Carrillo was continuing his efforts to emulate the PSUC's success in other parts of Spain. And as the PCE grew nearer to representatives of the Spanish bourgeoisie, so it grew further away from the USSR. At a Central Committee meeting in September 1973, Carrillo had pointed to the Carrero Blanco government as evidence of the decadence of the regime. Accordingly, he had sought and received formal permission for the executive committee to establish contacts with 'representatives of neo-capitalist groups' in order to take advantage of the discontent of the bourgeoisie. In fact, there had been prior contacts with bankers and senior members of the Catholic hierarchy. These had been initiated by the three senior PCE members in Madrid, the veteran Francisco Romero Marín, the novelist Armando López Salinas and Jaime Ballesteros Pulido. Indeed, Carrillo himself had met one of the principal advisers of Juan Carlos's father Don Juan de Borbón, the repentant ex-Francoist José María de Areilza, in Paris in 1969. Such contacts became more intense after the Carrero Blanco assassination.[12]

In the same session of the Central Committee, on Carrillo's instructions Manuel Azcárate delivered a report on the PCE's international policy in which he stated that the fusion of the CPSU and the Soviet state rendered true democratic socialism impossible in Russia. This was to provoke a broadside from the Soviet Party accusing him of being an enemy of the USSR.[13] Seriously displeased, Carrillo believed that Azcárate had gone too far and ensured that he never again delivered a report on the PCE's international policy. However, when in February 1974 the CPSU journal *Partiinaya Zhizn* made a scathing attack on Azcárate's report, Carrillo quickly arranged for the executive committee to publish and distribute a substantial and well-produced pamphlet containing Azcárate's report, the Russian reply and the PCE's counter-reply. He was fully aware that acrimonious exchanges with the Kremlin could attract valuable media attention. He thereby managed not only to publicize the rift as evidence of the PCE's independence but also to give the impression that the Party conducted all its affairs in public. As Azcárate himself explained, 'Carrillo remained as ever committed to the traditional ideas of a monolithic party but at the same time he was convincing himself that, without a critical attitude towards the Soviet Union and a close friendship with the PCI to help dispel the memory of what the PCE had been during the Civil War, it would not be possible for the Communists ever to occupy a significant space within Spanish democracy.'[14]

The ambiguity of his approach could be plainly discerned in his report to a plenary meeting of the Central Committee in late April 1974. Recounting the Soviet attack on Azcárate and his decision to publish both it and the offending report, he proudly praised his own approach to internal debate. It should be, he declared, 'not like something hidden in closed meetings or interviews but rather as a friendly criticism between comrades, without distortions or simplifying things into black and white, and of course without anathemas or excommunications'. He had apparently already forgotten how he had dealt with Antón, Uribe, Claudín and Semprún, Gómez, García and Líster, and many more less prominent comrades. Interestingly, he went on to express a firm desire to see an improvement in relations between the PCE and the CPSU. Nevertheless, he stressed his view that every Communist Party was free to elaborate its own policy in accordance with the circumstances of its own country.[15]

After the death of Carrero Blanco, various Francoist elements began to jockey for power. As the regime's forces began to fragment, the Pact for Liberty suddenly seemed to have acquired wider relevance than it had had before. Several events elsewhere in Europe in the first half of 1974 reinforced the impression that the initiative was slipping away from the right: in Portugal the fall of Marcelo Caetano (25 April), in Italy the overwhelming defeat of the Christian Democrat Prime Minister Amintore Fanfani in the referendum on the proposed repeal of the divorce law (12 May), in France the good showing by the Socialist François Mitterrand in the presidential elections (5 and 19 May, in which he was defeated by Valéry Giscard d'Estaing by only 424,599 votes) and in Greece the collapse of the colonels' dictatorship (23 July, after the Turkish invasion of Cyprus). In particular, the events in Portugal gave an immense boost to the PCE and convinced Carrillo that his time was near. In his preface to the published version of his report to the meeting of the Central Committee in late April 1974, he hailed the victorious alliance of workers, the army and the 'most dynamic and liberal sectors of Portuguese capitalism'. He claimed that the provisional government formed in Lisbon was essentially identical to the PCE's Pact for Liberty and would be the formula for the transition from dictatorship to democracy in Spain.[16]

Spurred on by these events, many of Spain's economic elite began to consider that an understanding with the Communists could play a part in their own strategy for survival. Perhaps inspired also by the PCE's well-publicized spat with Moscow over Azcárate, important figures of the capitalist elite, representing both Spanish and multinational corporations, showed a readiness to open discussions with López Salinas, Ballesteros and Romero Marín.[17] At the same time, democratic round tables and juntas were gradually emerging on the model of the Assemblea de Catalunya, and everywhere Communists were driving them. Inevitably, possession of a nationwide organizational network ensured a dominant coordinating role for the PCE. The estrangement from the USSR was finally paying dividends. It was not simply events abroad which boosted Carrillo's confidence.

Useful contacts with businessmen and with other left-wing and also Christian Democrat opposition forces had been made throughout early 1974. Nevertheless, Carrillo remained concerned that the plans for a Francoist monarchy under Juan Carlos could still come to fruition. In Paris, the Opus Dei monarchist Rafael Calvo Serer and Antonio García Trevijano had encouraged him to bet instead on Don Juan de Borbón, who was in exile in Estoril in Portugal. Considering Juan Carlos to be a mindless puppet of Franco, Carrillo was delighted when his friend, the extremely wealthy lawyer Teodolfo Lagunero, was invited to meet Don Juan in a Paris hotel. He conveyed the message that the PCE would support a regency under Don Juan until a constitutional referendum could be held and would accept the result even if in favour of a monarchy. The pretender was not convinced, however, by Carrillo's promise that, if the vote favoured a republic, he would be treated with respect.[18]

Carrillo was now beginning to operate in a context unknown since the Civil War. As he returned to the surface, he was able to use to great effect his native cunning and the skills honed within the PCE's internal power struggles. The big difference was that the power that he wielded within the Party and the reverence that greeted his every utterance no longer applied. Indeed, he was faced at every turn with, at best, suspicion or, at worst, downright hatred. It was about this time that the subject of Paracuellos was resuscitated. Nevertheless, the political acumen and showmanship with which he led the PCE over the next three years was to be a major contribution to the transition to democracy and essentially was to constitute his finest hour. He missed no opportunity for public display. In June 1974, at a mass meeting in Geneva at which he was on stage but prevented from speaking live, a tape was played to several thousand emigrant Spanish workers from all over Europe. In his pre-recorded speech, he condemned as fascist the monarchical succession prepared by Franco: 'Faced by such a monarchy, Spaniards will have only one response: the democratic Republic! Even the cat will be republican!' Asking rhetorically 'For whom the bells toll?' he answered that 'the bells ring out the death of the fascist dictatorship'.[19]

One month later, Franco was diagnosed with phlebitis. He also had severe gastric ulcers caused by the medication taken to alleviate symptoms of Parkinson's disease. Given the complications arising from conflicts between the necessary treatments, he had been hospitalized and therefore obliged to name a reluctant Prince Juan Carlos as interim head of state. The government of Carlos Arias Navarro faced the virtually impossible task of adjusting the political mechanisms of the Franco regime to a changed social and economic situation – a job for which he had neither the will nor the power. His efforts to placate the Francoist old guard, the so-called 'bunker', destroyed his credibility and enhanced that of the opposition. In February, an attempt to silence the Bishop of Bilbao, Antonio Añoveros, had led to a humiliating climbdown and to an acceleration of the withdrawal of ecclesiastical support for the regime. The Minister of Information, Pío Cabanillas, relaxed press restrictions, as a result of which he was accused of opening the door to the reds and forced to resign. Meanwhile, there were widespread arrests and torture of dissidents as well as highly publicized executions, including that of the anarchist Salvador Puig Antich on 2 March. The consequence was steady growth in the popular movement all over Spain in favour of the so-called 'democratic break' that favoured Carrillo's policies of returning to the surface.[20]

In an effort to force the pace, Carrillo responded to news of Franco's illness by launching an apparently broad opposition front, the Junta Democrática, on 30 July 1974 in Paris. There was a simultaneous announcement in Madrid. The Junta consisted mainly of the PCE and the Workers' Commissions, together with the tiny Partido Socialista Popular of Enrique Tierno Galván, the Carlists and numerous individuals of whom the most notable were the monarchist and ex-Opus Dei theorist Rafael Calvo Serer and the publicity-hungry playboy José Luis de Vilallonga.[21] Despite the non-participation of the Partido Socialista Obrero Español and the various Christian Democrat groups, the Junta was a very considerable publicity coup for the Communists. The Pact for Liberty now had a focus. Opposition circles in Madrid and Barcelona buzzed with excitement. Non-aligned individuals looked to the Junta as a potential alternative at the moment when the regime's legitimacy was crumbling. Skilful diplomacy gained the Junta widespread recognition as the main opposition force and guaranteed the PCE a role in the transition process. Wildly optimistic as ever, Carrillo was convinced that the Junta would inspire the national political strike (the HNP) that would overthrow the regime. He anticipated the establishment of a provisional democratic government in which he would figure. Events were to show that yet again his optimism was misplaced.[22]

When the Junta Democrática was launched, it was the existence of real local organizations that gave significance to what might otherwise have been an empty gesture. Carrillo's idea was to put the PCE at the head of the regional juntas and *mesas* (round tables). In the early summer of 1974, various groups had already been negotiating a national framework for these organizations when Franco fell ill. It was to pre-empt any other group dominating proceedings that Carrillo, along with Calvo Serer, had launched the Junta. Its manifesto called for a provisional government, amnesty for *all* political offences, trade union liberties, the right to strike, a free press and media, an independent judiciary, the separation of Church and state, elections and entry into the EEC. The declaration implied that a broad spectrum of forces was involved, although the absence of the Socialists and Christian Democrats exposed this as an exaggeration.[23] Indeed, by the manner of its foundation, Carrillo had virtually guaranteed the hostility of the Socialists to the Junta. Always sensitive to any threat of Communist hegemony, they began to cast around for alliances, which within a year would lead to the formation of the rival Plataforma de Convergencia Democrática.

The extent of the change to the world in which Carrillo now found himself was illustrated in August 1974. José Mario Armero, the president of the Europa Press news agency, contacted Teodolfo Lagunero to ask him to arrange for Carrillo to come to Paris to meet an important, but unidentified, personage. Carrillo and his family were on holiday in Livorno with Natalia Calamai, the wife of Nicolás Sartorius, who had been imprisoned after the Proceso 1.001. Sartorius was regarded as one of Carrillo's potential successors, and Natalia and her brother Marco were key links to the PCI. Still a clandestine resident in France and having to use false passports, Carrillo tried to avoid airports whenever possible. Accordingly, the devoted Lagunero went to collect him by car. When they reached the elegant Parisian restaurant Le Vert Galant, they found Armero accompanied by the dictator's nephew, Nicolás Franco Pascual de Pobil. Carrillo politely asked him: 'How is your uncle?' When Franco replied, 'He is a bit better but, at his age, his condition is delicate,' Carrillo commented, 'Now you see, we Communists don't have horns and tails like the devil, we are normal people.' The visit may have been initiated in response to Carrillo's speech in Geneva since Nicolás Franco revealed that he had come as the emissary of Prince Juan Carlos. He brought a request that, when Franco died, the Communist Party should not organize mass demonstrations but give the new King six months to initiate political change. Carrillo responded that it would be Juan Carlos's responsibility to introduce an amnesty, permit the return to Spain of political exiles and call free elections. He declared that, as secretary general of the PCE, he was not prepared to give a blank cheque to anyone. However, he sent a message that the PCE was a serious party, that he would not engage in wild adventures and that he would develop policy in response to the evolution of Juan Carlos's rule.[24]

What made possible the meetings with representatives of Don Juan and of Juan Carlos and with bankers and businessmen was the massive popular pressure in favour of democracy. Increasing numbers of industrialists were convinced that the official vertical syndicates were incapable of preventing strikes. Moreover, they were unhappy with a political situation which forced workers to attack the regime by the only method open to them, strikes. Throughout 1974, Ramón Tamames and other Communists met members of the Madrid and Barcelona bourgeoisie, such as the prominent corporate lawyer Joaquín Garrigues Walker. As legal adviser to many important corporations, especially American ones, Garrigues was an accurate barometer of 'liberal capitalist' opinion. That figures like him should be interested in political change gave substance to Carrillo's claims.[25] Their concerns had intensified as Carrero Blanco's successor, Carlos Arias Navarro, made a series of errors which cast considerable doubt on his capacity to head the regime's campaign for survival without serious risk of bloody conflict.

Carrillo was sufficiently confident of his own position to risk disillusioning Party militants by reiterated assertions of the PCE's dependability as an ally of the bourgeoisie. Thus, with one eye on the oligarchy, Teodolfo Lagunero arranged for him to do a series of interviews with the fashionable left-wing intellectual Régis Debray and the novelist and historian Max Gallo. The interviews took place over several days in July 1974 in Teodolfo Lagunero's luxurious villa in Cannes, Villa Comète. Among the guests were Dolores Ibárruri, her daughter Amaya, her granddaughter Lola and the singer Joan Baez, who sang for them and flirted with Debray.[26] The interviews were published as the best-selling book *Demain l'Espagne*. It was the first of several highly sanitized, not to say fictionalized, accounts of Carrillo's own life, of his role in the Civil War and of the various expulsions from the PCE. In its total identification of Carrillo and the PCE, it could have been entitled 'Le parti c'est moi'.

Party members would have been surprised by his declared abhorrence of the cult of personality. 'If by personality cult you mean the dictatorship of a leader who does whatever he likes, who acts in an arbitrary manner and is put on a pedestal while incense is burned, then there has never been a personality cult in our party.' As if it were in the far distant past, he admitted that once upon a time a few people had had great power. Yet, despite 'being under enemy fire', he claimed that the PCE had gone as far as possible in the application of inner-party democracy. Having said that, he asserted the need for leaders, citing Lenin, Ho Chi Minh, Castro and Tito, with all of whom he implicitly ranked himself, but he declared himself against 'the party administration actually fabricating myths about leaders. I condemn it. It is repugnant and contrary to all norms of revolutionary action.' He then declared proudly that 'I will never permit propaganda being made about myself.'[27]

When it looked as if Claudín might be considering a return to the Party, alongside members of the factionalist Bandera Roja group, Carrillo altered the proofs of the book to stress that he had been right about the 1965 expulsions. This attempt to ensure that Claudín would not return as a wronged prophet provoked the disgust of his old comrade and a renewed breakdown in their relations.[28] In fact, Carrillo's flattery of the bourgeoisie in the interviews went far beyond the positions for which he had denounced Claudín and Semprún. The Junta Democrática, the working class and the great national general strike barely figured in his rhetoric. Indeed, to the intense chagrin of many further to the left than himself, he declared that 'it is necessary to have the courage to explain to the workers that it is better to pay a surplus value to the bourgeoisie than to risk creating a situation which could turn against them'. He was actually walking a tightrope because, at the same time, he was stating, with an eye on his supporters, and presumably in deference to his own beliefs, that such moderation was a short- to mid-term concession. The ultimate goal of socialism remained on the agenda.[29] However, the military coup that overthrew Chile's Socialist President, Dr Salvador Allende, on 11 September 1973 had inclined Carrillo to caution. The fact that the conservative middle classes had reacted to Allende's Socialist experiment by supporting the army's action convinced both Carrillo and his Italian counterpart Enrico Berlinguer of the need for broad alliances. Unfortunately, it was a policy which carried the risk of leaving him stranded between an incredulous bourgeoisie and an embittered rank and file. For a brief period of the transition to democracy, from 1975 to 1977, the quest for credibility would be successful. However, in the long run, it would lead to the PCE's electoral downfall.

Although Carrillo was presenting an ever more liberal image to the bourgeois press, he continued to rule the PCE with an iron hand. This was revealed when differences arose over the Portuguese revolution of 25 April 1974 which he had initially hailed as underlining the relevance of the Pact for Liberty. Carrillo's clash with Moscow over the Soviet invasion of Czechoslovakia had already provoked some conflict with the secretary general of the Portuguese Communist Party, Alvaro Cunhal. Now Carrillo felt obliged to distance himself from Cunhal's commitment to the creation of Eastern European-style socialism in Portugal. He described Cunhal's policy as 'a good example of how not to make a revolution'. In doing so, Carrillo not only incurred the further displeasure of Moscow, from which he was able to derive wider credibility, but also risked internal division inside his own Party. There was enthusiasm within the PCE for Cunhal among both the older Stalinists and the younger leftists who believed that his policy was crucial if the problems faced by Salvador Allende in Chile were to be avoided in Portugal.[30] Characteristically, Carrillo declared that he was more than able to handle internal dissidence over

Portugal: 'there may be Cunhalist tendencies within the PCE but I can say that so far I am in control of the situation.'[31]

Such statements contrasted strangely with the euphoric way in which he had first greeted the events of 25 April 1974. In fact, the terms of his initial welcome to the revolution provide the clue to his apparent volte-face. In a radio broadcast to Spain on 26 April Carrillo had described the Portuguese events as similar to his own scenario for Spain's future, a Pact for Liberty based on a broad coalition of the working-class and liberal bourgeois forces, with sectors of the Church, the army and the industrial-financial oligarchy, that would overthrow the dictatorship then establish a pluralist democratic socialism.[32] So long as Cunhal had appeared to be doing no more than this, he was warmly applauded by Carrillo. Once the Portuguese leader began to push for a more sectarian form of socialism, Carrillo's initial enthusiasm began to wane. Even before the Czech crisis, Carrillo had been trying anxiously to counter almost forty years of rabid anti-Communist propaganda and concerns in liberal circles about the lack of democracy in the Soviet bloc. He was determined to prevent his efforts being tarred with Cunhal's revolutionary brush after having claimed as long ago as 1967 that 'no one, and least of all the PCE, thinks today of making the "communist revolution" in Spain. The dilemma before the country today is either reactionary, fascist dictatorship or democracy.' As he had told Nicolás Franco in August 1974, the PCE would collaborate with any government that freed political prisoners, offered a general amnesty and established political freedoms.[33]

At this point, Carrillo was prepared to risk alienating many Party militants because he perceived his principal task as convincing his potential allies in Spain that he was anything but a dangerous revolutionary. Accordingly, he declared his readiness to work within the framework of a monarchy – 'we are not adventurers who will systematically wave the flag of social unrest'. He even accepted the possibility of participation by Francoist politicians in a future government of national unity.[34] Coming in the wake of the controversial and aggressively moderate *Demain l'Espagne*, these statements – particularly the suggestion that the PCE might abandon its commitment to the

Beijing, September 1956. PCE delegates to the Congress of the Chinese Communist Party, including Ignacio Gallego (far left), Enrique Líster (wearing beret) and Dolores Ibárruri (seated), watch a parade in Tiananmen Square.

Sixth Congress of the PCE, Prague, Christmas Day 1959. *Front row, left to right:* Vicente Uribe, Antonio Mije, Enrique Lister, Fernando Claudín. Behind Uribe, José Moix. Next to Moix and just visible behind Mije is Jorge Semprún. Santiago Alvarez is behind Líster and to his right. Ignacio Gallego is behind Lister and to his left, and to Gallego's left, leaning on the wall, is Manuel Delicado. Carrillo's forehead is just visible behind Delicado.

Jorge Semprún survived Buchenwald and became the intrepid liaison between the PCE apparatus in Paris and the militants in the interior of Spain. Expelled by Carrillo in 1965 along with Fernando Claudín, he went on to become an internationally celebrated novelist and script-writer.

The PCE hierarchy on holiday at Maxim Gorky's dacha, Foros, Crimea, summer 1960. *Back row, standing:* Carrillo (second from left), Dolores (in black dress, slightly left of centre), Líster (arms folded, slightly right of centre). *Middle row, seated:* Carmen Menéndez (fifth from right), Jorge Semprún (fourth from right). *Front row, sitting on floor:* Pedro Líster, and Carrillo's sons, José, Jorge and Santiago.

The Crimea, summer 1960. *Front row, left to right:* Líster's son Enrique López, Vladímir Sokolov (Soviet student leader), Santiago Carrillo, Enrique Líster. *Back row, left to right:* Jorge Semprún and a Siberian Communist named Mitiukhin.

A meeting to discuss drafting of the official history of the PCE, c.1960, attended by, among others, Julián Grimau (far left), Manuel Jimeno (second from left), Luis Fernández (third from left) and Dolores Ibárruri (third from right).

Paris, April 1963. Approximately fifteen thousand Parisians demonstrated against General Franco in front of the Central Bourse Du Travail (Trades Council) after the execution of Julián Grimau on 20 April.

Madrid, 6 April 1974. Police photographs of two suspected PCE leaders, Francisco Romero Marín and Pilar Brabo Castells.

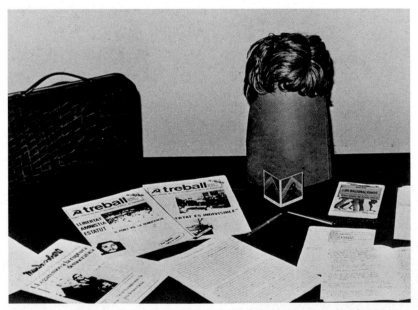

Carrillo was arrested in Madrid on 22 December 1976. Seen here are items taken from him by the Spanish police, including his PCE membership card and his wig.

Madrid, 25 October 1977. A meeting of the principal party leaders in the Moncloa Palace to sign the austerity pact. *Left to right:* Enrique Tierno Galván (PSP), Santiago Carrillo (PCE), José María Triginer (Federación catalana PSOE), Joan Raventos (PSC), Felipe González (PSOE), Juan Ajuriaguerra (PNV), Adolfo Suárez (UCD), Manuel Fraga Iribarne (AP), Leopoldo Calvo Sotelo (UCD) and Miguel Roca (Minoría Catalana).

Santiago Carrillo, Felipe González and Adolfo Suárez in 1978.

In the newly elected Cortes, on 26 July 1977, Carrillo makes his voice heard. To his right Ignacio Gallego, and to his left a sleepy Dolores Ibárruri.

The Cortes, Madrid, 4 July 1978. Pilar Brabo sits at Carrillo's side during the debate on the draft text of the Constitution. To his left can be seen Dolores Ibárruri and in the front row the Comisiones Obreras leader Marcelino Camacho.

Madrid, 23 February 1981. When Lieutenant-Colonel Antonio Tejero seized the Cortes, Carrillo was one of only three deputies who ignored the order to lie on the floor. He remained seated (top of photograph, being approached by a Civil Guard).

Madrid, 25 November 1982. King Juan Carlos meets Carrillo to discuss the results of the recent elections, won by the Socialist Party under Felipe González.

Madrid, 9 October 2012. Carrillo's devoted Secretary Belen Piniés, in the Círculo de Bellas Artes, just one week before her death.

Madrid, 20 September 2012. Mourners watch the cortège taking the body of Santiago Carrillo to the crematorium in the capital's Almudena cemetery.

Gijón, 28 October 2012. As requested in his will, Carrillo's widow came to the town of his birth to scatter his ashes into the sea.

re-establishment of the Republic – caused deep unease within the Party's ranks.[35] This internal tension was the most serious experienced by the PCE since its traumatic clash with Moscow over the Czech invasion. Although Carrillo's reaction to the Portuguese revolution and his emollient comments about a future monarchy had less dramatic consequences than those experienced by the Party in 1968, the two had certain features in common. Anxious to safeguard the credibility of the Pact for Liberty, Carrillo could hardly claim to the bourgeois allies he was pursuing that he was a democratic socialist while at the same time condoning anti-democratic activities by other Communists elsewhere.

The extreme left was loud and rancorous in its denunciation of the Junta, which was hardly surprising given its manifesto's effective denial of the realities of the class struggle. Maoists, Trotskyists, anarchists and even the PCE's own internal left opposition joined in condemning what was described as Carrillo's sell-out to the haute bourgeoisie.[36] Carrillo could argue plausibly that realism demanded such compromise. He had come to believe, as Claudín and Semprún had done before him, that alliance with the bourgeoisie was the essential prerequisite of the overthrow of the regime. If the price to be paid was ideological disarmament, then it had to be paid. Carrillo believed that it made more sense to aim at the possible target of establishing a regime of democratic liberties than at the impossible one, at least in the immediate future, of overthrowing Spanish capitalism. Nonetheless, his discordant claims that he was applying 'Marxist-Leninist method' suggest that he was desperate to maintain some ideological legitimacy in the face of the criticism from within his own Party. It was precisely this awareness of the needs of his Party's image which drew Carrillo nearer to Enrico Berlinguer, secretary general of the Italian Communist Party (PCI).

On 11 June 1975, Carrillo and Berlinguer both made speeches at a mass meeting at Livorno and the two parties then issued a joint declaration. Its moderate and liberal language constituted a clear attempt by the Italian and Spanish parties to establish a demarcation between themselves and the Portuguese and even the French parties. Carrillo benevolently declared that, if the PCE attained power, in the event of electoral defeat it would respect the voters' decision and leave government.[37] The PCI had a major advantage over the PCE. As a legal opposition party, it could freely publicize ideas and create concrete examples of Communist municipal administration such as that in Bologna. In his criticisms of Cunhal and in his speeches in Italy, Carrillo was staking everything on proving his commitment to pluralist socialism. Nevertheless, his commitment to pluralism certainly did not apply within his own Party. When the PCE eventually disappeared from the democratic landscape in the 1980s, as other Communist parties would do, the cause would be not just, as in other countries, the collapse of the Soviet Union. In Spain, it was to have a lot to do with rank-and-file disillusionment with Carrillo himself and his autocratic methods.

With Franco still alive, there was something of a stalemate. Ultimately confident in its powers of repression, if somewhat confused about its future evolution, the government adopted an increasingly hard line throughout 1975. A three-month state of emergency in the Basque Country decreed on 25 April unleashed an operation of mass police terror against the population at large. In June, the creation of the Plataforma de Convergencia Democrática united the PSOE with Dionisio Ridruejo's Unión Social Demócrata Española, the left Christian Democrats of Joaquín Ruiz Gimenez's Izquierda Demócrata Cristiana and a number of regionalist groups, including the Partido Nacionalista Vasco. Dominated by the PSOE, the Plataforma was more open to the possibility of dialogue with the regime reformists than the Junta Democrática, which remained committed to Carrillo's eternal strategy of strikes and mass demonstrations. However, the regime's bloodlust helped overcome the Socialists' residual suspicions of the PCE to such an extent that the two opposition fronts began negotiations for their eventual unification.

On 26 August, the government passed a sweeping anti-terrorist law which exposed the entire left to indiscriminate and draconian police action. Along with intensification of censorship and the seizure of many publications, the regime seemed to be returning to the habits of the 1940s, something made brutally clear by the execution of five alleged terrorists of ETA and FRAP on 27 September. A wave of fear and disgust thus accompanied the death agony of Franco and strengthened the prestige of the Junta. Nevertheless, despite the relative success in Madrid of the three days of democratic action convoked by the Junta, it was not remotely near to the great national political strike which Carrillo dreamed would topple the regime.[38] The brutal ineptitude of the regime's behaviour made Carrillo's call for a broad front to impose the 'democratic break' seem more attractive. The executions helped dissipate the Socialists' distrust of the PCE. In the hope of accelerating the breakdown of the dictatorship, ever more frantic efforts were made to unite the Junta and the Plataforma. A liaison committee was set up and a joint communiqué on 30 September called for a 'democratic rupture' with the regime.[39] It was ironic to see the Franco dictatorship helping Carrillo in his battle for credibility.

The opposition's confidence grew after Franco died on 20 November 1975. It was hardly surprising that the left greeted the coronation of Juan Carlos with headlines in its clandestine press that proclaimed 'No to an imposed King!' and 'No to the Francoist King'.[40] Despite a notable increase in right-wing terrorist activity, the PCE stepped up its calls for 'national democratic action', a slogan which, as a gesture to the Plataforma, replaced what had once been the national political strike. Mass demonstrations in favour of amnesty for political prisoners and large-scale industrial strikes spread during the first months of 1976, partly in response to the PCE's calls but, in the main, as a reflection of a widespread popular urge for political change. In January, Madrid was paralysed by a strike wave mounted by the Workers' Commissions.[41] In February, the Assemblea de Catalunya mobilized 100,000-strong amnesty demonstrations on successive Sundays in Barcelona.[42] The Francoist instincts of both Arias Navarro and his Minister of the Interior, Manuel Fraga, were reflected in the violence of police charges to break up amnesty demonstrations and groups of strikers. Railwaymen, postmen and workers on the Madrid underground were deterred from strike action by the device of 'militarization'. By declaring their work to be of national importance and co-opting them all into the armed forces, the government equated strikes with mutiny, which was subject to harsh punishment. Labour unrest was intensified even further by the government's imposition of a wage freeze. In the light of this ferment, Carrillo boldly announced to an astonished executive meeting on 6 January 1976 that his place was in Spain.[43] It was a virtually risk-free way of filling a gap in his CV, which permitted him to present himself later as a courageous clandestine combatant in enemy territory.

Several executive committee members, including Manuel Azcárate and Ignacio Gallego, had already acquired passports and were inside the country. However, it was impossible for Carrillo to get a legal passport since its concession would have been tantamount to the legalization of the PCE. Accordingly, false papers would be provided by Domingo Malagón, the PCE's expert forger. Transport would be arranged by Teodulfo Lagunero. Insisting that his cover as a businessman required that he be properly dressed, Lagunero took Carrillo to one of the most fashionable men's outfitters in Cannes and bought him a suit, shoes, shirts, ties and a magnificent cashmere overcoat. Wearing a wig and contact lenses by way of disguise, he was driven across the frontier on 7 February by Teodulfo Lagunero's wife, Rocío, in her Mercedes. They had a fright when the car was thoroughly searched at the customs post but reached Barcelona without further incident and had a meal in the port before continuing on to Madrid. Thirty-seven years had passed since Carrillo's flight from Spain. The next day, Carrillo was installed in a house purchased by Lagunero in the secluded Calle Leizarán in the elegant El Viso barrio of the capital. Shortly afterwards, he was joined there by a young PCE militant, Belén de Piniés y Nogués, who was to act as his secretary and also to provide cover for him. Belén came from a well-known conservative family. She had been selected for the role by one of the leading young executive committee members resident in Madrid, Pilar Brabo, whose relationship with Carrillo had grown closer in recent years. It was hoped that Belén's family background would diminish any possible suspicion of her. Her father, Vicente, was a follower of Don Juan who had been at the Munich meeting in 1962, and her uncle, Jaime de Piniés, had been Franco's Ambassador both to the United Nations and in London. Belén had previously been the partner of another prominent PCE member, Enrique Curiel, but henceforth would dedicate her life to Carrillo. In doing so, she would eventually displace Pilar Brabo, who had hitherto occupied the role of handmaiden to the great man. Within a few years, Pilar's one-time adoration of Carrillo would have turned into personal and political animosity.[44]

Carrillo had to come to terms with the fact that possibilities for 'national democratic action' were effectively limited to Madrid and Barcelona, the situation in the Basque Country being beyond Communist control. This was brought home not long after his arrival in Spain. A two-month strike in the town of Vitoria culminated in a massive demonstration on 3 March 1976. As the workers left the Church of San Francisco, they were charged by riot police. Three were killed instantly and over seventy badly hurt, of whom two died some days later. In protest, a general strike was called throughout the Basque Country, organized by a broad spectrum of local forces including ETA. Carrillo concluded that Fraga, whom he remembered from the Grimau case, had 'the instincts of a bloodthirsty despot' – something he would conveniently forget when he became a parliamentary deputy. He already realized that securing closer unity with the Plataforma was an urgent task. Two weeks earlier, on 20 February, after a joint meeting in Madrid University involving Pablo Castellanos of the PSOE, the Christian Democrat Joaquín Ruiz Giménez and Simón Sánchez Montero, only the latter had been arrested. Carrillo perceived this as a message from the government that only groups to the right of the PCE would be tolerated. Accordingly he decided that, in order to challenge the government, unity was crucial.[45] To achieve it would pose an acute problem.

Already, in the quest for opposition unity, Carrillo had moderated his declarations to such an extent that he was exposed to accusations from groups to the left that he was simply playing the game of the oligarchy.[46] Too much moderation could interrupt the momentum of the mass-mobilization campaign as well as blur the PCE's identity. As shown by the arrest of Sánchez Montero but not Castellanos and Ruiz Giménez, the relative success of the campaign was pushing the government into trying to buy off the PSOE or the Christian Democrats. Juan Carlos's first government was presided over by the reactionary Arias

Navarro but also included nominally 'liberal' Francoists like José María de Areilza. If Arias hoped to be able to resolve the crisis by means of timid and cosmetic reform, the evidence of popular militancy was forcing some members of his cabinet to accept that the survival of the monarchy required a more positive commitment to democratic change. That might well involve compromise with the component forces of the Plataforma and the exclusion of the PCE from the subsequent arrangements. The fear of being betrayed by other opposition groups was thus uppermost in Carrillo's mind.[47]

To counter the Francoist image being projected by Arias and Fraga, in March 1976 Juan Carlos sent an unofficial diplomatic envoy, his friend Manuel Prado y Colón de Carvajal, on a clandestine mission to Bucharest. Since the President of Romania Nicolai Ceauşescu was believed to have great influence with Carrillo, Prado's task was to convince him of the King's genuine democratic intentions. Ceauşescu was asked to urge Carrillo to be patient and not push for legalization of the Communist Party for at least two years. In order to give him the message in person, Ceauşescu asked Carrillo to come to Bucharest, which he could not do until early May. Then, while pleased to hear of the King's reforming aspirations, he asked Ceauşescu to relay back his reply that the PCE would continue to press for legalization at the same time as other parties. Carrillo was determined to do everything possible to keep up the popular pressure for change – although in some extremely perceptive editorials in *Mundo Obrero* he revealed a readiness for compromise.[48]

Although Carrillo was living clandestinely in Madrid, he made numerous foreign visits in order to maintain the fiction of his residence in Paris. They involved complex travel arrangements requiring the services of Teodulfo Lagunero.[49] On one of these trips, to Rome, he would make an important public declaration. Aware of the possibility of being edged out of the game, he had decided to modify the PCE's position on a number of issues in the hope of pre-empting any government effort to attract the moderate left. At a meeting of the PCE executive on 20 March, he dropped the Party's hitherto insistent calls for an outright break with the regime (the *ruptura democrática*), for the departure of Juan Carlos and for the creation of a provisional government. Now he proposed a unity pact behind the slogan of 'negotiated break' (*ruptura pactada*).[50] That this was a wise strategy was demonstrated inadvertently by Manuel Fraga. Against the advice of the growing liberal camp in the cabinet, on 29 March Fraga ordered the arrest of Antonio García Trevijano, the Juanista lawyer, Marcelino Camacho, the leader of the Comisiones Obreras, and others when they met to announce the launch of the united Plataforma and Junta Democrática.[51]

The formal announcement of the fusion of the Junta and the Plataforma into Coordinación Democrática was made on 4 April. This really meant the end of Carrillo's hopes of overthrowing the regime. Henceforth, the emphasis would be on negotiation with the government and the widening of the opposition front to embrace centre and right-of-centre groups. By accepting that all of his previous predictions were wrong, Carrillo ensured that the PCE would not simply be ignored. In return for his Party's capacity for popular mobilization, he was securing a role in a negotiated transition. He was effectively recognizing that popular pressure for change had coincided with the economic elite's dissatisfaction with Francoist structures predicted twelve years previously by Claudín. The combination of mass mobilization and the emergence of a broad and respectable coalition of forces was to ensure that there would be change and that it would take place without bloodshed.[52]

At the beginning of July, Carrillo attended a Conference of Communist and Workers' Parties in East Berlin. Although the meeting had been jointly inspired by the Italian Communist Party and the Polish United Workers' Party, his intervention was the one that made the greatest impact. He expressed a commitment to a liberal, pluralist view of socialism and affirmed roundly that Europe's Communists were subject to no central authority and followed no international discipline. Much as it dismayed comrades who still accepted the guiding role of Moscow, Carrillo's speech was hardly surprising given the need to consolidate Coordinación Democrática and to put pressure on the government. What was extraordinary, in retrospect, was his contemptuous dismissal of the journalistic label 'Eurocommunism' for such moderation. 'The term is most unfortunate,' he declared.

'There is no such thing as Eurocommunism because non-European Communist Parties, like the Japanese, are excluded.'[53] Hindsight made that rejection seem distinctly ironic since, at the time of making it, Carrillo was writing two works which were, in their different ways, to become fundamental texts of the Eurocommunist doctrine. In hiding in Madrid, he was using his enforced idleness to write the book 'Eurocommunism' and the State and a long report, From Clandestinity to Legality.

On his return to Spain, he found that the existence of a unified opposition with the capacity to call strikes and mass demonstrations had obliged Juan Carlos to speed up his programme of political liberalization. At the beginning of July, apparently on American advice, the King called for Arias's resignation and replaced him with Adolfo Suárez. In view of Suárez's Falangist past, the opposition was horrified. Massive demonstrations for political liberties and amnesty were thus called in the second week of July with considerable success. Suárez was left in no doubt that swift and thoroughgoing reform was necessary if the crisis was to be resolved without appalling violence.[54] In fact, having hoped that Juan Carlos would replace Arias with Areilza, Carrillo expected little from Suárez. Nevertheless, in response to Suárez's televised declaration that he would not try to perpetuate Francoism, Carrillo intelligently held out a tiny olive branch. Writing about 'the precarious rise of Suárez', he observed, 'I recognize that his words on television were sensible,' and speculated on the possibility that he might be the instrument of the ruptura pactada. 'As I write, there is still no cabinet or government programme and I would rather give the prime minister the benefit of the doubt. This is the dilemma in which both Suárez and King Juan Carlos find themselves.'[55]

Carrillo now decided to test Suárez by having those members of the executive who were legally in Spain request formal permission to hold a meeting of the Central Committee in Madrid. The idea was that the government would be damaged by the publicity surrounding its inevitable refusal. When that refusal duly arrived, the meeting was held openly in Rome from 28 to 31 July 1976, with all present using their real names. It was a clever challenge to the government to dare arrest, on their return to Spain, some quite famous people. Carrillo's speech to the meeting, the text of *From Clandestinity to Legality*, constituted a direct application to Spain of the ideas and ideals associated with Eurocommunism. Less theoretical and less universal than the book *'Eurocommunism' and the State*, his report was a clear statement of how the PCE wished to be seen in Spain: as a Party totally independent of Moscow, committed to a pluralistic model of socialist democracy and to peaceful and democratic means of obtaining power, and willing to respect ideological and religious differences and even hostile verdicts of the electorate. As well as being a significant publicity coup, the Rome plenum formed part of the PCE's long-term policy of returning to the surface, capturing democracy by challenging the government either to tolerate the Party's existence or else reveal its true colours by taking repressive action. Carrillo used his Rome speech to cast doubt on the reforming capacity of Suárez and to call for amnesty, a provisional government of national reconciliation and the election of a constituent assembly. He also made it clear that the process of the return to the surface would continue by announcing that the PCE would begin the open distribution of Party membership cards in the autumn.[56]

As it was, none of the delegates was arrested on return to Spain, perhaps because of the presence at the plenum of a broad range of Italian and Spanish political personalities. Indeed, at the beginning of August, a wide-reaching amnesty for political prisoners (other than terrorists convicted of crimes of blood) was announced by Suárez. Nevertheless, as his remarks in Rome had made clear, Carrillo still optimistically conceived of the *ruptura pactada* as a deal between government and opposition for a provisional cabinet to preside over free elections to a constituent Cortes. If Carrillo's faint hopes regarding Suárez were boosted by the amnesty, they were severely undermined by a minor incident shortly after the Rome meeting. He applied for a passport at the Spanish Embassy in Paris, was received cordially by the Ambassador, Miguel María de Lojendio Irure, and revealed to him that he had been clandestinely inside Spain already. Lojendio told him that he thought a passport was possible but that he would have to consult with the Foreign Ministry. On receiving Lojendio's report, Suárez immediately relieved him of his post.[57] It was hardly surprising then that Suárez's legislative programme was greeted with incredulity by the PCE, his intentions of seeking dialogue with the opposition denounced as mere words.[58]

Carrillo's threat to order the distribution of Party cards saw 200,000 issued by the end of October. Moreover, the PCE now had offices in Madrid in the Calle Peligros. Although there was no large sign outside, there was no secret about its nature.[59] Shortly afterwards, Carrillo made another threat. While holidaying at Lagunero's house in Cannes, he sent Lagunero to Madrid to speak with his friend Arturo Menéndez, Minister of Education in Suárez's cabinet. His message was that, if Carrillo did not receive a passport, he would hold a press conference in Madrid in the presence of internationally famous and influential journalists like Oriana Fallaci and Marcel Niedergang. Menéndez urged Lagunero to tell Carrillo to bear in mind how easy it would be to provoke the bunker. A struggle was thus developing between Suárez on the one hand and Carrillo and the rest of the opposition for control of the transition process. Suárez could take the initiative only by embarking on a combination of substantial concessions and efforts to split the united front of the opposition. He hoped that Carrillo would thereby be forced back from setting the pace of opposition demands for change to a more defensive position of avoiding the isolation of the PCE. Suárez sent José Mario Armero to Cannes to try to persuade Carrillo not to make the transition impossible by provocative actions.[60]

Nevertheless, the pressure was on Suárez. On 4 September, a wide range of liberal, Social Democrat and Christian Democrat groups gathered in Madrid's Eurobuilding to discuss unity with Coordinación Democrática and with a number of regional opposition fronts.[61] All that came out of the meeting was the creation of a liaison committee, but Suárez was obliged to hasten his preparations for the presentation of his project of political reforms. On 8 September, he outlined his plans to the high command of the armed forces, all men steeped in the visceral anti-communism of the dictatorship. Stressing that he would proceed at all times in accordance with the law, Suárez assured them that the Communist Party could not be legalized because the internationalist loyalty enshrined in the PCE's statutes constituted a breach of the penal code. He omitted to tell them that his indirect contacts with Carrillo through Armero had raised the possibility of a change in those statutes and thus an eventual legalization of the Communist Party. Enjoying the backing of Juan Carlos, Suárez's plans as outlined were reluctantly accepted by the officers present. The majority of the high command would later be convinced that Suárez had cheated them.[62]

On 10 September, having gained the agreement of the military, Suárez presented his project for reform to the country. Since it was to be his cabinet holding elections before mid-1977, and since there was to be no question of Suárez resigning to be replaced by a provisional government of opposition forces, Carrillo issued a declaration on 15 September, nominally from the PCE executive committee, vehemently denouncing the text as 'an imposed law that aims to cheat liberty and popular sovereignty'.[63] The PCE demanded the prior legalization of all political parties, but Suárez simply pressed ahead with his project. Many within the opposition were pleasantly surprised by the extent to which daily life was being liberalized. The press was functioning normally, political groups to the right of the PCE were unhindered, the PSOE was preparing to hold its Seventeenth Congress and even the PCE was allowed unofficially to go about its business inside Spain. The initiative was swinging Suárez's way. He was able to insinuate to Socialists and Christian Democrats that he could make greater concessions to them if only they would not rock the boat and provoke the army by insisting on legalization of the PCE.[64] He was skilfully trying to use the issue to drive a wedge into the opposition and to impose caution on Carrillo. Thus, while in late September the Socialist leader Felipe González was adamant that legalization of the Communist Party was a non-negotiable prerequisite of democracy, by the end of November he was arguing that it was unrealistic to insist on it.[65] Faced with evidence of the impossibility of imposing change against the will of the army and seeing that things were moving along steadily under Suárez's guidance, the opposition could do little but acquiesce.

Nevertheless, Carrillo had some small victories. On 21 October, his wife Carmen and his sons returned legally to Spain, although he remained in hiding. On 27 October, when Ignacio Gallego made an appearance in his native Jaén, 10,000 people came out to greet him. In the meantime, on 23 October Coordinación Democrática united with five regional fronts, the Taula de Forces Polítiques i Sindicals del País Valencià, the Assembleas de Mallorca, Menorca i Eivissa, the Assemblea de Catalunya, the Coordinadora de Fuerzas Democráticas de las Islas Canarias and the Táboa Democrática de Galiza. Knowing that Suárez intended to hold a referendum on his reform project, the new united opposition front, called the Plataforma de Organismos Democráticos, issued a statement on 5 November that it would boycott the referendum unless the government conceded the legalization of political parties and trade unions, amnesty for political prisoners and exiles, recognition of the freedoms of expression, association and assembly and repeal of the anti-terrorist law.[66]

Both Suárez and Juan Carlos knew that for democracy to be credibly established the Communist Party would have to be legalized. The difficulties for the King were illustrated at a dinner party that he attended in Madrid on 10 November at the home of his sister, the Infanta Doña Pilar. Apart from Juan Carlos and the Queen, the guests included Don Juan, José Mario Armero and the head of Suárez's private office, the elegant blonde aristocrat Carmen Díez de Rivera. An extremely close friend of the King, the willowy Carmen had been asked by him to broach the topic of the legalization of the PCE. Years later, she commented: 'I had been commanded to let it slip, to see what would happen.' When she did, a glacial silence fell over the room.[67] The reactions of those around the table reflected the views of Madrid high society, which did not significantly differ from those of the military establishment.

The great general strike called for 12 November was posed in economic rather than political terms. Its slogans were protests against the wage freeze and redundancies, although the political implications were clear enough. In the event, more than a million workers were involved, but the strike never spilled over into the great national action against the Suárez reform that Carrillo had hoped for. That was in large part because of the elaborate precautions taken by the Minister of the Interior, Rodolfo Martín Villa. As soon as he received intelligence reports about the strike's preparation, he set up a committee to elaborate a counter-strategy. It was composed of senior public order, telecommunications, traffic and intelligence experts. The police arrested workers' leaders in Madrid, Barcelona, Valencia, Bilbao and Seville. They thereby neutralized the nerve-centres of the movement and so appreciably limited its impact. Carrillo did not perceive it to have been a failure.[68] In his diary, he described it as a great success, almost as if it had been the fulfilment of his dreams of HNP.[69]

The failure of the strike allowed Suárez to proceed with steering his project through the Francoist Cortes. A summit meeting of the Plataforma de Organismos Democráticos and other groups held on 27 November reaffirmed many of the demands of the Plataforma's inaugural declaration of 4 November. However, the crucial condition of a provisional government of 'democratic consensus' to oversee the forthcoming elections was dropped. The way was now open for a 'committee of personalities' from the opposition to negotiate with the government. Carrillo was becoming increasingly concerned about the PCE being isolated. Henceforth, his central objective would be legalization. Rumours had begun to circulate in mid-November that he was resident somewhere in Madrid. Via Armero, he had informed the government that he was in Spain and about to publicize the fact. On 20 November, at a massive demonstration on the first anniversary of Franco's death, extreme rightists had chanted: 'Come back, Carrillo, we'll make mincemeat of you.' Despite concerns for his safety, on 22 and 23 November film of him being driven around Madrid by Belén Piniés appeared on French television.[70]

On Friday 10 December, he held a clandestine press conference in Madrid. It was a remarkable organizational achievement to bring together seventy Spanish and foreign journalists under the noses of the police. It was a deliberate ploy to put pressure on the government. The event was in itself a provocation, but Carrillo's words were concil-iatory: 'everyone knows we disapproved of the way the King came to the throne … [but] the King is there, that is a fact … If a majority of the Spanish people vote for a constitutional and parliamentary monarchy, we Communists will respect as always the decision of the Spanish people.' He insinuated that, provided the PCE were allowed to take part in the elections, it would collaborate in the negotiation of a social contract to deal with the economic crisis. With characteristic dry humour, he even offered to meet Juan Carlos in order to explain in person the Communists' position. The press coverage was massive. He commented in his diary, 'this appearance more than repays ten months in the catacombs'.[71]

When the referendum was held on 15 December, despite abstention calls from the Plataforma de Organismos Democráticos and particularly from the Communists the project was approved by 94 per cent of the vote. A month earlier, Carrillo had already accepted privately that the government would get the result it wanted.[72] The fact that such a project was being put to a referendum at all was in general terms a great triumph for the opposition. Nevertheless, the tactical error of the abstention call highlighted the extent to which Suárez was now setting the pace. However, the press conference had been a masterstroke on Carrillo's behalf which allowed him to recover some of the initiative. The government was furious and ordered his arrest, although it took the police until 22 December to find him. The Communist Party had used the time to prepare a huge campaign in favour of his release. Within hours, there was graffiti all around Madrid demanding his release and messages to the government from foreign ambassadors. A delegation of senior Party members was received at Suárez's office by Carmen Díez de Rivera. To Suárez's discomfort, this was interpreted by the press as a major step towards legalizing the PCE. In any case, to keep Carrillo imprisoned, or to put him on trial, would have fatally undermined Suárez's credibility. Nevertheless, while in custody in the Dirección General de Seguridad, Carrillo was subjected to humiliation by some of the policemen guarding him. After a week, Suárez had to order his release and that constituted a substantial step towards legalization. Henceforth, Carrillo had no need of his wig, which he had given to one of the policemen who questioned him after his arrest. He decided to go and live with his family, but, faced with numerous death threats, he returned to the house in El Viso.[73]

Throughout January 1977, Carrillo and Suárez negotiated at arm's length through José Mario Armero and Jaime Ballesteros of the PCE's

Madrid apparatus. The PCE pushed for authorization for its meetings; the government pressed the PCE to use its influence in the Workers' Commissions to restrain industrial militancy. However, the release of Carrillo and ever stronger indications that the PCE was on the road to regaining legal status led to a vicious backlash from the extreme right. Already, in response to the amnesty and the growing public presence of the PCE, right-wing efforts were mounted to block Suárez's political reform programme. One of the most effective was the mysterious and allegedly Marxist-Leninist splinter group GRAPO (Grupos de Resistencia Antifascista Primero de Octubre), which initially announced its emergence with a bombing campaign. At least three of Suárez's ministers, General Manuel Gutiérrez Mellado (Defence), Rodolfo Martín Villa (Interior) and Enrique de la Mata Gorostizaga (Sindicatos), as well as senior members of the PCE, were convinced that GRAPO was infiltrated by, or even the creation of, the extreme right and elements of the police. The emergence several years later of one of its leaders, Pío Moa, as a successful rightist media celebrity renewed these suspicions. Significantly, both Moscow and Beijing had refused to recognize GRAPO.[74] The day after Carrillo's press conference and just four days before the December referendum, GRAPO had kidnapped Antonio María de Oriol y Urquijo, president of the Consejo del Estado (Council of State), one-time Minister of Justice under Franco and a key figure of the conservative establishment. His kidnapping was a provocation directly aimed at persuading orthodox Francoists that Suárez's reform project and increasing tolerance of the Communists meant a return to the disorder and violence which they associated with the pre-Civil War Republic.

GRAPO's efforts to derail the transition would continue, on 24 January 1977, with the kidnapping of General Emilio Villaescusa Quilis, president of the Supreme Council of Military Justice (Consejo Superior de Justicia Militar). To the astonishment of the media, this tiny group of alleged extremists had managed to carry out two sophisticated operations, pour out a stream of communiqués and yet evade the police. Villaescusa and Oriol remained in captivity until freed by the police on 11 February.[75] Neither kidnapping made any sense from a left-wing perspective. GRAPO claimed to be the armed wing of the previously non-existent Partido Comunista de España (Reconstruido), a splinter of one of the pro-Chinese groupuscules, the Organización Marxista. It was far from a secret that Suárez was in touch with the real PCE about its eventual legalization within a democratic Spain. In that context, the only logic of GRAPO's actions was to smear Carrillo and damage the Prime Minister by implying that he was risking Franco's achievements. Carrillo himself was told by Areilza that the CIA was behind the operation.[76]

As part of the rightist strategy of tension, on the same day as the kidnapping of Villaescusa ultra-right-wing terrorists murdered five people, four of whom were Communist labour lawyers, in an office in the Atocha district of Madrid. It was immediately realized within the Party leadership that the intention was to provoke a violent Communist reaction which would scupper any possibility of legalization.[77] Carrillo refused to take the bait and instead the PCE issued appeals for calm. In what was to be a key moment of the transition to democracy, Communist Party members and sympathizers marched in silence in a gigantic display of solidarity. Both Suárez and the King himself, who was said to have been flown over the march in a helicopter, were deeply impressed by the demonstration of Communist strength and discipline. Certainly, much popular hostility to the legalization of the PCE was dissipated by the restraint with which its supporters responded to the tragedy. A delegation of opposition leaders negotiated with Suárez and, in return for promises of action against the bunker's violence, they offered him a joint government–opposition declaration denouncing terrorism and calling for national support for the government. The gesture signified that Suárez had been publicly accepted by the left as belonging to the democratic forces in Spain.[78]

The shrewdness with which Carrillo pursued the immediate goal of legalization was illustrated by his readiness to make all possible concessions to the Crown. After a dinner on 20 January 1977 at the Ritz Hotel in Barcelona at which the magazine *Mundo* was presenting prizes to various politicians, Suárez's chef de cabinet, Carmen Díez de Rivera, on her own initiative took Carrillo to one side. They were photographed while talking and the press made much of the encounter. Although deeply embarrassed, Suárez was astute enough to refuse her resignation and then to use her as his intermediary with Carrillo. They met again on 31 January and she told Carrillo of her boss's commitment to change and the difficulties that he faced. She then arranged a secret meeting between Carrillo and the Prime Minister at the home of José Mario Armero on 27 February.

Suárez began the meeting with the flattering remark 'We've been playing a game of chess in which I have had to move my pieces in response to your moves.' He then went on to outline the difficulties that he faced in terms of the military high command and other Francoist elements and suggested that the Communists run in the elections as 'independent' candidates. Carrillo refused point blank and threatened to ensure international uproar. Finally, however, in return for legal status, he undertook to recognize the monarchy, adopt the red-yellow-red monarchist flag of Spain and offer his support for a future social contract. These astonishing concessions were made entirely on his own initiative and were related afterwards only to his closest cronies in the executive.[79] The meeting saw a process of mutual seduction between these two heavy smokers and consummate cynics. Carrillo was thrilled when Suárez said: 'In this country, there are only two real politicians, you and me.' He would henceforth believe that his special relationship with Suárez gave him a unique importance in national politics. Moreover, he informed the PCE executive that he could not tell them everything that had been said at the meeting because it constituted a 'state secret'.[80]

After their agreement on legalization, Suárez had little choice but to allow a Eurocommunist summit to take place on 2 March at the Hotel Meliá Castilla in Madrid. Carrillo convinced him that worldwide outrage would ensue if he tried to block the entry into Spain of the leaders of the Italian and French parties, Enrico Berlinguer and Georges Marchais. Thus, with full press coverage, Carrillo was able to meet Berlinguer and Marchais. Carrillo repaid Suárez in full. At the end of the meeting, he declared, again without prior discussion in the executive committee, that the PCE accepted the existence of American bases in Spain. It was another step closer to legalization.[81] Over recent months, Suárez had hastily cobbled together a new party, the Unión del Centro Democrático, composed of a disparate group of liberals,

Christian Democrats and Francoist bureaucrats, rather like himself. They had united around Suárez because his access to state funds and his control of government patronage and the radio and television networks offered the probability of electoral success. Many in the PCE were concerned that the UCD had been created as an instrument to ensure that, in the transition to a democratic regime, real government power would be in sufficiently conservative hands to protect the existing structure of economic and social power. Most PCE members were astonished when Carrillo airily declared that he would be happy to see Suárez continue as Prime Minister after the next elections. He felt able to make the remark because of his misplaced optimism that the real electoral battle would be between the PCE and Fraga's Alianza Popular.[82]

To facilitate legalization, the PCE's statutes as presented to the Supreme Court (Junta de Fiscales Generales del Tribunal Supremo) were carefully edited. Marxism-Leninism, proletarian internationalism and the struggle to overthrow capitalism were all concepts missing from the submitted text and would not be officially removed from the statutes until the Ninth Congress in April 1978.[83] Suárez could thus claim that he was not going back on the assurances given to the assembled generals in September. On Good Friday, 8 April, the court issued a judgement to the effect that there was nothing in the statutes to prevent the PCE's inclusion in the Register of Political Associations. Both the King and Suárez were concerned that the scale of anti-Communist feeling within the army signified a real danger of a military coup. However, both knew that without the legalization of the PCE, there would not be full-scale democracy in Spain. It was a massive gamble, but one that had to be taken. On Holy Saturday, 9 April, Suárez, mistakenly confident of army acquiescence, announced the legalization of the PCE. Carrillo received the news in Cannes, at the home of Teodulfo Lagunero.[84] Most of the Madrid political and military elite were out of town for the Easter weekend but that merely delayed a fiercely negative reaction that ultimately would be far more damaging for Suárez than it would ever be for Carrillo.[85]

Carrillo was understandably delighted with the completion of the Communist return to the surface, but he still had some secrets to reveal and some difficult explanations to make to his comrades. The first legal plenum of the Central Committee was arranged to start on 14 April, the forty-fifth anniversary of the foundation of the Second Republic. It took place in a hotel surrounded by police whose job was to prevent an attack by extreme rightists. Rumours were buzzing of the simmering opposition to the legalization among the officer corps of the armed forces. Nevertheless, Carrillo's dramatic announcement on 15 April that the PCE had to drop the Republican flag caused consternation and some opposition. He argued that the decision was inevitable and indeed it was, since Suárez was anxiously waiting to hear if Carrillo could fulfil his half of the bargain made on 27 February.

Presenting the measure as a demonstration of 'revolutionary responsibility', he stressed the considerable danger that the PCE still faced. In defence of his moderation, he asked rhetorically: 'Did we have any alternative? What? Bring the masses on to the streets to confront the apparatus of the state? Where would that have led us other than to a brutal defeat for which the first to reproach us would probably be those who today criticize our moderation?' Given the delicate nature of democracy in Spain, he said destabilization and military intervention were a risk to be avoided at all costs. He emphasized the vocal opposition to the legalization that had been expressed by Manuel Fraga, who had called it a threat to Spain. He commented dryly that Fraga's insults made Spanish politics seem like a lunatic asylum. 'We know that it is useless to ask Sr Fraga to calm down. But we want to reassure those who in good faith let themselves be affected by his shock tactics that we pose no threat to Sr Fraga.' Far from seeking partisan benefit, Carrillo wanted the PCE to form part of a broad 'constructional pact', until a new democratic constitution was established. When he carried the day, a curtain was flung aside to reveal a large Spanish monarchist flag and that of the Republic was removed.[86] His speech was the final goodbye to the triumphalist rhetoric of the HNP. It would be replaced by a new set of triumphalist predictions.

The price paid for legalization had been high, but Carrillo had had little choice. His pact with Suárez was intended to prevent the marginalization of the PCE and its eclipse by the PSOE in the upcoming elections. Nevertheless, the abandonment of the PCE's commitment to a republic, or at least to a referendum on the future constitutional framework, shocked many of the rank and file. Moreover, the fact that Carrillo had entered negotiations and taken decisions without discussion with the executive, let alone with the rest of the Central Committee, planted the seeds of serious future conflict. Already in March, a group of Party lawyers had complained about the dictatorial nature of his leadership: 'We have read many times that clandestinity imposed a certain predominance of centralism over democracy and that this situation would come to an end with legalization. Now we are virtually legal and yet we must lament that, far from seeing a move to democratic criteria, we are facing exactly the opposite.' The lawyers also called for elections to all the leadership positions in the PCE. Needless to say, they were ignored and most drifted away. In 1977, there were 138 lawyers in the Party in Madrid, and by 1981 there remained only twenty.[87]

As Manuel Azcárate later protested, 'All that was left for us to do was confirm after the fact that Carrillo could undertake whatever commitments he thought fit and the executive and Central Committee would trot along behind like lambs … It is not a question of honour, of good faith or deception … There is a serious political problem that has probably affected the subsequent weakness of the PCE throughout the transition period.' In Azcárate's view, Carrillo had sold the Party's principles too cheaply and demonstrated his contempt for the rest of the leadership along the way.[88]

Despite simmering internal discontent, Carrillo wasted no time in preparing for the future electoral battle. Another step on the road to the elections was the presentation in Madrid on 25 May of his book 'Eurocommunism' and the State, written during the months in El Viso.[89] By the time of his arrest, he had decided to allow himself to be internationally acclaimed as the champion of 'Eurocommunist' positions, having forgotten his earlier rejection of the term. He was intensely aware of the propaganda value of such a modern and unRussian-sounding term. For nearly forty years, the Franco regime, with help from the Catholic Church and the Western media, had denounced the Communists as torturers and assassins subject to the orders of the Kremlin. If the PCE was to play a role in Spain's new democracy, Carrillo had to convince the world that he and his followers were not simply waiting for the chance to build a Mediterranean Gulag. The publication of the book went a long way towards solving the PCE's remaining credibility problems.[90]

The favourable impression created in the bourgeois press was increased a hundredfold when Carrillo and his book immediately became the targets of a series of savage and anonymous articles in the Soviet ideological journal *Novoye Vremya*. The speed of the Russian response was made possible by the fact that early in 1977, through a KGB agent in the PCE leadership, the Madrid KGB *rezidentura* received a copy of the manuscript of Carrillo's forthcoming book. The Kremlin was scandalized by the scale of its criticism of the Soviet Union. Until March 1976, secret Soviet subsidies had still been forwarded to Carrillo via the French Communist Party. Now, by politburo decision no. P-I/84 of 16 March 1976, the KGB was instructed to make all further payments to Ignacio Gallego, code-named 'Kobo', the most pro-Soviet member remaining on the executive committee. The Madrid KGB station's main source within the PCE, Gallego had leaked Carrillo's manuscript. On 6 December 1976, the Soviet politburo had approved payment to Gallego of $20,000 for the purchase of a flat in Madrid. In public, Gallego was restrained in his criticisms of Carrillo, but privately he denounced him to the Madrid KGB *rezidentura* as 'a danger to the Spanish Communist Party and the international communist movement'.[91] It did the PCE's secretary general no harm at all in Spain for the Russians to accuse him of waging 'a determined and crude campaign against the Soviet Union and the CPSU' and of being at the service of 'the interests of imperialism and the forces of aggression and reaction'. The intensity of the split between Moscow and the PCE made headline news throughout Europe and the United States, and the PCE even published a substantial dossier of newspaper reactions.[92] In private, Carrillo displayed a penchant for anti-Soviet jokes.

What particularly infuriated the Russians was Carrillo's open insistence that the success of democratic socialism among the

Western Communist parties would have a considerable impact on the Eastern bloc and lead to a number of Prague springs. Carrillo pushed this view in interviews with the press in various European countries.[93] Russian displeasure was made clear not just in the Soviet press. The secretary of the fiercely pro-Moscow Communist Party of the USA, Henry Winston, was wheeled out to attack Carrillo.[94] Hostility was not confined to the devotees of the Kremlin. Conservative journalists, politicians and scholars in the Western world also denounced Carrillo's approach as a cynical tactic to win votes by waving the flag of socialism with a human face, to breach the gates of democratic Europe and then to erect a regime of totalitarian communism. This view of Eurocommunism as a Russian Trojan horse was expressed in speeches at a number of American universities by Harold Wilson, the former Labour Prime Minister of Great Britain. He argued that Eurocommunism in France, Italy and Spain was a threat to Western solidarity and defence capabilities.[95] His comments were echoed in less apocalyptic terms in Cambridge in November 1977 by David Owen, the British Foreign Secretary, and later in an article in the *Washington Review of Strategic and International Studies*, which was published by Georgetown University, an institution linked to the CIA.[96]

That June, Carrillo was to lead his Party into Spain's first democratic elections since 1936. His readiness to sacrifice immediate profit in order to consolidate the democratic process was evident during this election campaign. He made speeches all over Spain, sometimes as many as three each day. His fire was concentrated neither on Suárez's Unión del Centro Democrático nor on the PCE's immediate rivals, the Partido Socialista Obrero Español (PSOE), but on Fraga's neo-Francoist Alianza Popular. This was a mistake, evoking as it did memories of the Civil War. With the photogenic Felipe González at its head, the PSOE projected a far more dynamic image than the combination of Carrillo, Pasionaria and the other recently returned veterans to whom he gave priority in the PCE electoral lists.[97] It was one of the reasons why, on 15 June 1977, the PCE received only 1,634,991 votes, 9.2 per cent of the total, coming third after Suárez's UCD (35 per cent) and the PSOE (29 per cent). Carrillo himself became a member of the Congress of Deputies. This was a consider-able achievement, but he had already passed his zenith.

Given the pre-eminent role that the Party had played in thirty-eight years of struggle against the dictatorship, it was a disappointing result. To many militants, it appeared that Carrillo, in the interests of establishing a democratic regime and his own position within it, had let the Party become the victim of his moderate and accommodating policies. The PSOE, as well as exploiting the semi-paralysis of the PCE while awaiting legalization, used its ample financing to present a more positive left-wing image and seemed unjustly to have harvested the fruits of the PCE's long struggle for democracy. The polls had predicted that the PCE would not get more than 10 per cent of the vote, but expectations among militants had been much higher. Until the very last minute, Carrillo himself was sure that the PCE would be the second party with around 20 per cent of the vote.[98]

After recovering from the traumatic shock of the results, Carrillo declared that all had transpired as he had predicted. The fact that the dictatorship had not been overthrown by the Huelga Nacional Política nor by a Communist-led Pact for Liberty was conveniently over-looked.[99] Nevertheless, he was to make a considerable contribution in terms of the consolidation of the new democratic regime. Despite his years of triumphalist predictions, Carrillo had acquired an acute sense of the fragility of democracy. While trying to deal with a substantial economic crisis, the new regime was caught in a pincer between the terrorism of ETA and mounting extreme right-wing subversion.

The immediate priority was the elaboration of a democratic consti-tution. An initial proposal from Suárez and Felipe González was for the creation of a five-man drafting committee with three members from UCD and two from the PSOE. Carrillo made three perceptive objections to this – that it was a big mistake to leave out the regions, especially the Basques and Catalans, that it would be a huge error to exclude Fraga's Alianza Popular because not to implicate them in the construction of the new democracy would make them a banner for all right-wing discontent, and that the Communists as the third-biggest group in parliament could not be left out. When the Socialists agreed to cede one of their representatives to a representative of the regions, Suárez agreed to the formation of an all-party drafting committee, the Ponencia, consisting of seven parliamentary deputies. Elected at the beginning of August 1977, the Ponencia comprised Gabriel Cisneros, Miguel Herrero y Rodríguez de Miñon and José Pedro Pérez Llorca of UCD, Gregorio Peces Barba of the PSOE, Miquel Roca of Convergencia i Uniò representing the regions, Manuel Fraga of Alianza Popular and Jordi Solé Tura of the PSUC. Despite inevitable frictions over such issues as abortion, the rights of the autonomous regions such as Catalonia, the Basque Country and Galicia, private education and the death penalty, the seven carried out their labours in a spirit of compromise and cooperation and by the beginning of 1978 had delivered a draft to the thirty-six members of the parliamentary Constitutional Committee. The work of that larger committee, on which Carrillo led the Communist group, was greatly facilitated by his acceptance of a monarchy. This renunciation of the PCE's long-declared aim of a referendum on the subject seriously disillusioned the rank and file. Nevertheless, it symbolized the extent to which Carrillo was prepared to make a priority of the consolidation of democracy.[100]

Despite the disappointments accruing from his moderation, Carrillo would persist with the same line until the autumn of 1979 when evidence of dwindling Party membership would oblige him to opt for a more dynamic policy. Carrillo had spent the summer of 1977 frenetically trying to make good the PCE's disappointing showing in the elections by pushing in his first speeches in the new democratic Cortes for a 'national democratic coalition government'. He claimed that the country was economically too weak and the health of the new-born democracy too fragile to stand right–left polarization. Accordingly, he argued that the strength of anti-democratic forces in Spain required the parliamentary parties to work together. To build a strong framework for democracy, he called on them to emulate the cooperation between the Christian Democrats and Communists in Italy, the so-called 'historic compromise'.[101] Neither Suárez nor Felipe González was prepared to share power. However, Suárez was keen to take advantage of Communist influence in the workers' movement. Moreover, both he and Carrillo were happy to diminish the influence of the PSOE. In secret negotiations, Suárez exploited Carrillo's anxiety to be near the levers of power and secured his backing for an austerity package. Thus, in late October 1977, along with thirty representatives of virtually all parties, Carrillo signed Spain's social contract, the Pacto de la Moncloa, which aimed to establish a common response to the problems of terrorism, inflation, unemployment and the growing trade deficit. The fact that he showed greater readiness to collaborate with Suárez than did Felipe González laid him open to accusations of collaborating in an operation to heap the costs of the economic crisis on to the working class.[102]

The pact saw the left accept a wage ceiling of 20–22 per cent, at a time when inflation was 29 per cent, together with a series of monetarist measures to restrict credit and public spending. In return, the government made promises of major structural reform, especially in agriculture and the tax system, and undertook to return the *patrimonio sindical* – the buildings, newspapers and funds of the trade unions confiscated by the Francoists after the Civil War. In fact, the government fulfilled few of its promises and, in consequence, the Spanish working class bore the brunt of the economic crisis. UCD's monetarist policies led to a flood of bankruptcies and plant closures. In a return to his triumphalist habits, Carrillo acclaimed the Moncloa Pact as a colossal victory at the PCE's great carnival, the Fiesta de *Mundo Obrero*. He did much the same in a speech in the Cortes on 27 October. The ovation that he received from the UCD deputies in the Cortes may have given him personal satisfaction but did little to calm concerns among the younger members of the executive. His incorporation into the political establishment continued a few days later with a speech at the debating society, Club Siglo XXI, presented by Manuel Fraga. His evident delight at such an accolade was shared by few rank-and-file militants.[103]

Neither the PCE nor the PSOE would be able to force the government to fulfil its side of the bargain. The pact was a necessary evil but such an austerity programme was hardly likely to generate popular enthusiasm. Within six months of the signature of the Moncloa agreement, in a speech in the Cortes on 6 April, Carrillo was obliged to denounce the government's failure to keep its promises.[104] The subsequent increase in unemployment provoked deep popular discontent that was eventually reflected in the PCE's electoral fortunes since Carrillo's policies sat ill with an ostensibly revolutionary party. Fellow members of the executive complained that Carrillo made policy on the hoof in the Cortes, merely leaving them to sell it to the militants.[105] Combined with dissipation of the initial excitement about the establishment of the parliamentary regime, this led to a dramatic fall in PCE membership. Members of the Communist Youth complained that the only political activity left for them was to stick posters on walls or sweep out Party headquarters. Veterans of the anti-Franco struggle joked nostalgically that 'Against Franco, we lived better' (Contra Franco, vivíamos mejor) – a bon mot attributed to the journalist Manuel Vázquez Montalbán, a member of the Catalan Communist Party, the PSUC.

According to Party figures, membership strength dropped off from the 1977 high point of 201,757 to 171,332 in 1978 – both figures almost certainly exaggerated.[106] That 15 per cent loss contrasted dramatically with the steady increase of membership throughout the 1970s. The departure of 30,000 members reflected disenchantment with the continuing caution of Carrillo's policy. At a time of increasing unemployment and rampant inflation, his moderation seemed like a betrayal to working-class Party members. Moreover, during years of struggle against the dictatorship and the sacrifices of 1976 and 1977, inordinate hopes had been raised by Carrillo's endless triumphalism about the post-Franco democratic regime. It was difficult for the average rank-and-file militant to accept that the Party had to maintain a low profile and even to give its parliamentary support so willingly to the UCD.

At the same time, by the autumn of 1977 Carrillo's moderation in the Cortes, his Eurocommunist pronouncements and the Kremlin's hostility had started to roll back the distrust of Carrillo in some of the Spanish press. However, the more respectable he was becoming in the mainstream media, the more problems he faced on the left. Just when his image was reaching a peak of popularity, he received what could only seem like a stab in the back. The seeming treachery was the publication in November of the memoirs of Jorge Semprún, recalling

his time in the 1950s and early 1960s as organizer of the PCE's clandestine network inside Spain. A few perceptive readers of
'*Eurocommunism*' *and the State* had already noted that Carrillo's
enthusiasm for political and philosophical pluralism was expressed
more by repetition of the word 'liberty' than by close reasoning. Now
Semprún's book argued that the PCE's adoption of Eurocommunism
was merely tactical and was rendered valueless by the basically
Stalinist methods with which Carrillo continued to rule the Party.
Despite the fact that the PCE had undergone considerable sacrifices
and played a major role in bringing back democracy to Spain in the
1970s, Semprún was to be proved right in the 1980s.

The charge that Carrillo had consistently falsified his own and the
Party's history by creating a democratic image and was in reality a
servile lackey of the Kremlin had hitherto been heard only on the lips
of Francoists. More dramatic was Semprún's insinuation that the
death of the PCE's last great martyr, Julián Grimau, executed by the
dictatorship on 20 April 1963, was in some way the consequence of
Carrillo's irresponsibility.[107] Such accusations were normally ignored
by the Communist leadership. However, the repercussions in this
case were so enormous that some reaction was called for. Before
December 1977 was out, Semprún's *Autobiografía de Federico Sánchez*
had sold over 150,000 copies and was the centre of frantic press and
media interest. As author of novels such as *Le Long Voyage* and *La
Deuxième Mort de Ramón Mercader* and of the scripts for films such
as *Z*, *L'Aveu* and *État de siège* for Costa-Gavras and *La Guerre est finie*
for Alan Resnais, Semprún was already a major international celebrity. More importantly, he was a Party hero. The son of a Spanish
diplomat exiled in France, he joined the resistance at the age of seventeen in 1940. After being captured by the Gestapo in 1943, his linguis-
tic abilities helped him not only to survive Buchenwald but also to
organize the Communist network within the camp. After the war, he
joined the PCE and, as 'Federico Sánchez', carried out clandestine
work in Spain with panache, courage and intelligence, eventually
being co-opted on to the politburo.

As the polemic over Semprún's book was building up steam, the
documents published privately in Paris by Claudín in 1965 were

reissued commercially in Spain by a dissident Communist publisher.[108] This made it even more difficult for Semprún's accusations to be ignored. Carrillo consistently denied having read the memoirs. If he had not already devoured them, which would have been logical, he took a copy with him when he made a tour of American universities in November 1977. Perhaps the need to counter the book's impact influenced him in going further than ever before in anti-Soviet declarations in speeches made at Yale, Harvard and Johns Hopkins which, he said later, 'gave me respectability'.[109]

It was understandable that Semprún's attacks should be felt by Carrillo as a stab in the back. The consequent hurt reaction came over as a rather ham-fisted attempt to ensure that past issues would not tarnish the Party's newly won image. At first, Vázquez Montalbán, the immensely influential journalist and good friend of Semprún, was permitted to state in the PCE newspaper *Mundo Obrero* that, if the Party was really committed to internal democracy, it should come to terms with the accusations made and with its own past mistakes.[110] That intelligent tolerance was quickly swamped by a furious reply from Fernando Soto, Communist deputy for Seville, who denounced Semprún's book as 'a load of rubbish dumped on the highest peaks of human dignity'.[111]

Shortly thereafter bigger guns were brought into action. Manuel Azcárate of the Party executive produced a reply to Semprún in a national newspaper.[112] While more diplomatic in tone than Soto's intervention, it was every bit as ill considered. Indeed, Azcárate's rebuttal inadvertently went some way to substantiating Semprún's original case. Semprún had accused the PCE leadership of having blotted out its collective memory. Admitting his own defective recollections and claiming not to have the time necessary to check the documents, Azcárate began by so grossly distorting the issues of the 1964 schism as to imply that Claudín had been proposing collaboration with the dictatorship. He went on to give a mendacious account of the allegedly democratic procedures which had accompanied the Claudín–Semprún expulsions. Finally, he accused Semprún of simply repeating the worst kind of Francoist propaganda. It was not difficult for Semprún to demolish these arguments a few days later.[113]

Nor was Semprún seriously challenged by the laughable declaration made on 8 January 1978 by the president of the PSUC, Gregorio López Raimundo. In an interview which reflected the stance of the leadership group created by Carrillo, the Catalan Communist leader explained Semprún's motive as 'pure and simple envy. Carrillo is so superior to everyone else. Carrillo's political creativity is beyond any of us. The trouble with Semprún and Claudín is just bad-tempered jealousy of the political, ideological, moral and intellectual superiority of Carrillo. They should be humble and accept reality.' In the short term, the damage done to PCE credibility by the scandal surrounding the Semprún book was considerable – to such an extent, indeed, that Claudín himself and the ex-Claudinista Javier Pradera, one of the *Autobiografía*'s dedicatees, felt obliged to dissociate themselves from some of its more sweeping accusations.[114]

Among the charges hurled at the PCE in the ensuing media coverage, the one which hit hardest was that Carrillo's Eurocommunism positions reflected not democratic conviction but opportunistic tactics. In consequence, Carrillo himself was eventually forced to enter the arena. Unlike the incompetent efforts of Soto and Azcárate, his characteristically cunning comments did not engage with any of the specific accusations of the *Autobiografía*. He continued to maintain that he had not read the book but nevertheless told journalists that 'what he had been told was in it' was 'legally actionable'. He declared airily that he would not lower himself to get involved in a slanging match but that he would make available documents that would disprove Semprún's accusations. Needless to say, these never materialized. He tried to divert attention from Semprún's accusations by urging a wider consideration of the disproportionate damage that they were doing. Justifiably stressing the PCE's paramount role in the struggle for democracy in Spain, he claimed that the press furore aroused by the book had become part of an orchestrated campaign against Eurocommunists in general and ultimately against Spain's nascent democracy. The absurd implication was that Semprún was somehow darkly linked with Henry Kissinger, the former US Secretary of State, and Brezhnev in a global anti-Eurocommunist plot.[115]

He followed up his remarks to the press with an utterly manipulative article in *Mundo Obrero* entitled 'We shall not be moved'. Despite still claiming that lack of time had prevented his reading the *Autobiografía*, he produced a series of distorted claims about it. He repeated his allegation that Semprún's book was a key element of a great international and national anti-Communist offensive against the PCE and thus damaging to Spain's fledgling democracy. Ignoring Semprún's criticisms of his own activities, he presented the book as a nauseating attempt to besmirch the memory of those who had died fighting Francoism. He even went so far as to describe Semprún's own method as Stalinist, comparing it to that of the interrogations carried out by the disciples of Beria.[116] Finally, in a long interview in *El País*, while maintaining his fatuous claim not to have read the book, he complained that Semprún was motivated by hatred. At no point in his various responses did he attempt to dispute any of the book's allegations nor did he respond when Semprún challenged him to a public debate.[117]

In fact, Carrillo's assertion that recriminations about the PCE's internal history unfairly obscured the Communists' role in the fight for democracy underscored the ambivalence of the entire polemic. Virtually everything that Semprún said about Carrillo's methods was true, but that did not obliterate the PCE's central contribution to the struggle against Franco. Carrillo's defence against accusations of his authoritarian practices was that they had been a necessity in the context of the clandestinity imposed by the dictatorship. He was understandably reticent about the details of his stewardship of the Party. The long battle for democratic credibility had finally been won and Carrillo had no interest in risking his fragile triumph by disinterring discreditable incidents from the past.

The PCE's enemies felt that if, as Semprún maintained, Eurocommunist positions were not a fundamental aspiration of the entire Party but simply a tactic imposed from above with Stalinist methods, the commitment to a pluralist, democratic socialism was highly suspect. For Semprún, Carrillo's reluctance to recognize the more unsavoury elements of his past showed that the Party was incapable of real change. Carrillo, on the other hand, claimed that changes of strategy were in themselves a form of self-criticism.[118] Semprún, however, argued that such changes were no more than desperate *post factum* measures to cover his failure to make any correct analyses of political and economic development in Spain since the Civil War. In the view of Semprún, the only real achievement of Carrillo and his entourage was to have survived the consequences of their mistakes.

After the elections of June 1977 and the transfer of the political arena from the streets to the Cortes, the importance of the Communists diminished considerably. Nevertheless, the fact remains that Carrillo's moderation backed by the PCE's mass strength was a central factor in consolidating the Spanish transition to democracy. There can be no doubt that Suárez would not have gone as far as he did down the democratic road without popular pressure, some, if far from all, of which had been orchestrated by Carrillo. The modesty of Communist electoral success was, in part, a tribute to the success of American and West German sponsorship of the two most successful mass parties of right and left – the UCD and the PSOE. However, Carrillo's critics on the Spanish left would argue that the poor Communist vote was to be attributed to working-class disillusionment with a scale of moderation sold too cheaply.[119] Of course, there were many reasons for the electoral results: the enormous disproportion between propaganda budgets; a loaded electoral law favouring the conservative countryside; the fears consciously engendered for forty years by the virulently anti-Communist Franco regime; the way in which Carrillo's aged leadership team inadvertently evoked memories of the Civil War. However, taking up the leftist critique of Communist moderation, it might be argued that, from mid-1976 until mid-1979, Carrillo, not entirely disinterestedly, certainly making a virtue of a necessity, took the longer-term view and sacrificed the PCE's vanguard position in order to strengthen the new democratic regime.

The element of sacrifice in the PCE's self-imposed moderation, and particularly Carrillo's support of the Pacto de la Moncloa, led to considerable internecine dispute which surfaced at the Ninth Congress of the PCE, held in Madrid in April 1978. Knowing that discontent was simmering over his sycophantic and heavy-handed bureaucracy, Carrillo had declared in his interview about Semprún's book that there was no such thing as 'Carrillismo' in the PCE. There was a barely concealed warning to dissidents in his remark 'I don't know if there will be any sector ready to question my position as secretary general. The party is free to do so but I'm not worried.' He ended with the disingenuous comment: 'I'm just a simple man and a humble politician.' That interview coincided with a meeting of the Central Committee called to discuss the line to be presented to the forthcoming congress. He was criticized for the fact that, while on his tour of American universities, accompanied by Belén Piniés, in November 1977, he had suggested to the press – without any prior consultation with the rest of the executive – that the concept of Leninism would be dropped from the Party's statutes at the next congress. His reply was a perfect summary of his autocratic views: 'The job of the party leader is to be at the top, to take the responsibility of choosing the right road. If he is mistaken, the party gets rid of him, expels him and that's that.'[120] At the Ninth Congress itself, discontent centred on two issues linked by Carrillo's tendency to make policy without discussion. On the one hand, there was consternation at the official line that 'the Moncloa agreements represent a success for the PCE's policy of national democratic coalition government'. On the other, the proposal to remove Leninism from the PCE's self-definition caused outrage among many delegates.[121] Along with the incorporation of substantial numbers of working-class militants into the Central Committee, this constituted an attempt by Carrillo to adjust both the PCE's theoretical positions and its organizational composition to its day-to-day political practice. However, the costs of the Moncloa accords saw loud rumblings of rebellion, especially in Asturias and Catalonia, where rank-and-file sentiment was in favour of militant strike action. In the Andalusian sections of the Party, and indeed elsewhere, deep discontent was not just confined to the fact that the operation to drop Leninism had been taken on Carrillo's own initiative without prior consultation. There was also outrage that he treated the entire issue simply as a question of rebranding for public relations purposes. He did not engage in theoretical discussion, merely imposed a change of label in order to emphasize the decoupling of the PCE from its Soviet links.[122]

If he planned to de-Leninize the PCE, he certainly did not intend to de-Stalinize it. The new label might mean that there was no longer any vague commitment to the seizure of power in order to impose the dictatorship of the proletariat. However, he inadvertently revealed his determination to keep Party management centrally controlled when he declared that if the Party enjoyed democratic features, it was as the gift of the leadership: 'It is clear that if the leadership team of the party, formed in the long years of struggle, by dint of a process of natural selection, had wanted to create not this open, transparent and democratic party but rather a closed, hermetic one, without contrasting opinions, it could have done so.'[123] Moreover, at the congress, the veterans from the exile, Stalinists one and all, were confirmed in their positions.

The Ninth Congress confirmed that there was serious trouble brewing within the PCE despite the fact that several developments in Spanish politics went some way to justifying Carrillo's moderation. Terrorist activities, first by the ostensibly ultra-leftist but almost certainly police-manipulated GRAPO, and then by the Basque revolutionary separatist organization ETA, ensured that as the new constitution was being elaborated great strain was put on the fragile loyalties of the forces of order. Various attempts at a military coup finally culminated in the abortive putsch of 23 February 1981, the so-called 'Tejerazo' described below. The combination of terrorism and military sedition gave credence to Carrillo's assertion that Spanish democracy was in need of all the cosseting it could get. Moreover, while this caution necessitated curtailing rank-and-file militancy, it was rewarded in the elections of 1 March 1979 by a small increase in the PCE vote from 9.2 per cent to 10.9 per cent, which has to be set against a 2 per cent drop in the PSOE vote.

Within the Party, the way Carrillo gave priority to his role in national politics, and particularly the way he had railroaded through the abandonment of Leninism, had provoked a growing discontent with his leadership. The old excuse that clandestinity imposed the most rigid democratic centralism was no longer valid. Even the life-long loyalty of his friend Manuel Azcárate was stretched to breaking point by Carrillo's increasing contempt for the rest of the leadership:

Authoritarianism, arrogance, was a marked characteristic of Santiago within the leadership. He tended to lead by giving orders with total confidence that he was always right. He would never permit disagreement. He could be incredibly rude if something displeased him. For him, a *normal* discussion was one in which one could comment or expand on what he had said but finally had to accept it. And this had created a habit that gave Santiago excessive power in the party. Above all, he was used to being the one who decided.[124]

Like Claudín and Semprún before him, Azcárate had finally woken up to the fact that Carrillo's despotic Party management prevented the PCE from renewing itself in relation to changing circumstances. Previously the problem had been that he was out of touch with the problems of militants because he was ruling the PCE from Paris. Now he was equally out of touch with the rank and file because he was ruling the Party from the Cortes and the smoke-filled rooms in which he made deals with Suárez. Carrillo was facing outright confrontation with erstwhile collaborators like Azcárate, Ramón Tamames, Carlos Alonso Zaldívar and Pilar Brabo, his once inseparable companion. They were beginning to give voice to a widespread dissatisfaction with the heavy bureaucratic style of the aged leadership team that Carrillo had brought from Paris in 1976. Mounting discontent derived from the fact that, on his return to Spain from exile, Carrillo had ignored the younger elements who had been prominent in recent years and given priority in electoral lists and administrative jobs in the PCE to those who had been with him in exile – Ignacio Gallego, Santiago Álvarez, Francisco Romero Marín, José Gros, Federico Melchor, Tomás García, José Sandoval and many others. There were also frustrations arising out of a series of errors attributable to this bureaucracy such as the decision in July 1980 to stop publishing *Mundo Obrero* as a daily. It had been a mistake to do so in the first place and the poor sales went hand in hand with the failure of the sixtieth-anniversary recruitment campaign. Its results were so poor that there were witticisms about it being a 'disbandment campaign', though, to general alarm, Carrillo seemed unconcerned. Although he had to accept that there had been a drop in Party membership, he claimed that very few of those who had left had done so because of disagreement with the leadership.[125]

Although his star had been waning throughout 1980, Carrillo's position as a figure of national importance was reasserted by his behaviour during the attempted military coup of 23 February 1981. Since 1978, Spain had experienced a debilitating cycle of economic crisis, Basque terrorism and military conspiracy. After a long process of attrition, in which personal exhaustion had combined with the fragmentation of his party, Suárez announced his resignation in a television broadcast on 29 January 1981. To Carrillo's displeasure, his successor as Prime Minister was to be Leopoldo Calvo Sotelo, whom he regarded as cold, snobbish and right-wing. He could not see any possibility of resurrecting the kind of relationship that he had had with Suárez.[126] When Calvo Sotelo appeared before the Cortes on 21 February, Carrillo voted against his investiture and told the press that his government had been born dead. Two days later, when Calvo Sotelo returned for a second vote, the proceedings were interrupted when 180 Civil Guards led by Colonel Antonio Tejero burst into the chamber. The deputies were ordered to the floor and only three refused. Great personal courage was demonstrated by General Manuel Gutiérrez Mellado, who ordered the Guards to leave and was violently jostled; by Adolfo Suárez, who went to Gutiérrez Mellado's assistance; and by Santiago Carrillo, who remained standing. As one of the people most hated by the extreme right in Spain, Carrillo was convinced that he was going to die. He reflected later, and there is no reason to doubt him, that his main concern was that no one should be able to say the head of the Communist Party had died like a coward. He, Gutiérrez Mellado, Suárez, Felipe González and other 'super-hostages' were taken at gunpoint and locked in different rooms. Suárez was kept isolated and the others were put in the so-called Salón de Relojes (Clock Room). As he sat opposite Gutiérrez Mellado, forbidden to speak, Carrillo reflected on the irony that they had both been in Madrid in 1936 – he himself committed to destroying the fifth column and Gutiérrez Mellado as a rebel fifth columnist.[127] The attempted coup collapsed less than twenty-four hours later after King Juan Carlos had made a televised address in support of democracy.

Out of the debacle of 23 February, the phoenix of Spanish democracy was to rise again. On 27 February, three million people demonstrated in favour of democracy in Madrid and other cities. The change of mood was evident too in the offers made by Felipe González, Manuel Fraga and Santiago Carrillo to support the government in the Cortes. Carrillo's place in history as one of the principal architects of the transition to democracy was now secure. However, this did nothing to dissipate the problems within the PCE. Since 1978, there had been emerging a serious challenge to Carrillo's leadership on two fronts. First, an 'ultra-Eurocommunist' group, known as the *renovadores* (renovators) and led by Carlos Alonso Zaldívar, Pilar Brabo and Azcárate, argued that the only way in which the PCE could prosper was by facing fully the implications of Eurocommunism and introducing internal democracy as the basis of realistic and flexible policies. Secondly, there were those who had never been happy about the adoption of Eurocommunism and the abandonment of Leninism. A Soviet-sponsored opposition, which was especially successful in Catalonia, pushed for a more revolutionary, combative line. Because of their support for the Soviet invasion of Afghanistan, they came to be known as *afganos* or *pro-Soviéticos*. Over the next two years, the Party was torn apart in a destructive three-way feud between Eurocommunist *renovadores*, pro-Soviet *afganos* and the Party bureaucrats loyal to Carrillo. The secretary general himself was concerned less with the theoretical issues than with the need to reassert his own control. His efforts began with malicious comments that, while he had been held prisoner in the Cortes, those in charge of the PCE, Manuel Azcárate and Carlos Alonso Zaldívar, had failed to organize mass mobilizations such as those which had greeted the military coup of 1936. Speaking of 'insufficient unity', he was insinuating that the reason was that they were too busy with divisive theoretical debates.[128]

By the time the Tenth Congress was held in Madrid in July 1981, Party membership had fallen, according to official figures, from 171,332 to 132,069, although real numbers were probably dramatically lower. While the *pro-Soviéticos* pushed for a return to a harder line, the 'ultra-Eurocommunist' *renovadores*, with the support of Roberto Lertxundi of the Basque Communist Party (Partido Comunista de Euskadi-EPK, Euskadiko Partidu Komunista), demanded that Carrillo go further towards the Eurocommunist ideal of internal democracy. Since this implied an end to his monolithic method of Party leadership and the removal of his bureaucratic team, it led to a bitter fight both in the build-up to the congress and in the proceedings of the congress itself. At the Central Committee meeting on 5 May convened to discuss the forthcoming congress, Carrillo revealed his unshakeable commitment to democratic centralism when he stated that those who did not accept the majority resolutions would be expelled. He justified this by saying that popular faith in democracy would be undermined by the sight of dissent within the Party. In fact, faced with a pointless struggle, Tamames left the PCE before the congress.[129] On the eve of the congress, Carrillo declared in a press interview: 'Those who do not respect the decisions of the Congress will be expelled.' The clear implication that he could decide on expulsions without consulting the executive or the Central Committee was hardly appropriate when so much of the opposition to his role in the Party was about his despotic leadership.[130] In his inadequate and self-congratulatory report to the congress itself, Carrillo claimed that, if the PCE was still a Stalinist Party, the current debate would have been impossible. Nevertheless, he rejected a pluralist model for the Party, insisting instead on discipline, authority from the top and the maintenance of democratic centralism. His report was approved by 689 votes to 64 against, with an astonishing 266 abstentions.[131]

This result, not at all what Carrillo required, was despite what Azcárate described as 'the most militarized' congress he had ever known. Inevitably, Carrillo reverted to his most Stalinist instincts. In the autumn of 1981, the bulk of the Partido Comunista de Euskadi-EPK broke away under Roberto Lertxundi and joined up with the former ETA leader Mario Onaindia in Euskadiko Eskerra (the Basque Left). Both spoke at a huge meeting in Madrid on 4 November to explain the unification. The event, convened by the *renovadores*, was

a resounding success despite the fact that Carrillo had even tele-
phoned the Minister of the Interior in a vain attempt to have the event
prohibited. When the executive committee met two days later, he
dismissed suggestions that the Party was Eurocommunist on the
outside but Stalinist on the inside. By dint of threatening his own
resignation, he secured the application of 'administrative sanctions'
to expel many of the PCE's most talented elements and several of his
own once closest collaborators, including Azcárate, Pilar Brabo and
Carlos Alonso Zaldívar.[132] The resulting publicity exposed his residual
Stalinism to the general public. It was deeply significant that Azcárate's
replacement as editor of *Nuestra Bandera* was José Sandoval, who was
far from being an intellectual and was notable principally for his years
in Moscow and his loyalty to Carrillo. In a procedure reminiscent of
what had followed Claudín's expulsion, the Party put difficulties in the
way of Azcárate collecting unemployment benefit.[133]

After the Tenth Congress, the divisions between the *renovadores*
and the Carrillista bureaucracy intensified. There were constant crises
in the Catalan, Basque and Asturian parties. This, together with the
endless drifting away of Party intellectuals, led to a widespread
conviction that the PCE was moribund and likely to be annihilated in
the next elections, as indeed was to be the case. Carrillo's later, and
utterly ludicrous, explanation of this was that militants had been
demoralized by the way in which the exaggerated variant of
Eurocommunism pushed by the *renovadores* had degenerated into
petit-bourgeois social democracy.[134]

The expulsions left Carrillo with a tenuous grip on the Party. In the
summer of 1982, he rejected proposals from Nicolás Sartorius for the
reincorporation of the *renovadores* expelled eighteen months previously. At a meeting of the executive committee on 7 June, held to
discuss the fact that, despite Carrillo's predictions of victory, the PCE
had been defeated in the Andalusian regional elections, Marcelino
Camacho tentatively proposed that Carrillo accept the symbolic post
of president with Sartorius becoming secretary general. This would
have required persuading the now eighty-seven-year-old Dolores
Ibárruri to relinquish the post. In the event, it was not necessary since
Carrillo responded to the suggestion, and briefly held on to power, by

the dangerous gesture of resigning. Although his resignation was not accepted at the immediately following meeting of the Central Committee, it presaged his ultimate loss of control of the Party apparatus. Sartorius himself resigned from the executive and with his departure went the best chance of a major renovation of the PCE.[135] The elections of 28 October 1982 took place under the shadow of military intervention but fear did not deter the population from granting the PSOE a substantial mandate with 10,127,092 votes, 47.26 per cent of those cast, which gave them 202 seats. Alianza Popular came second with 5,548,335 votes, 25.89 per cent, and 107 deputies, thereby substantiating Fraga's predictions about a two-party system. The UCD limped home behind the Catalan regional party Convergencia i Unio with 1,323,339 votes, 6.17 per cent, and eleven deputies. Calvo Sotelo failed to win a seat.

Carrillo did get a seat but the PCE saw its vote drop from nearly 11 per cent to 3.6 per cent and lost three-quarters of its deputies.[136] The results ensured that, at the subsequent meeting of the executive committee between 2 and 7 November, Carrillo did indeed resign. He suggested as his successor Gerardo Iglesias, a young leader from Asturias. Five weeks later, the Central Committee was convened to confirm the change. On the eve of the meeting, Iglesias told Simón Sánchez Montero that when Carrillo had informed him that he planned to propose him as secretary general he had said, 'You will be the secretary, but I will make all the decisions.' To Carrillo's disgust, Iglesias sided with the renovators. At the Eleventh Congress in February 1983, Carrillo was defeated when he opposed Iglesias. He subsequently decided that those who voted against him were the puppets of foreign intelligence services.[137] By that time, Party membership had fallen catastrophically from 132,069 to 84,652. Carrillo had forged the PCE in his own image and now, without him, it began to disintegrate. Carrillo himself was dropped from the Central Committee in April 1985. He founded a new party, the Partido de los Trabajadores de España-Unidad Comunista, and Ignacio Gallego formed a pro-Soviet party called the Partido Comunista de los Pueblos de España, which confirmed long-standing suspicions of his Muscovite loyalties. Neither enjoyed any success.[138]

Carrillo stood unsuccessfully for parliament in the 1986 elections, in the 1989 European elections and for parliament again in 1989. Two years later, he agreed to the mass incorporation of the Partido de los Trabajadores de España into the PSOE. He did not go with it, on the grounds that his long track record as a Communist prevented him playing an active role in the PSOE. However, his wife Carmen Menéndez did join. After losing his position in the PCE, Carrillo accepted his departure from the top table of the political establishment with some dignity. He made a living as a writer, scoring a notable commercial success in 1993 with his rather anodyne memoirs in which he proclaimed: 'one does not take decisions entirely on the basis of one's own inclinations; the circumstances surrounding one sometimes weigh more than one's own feelings and dictate what one does. I am convinced that I always acted honestly.'[139] A stream of other volumes followed, on the Second Republic and the Civil War, but he never gave away the secrets which could have done so much to illuminate the history of the period. Indeed, the underlying theme of his many books was that he had been right all along about everything. Carrillo also became a regular interviewee on television and radio, recognizable by his slow-talking style and a gruff, knowing voice that reflected seven decades of chain-smoking. He attributed his iron constitution to the advice given him in Moscow in 1936 to take an aspirin every day. His participation in media debates consolidated his reputation as one of the principal architects of Spanish democracy.

On 19 October 2005, the ninety-year-old Carrillo was awarded an honorary doctorate by the Universidad Autónoma de Madrid in recognition of his role in the struggle for democracy and of his 'extraordinary merits, and particularly his contribution to the policy of national reconciliation, and his decisive contribution to the process of democratic transition in Spain'. Carrillo had come to be widely revered for his moderate and moderating role at a crucial stage in the transition from the dictatorship to democracy. However, his role in the Junta de Defensa de Madrid was still a burning issue among rightists. Accordingly, the degree ceremony was disrupted by militants chanting '¡Paracuellos Carrillo asesino!'[140] It was not the first time that Carrillo had been the target of violent ultra-right-wing attacks.

Ever since his return to Spain in 1976, he had been the object of abuse for his alleged role in the killings at Paracuellos. On 16 April 2005, when he was scheduled to speak at the launch of *Historias de las dos Españas*, a book by the historian Santos Juliá Díaz, the event was interrupted when the bookshop was ransacked by extreme rightists. Barely a week later, a wall adjacent to his apartment block was scrawled with the words 'This is how the war began and we won', 'Carrillo, murderer, we know where you live' and 'Where is the Spanish gold'.[141]

In June 2008, he was taken to the Hospital Clínico in Madrid with cardiac arrhythmia related to problems with the pacemaker with which he had been fitted earlier.[142] His iron health began to show increasing signs of deterioration. In October 2011, he was hospitalized with a urinary tract infection. The following April, he had his appendix removed at the Gregorio Marañón Hospital in Madrid. In July, he was taken again to the neurology department of the same hospital with a circulatory problem.[143] He died in his sleep of cardiac insufficiency on the afternoon of 18 September 2012. He was ninety-seven years old. Twenty-five thousand people visited the chapel of repose where his body was laid out for two days. Belén Piniés, who had remained his secretary until the day he died, stayed with the body throughout those days. Forty-five years younger than him, she herself died on 15 October, less than one month later.[144] It was as if, with the death of the man to whom she had dedicated more than half of her life, she finally gave in to the cancer that she had fought for so long.

Carrillo's body was cremated at the Almudena Cemetery and his ashes were scattered in the sea off Gijón. At the end of October, on the initiative of the PSOE, and with the abstention of the ruling conservative party, the Partido Popular, it was proposed that a street in Madrid be named after him.[145]

EPILOGUE

One of Carrillo's most quoted remarks was: 'In politics, repentance does not exist. You are either right or wrong but there is no room for repentance.' In an interview in 1991, when the journalist Feliciano Fidalgo commented, 'Your eldest son said recently that your vitality derived from your self-satisfaction,' Carrillo replied, 'Looking back over my life, I don't regard it negatively. If I had to live it all over again, I think that, some small change aside, I would do it all exactly the same as before.'[1] The things that he was prepared to do again included his attack on his father: 'I broke with my father and I would do it a thousand times if I had to.'[2] From the early 1980s until his death, Carrillo wrote several sets of recollections, most notably the huge tome that he described as the 'memoirs of a survivor'.[3] In none of those volumes could there be found anything resembling repentance, but there was certainly ample falsification and obfuscation. The conclusion might be drawn that any small changes he would make if he could live his life over again would be in the record of his deeds.

The brilliant columnist and novelist Rosa Montero captured Carrillo's complacency when she wrote: 'He looks a bit like a sinful country priest who has enjoyed his sins.'[4] If Carrillo was really as self-satisfied as he presented himself in his writings and in countless interviews, it would certainly account for his rejection of any need for repentance. However, it would not account for the way in which he consistently felt the need to reinvent his own life-story. It was a life of different phases, which were linked by a successful blend of ruthless ambition and pragmatism. He went from being revolutionary firebrand to Communist apparatchik to Stalinist leader and finally to national hero as a result of his contribution to the restoration of democracy. Along the way, there were betrayals – of Largo Caballero, Wenceslao Carrillo, Jesús Monzón, Carmen de Pedro, Joan Comorera, Francisco Antón, Fernando Claudín, Jorge Semprún, Javier Pradera and many, many more. And there were lies, about Paracuellos, about the Val d'Aran, about the guerrilla, about the several variants of the great national general strike, about his relationship with the Soviet Union. In the interviews and books, the betrayals continued, as when, in the celebrated interview with Rosa Montero, alongside several bizarre and unsolicited affirmations of his heterosexuality, he blamed Claudín both for the failure of the national general strike of 1959 and for the capture of Julián Grimau.[5] And there were silences when awkward questions were asked, and interviews refused when such questions were expected.[6]

Carrillo's own perception of his achievements was laid out in his report to the Rome meeting of the Central Committee in 1976. Using the royal 'we', he made a number of claims in a balance sheet of his stewardship of the PCE, of which the two most striking were that he had avoided conflicts both between militants in the Spanish interior and the exiled leadership and between generations. In what, at best, was a considerable exaggeration, he declared: 'We have been inspired by the determination to establish a harmonious relationship between the different generations, balancing their representation in the leadership team.'[7] He had conveniently forgotten that the issues that arose in relation to Monzón, Pradera, Grimau, Claudín, Semprún and others were concerned with the failure of the exiled leadership team to comprehend the reality of Spain. Moreover, if his second claim about the incorporation of young elements had been true, Carrillo would not eventually have clashed in the 1980s with those younger militants who had risen to prominence inside Spain, away from the control of his Parisian clique. Yet another of his claims was that he had secured the Party's independence from Moscow and been in the front rank of the movement to renovate world communism. Ironically, his destructive conflict with those younger elements came about because they had believed his Eurocommunist boasts and so pushed for a degree of internal Party democracy that he had found unacceptable. The way in which he dealt with their dissent virtually destroyed the PCE as an effective political force in the democracy established in 1977.

Long before the explicit boasts of the Rome meeting, his reports to successive meetings of the politburo and the Central Committee were larded with triumphant and often mistaken predictions. From 1944 until 1976, he regularly announced the imminent overthrow of the Franco dictatorship first by popular uprisings and guerrilla warfare and later by armed violence and nationwide general strikes. None of these predictions came true. Similarly, he had announced that nothing could be expected of a monarchy invented by Franco.[8] Yet, despite the mistakes, by the time of his death, Carrillo had been converted into a national treasure, hailed by major figures of the right.

Certainly, it was a life of failures seasoned with eternal optimism and reflected on with lies. After leaving the Party in 1985, Carrillo became a full-time media commentator and writer. He published several books and many dozens of articles, but little of lasting value. The most credible among them was his account of his year on the run after he returned to Spain clandestinely in early 1976, *El año de la peluca* (*The Year of the Wig*, 1987). In 1993, he garnered considerable media attention with his lengthy, unrevealing and often mendacious memoirs. There were other volumes, such as *La memoria en retazos* (2003), *Los viejos camaradas* (2010) and the posthumous *Mi testamento político* (2012), which continued the pattern of whitewashing his past but were more explicit in their settling of accounts with those who had criticized him.

His innumerable contributions to radio and television programmes enhanced his image as a thoughtful national figure. Chain-smoking to the last, his media performances projected deep satisfaction with his career. He gave every appearance of believing his own, often contradictory, versions of his past. Yet his hurt reaction to criticism revealed something else, a shadow of guilt perhaps. After the disputes that had led to the expulsion of Fernando Claudín from the PCE, Carrillo had treated him brutally, having him evicted from his home and putting difficulties in the way of his earning a living. Conveniently forgetting this, he consistently claimed that he had maintained a warm friendship with his old comrade. Thus he was outraged by the eminently even-handed biography produced by Claudín, *Santiago Carrillo: crónica de un secretario general*, describing it as an ugly political attack.[9] A similar development can be discerned in relation to his one-time protégé Jorge Semprún. Carrillo always claimed to have had a cordial relationship with Semprún after his expulsion. He claimed with equal consistency that he had not read *Autobiografía de Federico Sánchez*. However, in 1996, he unleashed a vicious attack not just on the book, which he clearly had read, but on Semprún's entire career as a novelist and his record as Spanish Minister of Culture. Four years later, his festering resentment of Semprún went even further. In an interview with the journalist José Luis Losa, Carrillo absurdly accused Semprún of cowardice and blamed him for Grimau's death.[10]

The efforts that Carrillo made to acquire power within the PCE and to hold on to it were replaced after 1985 by equally tireless efforts to justify his actions. A pathological need to remodel the past could be seen as a way of avoiding guilt. The scaffolding of lies was so well constructed that it is likely that Carrillo did believe them. The lies, the half-truths, the treachery all demonstrate, along with the intelligence, the stamina and the daring, that the key to Carrillo was ambition. The best that can be said about him is that he played a key role in the transition to democracy by helping to convince the right of the moderation of the left. The worst that can be said about him is that while the central objective of most of those with whom he worked and sometimes clashed was the struggle against Franco, his main priority was always his own eminence. Accordingly, he betrayed comrades and appropriated their ideas. To put it another way, his ambition and the rigidity with which he pursued it squandered the sacrifices and the heroism of the tens of thousands of militants who suffered in the struggle against Franco.

ABBREVIATIONS

ACNP: Asociación Católica Nacional de Propagandistas (National Catholic Association of Propagandists – secular Catholic political organization of elite lawyers, professors, bankers etc)

AGL: Agrupación Guerrillera de Levante (Communist Guerrilla Group of the Levante – created in 1945)

AGLA: Agrupación Guerrillera de Levante y Aragón (the name of the AGL above was changed in 1948 to disguise the failure of the guerrilla in Aragón)

ANFD: Alianza Nacional de Fuerzas Democráticas (National Alliance of Democratic Forces – non-Communist anti-Franco front)

CEDA: Confederación Española de Derechas Autónomas (Spanish Confederation of Autonomous Right-Wing Groups – mass party of the right created in 1933 by José María Gil Robles)

CGTU: Confederación General de Trabajo Unitaria (United General Confederation of Labour – small Communist trade union which aspired to merge with, and take over, the UGT (q.v.))

CNT: Confederación Nacional del Trabajo (National Confederation of Labour – anarcho-syndicalist trade union)

CPSU: Communist Party of the Soviet Union

EEC: European Economic Community

ETA: Euskadi Ta Askatasuna (Basque Homeland and Freedom – Basque separatists)

FAI: Federación Anarquista Ibérica (Iberian Anarchist Federation – direct action group created in 1926)

FJS: Federación de Juventudes Socialistas (Socialist Youth Federation – merged in 1936 with the Communist Youth to form the JSU (q.v.))

FLP: Frente de Liberación Popular (Popular Liberation Front – small Castroist anti-Franco group created in 1959)

FNTT: Federación Nacional de Trabajadores de la Tierra (National Federation of Landworkers – Socialist union of agricultural labourers)

FRAP: Frente Revolucionario Anti-fascista y Patriota (Revolutionary Anti-Fascist and Patriotic Front – small revolutionary group consisting largely of the FUDE (q.v.) and the PCE-ML (q.v.))

FUDE: Federación Universitaria Democrática Española (Federation of Democratic University Students – the student group of the PCE-ML (q.v.))

GRAPO: Grupos de Resistencia Antifascista Primero de Octubre (First of October Anti-Fascist Resistance Groups)

GRU: Glavnoe Razvedupravlenie (Soviet Military Intelligence)

HNP: Huelga Nacional Pacífica (National Peaceful Strike)

HOAC: Hermandad Obrera de Acción Católica (Workers' Fraternity of Catholic Action)

JAP: Juventud de Acción Popular (the CEDA youth movement)

JOC: Juventud Obrera Católica (Catholic Workers' Youth Movement)

JSU: Juventudes Socialistas Unificadas (United Socialist Youth – created in 1936 from the fusion of Socialist and Communist youth movements)

KGB: Komitet Gosudarstvennoi Bezopasnosti (Committee for State Security – Soviet security and intelligence organization, successor to the NKVD (q.v.))

KIM: Kommunisticheskii International Molodyozhy (Communist Youth International)

NKVD: Narodnyi Komissariat Inostrannykh Del (People's Commissariat for Internal Affairs – Soviet security and intelligence organization)

PCE: Partido Comunista de España (Spanish Communist Party)

PCE-ML: PCE-Marxista-Leninista (Maoist faction that appeared in the late 1960s)

PCI: Partido Comunista Italiano (Italian Communist Party)

PCOE: Partido Comunista Obrero Español (Spanish Workers' Communist Party – pro-Soviet breakaway created by Enrique Líster in 1970)

POUM: Partido Obrero de Unificación Marxista (Workers' Marxist Unification Party – anti-Stalinist Marxist group persecuted during the Civil War as Trotskyist)

PSOE: Partido Socialista Obrero Español (Spanish Socialist Party)

PSUC: Partit Socialista Unificat de Catalunya (Catalan Communist Party)

UCD: Unión del Centro Democrático (Union of the Democratic Centre – party created by Adolfo Suárez in 1977 to contest the first post-Franco election)

UGT: Unión General de Trabajadores (General Union of Workers – Socialist trades union federation)

UJC: Unión de Juventudes Comunistas (Communist Youth – merged with the FJS (q.v.) in 1936 to form the JSU (q.v.))

NOTES

Abbreviations Used in Notes
AHN: Archivo Histórico Nacional; AHPCE: Archivo Histórico del Partido Comunista de España; *BUGT: Boletín de la Unión General de Trabajadores de España*; FPI: Fundación Pablo Iglesias

Preface

1 Santiago Carrillo, *Demain l'Espagne: entretiens avec Régis Debray et Max Gallo* (Paris: Éditions du Seuil, 1974) pp. 115–17.

2 Rosa Montero, 'Entrevista con Santiago Carrillo', *El País Semanal*, 18 June 1978.

3 His own books are listed in the Bibliography. The dictated ones are the interviews with Debray and Gallo, and María Eugenia Yagüe, *Santiago Carrillo: perfil humano y político* (Madrid: Editorial Cambio 16, 1977).

4 Fernando Claudín, *Santiago Carrillo: crónica de un secretario general* (Barcelona: Editorial Planeta, 1983) p. ix. See, *inter alia*, subsequent references to his first wife and his daughter.

Chapter 1: The Creation of a Revolutionary: 1915–1934

1 Santiago Carrillo, *Memorias*, 2nd edn (Barcelona: Editorial Planeta, 2006) pp. 15–16.

2 Santiago Carrillo, *Demain l'Espagne: entretiens avec Régis Debray et Max Gallo* (Paris: Éditions du Seuil, 1974) pp. 29–30; Carrillo, *Memorias*, pp. 3–6.

3 Carrillo, *Memorias*, pp. 6–16; Fernando Claudín, *Santiago Carrillo: crónica de un secretario general* (Barcelona: Editorial Planeta, 1983) pp. 10–13, 22. Andrés Carabantes and Eusebio Cimorra, *Un mito llamado Pasionaria* (Barcelona: Editorial Planeta, 1982) p. 163.

4 Carrillo, *Memorias*, pp. 17–18, 23–8. On Hildegart and Aurora, see Rosa Cal, *A mi no me doblega nadie: Aurora Rodríguez: su vida y su obra (Hildegart)* (Sada-A Coruña: Edicios do Castro, 1991), and Joan Llarch, *Hildegart: la vírgen roja* (Barcelona: Producciones Editoriales, 1979) pp. 89–95; Carmen Domingo, *Mi querida hija Hildegart* (Barcelona: Editorial Destino, 2008) pp. 69–73; Eduardo de Guzmán, *Mi hija Hildegart* (Barcelona: Plaza y Janés, 1997) pp. 111–25; Alison Sinclair, *Sex and Society in Early Twentieth-Century Spain: Hildegart Rodríguez and the World League for Sexual Reform* (Cardiff: University of Wales Press, 2007) pp. 71–2.

5 On Besteiro, see Andrés Saborit, *Julián Besteiro* (Buenos Aires: Losada, 1967); Emilio Lamo de Espinosa and Manuel Contreras,

Filosofía y política en Julián Besteiro, 2nd edn (Madrid: Editorial Sistema, 1990) ch. 6; Paul Preston, *¡Comrades! Portraits from the Spanish Civil War* (London: HarperCollins, 1999).

6 On Prieto in this period, Octavio Cabezas, *Indalecio Prieto, socialista y español* (Madrid: Algaba Ediciones, 2005) pp. 49–152; Preston, *¡Comrades!*, ch. 7.

7 On Largo Caballero, see the forthcoming study by Julio Aróstegui.

8 Juan Pablo Fusi, *Política obrera en el País Vasco* (Madrid: Ediciones Turner, 1975) pp. 105, 333–58.

9 Carolyn P. Boyd, *Praetorian Politics in Liberal Spain* (Chapel Hill: University of North Carolina Press, 1979) pp. 84–5, 286; Enrique Moradiellos, *El Sindicato de los Obreros Mineros Asturianos 1910–1930* (Oviedo: Universidad de Oviedo, 1986) pp. 58–9; Juan Antonio Lacomba Avellán, *La crisis española de 1917* (Madrid: Editorial Ciencia Nueva, 1970) pp. 269–74.

10 Llaneza, letters from prison, published in *El Minero de la Hulla*, August and September 1917, reprinted in Manuel Llaneza, *Escritos y discursos* (Oviedo: Fundación José Barreiros, 1985) pp. 206–14. On Franco's role, see Francisco Aguado Sánchez, *La revolución de octubre de 1934* (Madrid: Editorial San Martín, 1972) p. 193; Luis Galinsoga and Francisco Franco-Salgado, *Centinela de occidente (Semblanza biográfica de Francisco Franco)* (Barcelona: Editorial AHR, 1956) pp. 35–6; Brian Crozier, *Franco: A Biographical History* (London: Eyre & Spottiswoode, 1967) p. 50.

11 Gerald H. Meaker, *The Revolutionary Left in Spain, 1914–1923* (Stanford: Stanford University Press, 1974) pp. 225–384; Paul

Heywood, *Marxism and the Failure of Organised Socialism in Spain 1879–1936* (Cambridge: Cambridge University Press, 1990) pp. 62–83; Manuel Tuñón de Lara, *El Movimiento obrero en la historia de España* (Madrid: Taurus, 1972) pp. 681–717.

12 José Carlos Gibaja Velázquez, *Indalecio Prieto y el socialismo español* (Madrid: Editorial Pablo Iglesias, 1995) p. 13.

13 *El Socialista*, 14 September 1923; Francisco Largo Caballero, *Presente y futuro de la Unión General de Trabajadores de España* (Madrid: Javier Morata, 1925) pp. 30–40; Francisco Largo Caballero, *Mis recuerdos: cartas a un amigo* (Mexico City: Editores Unidos, 1954) pp. 90–1.

14 Largo Caballero, *Presente y futuro*, pp. 7, 41–3; PSOE, *Convocatoria y orden del día para el XII congreso ordinario del Partido Socialista Obrero Español* (Madrid: Gráfica Socialista, 1927) p. 91; Antonio Ramos Oliveira, *Nosotros los marxistas: Lenin contra Marx*, 2nd edn (Madrid: Ediciones Júcar, 1979) pp. 144–66.

15 *El Socialista*, 2 October and 1 November 1923.

16 Tuñón, *Movimiento obrero*, p. 776; Ramos Oliveira, *Nosotros los marxistas*, p. 158.

17 Manuel Tuñón de Lara, *La España del siglo XX*, 2nd edn (Paris: Librería Española, 1973) p. 151.

18 PSOE, *Convocatoria y orden del día para el XII congreso ordinario del PSOE*, pp. 103–4; PSOE, *XII Congreso del Partido Socialista Obrero Español, 28 de junio al 4 de julio de 1928* (Madrid: Gráfica Socialista, 1929) pp. 140–53.

19 Largo Caballero, *Mis recuerdos*, pp. 90–2.

20 Enrique de Santiago, *La Unión General de Trabajadores ante la*

revolución (Madrid: Tipografía Sáez Hermanos, 1932) pp. 44–5; Tuñón, *Movimiento obrero*, pp. 721, 775, 784; Joaquín Maurín, *Los hombres de la Dictadura* (Madrid: Editorial Cénit, 1930) pp. 197–8.

21 Tuñón, *Movimiento obrero*, p. 784.

22 *El Socialista*, 3 January 1929.

23 *Boletín de la Unión General de Trabajadores de España* [henceforth *BUGT*], August 1929; *El Socialista*, 1 September 1929.

24 Saborit, *Besteiro*, pp. 172–80.

25 *BUGT*, September 1929; *El Sol*, 17 September 1929; *El Socialista*, 14 January 1930.

26 Emilio Mola Vidal, *Obras completas* (Valladolid: Librería Santarén, 1940) pp. 352–4. On the strike wave, see Tuñón, *Movimiento obrero*, p. 790.

27 Gabriel Mario de Coca, *Anti-Caballero: una crítica marxista de la bolchevización del Partido Socialista Obrero Español* (Madrid: Ediciones Engels, 1936) p. 11.

28 Largo Caballero, *Mis recuerdos*, pp. 107–8; Miguel Maura, *Asi cayó Alfonso XIII* (Mexico City: Imprenta Mañez, 1962) p. 83.

29 Carrillo, *Memorias*, pp. 23–4, 31.

30 *Ibid.*, pp. 31–2.

31 *Ibid.*, pp. 33–4.

32 Graco Marsá, *La sublevación de Jaca: relato de un rebelde* (Madrid: Zeus, 1931) *passim*; José María Azpíroz Pascual and Fernando Elboj Broto, *La sublevación de Jaca* (Zaragoza: Guara Editorial, 1984) pp. 27–36, 109–17.

33 Julio Alvarez del Vayo, *The Last Optimist* (London: Putnam, 1950) p. 198; Mola, *Obras*, p. 543; Largo Caballero, *Mis recuerdos*, pp. 111–12; *El Socialista*, 8–13 October 1932; Carrillo, *Memorias*, pp. 34–9; Claudín, *Santiago Carrillo*, p. 13.

34 Carrillo, *Memorias*, pp. 40–3.

35 Dámaso Berenguer, *De la Dictadura a la República* (Madrid: Editorial Plus Ultra, 1946) pp. 349–51, 394–7.

36 Ángeles Barrio Alonso, *Anarquismo y anarcosindicalismo en Asturias (1890/1936)* (Madrid: Siglo XXI, 1988) pp. 314–19; Enrique Montañés, *Anarcosindicalismo y cambio político: Zaragoza, 1930–1936* (Zaragoza: Institución Fernando el Católico, 1989) pp. 47–60; Enric Ucelay Da Cal, *La Catalunya populista: imatge, cultura i política en l'etapa republicana (1931–1939)* (Barcelona: Edicions de La Magrana, 1982) p. 135; Julián Casanova, *De la calle al frente: el anarcosindicalismo en España (1931–1939)* (Barcelona: Editorial Crítica, 1997) pp. 14–17.

37 Paul Preston, *The Spanish Holocaust: Inquisition and Extermination in Twentieth-Century Spain* (London: HarperCollins, 2012) pp. 37–51.

38 *Renovación*, 20 April, 10 May 1931.

39 Eugenio Vegas Latapie, *El pensamiento político de Calvo Sotelo* (Madrid: Cultura Española, 1941) pp. 88–92; Eugenio Vegas Latapie, *Escritos políticos* (Madrid: Cultura Española, 1941) pp. 9–12; Eugenio Vegas Latapie, 'Maeztu y Acción Española', *ABC*, 2 November 1952; Pedro Carlos González Cuevas, *Acción Española: teología política y nacionalismo autoritario en España (1913–1936)* (Madrid: Editorial Tecnos, 1998) pp. 144–5, 165–8, 171–5.

40 Paul Preston, *The Coming of the Spanish Civil War: Reform, Reaction and Revolution in the Second Spanish Republic*, 2nd edn (London: Routledge, 1994) ch. 2.

41 Carrillo, *Memorias*, pp. 49–53, Claudín, *Santiago Carrillo*, p. 14.

42 Federación de Juventudes Socialistas de España, *Resoluciones del IV Congreso* (Madrid: Gráfica Socialista, 1932) pp. 17, 32, 40 (quoted by Sandra Souto Kustrín, *Paso a la juventud: movilización democrática, estalinismo y revolución*

en la República Española (Valencia: Publicacions de la Universitat de València, 2013) pp. 43–4); Claudín, *Santiago Carrillo*, p. 14; Carrillo, *Memorias*, pp. 56, 58–61; Santiago Carrillo, *La memoria en retazos: recuerdos de nuestra historia más reciente española* (Barcelona: Plaza y Janés, 2003) pp. 115–16.

43 *El Socialista*, 11 August 1932; Carrillo, *Memorias*, pp. 63–4.

44 *El Socialista*, 14, 16, 17, 18 August 1932.

45 Carrillo, *Memorias*, pp. 63–8.

46 Manuel Azaña, *Obras completas*, 4 vols (Mexico City: Ediciones Oasis, 1966–8) IV, pp. 36–7; Eulàlia Vega, *Anarquistas y sindicalistas durante la segunda República: la CNT y los Sindicatos de Oposición en el País Valenciano* (Valencia: Edicions Alfons el Magnànim, 1987) pp. 98–101; Carrillo, *Memorias*, pp. 63–8.

47 Luis Araquistáin, 'Los socialistas en el primer bienio', *Leviatán*, No. 18, October–November 1935, pp. 24–5.

48 *El Socialista*, 8, 9 October 1932; Lamo de Espinosa, *Besteiro*, pp. 86–7; Saborit, *Besteiro*, pp. 227–8; Juan-Simeón Vidarte, *Las Cortes Constituyentes de 1931–1933* (Barcelona: Grijalbo, 1976) pp. 485–93; Coca, *Anti-Caballero*, pp. 62–5.

49 *El Sol*, 23 October 1932; *El Socialista*, 23, 25 October 1932; Coca, *Anti-Caballero*, pp. 66–70; Lamo de Espinosa, *Besteiro*, pp. 87–8; Vidarte, *Cortes Constituyentes*, pp. 495–7; Amaro del Rosal, *Historia de la UGT de España 1901–1939*, 2 vols (Barcelona: Grijalbo, 1977) I, pp. 350–2.

50 Juan-Simeón Vidarte, *El bienio negro y la insurrección de Asturias* (Barcelona: Grijalbo, 1978) p. 188.

51 *El Socialista*, 25 July 1933; Segundo Serrano Poncela, *El Partido Socialista y la conquista del poder* (Barcelona: Ediciones L'Hora, 1935) pp. 47–9.

52 On the origin of the summer schools, see Souto Kustrín, *Paso a la Juventud*, pp. 37–8. Besteiro's speech is reproduced almost in its entirety in Saborit, *Besteiro*, pp. 237–40; Coca, *Anti-Caballero*, pp. 100–1.

53 For the text, see Indalecio Prieto, *Discursos fundamentales* (Madrid: Ediciones Turner, 1975) pp. 160–80, and for the reception, Indalecio Prieto, *Convulsiones de España: pequeños detalles de grandes sucesos*, 3 vols (Mexico City: Ediciones Oasis, 1967–9) III, pp. 160–5.

54 *El Socialista*, 13 August 1933; Serrano Poncela, *El Partido Socialista*, pp. 50–1; *El Debate*, 15 August 1933. On the nickname, see Claudín, *Santiago Carrillo*, pp. 15–16; Juan Francisco Fuentes, *Largo Caballero: el Lenin español* (Madrid: Editorial Síntesis, 2005) pp. 14–18.

55 *Renovación*, 23 September 1933; Coca, *Anti-Caballero*, pp. 109–10.

56 *Renovación*, 30 September, 7, 14, 21, 28 October, 4 November 1933.

57 Claudín, *Santiago Carrillo*, pp. 22–3; Carrillo, *Memorias*, p. 88.

58 José Antonio Primo de Rivera, 'Discurso de la fundación de Falange Española', in *Textos de doctrina política*, 4th edn (Madrid: Sección Femenina de FET y de las JONS, 1966) pp. 61–9.

59 *Renovación*, 25 November 1933.

60 Vidarte, *El bienio negro*, pp. 109–10; appendix to Francisco Largo Caballero, *Discursos a los trabajadores* (Madrid: Gráfica Socialista, 1934) pp. 163–6.

61 Actas de la Comisión Ejecutiva del PSOE, 25 November 1933, Fundación Pablo Iglesias [henceforth FPI], AH 20–2; *BUGT*, December 1933 and January 1934; Francisco Largo Caballero, *Escritos*

de la República (Madrid: Fundación Pablo Iglesias, 1985) pp. 42–8; Largo Caballero, Mis recuerdos, pp. 131–3. Cf. Vidarte, El bienio negro, pp. 110–11.

62 El Socialista, 26, 28 November, 1 December 1933; Renovación, 2, 9 December 1933.

63 Renovación, 23 December 1933.

64 Amaro del Rosal, 1934: el movimiento revolucionario de octubre (Madrid: Akal, 1983) pp. 35–93.

65 BUGT, January 1934; Rosal, 1934, pp. 93–150.

66 Renovación, 4 November 1933, 30 December 1933; Carrillo, Memorias, pp. 82–3; Sandra Souto Kustrín, 'Y ¿Madrid? ¿Qué hace Madrid?' Movimiento revolucionario y acción colectiva (1933–1936) (Madrid: Siglo XXI, 2004) pp. 176–200.

67 Rosal, 1934, pp. 151–87; Largo Caballero, Mis recuerdos, pp. 134–5; Coca, Anti-Caballero, p. 133.

68 Largo Caballero, Escritos, pp. 64–75; Dolores Ibárruri et al., Guerra y revolución en España 1936–39, 4 vols (Moscow: Editorial Progreso, 1967–77) I, pp. 52–7; Santos Juliá Díaz, 'Los socialistas y el escenario de la futura revolución', in Germán Ojeda, ed., Octubre 1934: cincuenta años para la reflexión (Madrid: Siglo XXI, 1985) p. 122.

69 Largo Caballero, Escritos, pp. 76–141; El Socialista, 25, 26, 28, 30 January 1934; BUGT, February 1934; El Obrero de la Tierra, 3 February 1934; Rosal, 1934, pp. 188–200; Coca, Anti-Caballero, pp. 137–42; Juliá, 'Los socialistas y el escenario de la futura revolución', pp. 123–7; Santos Juliá Díaz, Historia del socialismo español (1931–1939) (Barcelona: Conjunto Editorial, 1989) pp. 101–2; Carrillo, Memorias, pp. 89–98.

70 Renovación, 6 January 1934.

71 Rosal, 1934, pp. 200–56.

72 Renovación, 6, 13, 20, 27 January, 3, 10 February, 3 March 1934.

73 On Salazar Alonso, see Preston, The Spanish Holocaust, pp. 20, 61–6, 71–9.

74 Rafael Salazar Alonso, Bajo el signo de la revolución (Madrid: Librería de San Martín, 1935) pp. 34–5.

75 Carrillo, Memorias, p. 77; Renovación, 17, 24 February, 3 March 1934; Souto Kustrín, 'Y ¿Madrid? ¿Qué hace Madrid?', p. 129.

76 Federación de Juventudes Socialistas, Memoria del V Congreso (Madrid: Gráfica Socialista, 1934) pp. 97, 110 (quoted by Souto Kustrín, Paso a la Juventud, p. 59); Renovación, 7 July 1934; Carrillo, Memorias, p. 83; Rosal, 1934, p. 326; Ricard Viñas, La formación de las Juventudes Socialistas Unificadas (1934–1936) (Madrid: Siglo XXI, 1978) pp. 14–15.

77 Renovación, 20 January, 3 March, 18 April 1934; El Debate, 21, 22, 24 April 1934; El Socialista, 22, 24 April 1934; Henry Buckley, Life and Death of the Spanish Republic (London: Hamish Hamilton, 1940) pp. 126–7.

78 Grandizo Munis, Jalones de derrota, promesa de victoria (Mexico City: Editorial Lucha Obrera, 1948) pp. 114–16; Carrillo, Memorias, p. 84.

79 Francesc Bonamusa, El Bloc Obrer i Camperol (1930–1932) (Barcelona: Curial, 1974) pp. 275–82, 341–2; Victor Alba, La Alianza Obrera: historia y análisis de un táctica de unidad en España (Gijón: Ediciones Júcar, 1977) pp. 83–131; Antoni Monreal, El pensamiento político de Joaquín Maurín (Barcelona: Ediciones Península, 1984) pp. 159–77.

80 El Socialista, 29 December 1933. Cf. Marta Bizcarrondo, 'De las Alianzas Obreras al Frente Popular', Estudios de Historia Social, Nos. 16–17, January–June 1981, pp. 83–7.

81 *Renovación*, 7 July 1934; Carrillo, *Memorias*, pp. 99–100; Preston, *The Coming of the Spanish Civil War*, pp. 147–55.

82 *Renovación*, 14, 21, 28 July 1934.

83 *Renovación*, 4, 11, 18 August 1934; Viñas, *La formación de las JSU*, pp. 7–22, 71–109; Claudín, *Santiago Carrillo*, pp. 21–5; Carrillo, *Memorias*, pp. 85–9; Souto Kustrín, 'Y ¿Madrid? ¿Qué hace Madrid?', pp. 96–101.

84 Carrillo, *Memorias*, pp. 85–7.

85 *Renovación*, 25 August, 1, 14, 22, 29 September 1934.

86 *BUGT*, August 1934; Largo Caballero, *Mis recuerdos*, p. 141; Carrillo, *Memorias*, pp. 102–4.

87 Largo Caballero, *Escritos*, pp. 86–110, 115–41; Rosal, *1934*, pp. 207–33; Vidarte, *El bienio negro*, p. 231.

88 *El Debate*, 28 September 1934; José María Gil Robles, *No fue posible la paz* (Barcelona: Ariel, 1968) p. 131.

89 *CEDA*, Nos. 36–7, December 1934.

90 *El Sol*, 12 September 1934; Salazar Alonso, *Bajo el signo*, pp. 316–20.

91 *El Socialista*, 13, 15, 16 September 1934; *Renovación*, 22 September 1934; Souto Kustrín, 'Y ¿Madrid? ¿Qué hace Madrid?', pp. 163–6; Claudín, *Santiago Carrillo*, pp. 25–6.

92 Largo Caballero, *Escritos*, pp. 150–8; Largo Caballero, *Mis recuerdos*, p. 136; Rosal, *1934*, pp. 257–61; Rosal, *UGT*, I, pp. 387, 401–2; Julio Alvarez del Vayo, *The Last Optimist* (London: Putnam, 1950) p. 266.

93 Manuel Grossi, *La insurrección de Asturias (Quince días de revolución socialista)* (Barcelona: Gráficos Alfa, 1935) pp. 23, 63; Vidarte, *El bienio negro*, pp. 267–85, 334.

94 Munis, *Jalones de derrota*, pp. 130–40; Joaquín Maurín, *Hacia la segunda revolución: el fracaso de la República y la insurrección de octubre* (Barcelona: Gráficos Alfa, 1935) pp. 144–67; testimony of Madrid CNT secretary, Miguel González Inestal, to the author; Enrique Castro Delgado, *Hombres made in Moscú* (Barcelona: Luis de Caralt, 1965) pp. 176–83; Andrés Nin, *Los problemas de la revolución española* (Paris: Éditions Ruedo Ibérico, 1971) pp. 156–7; Santos Juliá Díaz, 'Fracaso de una insurrección y derrota de una huelga: los hechos de octubre en Madrid', *Estudios de Historia Social*, No. 31, October–December 1984; Juliá, *Historia del socialismo*, pp. 126–9.

95 Paul Quintanilla, *Waiting at the Shore: Art, Revolution, War and Exile in the Life of the Spanish Artist Luis Quintanilla* (Rhode Island: Lulu Press, 2003) pp. 121–2; Luis Quintanilla, 'Pasatiempo': la vida de un pintor (Memorias) (Sada-A Coruña: Ediciós do Castro, 2004) pp. 317–19; Alvarez del Vayo, *The Last Optimist*, p. 263; Carrillo, *Memorias*, pp. 104–9.

Chapter 2: The Destruction of the PSOE: 1934–1939

1 Manuel Tagüeña Lacorte, *Testimonio de dos guerras* (Mexico City: Ediciones Oasis, 1973) pp. 67–72.

2 Grandizo Munis, *Jalones de derrota, promesa de victoria* (Mexico City: Editorial Lucha Obrera, 1948) pp. 136–7; Amaro del Rosal, *1934: el movimiento revolucionario de octubre* (Madrid: Akal, 1983) pp. 259–64, 286–7.

3 Rosal, *1934*, pp. 295–7.

4 Juan-Simeón Vidarte, *El bienio negro y la insurrección de Asturias* (Barcelona: Grijalbo, 1978) pp. 342–55; Rosal, *1934*, pp. 295–6; Amaro del Rosal, *Historia de la UGT de España 1901–1939*, 2 vols (Barcelona: Grijalbo, 1977) I, pp. 409–22.

5 Helen Graham, *Socialism and War: The Spanish Socialist Party in Power*

and Crisis, 1936–1939 (Cambridge: Cambridge University Press, 1991) pp. 18–19; Rafael Cruz, *El Partido Comunista de España en la II República* (Madrid: Alianza, 1987) pp. 103–9, 175–9.

6 Francisco Largo Caballero, *Mis recuerdos: cartas a un amigo* (Mexico: Editores Unidos, 1954) pp. 138–9; Santos Juliá Díaz, *Historia del socialismo español (1931–1939)* (Barcelona: Conjunto Editorial, 1989) pp. 127, 353–4.

7 Luis Araquistáin, 'Largo Caballero ante los jueces', *Leviatán*, No. 20, January 1936, p. 10.

8 Fernando Claudín, *Santiago Carrillo: crónica de un secretario general* (Barcelona: Editorial Planeta, 1983) p. 34; Santiago Carrillo, *Memorias*, 2nd edn (Barcelona: Editorial Planeta, 2006) p. 121.

9 Carrillo, *Memorias*, pp. 121–2; Burnett Bolloten, *The Spanish Civil War: Revolution and Counterrevolution* (Chapel Hill: University of North Carolina Press, 1991) p. 131.

10 Dolores Ibárruri *et al.*, *Guerra y revolución en España 1936–1939*, 4 vols (Moscow: Editorial Progreso, 1967–77) I, p. 62; Enrique Castro Delgado, *Hombres made in Moscú* (Barcelona: Luis de Caralt, 1965) pp. 192–3.

11 Carrillo, *Memorias*, pp. 114–21; María Eugenia Yagüe, *Santiago Carrillo: perfil humano y político* (Madrid: Editorial Cambio 16, 1977) p. 26; Claudín, *Carrillo*, p. 33.

12 Andrés Saborit, *Julián Besteiro* (Buenos Aires: Losada, 1967) p. 251.

13 Largo Caballero, *Mis recuerdos*, pp. 143, 145. See Araquistáin to Largo Caballero, 14 April 1935, reprinted in Juliá, *Historia del socialismo*, pp. 356–7; Ramos Oliveira to Largo Caballero, undated, quoted in Vidarte to Prieto, 10 July 1935, FPI,

AH 22–24 and reprinted in Francisco Largo Caballero, *Escritos de la República* (Madrid: Fundación Pablo Iglesias, 1985) pp. 171–2.

14 *La Libertad*, 30 March 1935; *Documentos socialistas* (Madrid: Publicaciones Índice, 1935) pp. 249–55; Vidarte, *El bienio negro*, pp. 393–8; Juliá, *Historia del socialismo*, p. 147.

15 Vidarte to Prieto, 20 March 1935, *Documentos socialistas*, pp. 17–18; Juan-Simeón Vidarte, *Todos fuimos culpables* (Mexico City: Grijalbo, 1973) p. 25; Prieto to PSOE executive, reprinted in Carlos de Baraibar, *Las falsas 'posiciones socialistas' de Indalecio Prieto* (Madrid: Ediciones Yunque, 1935) pp. 139–45. The original is in the FPI, AH 17.

16 The text of the letter is reprinted in Baraibar, *Prieto*, pp. 197–200, and in *Documentos socialistas*, followed by the unpublished message from González Peña to the Madrid section of the FJS, pp. 143–55, and the protests of the Asturian FJS, pp. 179–87. Cf. Largo Caballero, *Mis recuerdos*, p. 144; Largo Caballero, *Escritos*, pp. 167–71.

17 Indalecio Prieto, 'La coalición de izquierdas', *El Liberal*, 14 April 1935.

18 Andrés Nin, *Los problemas de la revolución española* (Paris: Éditions Ruedo Ibérico, 1971) pp. 155–8; Munis, *Jalones de derrota*, p. 183; Pelai Pagès i Blanch, *Andreu Nin: una vida al servicio de la clase obrera* (Barcelona: Laertes, 2011) pp. 228–37.

19 Carlos Hernández Zancajo, *Octubre: segunda etapa* (n.p., n.d. [Madrid, 1935]). There were two editions, of which the cheaper had no cover and smaller print. References given here are to that popular edition. On the authorship, see Amaro del Rosal quoted in Marta Bizcarrondo, ed., *Octubre del 34: reflexiones sobre una*

revolución (Madrid: Editorial Ayuso, 1977) p. 50; Carrillo, *Memorias*, pp. 128–30; remarks of Carrillo to the author on 5 October 1977.

20 Bizcarrondo, ed., *Octubre*, pp. 26–31, 39–46, 52–5, 94.

21 Vidarte, *Todos fuimos culpables*, p. 30; Largo Caballero, *Mis recuerdos*, pp. 141–2; Santiago Carrillo, *Demain l'Espagne: entretiens avec Régis Debray et Max Gallo* (Paris: Éditions du Seuil, 1974) p. 32; Carrillo, *Memorias*, p. 133.

22 *Claridad*, 7 December 1935.

23 Saborit, *Besteiro*, pp. 251–7.

24 Segundo Serrano Poncela, *El Partido Socialista y la conquista del poder* (Barcelona: Ediciones L'Hora, 1935) p. 156.

25 Julián Besteiro, *Marxismo y anti-marxismo* (Madrid: Gráfica Socialista, 1935). References are to the 4th edition (Madrid: Editorial ZYX, 1967) pp. 16–23, 93–102, 107–13, 130–1.

26 Luis Araquistáin, 'El marxismo en la Academia', 'Un marxismo contra Marx', 'La esencia del marxismo', *Leviatán*, Nos. 13–15, May–July 1935; Julián Besteiro, 'Leviatán: el socialismo mitológico', 'Mi crítico empieza a razonar', *Democracia*, 15 June, 6 July 1935.

27 Indalecio Prieto, 'Mi derecho a opinar', 'La Amnistía, base de la coalición electoral', 'El valor de la acción parlamentaria', 'Los roedores de derrotas', 'La planta exótica del caudillismo', *El Liberal* and *La Libertad*, 22–26 May 1935. In book form, Indalecio Prieto, *Posiciones socialistas: del momento* (Madrid: Publicaciones Índice, n.d. [1935]).

28 Prieto's replies to Enrique de Francisco of 30 April and 14 May are reprinted in *Documentos socialistas*, pp. 31–59. Baraibar, *Las falsas 'posiciones socialistas'*, pp. 22–6, 46, 67–9, 113. See also the refutation of Baraibar by Antonio Gascón and Victoria Priego, *Por hoy y por mañana (Leves comentarios a un libro firmado por Carlos Baraibar)* (Madrid: Publicaciones Índice, 1935).

29 *Claridad*, 29 July, 26 October, 30 November 1935.

30 *Democracia*, 13 September, 11 October 1935; Rosal, *1934*, p. 301.

31 José Díaz, *Tres años de lucha* (Toulouse: Ediciones Nuestro Pueblo, 1947) pp. 17–23, 35–43.

32 Carrillo, *Memorias*, pp. 133–6; Sandra Souto Kustrín, *Paso a la juventud: movilización democrática, estalinismo y revolución en la República Española* (Valencia: Publicacions de la Universitat de València, 2013) p. 85.

33 *Claridad*, 27 August, 12, 19 October 1935.

34 Luis Araquistáin, 'La nueva táctica comunista', *Leviatán*, No. 16, August 1935. Cf. Santos Juliá Díaz, *La izquierda del PSOE (1935–1936)* (Madrid: Siglo XXI, 1977) pp. 184–201.

35 *Claridad*, 7, 14 December 1935.

36 Carrillo, *Memorias*, p. 136; Antonio Elorza and Marta Bizcarrondo, *Queridos camaradas: la Internacional Comunista y España, 1919–1939* (Barcelona: Editorial Planeta, 1999) pp. 274, 277–8; Amaro del Rosal, *Historia de la UGT de España 1901–1939*, 2 vols (Barcelona: Grijalbo, 1977) II, pp. 621–2.

37 Souto Kustrín, *Paso a la juventud*, p. 85.

38 Archivo Histórico del Partido Comunista de España [henceforth AHPCE], Dirigentes, 3/1.2, Letter from Santiago Carrillo from the Cárcel Modelo in Madrid, 22 November 1935. Margarita Nelken later referred to these photographs in her speeches – *El Socialista*, 26 March 1936; *Claridad*, 19 May 1936.

39 Minutes of meeting on 16 November 1935 of the executive committees of the UGT, FJS and PSOE, reprinted in Largo Caballero, *Escritos*, pp. 255–9; Juliá, *Historia del socialismo*, pp. 157–8; Graham, *Socialism and War*, pp. 18–21.

40 Vidarte to Prieto, 20 November 1935, Prieto to Vidarte, n.d. [November 1935], in Largo Caballero, *Escritos*, pp. 276–81.

41 Santiago Carrillo, 'Hacia la unidad orgánica a marchas rápidas', *Claridad*, 7 December 1935, reprinted in Ricard Viñas, *La formación de las Juventudes Socialistas Unificadas (1934–1936)* (Madrid: Siglo XXI, 1978) pp. 137–40.

42 Minutes of the meeting of the Comité Nacional del PSOE, 16 December 1935, FPI, AH 24–1; *El Socialista*, 18, 19, 25 December 1935; *Claridad*, 23 December 1935, 15 January 1936; Vidarte, *Todos fuimos culpables*, p. 26; Largo Caballero, *Mis recuerdos*, p. 148; Gabriel Mario de Coca, *Anti-Caballero: una crítica marxista de la bolchevización del Partido Socialista Obrero Español* (Madrid: Ediciones Engels, 1936) pp. 193–8; Juliá, *La izquierda*, pp. 22–3, 82–5; Paul Preston, *The Coming of the Spanish Civil War: Reform, Reaction and Revolution in the Second Spanish Republic 1931–1936*, 2nd edn (London: Routledge, 1994) pp. 230–7; Carrillo, *Memorias*, pp. 137–9.

43 *Renovación*, 1 February 1936.

44 *Claridad*, 25, 30 January, 6 February 1936; *El Socialista*, 12 February 1936.

45 Carrillo, *Memorias*, pp. 141–3.

46 *Ibid.*, pp. 148–9; Bolloten, *The Spanish Civil War*, pp. 130–1; Carrillo, *Demain l'Espagne*, p. 43.

47 Carrillo, *Demain l'Espagne*, pp. 45–7; Carrillo, *Memorias*, pp. 149–53; Claudín, *Carrillo*, pp. 36–8.

48 Claudín, *Carrillo*, p. 32. Carmen later became the wife of Colonel Martínez Cartón of the PCE leadership (see David Wingeate Pike, *In the Service of Stalin: The Spanish Communists in Exile 1939–1945* (Oxford: Clarendon Press, 1993) p. 16).

49 Boris Volodarsky, 'Soviet Intelligence Services in the Spanish Civil War, 1936–1939' (unpublished doctoral thesis, London School of Economics and Political Science, 2010) pp. 134–6.

50 Carlos de Baraibar, 'La traición del Stalinismo: la experiencia española de la Juventud Socialista Unificada', *Timón* (Buenos Aires), No. 7, June 1940, p. 64.

51 Viñas, *La formación del JSU*, pp. 49–63.

52 Largo Caballero, *Escritos*, p. 307.

53 Helen Graham, 'The Socialist Youth in the JSU: The Experience of Organisational Unity 1936–1938', in Martin Blinkhorn, ed., *Spain in Conflict 1931–1939: Democracy and its Enemies* (London: Sage Publications, 1986) pp. 83–102; Graham, *Socialism and War*, pp. 31–2. Carrillo's speech, *Mundo Obrero*, 6 April 1936; Largo Caballero's tears, Graham, 'The Socialist Youth in the JSU', p. 101.

54 Fernando Hernández Sánchez, *Guerra o revolución: el Partido Comunista de España en la guerra civil* (Barcelona: Editorial Crítica, 2010) pp. 79, 489; Carrillo, *Memorias*, p. 169; Carrillo, *Demain l'Espagne*, pp. 42–9.

55 Carrillo, *Demain l'Espagne*, pp. 48–9.

56 Viñas, *La formación del JSU*, p. 64.

57 Araquistáin to Norman Thomas, president of the Socialist Party of the USA, 1 January 1939, reprinted in Luis Araquistáin, *Sobre la guerra civil y en la emigración* (Madrid: Espasa Calpe, 1983) p. 179.

58 Carrillo, *Memorias*, pp. 173–83; Claudín, *Carrillo*, pp. 42–3; Enrique Líster, *¡Basta! Una aportación a la lucha por la recuperación del Partido*, 2nd edn (Madrid: G. del Toro, 1978) pp. 173–4.

59 Giuseppe Loteta, 'Fratello, mio valoroso compagno …': Dall'Italia alla Spagna, la vita di Fernando De Rosa, socialista libertario (Venice: Marsilio, 1998) pp. 231–6; Carrillo, *Memorias*, pp. 183–7; Tagüeña Lacorte, *Testimonio*, p. 129.

60 Santiago Carrillo, *La Segunda República: recuerdos y reflexiones* (Barcelona: Plaza y Janés, 1999) p. 36.

61 According to Carlos Contreras, *Milicia Popular*, 10 October 1936, Mola's press conference took place a few days earlier.

62 Julio Aróstegui and Jesús A. Martínez, *La Junta de Defensa de Madrid* (Madrid: Comunidad de Madrid, 1984) pp. 54–61; Antonio López Fernández, *Defensa de Madrid: relato histórico* (Mexico City: Editorial A. P. Márquez, 1945) pp. 82–4.

63 *ABC*, 8 October 1936; Gregorio Gallego, *Madrid, corazón que se desangra* (Madrid: G. del Toro, 1976) pp. 173–80; Largo Caballero, *Mis recuerdos*, p. 189; Francisco Largo Caballero, *Obras completas*, 16 vols (Madrid and Barcelona: Fundación Largo Caballero/Instituto Monsa, 2003–9) IX, pp. 3512–19.

64 Helen Graham, *The Spanish Republic at War 1936–1939* (Cambridge: Cambridge University Press, 2002) pp. 168–9; General Vicente Rojo, *Así fue la defensa de Madrid* (Mexico City: Ediciones Era, 1967) pp. 32–6.

65 Gregorio Morán, *Miseria y grandeza del Partido Comunista de España 1939–1985* (Barcelona: Editorial Planeta, 1986) pp. 65–6.

66 Aróstegui and Martínez, *La Junta de Defensa*, pp. 61–3; Ibárruri *et al.*, *Guerra y revolución*, II, p. 142; Ian Gibson, *Paracuellos: cómo fue* (Barcelona: Argos Vergara, 1983) p. 192.

67 Santiago Carrillo, *Mi testamento político* (Barcelona: Galaxia Gutenberg, 2012) pp. 116–18.

68 Carrillo, *Memorias*, pp. 195–7; Paul Preston, *The Spanish Holocaust: Inquisition and Extermination in Twentieth-Century Spain* (London: HarperCollins, 2012) pp. 356–7. Carrillo was using the Spanish edition, *El holocausto español: odio y exterminio en la Guerra Civil y después* (Barcelona: Editorial Debate, 2011). See below for discussion of the report.

69 Declaration of Ramón Torrecilla Guijarro, Archivo Histórico Nacional [henceforth AHN], FC-Causa General, 1526–3, Exp. 5, p. 25. See also Gibson, *Paracuellos*, pp. 45, 260–6.

70 Gallego, *Madrid*, p. 222.

71 Carrillo, *Memorias*, pp. 192–3; Castro Delgado, *Hombres made in Moscú*, p. 390; Claudín, *Carrillo*, pp. 44–5.

72 Carrillo *Memorias*, pp. 274–5.

73 Carrillo, *Demain l'Espagne*, p. 51; Carrillo *Memorias*, pp. 251–2; Claudín, *Carrillo*, p. 45.

74 Andrés Carabantes and Eusebio Cimorra, *Un mito llamado Pasionaria* (Barcelona: Editorial Planeta, 1982) pp. 163–4.

75 Largo Caballero, *Obras completas*, VIII, p. 3247; Bolloten, *The Spanish Civil War*, p. 132.

76 Baraibar, 'La traición del Stalinismo', p. 68; Largo Caballero, *Obras completas*, VIII, p. 3248.

77 Declaration of Manuel Muñoz, AHN, FC-Causa General, 1530–1, Exp. 1, p. 305; Carlos Fernández Santander, *Paracuellos del Jarama:*

¿Carrillo culpable? (Barcelona: Argos Vergara, 1983) p. 102.

78 Félix Schlayer, *Diplomático en el Madrid rojo* (Seville: Espuela de Plata, 2008) pp. 143–4.

79 Graham, *The Spanish Republic at War*, p. 189.

80 Boris Volodarsky to the author, 14 June 2013.

81 Jorge M. Reverte, 'Paracuellos, 7 de noviembre de 1936: agentes de Stalin indujeron la matanza de presos sacados de las cárceles de Madrid', *El País*, 5 November 2006.

82 Aurora Arnaiz, *Retrato hablado de Luisa Julián* (Madrid: Compañía Literaria, 1996) p. 35.

83 Rojo, *Así fue la defensa de Madrid*, pp. 43–5.

84 Román Karmén, *¡No pasarán!* (Moscow: Editorial Progreso, 1976) pp. 276–8.

85 Mijail Koltsov, *Diario de la guerra de España* (Paris: Éditions Ruedo Ibérico, 1963) pp. 191–2; Gibson, *Paracuellos*, p. 83.

86 Contreras articles in *Milicia Popular*; Ángel Viñas, *El escudo de la República: el oro de España, la apuesta soviética y los hechos de mayo de 1937* (Barcelona: Editorial Crítica, 2007) pp. 61–2; Alexander I. Kolpakidi and Dmitri P. Prokhorov, *KGB: vsyo o vneshnei razvedke* (Moscow: Olimp, 2002) p. 168, quoted by Volodarsky, 'Soviet Intelligence Services', ch. 4, p. 134.

87 Castro Delgado, *Hombres*, pp. 390–1.

88 'V Madride ya rukovodil gruppoi, kotoroi polzovalsya dlya samykh raznykh del' – Grigulevich, interviewed by Shatunovskaya, *Latinskaya Amerika*, No. 3, 1993, pp. 63–9, quoted by Volodarsky, 'Soviet Intelligence Services', ch. 4, pp. 131–4.

89 Causa General, *La dominación roja en España* (Madrid: Ministerio de Justicia, 1945) pp. 279–80.

90 'Informe sobre la actuación de la policía en el servicio que permitió el descubrimiento en los meses de abril, mayo y junio de la organización de espionaje de cuyas derivaciones surgieron las detenciones y diligencias instruidas contra elementos destacados del POUM', 28 October 1937, FPI, AH 71–6; Declaration of Fernando Valentí Fernández in Proceedings of the Military Trial against José Cazorla Maure, AHN, FC-Causa General, 1525–1, pp. 28–9. I am grateful to Ángel Viñas for drawing my attention to the 'Informe' and to Aurelio Martín Nájera of the Fundación Pablo Iglesias for providing me with a copy. See also Viñas, *El escudo*, pp. 75–6.

91 'V Madride ya rukovodil gruppoi, kotoroi polzovalsya dlya samykh raznykh del' – Grigulevich, interviewed by Shatunovskaya, *Latinskaya Amerika*, No. 3, 1993, pp. 63–9, quoted by Volodarsky, 'Soviet Intelligence Services', ch. 4, p. 138.

92 Christopher Andrew and Vasili Mitrokhin, *The Sword and the Shield: The Mitrokhin Archive and the Secret History of the KGB* (New York: Basic Books, 1999) p. 300; Marjorie Ross, *El secreto encanto de la KGB: las cinco vidas de Iósif Griguliévich* (Heredia, Costa Rica: Farben Grupo Editorial Norma, 2004) pp. 164–81.

93 Aróstegui and Martínez, *La Junta de Defensa*, pp. 75–6, 292.

94 Schlayer, *Diplomático en el Madrid rojo*, pp. 138–40.

95 The original of the document is in the Archives of the International Institute for Social History, Amsterdam. Jorge Martínez Reverte, *La Batalla de Madrid* (Barcelona: Editorial Crítica, 2004) pp. 226–7; Gibson, *Paracuellos*, p. 12.

96 Padre Carlos Vicuña OSA, *Mártires Agustinos de El Escorial* (El Escorial:

Imprenta del Monasterio de El Escorial, 1943) pp. 168-9.

97 Adelardo Fernández Arias (El Duende de la Colegiata), *Madrid bajo el 'terror' 1936-1937 (Impresiones de un evadido, que estuvo a punto de ser fusilado)* (Zaragoza: Librería General, 1937) pp. 249-52; Gibson, *Paracuellos*, pp. 11-17.

98 There is considerable debate concerning the exact numbers; see Fernández Santander, *Paracuellos*, p. 47; Adelardo Fernández Arias (El Duende de la Colegiata), *La agonía de Madrid 1936-1937 (Diario de un superviviente)* (Zaragoza: Librería General, 1938) p. 64. For overall figures, see Gibson, *Paracuellos*, pp. 184-91; Javier Cervera Gil, *Madrid en guerra: la ciudad clandestina 1936-1939*, 2nd edn (Madrid: Alianza Editorial, 2006) pp. 91-3.

99 Declaration of Antonio Viqueira Hinojosa, AHN, FC-Causa General, 1526-1, Exp. 2, pp. 183-6; Gibson, *Paracuellos*, pp. 184-91; Cervera Gil, *Madrid en guerra*, pp. 88-93; Rafael Casas de la Vega, *El terror: Madrid 1936: Investigación histórica y catálogo de víctimas identificadas* (Madrid: Editorial Fénix, 1994) pp. 299-303, 311-95; Fernández Arias, *Madrid bajo el 'terror'*, pp. 248-52.

100 Declaration of José Cazorla Maure, AHN, FC-Causa General, 1525-1, pp. 9-10; Declaration of Ramón Torrecilla Guijarro, AHN, FC-Causa General, 1526-3, Exp. 5, p. 25; Gibson, *Paracuellos*, pp. 48, 52, 172.

101 Reproduced in Causa General, *La dominación roja*, between pp. 51 and 53. Gibson, *Paracuellos*, pp. 144-50.

102 *Heraldo de Madrid*, 10 November 1936; *La Voz*, 12 November 1936; Vicente Rojo, *Así fue la defensa de Madrid*, 35; Gibson, *Paracuellos*, pp. 36-8.

103 Declaration of Teodoro Illera Martín, AHN, FC-Causa General, 1505, Exp. 2, pp. 21-2; Casas de la Vega, *El terror*, pp. 114-15; Causa General, *La dominación roja*, pp. 104-5.

104 Declaration of Ramón Torrecilla Guijarro, AHN, FC-Causa General, 1526-3, Exp. 5, p. 25; Gibson, *Paracuellos*, p. 48.

105 *La Voz*, 1, 11 November 1936; *Informaciones*, 10, 11, 12 November 1936; Gibson, *Paracuellos*, pp. 38-45, 49, 52-3.

106 Declaration of Manuel Rascón Ramírez, AHN, FC-Causa General, 1530, Exp. 4, p. 145, 1526, Exp. 5, pp. 196-7; Gibson, *Paracuellos*, p. 49.

107 Declaration of Ramón Torrecilla Guijarro, AHN, FC-Causa General, 1526-3, Exp. 5, pp. 27-8.

108 Declaration of Álvaro Marasa Barasa, AHN, FC-Causa General, 1526-3, Exp. 5, pp. 16-17, 38-40, 124-5; Gibson, *Paracuellos*, pp. 256-9.

109 Libro de Actas de la Junta de Defensa de Madrid, Aróstegui and Martínez, *La Junta de Defensa*, pp. 295ff.

110 AHN, FC-Causa General, 1530, Exp. 12, p. 5; Cervera Gil, *Madrid en guerra*, pp. 105-6.

111 Declaration of the witness Melchor Rodríguez García, AHN, FC-Causa General, 1530-2, p. 6; declaration of Gabriel Callejón Molina, AHN, FC-Causa General, 1530-2, p. 32; Alfonso Domingo, *El ángel rojo: la historia de Melchor Rodríguez, el anarquista que detuvo la represión en el Madrid republicano* (Córdoba: Editorial Almuzara, 2009) pp. 172-83; Cervera Gil, *Madrid en guerra*, p. 89; AHN, FC-Causa General, 1530-2/5, pp. 6-7; Juan García Oliver, *El eco de los pasos* (Barcelona: Éditions Ruedo Ibérico, 1978) pp. 306; Schlayer, *Diplomático*

en el Madrid rojo, p. 163; Domingo, *El ángel rojo*, pp. 187–9.

112 AHN, FC-Causa General, 1530–2/5, pp. 6–7; García Oliver, *El eco de los pasos*, p. 306; Schlayer, *Diplomático en el Madrid rojo*, p. 163; Domingo, *El ángel rojo*, pp. 187–9.

113 Manuel Azaña, *Apuntes de memoria inéditos y cartas 1938–1939–1940* (Valencia: Pre-Textos, 1990) pp. 153–5.

114 *La Voz*, 13 November 1936; *Informaciones*, 13 November 1936; *ABC*, 13 November 1936; *Heraldo de Madrid*, 14 November 1936.

115 Aróstegui and Martínez, *La Junta de Defensa*, pp. 90–4; Largo Caballero, *Mis recuerdos*, pp. 191–2.

116 Jesús de Galíndez, *Los vascos en el Madrid sitiado* (Buenos Aires: Editorial Vasca Ekin, 1945) p. 68.

117 Serrano Poncela to the Central Committee of the PCE, FPI, AH 63–52, pp. 2–5; Serrano Poncela to Fidel Miró, 13 August 1939, FPI, AH 26–28, pp. 4–7. I am immensely grateful to Sandra Souto Kustrín for drawing my attention to these letters.

118 Souto Kustrín, *Paso a la juventud*, p. 123 n. 70.

119 Gibson, *Paracuellos*, pp. 198–209.

120 Santiago Carrillo, *Los viejos camaradas* (Barcelona: Editorial Planeta, 2010) pp. 37–8.

121 Carrillo, *Memorias*, p. 220.

122 Declaration of Ramón Torrecilla Guijarro, AHN, FC-Causa General, 1526–3, Exp. 5, p. 28.

123 Ministers in Adolfo Suárez's government demanded an investigation into Paracuellos which must have been extremely cursory since it produced no documentary proof of Carrillo's guilt: Joaquín Bardavío, *Sábado santo rojo* (Madrid: Ediciones UVE, 1980) pp. 130–6.

124 'No fui responsable', *Cambio 16*, 16 January 1977, pp. 12–14; Bardavío, *Sábado santo rojo*, p. 133.

125 Carrillo interview with Gibson, *Paracuellos*, pp. 196–7; *El País*, 28 October 2005.

126 Francisco Antón Sanz, *Madrid, orgullo de la España antifascista: discurso pronunciado en el Pleno del C.C. del Partido Comunista celebrado en Valencia los días 5, 6, 7 y 8 de Marzo de 1937* (Valencia: Ediciones del Partido Comunista de España, Comisión Nacional de Agit-Prop, 1937) p. 18; Santiago Carrillo, *La juventud, factor de la victoria: discurso pronunciado en el Pleno del C.C. del Partido Comunista celebrado en Valencia los días 5, 6, 7 y 8 de Marzo de 1937* (Valencia: Ediciones del Partido Comunista de España, Comisión Nacional de Agit-Prop, 1937) p. 3. Both texts and other interventions in AHPCE, Pleno ampliado del CC del PCE, Valencia, 5, 6, 7, 8 March 1937, carp. 18.

127 Elorza and Bizcarrondo, *Queridos camaradas*, p. 379; Ronald Radosh, Mary R. Habeck and Grigory Sevostianov, eds, *Spain Betrayed: The Soviet Union in the Spanish Civil War* (New Haven: Yale University Press, 2001) p. 223.

128 Ángel L. Encinas Moral, ed., *Las causas de la derrota de la República española: informe elaborado por Stoyán Mínev (Stepanov), Delegado en España de la Komintern (1937–1939)* (Madrid: Miraguano Ediciones, 2003) pp. 93, 111–12; Carrillo, *Mi testamento*, p. 121.

129 Cazorla's wife refers to this destruction of papers: Arnaiz, *Retrato hablado*, p. 113.

130 Ibárruri et al., *Guerra y revolución*, II, p. 187.

131 Carrillo, *Memorias*, pp. 239–40; Arnaiz, *Retrato hablado*, p. 35.

132 Aróstegui and Martínez, *La Junta de Defensa*, pp. 343–5; Gallego, *Madrid, corazón que se desangra*, pp. 272–5.

133 *Mundo Obrero*, 26, 27, 29, 31
December 1936, 2 January 1937;
CNT, 29 December 1936, 1 January
1937; Aróstegui and Martínez, *La
Junta de Defensa*, pp. 92–3, 252, 228,
233, 236–8; Julián Zugazagoitia,
Guerra y vicisitudes de los españoles,
2nd edn, 2 vols (Paris: Librería
Española, 1968) I, pp. 219–21;
Gallego, *Madrid*, pp. 211–12.

134 Viñas, *La formación del JSU*, pp.
64–6; Graham, *Socialism and War*,
pp. 69–74.

135 Escribano to Bolloten, 28 May 1950,
quoted Bolloten, *The Spanish Civil
War*, pp. 134–6.

136 Santiago Carrillo, *En marcha hacia
la victoria* (Valencia: JSU, 1937) p. 9.

137 *Ibid.*, pp. 3–5, 7–12, 33–5, 67;
Claudín, *Carrillo*, p. 50; Hernández
Sánchez, *Guerra y revolución*, p. 216.
For newsreel pictures, see http://
www.abelmartin.com/album/imag/
jsu.html.

138 Carrillo, *En marcha*, pp. 13–14, 49;
Ramón Casterás Archidona, *Las
Juventudes Socialistas Unificadas de
Catalunya ante la guerra y la
revolución (1936–1939)*, 2nd edn
(Barcelona: Hogar del Libro, 1982)
pp. 168–84.

139 Carrillo, *La juventud, factor de la
victoria*; Claudín, *Carrillo*, pp. 50–2.

140 Claudín, *Carrillo*, pp. 56–7;
Carrillo, *Memorias*, pp. 246–7,
273–82; Hernández Sánchez,
Guerra o revolución, pp. 214,
473–4.

141 Souto Kustrín, *Paso a la juventud*,
pp. 147–8; Viñas, *La formación del
JSU*, pp. 66–8; Graham, *Socialism
and War*, pp. 69–74, 116, 224–6.

142 Carrillo, *Memorias*, pp. 287, 296;
Líster, *¡Basta!*, pp. 174–5.

143 'Informe del camarada Santiago
Carrillo, Secretario General de las
Juventudes Socialistas Unificadas de
España, al Comité Ejecutivo de la
Internacional Juvenil Socialista',
quoted by Souto Kustrín, *Paso a la

juventud*, p. 287; Carrillo, *Memorias*,
pp. 242–50.

144 Souto Kustrín, *Paso a la juventud*, p.
133 nn. 97–9.

145 Graham, *Socialism and War*, pp.
226–31, 297 n. 31.

146 Hernández Sánchez, *Guerra o
revolución*, p. 440.

147 Carrillo, *Memorias*, pp. 298–303.

148 Carrillo, *Demain l'Espagne*, p. 65;
Teresa Pàmies, *Quan érem capitans:
memòries d'aquella guerra*
(Barcelona: Dopesa, 1974) pp.
147–51; Carrillo, *Memorias*, pp.
305–19.

149 Carrillo, *Memorias*, pp. 318–19.

150 Elorza and Bizcarrondo, *Queridos
camaradas*, p. 433.

151 On the Casado coup, the fullest
account is by Ángel Viñas and
Fernando Hernández Sánchez, *El
desplome de la República* (Barcelona:
Editorial Crítica, 2009). For
Carrillo's reaction, Carrillo,
Memorias, p. 319.

Chapter 3: A Fully Formed Stalinist: 1939–1950

1 Enrique Líster, *¡Basta! Una
aportación a la lucha por la
recuperación del Partido*, 2nd edn
(Madrid: G. del Toro, 1978) pp.
169–71; Santiago Carrillo, *Demain
l'Espagne: entretiens avec Régis
Debray et Max Gallo* (Paris: Éditions
du Seuil, 1974) pp. 70, 73; Manuel
Tagüeña Lacorte, *Testimonio de dos
guerras* (Mexico City: Ediciones
Oasis, 1973) pp. 303–4.

2 Joan Estruch Tobella, *El PCE en la
clandestinidad 1939–1956* (Madrid:
Siglo XXI, 1982) pp. 11–12.

3 Gregorio Morán, *Miseria y
grandeza del Partido Comunista de
España 1939–1985* (Barcelona:
Editorial Planeta, 1986) pp. 68–9;
Fernando Claudín, *Santiago
Carrillo: crónica de un secretario
general* (Barcelona: Editorial
Planeta, 1983) pp. 58–9.

4 Tagüeña Lacorte, *Testimonio*, pp. 357–9.

5 Claudín, *Santiago Carrillo*, pp. 60–2

6 Carrillo, *Demain l'Espagne*, pp. 70–2; Villa's account at http://www.lne.es/asturama/2012/09/19/abril-1958-ingrese-psoe-aval-wenceslao-carrillo-padre-santiago-carrillo/1300159.html.

7 Ángel L. Encinas Moral, ed., *Las causas de la derrota de la República española: informe elaborado por Stoyán Mínev (Stepanov), Delegado en España de la Komintern (1937–1939)* (Madrid: Miraguano Ediciones, 2003) pp. 263–81; Palmiro Togliatti, *Opere 1935–1944* (Rome: Editori Riuniti, 1979) pp. 343–410; Ángel Viñas and Fernando Hernández Sánchez, *El desplome de la República* (Barcelona: Editorial Crítica, 2009) pp. 47–63; Líster, *¡Basta!*, pp. 163–71; Antonio Cordón, *Trayectoria (Recuerdos de un artillero)* (Seville: Espuela de Plata, 2008) pp. 651–728.

8 Viñas and Hernández Sánchez, *El desplome*, pp. 413–40; the secret report for Stalin, *ibid.*, pp. 471–626; Tagüeña Lacorte, *Testimonio*, pp. 343–5.

9 Jesús Hernández, *En el país de la gran mentira* (Madrid: G. del Toro, 1974) pp. 41–60; Enrique Castro Delgado, *Mi fe se perdió en Moscú* (Barcelona: Luis de Caralt, 1964) pp. 28–32.

10 Claudín, *Santiago Carrillo*, pp. 62–3; Santiago Carrillo, *Memorias*, 2nd edn (Barcelona: Editorial Planeta, 2006) pp. 332–3.

11 Carrillo, *Demain l'Espagne*, p. 75.

12 María Eugenia Yagüe, *Santiago Carrillo: perfil humano y político* (Madrid: Editorial Cambio 16, 1977) pp. 37, 49–50; Carrillo, *Memorias*, pp. 322–3, 360.

13 Carrillo, *Memorias*, p. 338; Enrique Líster, *Así destruyó Carrillo el PCE* (Barcelona: Editorial Planeta, 1983)

pp. 90–1. On Albatera, see Paul Preston, *The Spanish Holocaust: Inquisition and Extermination in Twentieth-Century Spain* (London: HarperCollins, 2012) pp. 480–1; Llum Quiñonero, *Nosotras que perdimos la paz* (Madrid: Foca, 2005) p. 180.

14 See José Díaz, *Las enseñanzas de Stalin: guía luminoso para los comunistas españoles* (Mexico City: Editorial Popular, 1940) *passim*.

15 For a gloss on Carrillo's articles in *Nuestra Bandera*, see Claudín, *Santiago Carrillo*, pp. 69–70.

16 *Ibid.*, pp. 64–5; Carrillo, *Memorias*, pp. 338–40.

17 'V Madride ya rukovodil gruppoi, kotoroi polzovalsya dlya samykh raznykh del' – Grigulevich, interviewed by Olga Shatunovskaya, *Latinskaya Amerika*, No. 3, 1993, pp. 63–9, quoted by Boris Volodarsky, 'Soviet Intelligence Services in the Spanish Civil War, 1936–1939' (unpublished doctoral thesis, London School of Economics and Political Science, 2010) p. 134.

18 Christopher Andrew and Vasili Mitrokhin, *The Sword and the Shield: The Mitrokhin Archive and the Secret History of the KGB* (New York: Basic Books, 1999) p. 300.

19 I am indebted to Boris Volodarsky for this information about Grigulevich's whereabouts and about the military-political school in Moscow. Tagüeña Lacorte, *Testimonio*, pp. 350, 384–5, 427.

20 Claudín, *Santiago Carrillo*, p. 65; David Wingeate Pike, *In the Service of Stalin: The Spanish Communists in Exile 1939–1945* (Oxford: Clarendon Press, 1993) p. 33; Carrillo, *Demain l'Espagne*, pp. 76–8; Carrillo, *Memorias*, pp. 343–53, 367.

21 Pavel Sudoplatov, *Special Tasks: Memoirs of an Unwanted Witness* (London: Little, Brown, 1994) pp.

72–8, 192–3; Andrew and Mitrokhin, *The Sword and the Shield*, pp. 86–7, 587–8; Marjorie Ross, *El secreto encanto de la KGB: las cinco vidas de Iósif Griguliévich* (Heredia, Costa Rica: Farben Grupo Editorial Norma, 2004) pp. 82–3, 97, 104–9, 115–23; communications of Enrique Líster López to author, 18 September 2013 and 5 January 2014.

22 Morán, *Miseria y grandeza*, p. 69; Carrillo, *Memorias*, pp. 357–73; Claudín, *Santiago Carrillo*, pp. 67–8.

23 Carrillo, *Demain l'Espagne*, pp. 79–80; Carrillo, *Memorias*, pp. 389–90.

24 Yagüe, *Santiago Carrillo*, pp. 37, 49–50; Carrillo, *Memorias*, p. 360; 'El secreto familiar de Carrillo', *El Mundo*, 23 September 2012.

25 Claudín, *Santiago Carrillo*, p. 75; Carrillo, *Memorias*, p. 391.

26 For Líster's allegations, Enrique Líster, 'Carta a la ¿Señora o Señorita? María Eugenia Yagüe', *Mundo Obrero* (PCOE), No. 4, April 1977; 'El secreto familiar de Carrillo', *El Mundo*, 23 September 2012; author's conversations with Jorge Semprún and Enrique Líster López.

27 Tagüeña Lacorte, *Testimonio*, pp. 411, 439–40; Morán, *Miseria y grandeza*, pp. 62–4; Pike, *In the Service of Stalin*, pp. 156–7; Carrillo, *Memorias*, p. 383.

28 David Wingeate Pike, *Jours de gloire, jours de honte: le Parti Communiste d'Espagne en France depuis son arrivée en 1939 jusqu'à son départ en 1950* (Paris: Société d'Édition d'Enseignement Supérieur, 1984) pp. 97–100; Tagüeña Lacorte, *Testimonio*, p. 400; Antonio Vilanova, *Los olvidados: los exilados españoles en la segunda guerra mundial* (Paris: Éditions Ruedo Ibérico, 1969) pp. 466–7; Hernández, *En el país de la gran mentira*, pp. 86–111.

29 Morán, *Miseria y grandeza*, pp. 70–4; Pike, *In the Service of Stalin*, p. 157; Carrillo, *Memorias*, pp. 383–5.

30 Morán, *Miseria y grandeza*, pp. 64–6.

31 Tagüeña Lacorte, *Testimonio*, pp. 456, 465–76; Irene Falcón, *Asalto a los cielos: mi vida junto a Pasionaria* (Madrid: Temas de Hoy, 1996) pp. 212–17, 227–32; Jesús Hernández, *Yo fui un ministro de Stalin* (Madrid: G. del Toro, 1974) pp. 177–8, 216–21; Santiago Álvarez, *Memorias III: La lucha continúa ... El exílio: la 2ª Guerra Mundial: el regreso clandestino a España (1939–1945)* (Sada-A Coruña: Ediciós do Castro, 1988) pp. 319–21; Fernando Hernández Sánchez, *Comunistas sin partido: Jesús Hernández, Ministro en la guerra civil, disidente en el exilio* (Madrid: Editorial Raíces, 2007) pp. 73–9, 121–32, 151–3; Declaration of the Central Committee of the PCE in respect of the expulsión of Jesús Hernández, 21 July 1944, AHPCE, Documentos PCE/Comunicados-Declaraciones-Llamamientos, carp. 25.

32 Morán, *Miseria y grandeza*, pp. 66–7; Claudín, *Santiago Carrillo*, p. 72.

33 Hartmut Heine, *La oposición política al franquismo* (Barcelona: Editorial Crítica, 1983) pp. 62–7; Carlos Fernández Rodríguez, *Madrid clandestino: la reestructuración del PCE (1939–1945)* (Madrid: Fundación Domingo Malagón, 2002) pp. 67–82; Carlos Fonseca, *Trece rosas rojas: la historia más conmovedora de la guerra civil española* (Madrid: Ediciones Temas de Hoy, 2004) pp. 103–19, 209–34; Morán, *Miseria y grandeza*, pp. 37–43; David Ginard i Ferón, *Matilde Landa: de la Institución Libre de Enseñanza a las prisiones franquistas* (Barcelona: Flor de Viento Ediciones, 2005) pp. 79–89;

AHN, FC-Causa General, 1525-1, pp. 2-3, 5-6, 19-25; Aurora Arnaiz, *Retrato hablado de Luisa Julián* (Madrid: Compañía Literaria, 1996) pp. 111-42, 158-9.

34 Dolores Ibárruri *et al.*, *Historia del Partido Comunista de España (Versión abreviada)* (Warsaw: Ediciones 'Polonia', 1960) p. 218.

35 Carrillo, *Demain l'Espagne*, p. 75.

36 Tagüeña Lacorte, *Testimonio*, pp. 360-1.

37 José Díaz and Dolores Ibárruri, *España y la guerra imperialista: llamamiento del PCE a la emigración española* (Mexico City: Delegación del PCE, 1939) pp. 5-12; PCE, *El heroico pueblo español lucha contra el franquismo y por la victoria de la Unión Soviética* (Bogotá: Ediciones Sociales, 1941) pp. 6-13; PCE, *¡Por la Unión Nacional de todos los españoles contra Franco, los invasores germano-italianos y los traidores!* (n.p., n.d. [Mexico City, 1941]) pp. 3-7; PCE, *¡Adelante por la libertad y la independencia de España!* (Santiago de Chile: DIAP, 1942) pp. 5-6, 18-23.

38 Morán, *Miseria y grandeza*, pp. 43-61; Ángel Ruiz de Ayúcar, *El partido comunista: treinta y siete años de clandestinidad* (Madrid: Editorial San Martín, 1976) pp. 112-29; David Ginard i Ferón, *Heriberto Quiñones y el movimiento comunista en España (1931-1942)* (Palma de Mallorca and Madrid: Documenta Balear/Compañía Literaria, 2000) pp. 15-22, 49-52, 75-118; Heine, *La oposición*, pp. 68-84; Fernández Rodríguez, *Madrid clandestino*, pp. 129-99; Estruch Tobella, *El PCE en la clandestinidad*, pp. 23-6. The full text of Quiñones's strategy document is in 'Documento tomado a Heriberto Quiñones para reorganizar el PCE', *Documentos inéditos para la historia del*

Generalísimo Franco, 4 vols (Madrid: Fundación Nacional Francisco Franco, 1992) II-2, pp. 186-294.

39 Ginard i Ferón, *Heriberto Quiñones*, pp. 137-52; Fernández Rodríguez, *Madrid clandestino*, pp. 200-2. See also the anonymous article, by Carrillo, regarding the capture of the Diéguez group, *Nuestra Bandera*, No. 1, January 1945, pp. 80-95; and see the anonymous editorial, also written by Carrillo, 'Hay que aprender a luchar mejor contra la provocación', *Nuestra Bandera*, No. 4, February-March 1950, pp. 97-146; Carrillo, *Demain l'Espagne*, p. 97; Ibárruri *et al.*, *Historia del Partido Comunista de España*, p. 217.

40 Líster, *¡Basta!*, pp. 240-1; Santiago Álvarez, *Memorias IV: Más fuertes que la tortura y la pena de muerte (1945-1954)* (Sada-A Coruña: Ediciós do Castro, 1990) pp. 39-42; Falcón, *Asalto a los cielos*, pp. 179-80; Carrillo, *Memorias*, pp. 386-7, 435-8.

41 Manuel Azcárate, *Derrotas y esperanzas* (Barcelona: Editorial Tusquets, 1994) pp. 205-6; Manuel Martorell, *Jesús Monzón: el líder comunista olvidado por la Historia* (Pamplona: Pamiela, 2000) pp. 58-67.

42 Carmen de Pedro, Report on Monzón, Toulouse, 5 August 1945, AHPCE, Caso Monzón/Jacqs. 46 and 47; Martorell, *Jesús Monzón*, pp. 72-83; Azcárate, *Derrotas y esperanzas*, pp. 218-22, 227-45; Fernández Rodríguez, *Madrid clandestino*, pp. 203-97, 316-34.

43 Manifesto of Unión Nacional, Dolores Ibárruri, 1942, AHPCE, Documentos PCE/Manifiestos/Film XXI Apartado 258; Jesús Hernández, *En el país de la gran mentira* (Madrid: G. del Toro, 1974) pp. 179-84; Enrique Castro

Delgado, *Mi fé se perdió en Moscú* (Barcelona: Luis de Caralt, 1964) pp. 222–6, 245–6; Morán, *Miseria y grandeza*, pp. 80–3; Antonio Mije, 'Un ano de Junta Suprema de Unión Nacional: lecciones y experiencias de un gran órgano de combate', *Nuestra Bandera*, No. 1, January 1945.

44 Morán, *Miseria y grandeza*, pp. 83–92; Daniel Arasa, *Años 40: los maquis y el PCE* (Barcelona: Argos Vergara, 1984) pp. 42–6; Martorell, *Jesús Monzón*, pp. 89–90, 113–19; Azcárate, *Derrotas y esperanzas*, pp. 245–9, 259–65, 271–4; Castro Delgado, *Mi fé se perdió*, pp. 289–90; Heine, *La oposición*, pp. 202–8; Manuel Vázquez Montalbán, *Pasionaria y los siete enanitos* (Barcelona: Editorial Planeta, 1995) p. 132.

45 Pilar Soler interviewed by Emilia Bolinches in 1998; Daniel Arasa, *La invasión de los maquis* (Barcelona: Belacqua de Ediciones, 2004) p. 53; Carmen de Pedro, Report on Monzón, Toulouse, 5 August 1945, AHPCE, Caso Monzón/Jacqs. 46 and 47.

46 Martorell, *Jesús Monzón*, pp. 132–3, 152–3, 198–9; Morán, *Miseria y grandeza*, p. 100; Líster, *Así destruyó Carrillo al PCE*, pp. 63–4.

47 Carrillo to Ibárruri from Argel, 14 August 1944, AHPCE, Dirigentes/Dolores Ibárruri/Correspondencia/Caja 31, carp. 13.1.

48 Morán, *Miseria y grandeza*, pp. 96–7; Carrillo, *Demain l'Espagne*, pp. 80–3; Carrillo, *Memorias*, pp. 394–406; Claudín, *Santiago Carrillo*, pp. 76–8.

49 Enrique Líster, 'Combates y experiencias de la Agrupación Guerrillera de Levante', *Nuestra Bandera*, No. 24, January–February 1948, pp. 25–32, and 'Lessons of the Spanish Guerrilla War', *World Marxist Review*, February 1965, pp.

35–6; Ibárruri et al., *Historia del Partido Comunista de España*, p. 220.

50 Dolores Ibárruri, *Memorias de Pasionaria 1939–1977: me faltaba España* (Barcelona: Editorial Planeta, 1984) pp. 86–7; Carrillo, *Memorias*, pp. 407–10.

51 Carrillo, *Memorias*, pp. 411–13.

52 Carrillo to Monzón, 27 July, Monzón to Carrillo, 2 August 1944, AHPCE, Caso Monzón, Correspondencia/Sign. Jacq 10. Adela Collado was the partner of Manuel Jimeno, one of Monzón's closest collaborators – Mariano Asenjo and Victoria Ramos, *Malagón: Autobiografía de un falsificador* (Barcelona: El Viejo Topo, 1999) p. 103.

53 Dolores Ibárruri, 'El movimiento guerrillero vanguardia de la lucha por la reconquista de España', 20 September 1944, AHPCE, Dirigentes/Dolores Ibárruri/Escritos, 16/2.

54 Azcárate, *Derrotas y esperanzas*, pp. 281–7; Fernández Rodríguez, *Madrid clandestino*, pp. 334–43; Fernanda Romeu Alfaro, *Más allá de la utopía: Agrupación Guerrillera de Levante* (Cuenca: Ediciones de la Universidad de Castilla-La Mancha, 2002) pp. 25–6; Ruiz Ayúcar, *El partido comunista*, pp. 80–1; Carrillo, *Memorias*, p. 413; Claudín, *Santiago Carrillo*, pp. 78–9; Carrillo, *Demain l'Espagne*, pp. 95–8.

55 Azcárate, *Derrotas y esperanzas*, pp. 285–9; Heine, *La oposición*, p. 207; Estruch Tobella, *El PCE en la clandestinidad*, pp. 89–94.

56 Arasa, *Años 40*, pp. 187–96; Francisco Moreno Gómez, *La resistencia armada contra Franco: tragedia del maquis y la guerrilla* (Barcelona: Editorial Crítica, 2001) pp. 241–50; Pike, *Jours de gloire*, pp. 122–32; Asenjo and Ramos, *Malagón*, p. 139; Arasa, *La invasión* pp. 243–5, 299–306; Secundino

Serrano, *Maquis: historia de la guerrilla antifranquista* (Madrid: Ediciones Temas de Hoy, 2001) pp. 129–40; Tomás Cossías, *La lucha contra el 'maquis' en España* (Madrid: Editora Nacional, 1956) pp. 60–3; Fernando Martínez de Baños, *Hasta su total aniquilación: el Ejército contra el maquis en el Valle de Arán y en el Alto Aragón, 1944–1946* (Madrid: Almena Ediciones, 2002) pp. 137–8, 155–6; Mercedes Yusta Rodrigo, *Guerrilla y resistencia campesina: la resistencia armada contra el franquismo en Aragón (1939–1952)* (Zaragoza: Prensas Universitarias de Zaragoza, 2003) pp. 92–4; Carrillo, *Memorias*, pp. 411–14; Carrillo, *Demain l'Espagne*, pp. 95–8; López Tovar, Vicente, 'Coronel de los guerrilleros españoles en Francia: biografía' (unpublished manuscript).

57 Telegram from Carrillo to Ibárruri, October 1944, AHPCE, Dirigentes/Santiago Carrillo/Dirigentes – Correspondencia – Movimiento Guerrillero/Microfilm/Sign. Jacq. 9.

58 Santiago Carrillo, *Para echar del poder a Franco y Falange: unidad y lucha*, 'Conferencia de Santiago Carrillo, miembro del buró político del PCE, ante un grupo de militantes del partido emigrados en Francia' (Toulouse: Editorial España Popular, 1944) pp. 7–8, 10; Arasa, *La invasión*, pp. 310–11, 355–6; Heine, *La oposición*, pp. 216–17; Carrillo, *Memorias*, p. 413; Claudín, *Santiago Carrillo*, pp. 79–81.

59 Azcárate, *Derrotas y esperanzas*, pp. 289–90; Líster, *¡Basta!*, pp. 184–5; Morán, *Miseria y grandeza*, pp. 97–100; Estruch Tobella, *El PCE en la clandestinidad*, pp. 105–9; Fernández Rodríguez, *Madrid clandestino*, pp. 363–9; López Tovar, 'Biografía', pp. 174–80.

60 Carrillo to Monzón, 1, 4 December 1944, AHPCE, Caso Monzón, Correspondencia/Sign. Jacqs. 18 and 19/Jacq. 104.

61 Monzón to Carrillo, 28 December 1944, AHPCE, Caso Monzón, Correspondencia/Sign. Jacq. 10.

62 Carrillo, Report to Ibárruri, 6 February 1945, AHPCE, Dirigentes/Santiago Carrillo/Informes/Caja 30, carp. 1.2.

63 Telegram from Carrillo to Ibárruri, 4 May 1945, AHPCE, Dirigentes/Santiago Carrillo/Correspondencia/Caja 30, carp. 1.1.

64 Morán, *Miseria y grandeza*, pp. 102–7; Martorell, *Jesús Monzón*, pp. 157–64; Tagüeña Lacorte, *Testimonio*, p. 541.

65 Report from Carrillo to Dolores [Ibárruri], Vicente [Uribe], Antonio [Mije], 30 June 1945, AHPCE, Dirigentes PCE/Correspondencia/Jacqs. 1 and 2.

66 'Carta abierta de la Delegación del Comité Central a los miembros del Partido, simpatizantes y a todos los antifranquistas en general', *Nuestra Bandera*, No. 1, January 1945, pp. 1–33, especially pp. 10, 14–16, 20–2, 26–7; Morán, *Miseria y grandeza*, pp. 100–2; Serrano, *Maquis* p. 141; Fernández Rodríguez, *Madrid clandestino*, p. 358. The *Nuestra Bandera* article was actually issued some months after the published date of January 1945, perhaps as a retrospective justification of the planned attack on Monzón.

67 Tagüeña Lacorte, *Testimonio*, p. 427.

68 Daniel Arasa, *Los españoles de Stalin* (Barcelona: Editorial Vorágine, 1993) pp. 90–2, 97–9, 104–5, 193–206; José Gros, *Abriendo camino: relatos de un guerrillero comunista español* (Paris: Colección Ebro, 1971) pp. 46ff. One of the radio operators in the NKVD guerrilla group was Maria Luisa 'África' de las Heras, who became friendly with Carrillo when she used to visit her boyfriend in the

Cárcel Modelo in 1935: Javier Juárez, *Patria: una española en el KGB* (Barcelona: Editorial Debate, 2008) pp. 47–8, 186–206. On Sudoplatov's operation, see Pavel Sudoplatov, *Special Tasks: Memoirs of an Unwanted Witness* (London: Little, Brown, 1994) pp. 126–71.

69 Ange Álvarez, Iván Delicado and Roland Delicado, *Royo le guérillero éliminé: frère d'armes de Marcel Bigeard pendant la Libération de l'Ariège* (Nîmes: Ardeo, 2011) pp. 3–7, 10–15, 25–7; Romeu Alfaro, *Más allá de la utopía*, p. 453.

70 Asenjo and Ramos, *Malagón*, p. 150.

71 'Informe de Pilar Soler sobre la Junta Suprema de Unión Nacional y sobre Monzón', December 1945, AHPCE, Caso Monzón, Informes/ Jacqs. 84, 85, 86, 87, 88 and 89; Pilar Soler interview with Emilia Bolinches in 1998; Arasa, *La invasión*, p. 381.

72 Fernanda Romeu Alfaro, *El silencio roto: mujeres contra el franquismo* (Madrid: Edición de la autora, 1994) pp. 154–5; Martorell, *Jesús Monzón*, pp. 183–90; Arasa, *Años 40*, p. 300; Carmen de Pedro, Report on Monzón, Toulouse, 5 August 1945, AHPCE, Caso Monzón/Caso Monzón/Jacqs. 46 and 47.

73 Fernández Rodríguez, *Madrid clandestino*, pp. 347–60; Arasa, *La invasión*, pp. 373–87; Arasa, *Años 40*, pp. 294–7; Martorell, *Jesús Monzón*, pp. 172–82; Morán, *Miseria y grandeza*, p. 106.

74 Líster, *¡Basta!*, p. 237.

75 Serrano, *Maquis*, pp. 345–6; Carrillo to Monzón, 1 December 1944, AHPCE, Caso Monzón, Correspondencia/Jacq. 26; Claudín, *Santiago Carrillo*, p. 91.

76 Tagüeña Lacorte, *Testimonio*, p. 541; Líster, *¡Basta!*, pp. 215–17, 238–9; Jorge Semprún, *Autobiografía de Federico Sánchez* (Barcelona: Editorial Planeta, 1977) pp. 123–4;

Pike, *Jours de gloire*, p. 194; Claudín, *Santiago Carrillo*, pp. 47, 82–3; Morán, *Miseria y grandeza*, p. 107; Ruiz Ayúcar, *El partido comunista*, pp. 23, 141–2; Fernández Rodríguez, *Madrid clandestino*, pp. 370–6; Carrillo, *Memorias*, p. 447.

77 Serrano, *Maquis*, p. 312; Jorge Semprún in conversation with the author.

78 Santiago Carrillo, 'Somos el Partido de la destrucción del franquismo y también el Partido de la reconstrucción de una España grande y democrática (Informe ante el Pleno)', *Nuestra Bandera*, No. 4, January–February 1946, pp. 55–76 (see especially pp. 72–5).

79 Santiago Carrillo, '¡Desenmascaremos a los falsos resistentes!', *Nuestra Bandera*, No. 24, January–February 1948, pp. 13–23.

80 Pike, *Jours de gloire*, pp. 123, 134, 180; Jorge Marco Carretero, *Guerrilleros y vecinos en armas: identidades y culturas de la resistencia antifranquista* (Granada: Editorial Comares, 2012) pp. 29–33; Mercedes Yusta Rodrigo, *La guerra de los vencidos: el maquis en el Maestrazgo turolense, 1940–1950*, 2nd edn (Zaragoza: Institución Fernando el Católico, 2005) pp. 76–8.

81 José Manuel Montorio Gonzalvo, *Cordillera ibérica: recuerdos y olvidos de un guerrillero* (Zaragoza: Gobierno de Aragón, 2007) pp. 21–2.

82 Enrique Líster, *Nuestra guerra* (Paris: Colección Ebro, 1966) p. 100; Carrillo, *Memorias*, pp. 151, 194.

83 Enrique Líster López, 'Réflexions sur Fiodor Kravchenko (Antonio) combattant de l'ombre (1936–1950)', in Jean Ortiz, ed., *Rouges: maquis de France et d'Espagne: les guerrilleros* (Biarritz: Atlantica-Séguier, 2006) pp. 308–12; *Foreign Relations of the*

United States 1946 (Washington: Government Printing Office, 1969) V, pp. 1047-8.

84 Líster López, 'Reflexions sur Fiodor Kravchenko', pp. 312-15; Boris Volodarsky, *El caso Orlov: los servicios secretos soviéticos en la guerra civil española* (Barcelona: Editorial Crítica, 2013) p. 182.

85 Asenjo and Ramos, *Malagón*, p. 151; Semprún, *Autobiografía de Federico Sánchez*, pp. 111-14; Pike, *Jours de gloire*, pp. 188-9.

86 Santiago Carrillo, 'La situación en España y nuestras tareas después de la victoria de las Naciones Unidas', *Nuestra Bandera*, No. 2, June 1945, pp. 19-20.

87 David Wingeate Pike, *Spaniards in the Holocaust: Mauthausen, the Horror on the Danube* (London: Routledge, 2000) pp. 304-5; Pike, *In the Service of Stalin*, p. 282; Guy Hermet, *Los comunistas en España* (Paris: Éditions Ruedo Ibérico, 1972) p. 46; Andrés Sorel, *Búsqueda, reconstrucción e historia de la guerrilla española del siglo XX a través de sus documentos, relatos y protagonistas* (Paris: Éditions de la Librairie du Globe, 1970) p. 130; Líster, *¡Basta!*, pp. 30, 163-4; Fernando Claudín, *La crisis del movimiento comunista: de la Komintern al Kominform* (Paris: Éditions Ruedo Ibérico, 1970) pp. 494-5, 669.

88 Fernández Rodríguez, *Madrid clandestino*, pp. 363-4.

89 Marco Carretero, *Guerrilleros*, p. 35.

90 *Nuestra Bandera*, No. 16, February 1947, pp. 199-201, 217-20 (Ibárruri), 251-68 (Carrillo). The report by Dolores Ibárruri, *Por una España republicana, democrática e independiente: informe al III Pleno* (Paris: Nuestra Bandera, 1947) was published separately.

91 David J. Dunthorn, *Britain and the Spanish Anti-Franco Opposition,*

1940-1950 (London: Palgrave, 2000) pp. 74-5; José Borrás, *Políticas de los exilados españoles 1944-1950* (Paris: Éditions Ruedo Ibérico, 1976) pp. 184-91; José María Del Valle, *Las instituciones de la República española en exilio* (Paris: Éditions Ruedo Ibérico, 1976) pp. 157-63, 261; Enrique Marco Nadal, *Todos contra Franco: la Alianza Nacional de Fuerzas Democráticas 1944/1947* (Madrid: Queimada Ediciones, 1982) pp. 117-28.

92 Carrillo, *Memorias*, pp. 466-7.

93 *Mundo Obrero*, 29 January 1948.

94 *Arriba*, 30 November 1946.

95 *Foreign Relations of the United States 1946*, V, pp. 1080-2.

96 *Arriba*, 10 December 1946; *La Vanguardia Española*, 10 December 1946.

97 *ABC*, 10, 11, 12, 13 December 1946; Alberto J. Lleonart y Anselem and Fernando María Castiella y Maiz, *España y ONU I (1945-46)* (Madrid: Consejo Superior de Investigaciones Científicas, 1978) pp. 310-89.

98 Tagüeña Lacorte, *Testimonio*, pp. 539-40. I am also grateful to Enrique Líster López for information on this point.

99 José Antonio Rico, *En los dominios del Kremlin* (Mexico City: Atlántico, 1952) pp. 96-9, 106.

100 *Mundo Obrero*, 18 September, 2 and 9 October, 6 November, 11 and 18 December 1947; Luiza Iordache Cârstea, 'El exilio español en la URSS: represión y Gulag: entre el acoso comunista, el glacis estalinista y el caparazón franquista' (unpublished doctoral thesis, Universidad Autónoma de Barcelona, 2011) pp. 246-69, 456-68; Claudín, *Santiago Carrillo*, p. 88; Tagüeña Lacorte, *Testimonio*, pp. 540-1; Hernández Sánchez, *Comunistas sin partido*, pp. 153-5.

101 Líster, *Así destruyó Carrillo al PCE*, p. 94.

102 Morán, *Miseria y grandeza*, pp. 152–4; Tagüeña Lacorte, *Testimonio*, pp. 541–2.

103 *Arriba*, 14 January 1947; *ABC*, 14, 15, 16, 17 January 1947.

104 *Arriba*, 28 March 1947.

105 *Arriba*, 24 June 1947; *ABC*, 27 June 1947.

106 *Ya*, 6 July 1947; *Arriba*, 5, 6 July 1947.

107 Moreno Gómez, *La resistencia armada*, pp. 471–9, 506–45, 549–51; *Mundo Obrero*, 11 September 1947, 5, 19 August, 30 September 1948.

108 Moreno Gómez, *La resistencia armada*, p. 497.

109 Ibárruri, *Memorias*, pp. 89–90.

110 Carrillo, *Memorias*, pp. 449–51; Líster, *Así destruyó Carrillo el PCE*, p. 53; Morán, *Miseria y grandeza*, pp. 134–6; Moreno Gómez, *La resistencia armada*, p. 496; Santiago Carrillo, *¿Ha muerto el Comunismo? Ayer y hoy de un movimiento clave para entender la convulsa historia del siglo XX* (Barcelona: Plaza y Janés, 2000) pp. 200–2. On the language issue, I am grateful to both the son of Líster and the daughter and granddaughter of Dolores Ibárruri.

111 Ibárruri, *Memorias*, pp. 126–7; Carrillo, *Memorias*, pp. 452–6; Carrillo, *Demain l'Espagne*, p. 100; Líster, *¡Basta!*, pp. 123–4; Claudín, *Santiago Carrillo*, pp. 95–7.

112 Marco Carretero, *Guerrilleros*, pp. 125–6; Serrano, *Maquis*, pp. 235–43, 287–91; Romeu Alfaro, *Más allá de la utopía*, pp. 259–60. On the stomach ulcer, Claudín, *Santiago Carrillo*, p. 95.

113 Santiago Carrillo, 'Sobre las experiencias de dos años de lucha', *Nuestra Bandera*, No. 31, November–December 1948, pp. 824–39.

114 Moreno Gómez, *La resistencia aramada*, p. 533.

115 Líster, *¡Basta!*, p. 216.

116 Ange Álvarez, Iván Delicado and Roland Delicado, *Guérilla antifranquiste du Levant: Crimes et falsifications 1945–1952* (Nîmes: Ardeo, 2014) p. 23.

117 Carrillo to Monzón, 1 December 1944, AHPCE, Caso Monzón, Correspondencia/Jacq. 26.

118 Carrillo, *Memorias*, pp. 440–1; Morán, *Miseria y grandeza*, pp. 119–20.

119 Romeu Alfaro, *Más allá de la utopía*, pp. 445–56.

120 I am indebted to Iván Delicado for sending me the manuscript of his forthcoming book about his father's case. Ibáñez deliberately falsified a report to the PCE justifying the execution of Delicado, reproduced in Romeu Alfaro, *Más allá de la utopía*, pp. 447–8. See also Josep Sánchez Cervelló *et al.*, *Maquis: el puño que golpeó al franquismo* (Barcelona: Flor del Viento Ediciones, 2003) pp. 78–9, 88–92; Yusta Rodrigo, *Guerrilla y resistencia*, pp. 118–19, 128, 133, 137–9.

121 Álvarez and Delicado, *Guérilla antifranquiste du Levant*, pp. 205–8; Francisco Aguado Sánchez, *El maquis en España* (Madrid: Editorial San Martín, 1975) pp. 291–300.

122 Hartmut Heine, *A guerrilla antifranquista en Galicia* (Vigo: Edicións Xerais de Galicia, 1980) pp. 139–40, 196–7, 210, 234–8; Hartmut Heine, 'El Partido Comunista Español y la organización del fenómeno guerrillero', in Julio Aróstegui and Jorge Marco, eds, *El último frente: la resistencia armada antifranquista en España 1939–1952* (Madrid: Los Libros de la Catarata, 2008) pp. 92–3; Serrano, *Maquis*, pp. 263–4.

123 Ramón García Piñeiro, '¿Resistencia armada, rebeldía social o delincuencia? Huidos en Asturias (1937–1952)', in Aróstegui and Marco, eds, *El último frente*, pp. 235–40; Serrano, *Maquis*, pp. 265–6.

124 Líster, *¡Basta!*, pp. 227–8; Morán, *Miseria y grandeza*, pp. 161–3; Yusta Rodrigo, *Guerrilla y resistencia*, pp. 150–8.

125 Montserrat Roig, *Noche y niebla: los catalanes en los campos nazis* (Barcelona: Ediciones Península, 1978) p. 342; Pike, *Jours de gloire*, p. 195; Pike, *Spaniards in the Holocaust*, pp. 157, 165, 247–8.

126 Líster, *¡Basta!*, pp. 241–3; García Piñeiro, '¿Resistencia armada?', in Aróstegui and Marco, eds, *El último frente*, pp. 242, 244, 248–50; Serrano, *Maquis*, pp. 265–6; Silvia Ribelles de la Vega, *Luis Montero Sabugo: en los abismos de la historia: vida y muerte de un comunista* (Oviedo: Pentalfa Ediciones, 2011) pp. 43–72, 75–6, 82, 92–5, 100–1, 106; Mariano Peña Hernando, 'Propos recueillis auprès de Mariano Peña Hernando en deux entretiens en 1998', unpublished manuscript, p. 11. I am grateful to Michel Lefevbre for providing me with a copy of these interviews with his father.

127 Ribelles de la Vega, *Luis Montero Sabugo*, pp. 119–28.

128 Líster, *Así destruyó Carrillo el PCE*, pp. 58–9, 88–90; Ricardo de la Cierva, *Carrillo miente: 156 documentos contra 103 falsedades* (Madrid: Editorial Fénix, 1994) pp. 325–8; interview with Catalina Abad Tendero, *El Mundo*, 21 December 2008; Carrillo, *Memorias*, pp. 447–8.

129 Montorio Gonzalvo, *Cordillera ibérica*, pp. 122–3, 222, 233–9.

130 'Resumen de la discusión de la carta del CC con los camaradas de Levante (codificada). Códigos del acta sobre la discusión de la carta del CC', AHPCE, Nacionalidades y Regiones/Levante/Generalidades/Correspondencia, 1952/Jacqs. 767, 768; Romeu Alfaro, *Más allá de la utopía*, pp. 531–48; Montorio Gonzalvo, *Cordillera ibérica*, pp. 280–5, 291–5, 323–5.

131 Gros, *Abriendo camino*, pp. 196–7, 213–23, 264–6; Moreno Gómez, *La resistencia armada*, p. 533; Serrano, *Maquis*, pp. 288–91, 330; Sánchez Cervelló *et al.*, *Maquis*, pp. 367–74. On the deaths of 'Pepito el Gafas' and Francisco Bas Aguado 'Pedro', see Álvarez and Delicado, *Guérilla antifranquiste du Levant*, pp. 190–1, 199, 205, 208–13; Montorio Gonzalvo, *Cordillera ibérica*, pp. 237–8, 314, 322–3; José Antonio Vidal Castaño, *La memoria reprimida: historias orales del maquis* (Valencia: Publicacions de la Universitat de València, 2004) pp. 64–5, 144–5. For a fierce criticism of Gros, see the letter from Montorio to Gros, 30 April 1973, reproduced in Montorio Gonzalvo, *Cordillera ibérica*, pp. 363–8.

132 Pike, *Jours de gloire*, pp. 185–8.

133 *Mundo Obrero*, 11 March 1948; 'Comunicado del Buró Político del PCE', *Nuestra Bandera*, No. 28, June–July 1948, p. 473; Santiago Carrillo, 'A la luz del comunicado de Bucarest: las tendencias liquidacionistas en nuestro partido durante el período de la Unión Nacional en Francia', *ibid.*, pp. 495–516; Vicente Uribe, 'La penetración imperialista norteamericana pone en grave peligro la independencia nacional de España', *Nuestra Bandera*, No. 29, August 1948, pp. 597–601, 615.

134 Confession/Interrogation Carmen de Pedro, Report to PCE (Paris), 2 February 1950, AHPCE, Caso Monzón, Informes/Jacqs. 249, 250; Azcárate, *Derrotas y esperanzas*, pp. 220–3, 265–74, 327–30; Morán, *Miseria y grandeza*, p. 107; Martorell, *Jesús Monzón*, pp. 90–1, 203–15; Líster, *Así destruyó Carrillo el PCE*, pp. 63–4; Carrillo, 'Hay que aprender a luchar mejor contra la provocación', pp. 114–22.

135 Carrillo, 'Hay que aprender a luchar mejor contra la provocación', pp. 110–14; Semprún, *Autobiografía*, pp. 121–2.

136 Ignacio Gallego, 'La lucha contra el titismo es un deber revolucionario de los comunistas', *Nuestra Bandera*, No. 4, February–March 1950, pp. 169–91, especially pp. 189–91.

Chapter 4: The Elimination of the Old Guard: 1950–1960

1 Victor Alba, *El Partido Comunista en España: ensayo de interpretación histórica* (Barcelona: Editorial Planeta, 1979) pp. 291–2.

2 *Mundo Obrero*, 21 April, 20, 27 October 1949; Declaration of the Secretariat of the PSUC concerning the political conduct of Joan Comorera, 8 November 1949, AHPCE, Documentos PCE/Partido Socialista Unificado de Catalunya (PSUC), carp. 30; Joan Estruch Tobella, *El PCE en la clandestinidad 1939–1956* (Madrid: Siglo XXI, 1982) pp. 177–85; Miquel Caminal, *Joan Comorera III: Comunisme i nacionalisme (1939–1958)* (Barcelona: Editorial Empúries, 1985) pp. 253–85; Gregorio Morán, *Miseria y grandeza del Partido Comunista de España 1939–1985* (Barcelona: Editorial Planeta, 1986) pp. 169–78.

3 *Mundo Obrero*, 10 November 1949; David Wingeate Pike, *Jours de gloire, jours de honte: le Parti Communiste d'Espagne en France depuis son arrivée en 1939 jusqu'à son départ en 1950* (Paris: Société d'Édition d'Enseignement Supérieur, 1984) pp. 198–200.

4 *Mundo Obrero*, 10 November, 8 December 1949.

5 Manuel Tagüeña Lacorte, *Testimonio de dos guerras* (Mexico City: Ediciones Oasis, 1973) p. 579.

6 Alba, *El Partido*, pp. 293–4; Estruch Tobella, *El PCE en la clandestinidad*, pp. 189–91; Gregorio López Raimundo, *Primera clandestinidad: segunda parte* (Barcelona: Editorial Antártida/Empúries, 1995) p. 88.

7 Enrique Líster, *¡Basta! Una aportación a la lucha por la recuperación del Partido*, 2nd edn (Madrid: G. del Toro, 1978) pp. 228–9.

8 'El papel policiaco de los provocadores comoreristas', *Mundo Obrero*, 15 August 1951; Pike, *Jours de gloire*, pp. 201–6; Caminal, *Comorera*, pp. 289–317.

9 Caminal, *Comorera*, pp. 320–4; Enrique Líster, *Así destruyó Carrillo el PCE* (Barcelona: Editorial Planeta, 1983) pp. 74–9; Morán, *Miseria y grandeza*, pp. 178–82, 185–6; Estruch Tobella, *El PCE en la clandestinidad*, pp. 189–92; Hartmut Heine, *La oposición política al franquismo* (Barcelona: Editorial Crítica, 1983) pp. 452–3.

10 Santiago Carrillo, *'Eurocomunismo' y Estado* (Barcelona: Editorial Crítica, l977) p. l43.

11 Manuel Azcárate, *Derrotas y esperanzas* (Barcelona: Editorial Tusquets, 1994) pp. 332–3; Santiago Carrillo, *Memorias*, 2nd edn (Barcelona: Editorial Planeta, 2006) pp. 467–8; Líster, *Así destruyó Carrillo el PCE*, pp. 69–70; Morán, *Miseria y grandeza*, pp. 187–93; Mariano Asenjo and Victoria Ramos, *Malagón: autobiografía de un falsificador* (Barcelona: El Viejo Topo, 1999) pp. 177–8.

12 Carrillo, *Memorias*, pp. 463–4; José Luis Losa, *Caza de rojos: un relato urbano de la clandestinidad comunista* (Madrid: Ediciones Espejo de Tinta, 2005) pp. 59–67.

13 Enrique Castro Delgado, *Mi fé se perdió en Moscú* (Barcelona: Luis de Caralt, 1964) p. 85; Líster, *Así destruyó Carrillo el PCE*, p. 95; Azcárate, *Derrotas y esperanzas*, p. 232; Tagüeña Lacorte, *Testimonio*, p.

390; author's conversation with Irene Falcón.

14 Tagüeña Lacorte, *Testimonio*, pp. 411, 439–40, 456, 465–78; Irene Falcón, *Asalto a los cielos: mi vida junto a Pasionaria* (Madrid: Temas de Hoy, 1996) pp. 212–17, 227–32; Jesús Hernández, *Yo fui un ministro de Stalin* (Madrid: G. del Toro, 1974) pp. 99–100; Carrillo, *Memorias*, p. 384; Morán, *Miseria y grandeza*, pp. 188–9.

15 Falcón, *Asalto a los cielos*, pp. 261–2; Manuel Vázquez Montalbán, *Pasionaria y los siete enanitos* (Barcelona: Editorial Planeta, 1995) p. 125; PCE, *Carta a las organizaciones y militantes del Partido* (Mexico City: Ediciones España Popular, 1952) pp. 16–18; Morán, *Miseria y grandeza*, p. 141; Carrillo, *Memorias*, pp. 465–6.

16 Report/letter from Francisco Antón y Carrillo to Dolores Ibárruri and the politburo, June 1951, AHPCE, Dirigentes/Francisco Antón/Caja 29, carp. 4/4.

17 Carrillo, *Memorias*, p. 470.

18 Morán, *Miseria y grandeza*, pp. 190–3.

19 First and second reports on Antón; Interventions by Carrillo on Antón, AHPCE, Documentos/Dirigentes/Francisco Antón/Caja 29, carp. 4/4; Morán, *Miseria y grandeza*, pp. 191–3.

20 Intervention by Carrillo, 8 August 1952, AHPCE, Documentos/Dirigentes/Francisco Antón/Caja 29, carp. 4/4.

21 Resolution of politburo on Antón, AHPCE, Documentos/Dirigentes/Francisco Antón/Caja 29, carp. 4/4.

22 Fourth intervention by Carrillo, 9 August 1953, AHPCE, Documentos/Dirigentes/Francisco Antón/Caja 29, carp. 4/4.

23 Meeting of the politburo, July 1953, AHPCE, Documentos/Dirigentes/Francisco Antón/Caja 29, carp. 4/4.

24 Report by Dolores Ibárruri to the politburo, 13 November 1953, AHPCE, Documentos/Dirigentes/Francisco Antón/Caja 29, carp. 4/4.

25 Dolores Ibárruri, *Informe pronunciado ante un grupo de dirigentes del Partido, el 25 de octubre de 1951* (n.p.: Edición reservada del autor, 1951) pp. 32–3; Morán, *Miseria y grandeza*, pp. 194–205; Vázquez Montalbán, *Pasionaria*, pp. 127–8; Vittorio Vidali, *Diary of the Twentieth Congress of the Communist Party of the Soviet Union* (Westport, Conn.: Lawrence Hill, 1984) p. 50; Fernando Claudín, *Santiago Carrillo: crónica de un secretario general* (Barcelona: Editorial Planeta, 1983) pp. 101–2; Líster, *¡Basta!*, pp. 265–70; Fernando Hernández Sánchez, *Comunistas sin partido: Jesús Hernández, Ministro en la guerra civil, disidente en el exilio* (Madrid: Editorial Raíces, 2007) pp. 249–51.

26 Carrillo, *Memorias*, pp. 470–2; in conversation with the author, Carrillo said, 'lo que tiene que entender, amigo Preston, es que éramos como unos cruzados de una orden militar. Todos hacíamos lo que teníamos que hacer como los cruzados cristianos de la edad media.'

27 Carlos Semprún Maura, *El exilio fue una fiesta: memoria informal de un español de París* (Barcelona: Editorial Planeta, 1998) p. 78; 'Con la mentira en ristre', *ABC*, 9 April 1994; Losa, *Caza de rojos*, p. 89.

28 Claudín, *Santiago Carrillo*, p. 103.

29 Morán, *Miseria y grandeza*, pp. 166–9, 247; Falcón, *Asalto a los cielos*, pp. 284–5; Carrillo, *Memorias*, p. 466. On Claudín's efforts to acquire a theoretical background, I am grateful for information provided by Enrique Líster López.

30 *El Socialista*, 18 March, 31 May 1951; Ricard Soler, 'The New Spain', *New Left Review*, No. 58, November–December 1969.

31 *Mundo Obrero*, 12 January, 2 February 1950; Morán, *Miseria y grandeza*, pp. 158–9; Estruch Tobella, *El PCE en la clandestinidad*, p. 193.

32 Sebastian Balfour, *Dictatorship, Workers, and the City: Labour in Greater Barcelona since 1939* (Oxford: Clarendon Press, 1989) pp. 20–2.

33 *La Vanguardia Española*, 3 March 1951; Félix Fanés, *La vaga de tramvies del 1951* (Barcelona: Editorial Laia, 1977) pp. 28–33, 48–51.

34 *La Vanguardia Española*, 13, 14 March 1951; Fanés, *La vaga*, pp. 59–157; López Raimundo, *Primera clandestinidad: segundo parte*, pp. 208–27; Balfour, *Dictatorship*, pp. 22–30; Michael Richards, 'Falange, Autarky and Crisis: The Barcelona General Strike of 1951', *European History Quarterly*, October 1999, pp. 543–85.

35 López Raimundo, *Primera clandestinidad: segundo parte*, pp. 227–46, 270–386; *Mundo Obrero*, 15 September, 15 October, 1 December 1951; Dolores Ibárruri *et al.*, *Historia del Partido Comunista de España (Versión abreviada)* (Warsaw: Ediciones 'Polonia', 1960) p. 238; Morán, *Miseria y grandeza*, pp. 184–5 (Carrillo's auto-critique, pp. 191–3); Caminal, *Comorera*, p. 315.

36 Ibárruri, *Informe, 25 de octubre de 1951*, pp. 18–19; Fanés, *La vaga*, pp. 164–8; Manuel González Portilla and José María Garmendía, *La posguerra en el País Vasco: política, acumulación, miseria* (San Sebastián: Kriselu, 1988) pp. 275–84.

37 Morán, *Miseria y grandeza*, pp. 182–3.

38 Ibárruri, *Informe, 25 de octubre de 1951*, pp. 33–6, 41–2.

39 Sergo Beria, *Beria My Father: Inside Stalin's Kremlin* (London: Duckworth, 2001) pp. 269–72; Dmitri Volkogonov, *Stalin: Triumph and Tragedy* (London: Weidenfeld & Nicolson, 1991) pp. 574–6; Donald Rayfield, *Stalin and his Hangmen: An Authoritative Portrait of a Tyrant and Those Who Served Him* (London: Viking, 2004) pp. 442–50.

40 Estruch Tobella, *El PCE en la clandestinidad*, p. 207.

41 Azcárate, *Derrotas y esperanzas*, pp. 334–5; Claudín, *Santiago Carrillo*, pp. 104–6.

42 Dolores Ibárruri, *Informe al Comité Central al 5° Congreso del p. C. de España* (n.p., n.d. [Paris: Parti Communiste Français, 1955]) pp. 18–22, 46–51.

43 Ibárruri, *Informe, 25 de octubre de 1951*, pp. 52–8.

44 Ibárruri, *Informe al 5° Congreso*, pp. 10, 20, 70–91.

45 *Ibid.*, pp. 8, 11, 16–17, 116.

46 *Ibid.*, pp. 71, 99–104.

47 *Ibid.*, pp. 80–7.

48 Estruch Tobella, *El PCE en la clandestinidad*, p. 171; Morán, *Miseria y grandeza*, pp. 161–2.

49 Santiago Carrillo, 'Informe sobre problemas de organización y los estatutos del Partido', in AHPCE, 'Actas del V Congreso del Partido Comunista de España', 4 vols, typescript, III, pp. 0775–0826. A slightly expurgated version of his report was also published as a pamphlet with the same title. Cf. Fernando Claudín, *Documentos de una divergencia comunista* (Barcelona: El Viejo Topo, 1978) p. ii.

50 Santiago Carrillo, *Informe sobre problemas de organización y los estatutos del Partido* (n.p., n.d.) pp. 6–13, 41–3. The auto-censorship, AHPCE, 'Actas del V Congreso', III, pp. 0792–4, 0812–14.

51 AHPCE, 'Actas del V Congreso', III, 14th session, pp. 0909–0910; Carrillo, *Informe sobre problemas de organización*, pp. 26, 34–5, and AHPCE 'Actas del V Congreso', III, p. 0791.

52 AHPCE, 'Actas del V Congreso', III, 1, 3rd session, pp. 0178–0193 (Sánchez Montero), pp. 0201–20 (Semprún); Claudín, *Santiago Carrillo*, p. 106; Claudín, *Documentos*, p. ii.

53 AHPCE, 'Actas del V Congreso', IV, p. 1132; Azcárate, *Derrotas y esperanzas*, p. 335.

54 Claudín, *Santiago Carrillo*, pp. 107–8; Morán, *Miseria y grandeza*, pp. 247–8.

55 Morán, *Miseria y grandeza*, pp. 248–52.

56 Jorge Semprún, *Autobiografía de Federico Sánchez* (Barcelona: Editorial Planeta, 1977) pp. 36–7, 216–17; Claudín, *Documentos*, p. iii; Carrillo, *Memorias*, pp. 478 80.

57 Santiago Carrillo, 'Sobre la entrada de España en la ONU: la política de coexistencia ayuda a las fuerzas antifranquistas y de paz', *Mundo Obrero*, No. 2, January 1956; 'Sobre el ingreso de España en la ONU: una victoria de la política de paz', *Nuestra Bandera*, No. 15, January 1956, pp. 11–33.

58 However, Líster's son, who was present in the next room, says that he did not hear his father raise his voice – and that, on the occasions when he did, the walls trembled (correspondence with the author).

59 Semprún, *Autobiografía*, pp. 217–24.

60 Falcón, *Asalto a los cielos*, p. 304; Claudín, *Santiago Carrillo*, pp. 108–16; Líster, *¡Basta!*, pp. 275–87; Meetings of the politburo of the PCE, April–May 1956, AHPCE; Estruch Tobella, *El PCE en la clandestinidad*, pp. 222–5; Vidali, *Diary of the Twentieth Congress of the Communist Party of the Soviet Union*, pp. 6, 11–12, 52; Carrillo, *Memorias*, pp. 482–90; Dolores Ibárruri, *Memorias de Pasionaria 1939–1977: me faltaba España* (Barcelona: Editorial Planeta, 1984) p. 149; Morán, *Miseria y grandeza*, pp. 253–76.

61 Ibárruri's speech, 10 May 1956, AHPCE, Documentos PCE/Buró Político – Comité Ejecutivo/Política y Gobierno/Signatura: Reuniones CC, 5 vols, I, Tomo 7.

62 Claudín, *Santiago Carrillo*, pp. 116–17; Líster, *¡Basta!*, pp. 287–9.

63 Claudín's investigations resulted in his book *La crisis del movimiento comunista: de la Komintern al Kominform* (Paris: Éditions Ruedo Ibérico, 1970). See also Claudín, *Documentos*, p. iii.

64 Claudín, *Santiago Carrillo*, p. 117.

65 PCE, *Declaración por la reconciliación nacional, por una solución democrática y pacífica del problema español* (n.p., n.d. [Paris, 1956]) pp. 3, 5, 29–31, 37–40; Claudín, *Santiago Carrillo*, p. 118; Falcón, *Asalto a los cielos*, p. 319; Simón Sánchez Montero, *Camino de la libertad: memorias* (Madrid: Ediciones Temas de Hoy, 1997) pp. 228–9.

66 Santiago Carrillo, *La situación en la dirección del Partido y los problemas del reforzamiento del mismo* (Paris: Parti Communiste Français, 1956) pp. 23–4; Semprún, *Autobiografía*, p. 38.

67 Dolores Ibárruri, *Por la reconciliación de los españoles hacia la democratización de España* (Paris: Éditions Sociales, 1956) pp. 39–42, 83–9, 94–7.

68 Carrillo, *La situación en la dirección*, pp. 16–19, 25–31, 68–9, 87; Semprún, *Autobiografía*, pp. 222–4; Claudín, *Santiago Carrillo*, pp. 119–20; Estruch Tobella, *El PCE en la clandestinidad*, pp. 225–36.

69 Lister, *¡Basta!*, p. 288; Semprún, *Autobiografía*, pp. 131–2; Claudín, *Santiago Carrillo*, pp. 119–20; Falcón, *Asalto a los cielos*, pp. 309–10; Morán, *Miseria y grandeza*, pp. 288–301.

70 Morán, *Miseria y grandeza*, p. 294.

71 Claudín, *Santiago Carrillo*, pp. 120–1.

72 Carrillo, *Demain l'Espagne*, pp. 137–8; Carrillo, *Memorias*, pp. 496–9. On Carmen de Pedro and Antón, Carrillo, *Memorias*, p. 447

73 Carrillo, *Memorias*, pp. 499–502.

74 Manuel Azcárate, *Luchas y transiciones: memorias de un viaje por el ocaso del comunismo* (Madrid: El País Aguilar, 1998) p. 60.

75 Claudín, *Documentos*, p. iii; Claudín, *Santiago Carrillo*, pp. 125–9; '1956 Sobre una respuesta negativa', *Mundo Obrero*, November–December 1956; Estruch Tobella, *El PCE en la clandestinidad*, pp. 243–5.

76 Interview with Carrillo in *Nouvel Observateur*, 23–29 June 1975; 'Carrillo contra Cunhal', *Cambio 16*, 22–28 September 1975.

77 Claudín, *Santiago Carrillo*, pp. 129–31.

78 Carmen Grimau, 'Carrillo, el enterrador enterrado', *El Mundo*, 19 September 2012.

79 Federico Sánchez, 'Informe al VIº Congreso del PCE', *Nuestra Bandera*, No. 25, March 1960, pp. 63–74; Claudín, *Documentos*, pp. iv–v; Semprún, *Autobiografía*, pp. 204–7.

80 *Mundo Obrero*, mid-January 1957; Fernando Jáuregui and Pedro Vega, *Crónica del antifranquismo 1939–1975* (Barcelona: Editorial Planeta, 2007) pp. 237–8; Jordi Solé Tura, *Una historia optimista: memorias* (Madrid: Aguilar/El País, 1999) pp. 95–8; Luis Ramírez, *Nuestros primeros veinticinco años* (Paris: Éditions Ruedo Ibérico, 1964) pp. 111–12; Jaume Fabre, Josep M. Huertas and Antoni Ribas, *Vint anys de resistència catalana (1939–1959)* (Barcelona: Edicions de la Magrana, 1978) pp. 208–11.

81 Sánchez Montero, *Camino de la libertad*, pp. 232–3

82 'Algunas experiencias del boicot de Madrid', *Mundo Obrero*, No. 3, March 1957.

83 Semprún, *Autobiografía*, p. 243. For Sánchez Montero's report, Vicente Sainz (his pseudonym), 'Informe sobre la lucha de masas y la jornada nacional de demostración pacifica', *Nuestra Bandera*, No. 18, October 1957, p. 8.

84 'Declaración del Partido Comunista de España sobre la Jornada de Reconciliación Nacional', *Mundo Obrero*, 15–31 May 1958; Santiago Carrillo, 'Algunas cuestiones en torno a la jornada de 5 mayo', *Nuestra Bandera*, No. 21, July 1958, pp. 15–24; Fernando Claudín, *Las divergencias en el partido* (n.p., n.d. [Paris: author, 1965]) pp. 21–4; Solé Tura, *Una historia optimista*, pp. 107–8; Claudín, *Santiago Carrillo*, pp. 133–4.

85 Solé Tura, *Una historia optimista*, pp. 109–18.

86 Claudín, *Santiago Carrillo*, pp. 135–7; Jáuregui and Vega, *Crónica del antifranquismo*, pp. 249–50; Xavier Tusell, *La oposición democrática al franquismo 1939–1962* (Barcelona: Editorial Planeta, 1977) pp. 340–9; Letter from Tomás García (Juan Gómez) to Dolores Ibárruri, 1959, AHPCE, Dirigentes/Correspondencia/Tomás García/Caja 10, carp. 3.2 [n.d.], pp. 1–2.

87 Letter from Tomás García (Juan Gómez) to Dolores Ibárruri, 1959, AHPCE, Dirigentes/Correspondencia/Tomás García/Caja 10, carp. 3.2 [n.d.], pp. 3–5; Dolores Ibárruri to Santiago Carrillo, 1 June 1959, AHPCE,

Dirigentes/Dolores Ibárruri; Santiago Álvarez, *Memorias V: la larga marcha de una lucha sin cuartel (1954-1972)* (Sada-A Coruña: Ediciós do Castro, 1994) pp. 208–11; Semprún, *Autobiografía*, p. 8; Falcón, *Asalto a los cielos*, pp. 319–20; Ramírez, *Nuestros primeros veinticinco años*, pp. 169–71; Claudín, *Santiago Carrillo*, pp. 138–40; Sánchez Montero, *Camino de la libertad*, p. 241; Solé Tura, *Una historia optimista*, pp. 133–5; Morán, *Miseria y grandeza*, pp. 324–8; Losa, *Caza de rojos*, p. 299.

88 Claudín, *Las divergencias*, pp. 24–5; Semprún, *Autobiografía*, pp. 79–80; Jáuregui and Vega, *Crónica del antifranquismo*, pp. 242–5; Ramírez, *Nuestros primeros veinticinco años*, pp. 172–86; Eduardo G. Rico, *Queríamos la revolución: crónicas del FELIPE (Frente de Liberación Popular)* (Barcelona: Flor del Viento, 1998) pp. 55–61.

89 *Mundo Obrero*, 15 July 1959; Claudín, *Las divergencias*, pp. 25–8; Claudín, *Santiago Carrillo*, pp. 139–42.

90 Interview with Rosa Montero, *El País*, 18 June 1978.

91 Semprún, *Autobiografía*, pp. 7–9; Líster, *¡Basta!*, p. 289; Falcón, *Asalto a los cielos*, p. 320; Claudín, *Santiago Carrillo*, pp. 142–3; Ibárruri, *Memorias*, pp. 153–4; Álvarez, *Memorias V*, pp. 219–23. Carrillo denied that he had made the remark: Carrillo, *Memorias*, p. 515.

92 Claudín, *Santiago Carrillo*, pp. 142–3; author's conversations with both Semprún and Claudín.

93 Solé Tura, *Una historia optimista*, pp. 138–44; Claudín, *Santiago Carrillo*, p. 145; Morán, *Miseria y grandeza*, pp. 338–40; Líster, *Así destruyó Carrillo el PCE*, pp. 125–6; Carrillo, *Memorias*, p. 516.

94 The entire proceedings in typescript, AHPCE, VI Congreso del Partido Comunista de España 25–31 December 1959, 3 vols.

95 Carrillo's report, *ibid.*, I, pp. 6 101. It was also published as *VI Congreso del Partido Comunista de España: informe del Comité Central presentado por Santiago Carrillo* (Prague: Ediciones 'Boletín de Información', 1960) pp. 3–83; on the army and forces of order, see pp. 25–9, 39–47.

96 AHPCE, VI Congreso, I, pp. 108–256; II, pp. 251–97, 313–57, 361–78, 387–98, 407–8.

97 Gallego's report, *ibid.*, II, pp. 523–35; Solé Tura, *Una historia optimista*, p. 140.

98 Ibárruri's report, AHPCE, VI Congreso, II, pp. 472–521.

99 *Ibid.*, pp. 1740–7.

100 Claudín's report, *ibid.*, pp. 410–31; Solé Tura, *Una historia optimista*, p. 140.

101 Semprún's report, AHPCE, VI Congreso, III (Intervenciones no pronunciadas), pp. 45–56, Federico Sánchez, 'Informe al VIº Congreso del PCE', *Nuestra Bandera*, No. 25, March 1960, pp. 63–74; Semprún, *Autobiografía*, pp. 203–5.

102 Eduardo García, 'La organización de las masas', *Nuestra Bandera*, No. 27, July 1960; *Estatutos del PCE aprobados en su VI Congreso* (n.p., n.d. [Prague, 1960]) pp. 13–14; VI Congreso del PCE, *Programa del PCE* (n.p., n.d. [Prague, 1960]) p. 17; Claudín, *Santiago Carrillo*, pp. 143–5; closing session, AHPCE, VI Congreso, II, pp. 546–51.

103 *Informe del Comité Central presentado por Santiago Carrillo*, pp. 73–81.

104 The best account of the Maoist factions is Antonio Sala and Eduardo Durán, *Crítica de la izquierda autoritaria en Cataluña* (Paris: Éditions Ruedo Ibérico, 1975). See also 1er Congreso del PCE (M–L), *Informe del Comité Central* (Madrid: PCE-ML, 1973).

Chapter 5: The Solitary Hero: 1960–1970

1 Santiago Carrillo to Dolores Ibárruri, 23 March/7 May 1960, AHPCE, Dirigentes/Dolores Ibárruri/Correspondencia/Caja 16, carp. 4; Santiago Carrillo, interview in *France Nouvelle*, 11 March 1960.

2 Santos Juliá Díaz, *Camarada Javier Pradera* (Barcelona: Galaxia Gutenberg, 2012) pp. 96–101.

3 Fernando Claudín, *Santiago Carrillo: crónica de un secretario general* (Barcelona: Editorial Planeta, 1983) pp. 145–6; Notes from Javier Pradera to the executive committee, May 1960, AHPCE, Fuerzas de la cultura – Intelectuales – Profesionales – Artistas/ Correspondencia/Jacq. 233; Juliá Díaz, *Camarada Javier Pradera*, pp. 254–62; Gregorio Morán, *Miseria y grandeza del Partido Comunista de España 1939–1985* (Barcelona: Editorial Planeta, 1986) pp. 340–1.

4 Claudín, *Santiago Carrillo*, pp. 146–7; Letter from Federico Sánchez to Javier Pradera, June 1960, AHPCE, Fuerzas de la cultura – Intelectuales – Profesionales – Artistas/Correspondencia/Jacq. 107; also reprinted in Juliá Díaz, *Camarada Javier Pradera*, pp. 263–78.

5 Letter from Javier Pradera to Federico Sánchez, 18–20 July 1960, AHPCE, Fuerzas de la Cultura, Microfilm 108; also reprinted in Juliá Díaz, *Camarada Javier Pradera*, pp. 279–302.

6 Jorge Semprún, *Montand, la vida continua* (Barcelona: Editorial Planeta, 1983) pp. 72–3.

7 Esteve Riambau, *Ricardo Muñoz Suay: una vida en sombras* (Barcelona: Ediciones Tusquets, 2007) pp. 193–202, 265–6, 375–84; José Luis Losa, *Caza de rojos: un relato urbano de la clandestinidad comunista* (Madrid: Espejo de Tinta, 2005) pp. 325–7; Alicia Salvador Marañón, *De ¡Bienvenido, Mr. Marshall! a Viridiana: historia de UNINCI, una productora cinematográfica española bajo el franquismo* (Madrid: Egeda, 2006) pp. 533–69, 613–41, 649–53.

8 Santiago Carrillo, *Deberes del pueblo español en la presente situación internacional y nacional* (Paris: Parti Communiste Français, 1961) pp. 3–11, 14–20, 27–33, 39, 43–5, 52–7. Claudín, *Santiago Carrillo*, pp. 149–50, says that this meeting was actually held earlier but announced as having been in October to deceive the police. On the plan to attack the American air base at Morón, see Losa, *Caza de rojos*, pp. 331–2.

9 *VI Congreso del Partido Comunista de España, Informe del Comité Central presentado por Santiago Carrillo* (Prague: Ediciones 'Boletín de Información', 1960) pp. 42–3.

10 *Mundo Obrero*, 1 May 1962; Ignacio Fernández de Castro and José Martinez Guerricabeitia, eds, *España hoy* (Paris: Éditions Ruedo Ibérico, 1963) pp. 67–131, 206–22.

11 Santiago Carrillo, 'La clase obrera ha abierto el camino hacia la solución del problema político español', *Mundo Obrero*, 13 June 1962; Carrillo, 'The Working Class Paves the Way to Freedom for Spain', *World Marxist Review*, Vol. 5, No. 8, 1962, pp. 3, 7.

12 Parti Communiste Français, *2 meses de huelgas* (Paris: Parti Communiste Français, 1962) pp. 11–39, 84, 93–5, 114–17, 119–24; *Mundo Obrero*, No. 10, May 1962.

13 Fernández de Castro and Martínez Guerricabeitia, *España hoy*, pp. 235–56; Joaquín Satrústegui *et al.*, *Cuando la transición se hizo posible: el 'contubernio de Munich'* (Madrid: Editorial Tecnos, 1993) pp. 40, 48, 79

14 Xavier Tusell, *La oposición democrática al franquismo 1939–1962* (Barcelona: Editorial Planeta, 1977) pp. 388–432; José María Gil Robles, *Marginalia política* (Barcelona: Ariel, 1975) pp. 121–4.

15 *Mundo Obrero*, 13 June 1962; PCF, *2 meses de huelgas*, pp. 160–3; Claudín, *Santiago Carrillo*, p. 149; *ABC*, 9 June 1962; Francisco Franco Salgado-Araujo, *Mis conversaciones privadas con Franco* (Barcelona: Editorial Planeta, 1976) p. 343; Ramón Soriano, *La mano izquierda de Franco* (Barcelona: Editorial Planeta, 1981) pp. 151–2; Fernández de Castro and Martínez Guerricabeitia, *España hoy*, pp. 239–40.

16 *Mundo Obrero*, 13 June 1962; *L'Humanité*, 14 June 1967.

17 *Le Monde*, 13, 18, 19 April 1963; Amandino Rodríguez Armada and José Antonio Novais, *¿Quién mató a Julián Grimau?* (Madrid: Ediciones 99, 1976) pp. 17–26, 42–6, 113–47; Juan José del Águila, *El TOP: la represión de la libertad (1963–1977)* (Barcelona: Editorial Planeta, 2001) pp. 75–141.

18 Rodríguez Armada and Novais, *¿Quién mató a Grimau?*, pp. 11–13, 86–8, 130–2; Gabriel Avilés, *Tribunales rojos (Vistos por un Abogado defensor)* (Barcelona: Ediciones Destino, 1939) pp. 78, 96; Agustín Guillamón, 'La NKVD y el SIM en Barcelona: algunos informes de Gerö ("Pedro") sobre la Guerra de España', http://es.geocities.com/hbalance2000/pagina_n12.htm.

19 Jorge Semprún, *Autobiografía de Federico Sánchez* (Barcelona: Editorial Planeta, 1977), pp. 199–202, 205–12; Morán, *Miseria y grandeza*, pp. 360–1; Losa, *Caza de rojos*, pp. 134–5, 209–11.

20 Claudín, *Santiago Carrillo*, p. 155; Santiago Carrillo, *Memorias*, 2nd edn (Barcelona: Editorial Planeta,

2006) pp. 379, 529–32; Santiago Carrillo, *Los viejos camaradas* (Barcelona: Editorial Planeta, 2010) pp. 145–51.

21 Morán, *Miseria y grandeza*, pp. 359–60; Mariano Asenjo and Victoria Ramos, *Malagón: autobiografía de un falsificador* (Barcelona: El Viejo Topo, 1999) pp. 241–3. Grimau's role in the war had been mentioned in the minutes of the Fifth Congress AHPCE (ΛHPCE, 'Actas del V Congreso', carp. 35).

22 [Ángel Ruiz de Ayúcar], *¿Crimen o castigo? Documentos inéditos sobre Julian Grimau* (Madrid: Servicio de Información Española, 1963) pp. 3–21; Morán, *Miseria y grandeza*, pp. 361–2.

23 Claudín, *Santiago Carrillo*, p. 154.

24 *El País*, 18 June 1978.

25 Losa, *Caza de rojos*, pp. 463–7; José Luis Losa, 'Cuentas pendientes en el fusilamiento de Grimau: se cumplen 50 años de la ejecución del comunista', *El Confidencial*, 20 April 2013.

26 Carmen Grimau in correspondence with the author. See also her article, 'Carrillo, el enterrador enterrado', *El Mundo*, 19 September 2012, and Losa, *Caza de rojos*, pp. 450–1, 456. Francisco Romero Marín, 'Se ensañaron con Julián porque era comunista', in Justino Sinova, ed., *Historia del Franquismo*, 2 vols (Madrid: Información y Prensa, 1985) II, p. 572.

27 '1963 año critico', *Mundo Obrero*, January 1963; Fernando Claudín, *Las divergencias en el partido* (n.p., n.d. [Paris: author, 1965]) pp. 18–19

28 Claudín, *Santiago Carrillo*, pp. 153–4.

29 Semprún, *Autobiografía*, pp. 245–7.

30 Claudín, *Santiago Carrillo*, pp. 153–5; Morán, *Miseria y grandeza*, pp. 366–72.

31 Morán, *Miseria y grandeza*, pp. 375–6; Fernando Jáuregui and

Pedro Vega, *Crónica del antifranquismo, 1963-1975* (Barcelona: Editorial Planeta, 2007) pp. 360-2; Ángel Ruiz Ayúcar, *El Partido Comunista: treinta y siete años de clandestinidad* (Madrid: Editorial San Martín, 1976) pp. 322-8.

32 Ruiz Ayúcar, *El Partido Comunista*, p. 327.

33 Jordi Solé Tura, 'Unidad y diversidad en la oposición comunista al franquismo', in Joseph Fontana, ed., *España bajo el franquismo* (Barcelona: Editorial Crítica, 1986) p. 133.

34 Pau Costa, 'Organización e iniciativa revolucionaria', *Cuadernos de Ruedo Ibérico*, Nos. 13-14, June-September 1967, pp. 29-35; Julio Sanz Oller, *Entre el fraude y la esperanza* (Paris: Éditions Ruedo Ibérico, 1972) pp. 119-20; Carlos Prieto, 'La tactique du parti communiste a contribue a l'alfaiblissement des commissions ouvrières', *Le Monde*, 18 February 1970.

35 Santiago Carrillo, *Memoria de la transición* (Barcelona: Grijalbo, 1983) p. 194.

36 Federico Sánchez, 'Observaciones a una discusión'; Fernando Claudín, 'La revolución pictórica de nuestro tiempo', both in *Realidad*, No. 1, September-October 1963; Semprún, *Autobiografía*, pp. 277-9; Claudín, *Santiago Carrillo*, pp. 159-61; Morán, *Miseria y grandeza*, pp. 378-80; Jordi Solé Tura, *Una historia optimista: memorias* (Madrid: Aguilar/El País, 1999) pp. 201-2.

37 Claudín, *Santiago Carrillo*, pp. 161-2; Speeches of Fernández Inguanzo and Carrillo, 1-3 November 1963, AHPCE, Actas del Pleno del comité central del PCE; Santiago Carrillo, *La situación en el Movimiento Comunista* (Paris: P.P.I., 1963) pp. 37-8.

38 Carrillo, *Memoria de la transición*, pp. 189-95; Claudín, *Santiago Carrillo*, pp. 162-3.

39 Claudín, *Santiago Carrillo*, pp. 163-5; Semprún, *Autobiografía*, pp. 267-73, 279-80; Morán, *Miseria y grandeza*, pp. 381-4.

40 Fernando Claudín, *Documentos de una divergencia comunista* (Barcelona: El Viejo Topo, 1978) pp. 5-50; Semprún, *Autobiografía*, pp. 29-31, 231-2; Claudín, *Santiago Carrillo*, pp. 165-75; Claudín, *Las divergencias*, pp. 29-31, 43-9, 70-2; 'Dos concepciones de "la vía española al socialismo"', in Cuadernos de Ruedo Iberico, *Horizonte Español 1966*, 2 vols (Paris: Éditions Ruedo Iberico, 1966) II, pp. 66-7, 79-84, 92-6; Morán, *Miseria y grandeza*, pp. 384-92.

41 Acta del Comité Ejecutivo Asunto Claudín-Semprún, 3 September 1964, p. 3, AHPCE, Reuniones/Reunión Comité Ejecutivo/Caja 111, carp. 1; Santiago Carrillo, 'Discurso ante una Asamblea de militantes del Partido', 19 April 1964, AHPCE, Dirigentes/Santiago Carrillo/Discursos/Caja 4, carp. 1.1.1); Semprún, *Autobiografía*, pp. 190-5; Claudín, *Santiago Carrillo*, pp. 175-6; Solé Tura, *Una historia optimista*, pp. 203-4; Morán, *Miseria y grandeza*, pp. 392-4. The published version of Carrillo's speech, Santiago Carrillo, 'Discurso ante una Asamblea de militantes del Partido', *Boletín de Información*, Supplement to No. 9, June 1964, pp. 12, 14-23, 30-3, 37-43.

42 Solé Tura, *Una historia optimista*, pp. 206-8; Morán, *Miseria y grandeza*, pp. 395-7.

43 Interventions by Claudín and Semprún, AHPCE, Acta del Comité Ejecutivo Asunto Claudín-Semprún, 3-5 September 1964, pp. 2-6.

44 Letter from Fernando Claudín to the executive committee and the Central Committee, 22 September 1964, AHPCE, Divergencias Claudín–Semprún/Correspondencia/Caja 111, carp. 3; Semprún, *Autobiografía*, p. 185; Solé Tura, *Una historia optimista*, p. 208; Morán, *Miseria y grandeza*, p. 400.

45 'Sobre el reemplazamiento del camarada Jruschov', *Mundo Obrero*, 15 October 1964; Morán, *Miseria y grandeza*, pp. 397–9; Manuel Azcárate, 'The Prague–Moscow–Madrid Triangle', in G. R. Urban, ed., *Communist Reformation: Nationalism, Internationalism and Change in the World Communist Movement* (New York: St Martin's Press, 1979) p. 174; Carrillo, *Memorias*, pp. 536–42.

46 *Nuestra Bandera*, No. 40, January 1965; 'Resolución sobre la expulsión de Fernando Claudín y Federico Sánchez', *Mundo Obrero*, April 1965; Claudín, *Santiago Carrillo*, pp. 176–7.

47 Letter from Ignacio Gallego to Santiago Carrillo, 17 November 1965, AHPCE, Dirigentes/Ignacio Gallego/Caja 10, carp. 10.2.

48 Minutes of meeting between Pepe and Claudín, 26 November 1965, Conversation between 'Pepe' and Fernando Claudín, 26 November 1965, AHPCE, Divergencias/Informes/Caja 110; Letter from Fernando Claudín to the executive committee, 26 November 1965, AHPCE, Divergencias Claudín–Semprún/Correspondencia/Caja 111, carp. 3.

49 Author's conversations with Francesc Vicens and Fernando Claudín.

50 Claudín, *Las divergencias*, p. 124; Claudín, *Documentos*, pp. 215–16.

51 Claudín, *Santiago Carrillo*, pp. 87–8; Santiago Carrillo, *Mi testamento*

político (Barcelona: Galaxia Gutenberg, 2012) p. 236.

52 Solé Tura, *Una historia optimista*, pp. 205–6.

53 Santiago Carrillo, *Hacia el post-franquismo* (Paris: Colección Ebro, 1974) pp. 35–7.

54 Santiago Carrillo, *Demain l'Espagne: entretiens avec Régis Debray et Max Gallo* (Paris: Éditions du Seuil, 1974) pp. 117–21; Carrillo, *Memorias*, pp. 517–22; Carrillo, *Mi testamento político*, pp. 236, 241; Carrillo, *Los viejos camaradas*, pp. 70–2, 175–80; Claudín, *Santiago Carrillo*, p. 175.

55 Carrillo, *Memoria de la transición*, pp. 93–5, 189–95.

56 Letter from Santiago Carrillo to Dolores Ibárruri, 20 May 1964, AHPCE, Dirigentes/Correspondencia/Caja 16/4.

57 Carrillo's report, '¿Qué queremos los comunistas para España? Hacia una democracia política y social', in AHPCE, 'Actas del VII Congreso del Partido Comunista de España', 3 vols (unpublished typescript) I, pp. 049–238. It was published with minor alterations as *Después de Franco, ¿Qué? La democracia política y social que preconizamos los comunistas* (Paris: Éditions Sociales, 1965). Cf. especially pp. 11, 23, 32–6, 156–63. See also Claudín, *Santiago Carrillo*, pp. 178–81; Morán, *Miseria y grandeza*, pp. 420–4.

58 Eduardo García, AHPCE, 'Actas del VII Congreso', III, pp. 656–77.

59 Santiago Carrillo, closing session, AHPCE, 'Actas del VII Congreso', III, pp. 798–802.

60 León Lorenzo, 'Para hacer una información al Congreso', AHPCE, 'Actas del VII Congreso', III, pp. 807–19.

61 Interviews with Antoni Gutiérrez Díaz, Barcelona, 23 September 1980; with Miguel Núñez, *El Escorial*, July

2007; Santiago Carrillo, Intervention in Second Plenum of the Central Committee of the PCE, 11 August 1965, AHPCE, Comité Central; Morán, *Miseria y grandeza*, pp. 411–20.

62 'Il testo integrale dell'ultimo scritto di Togliatti a Yalta: promemoria sulle questioni del movimento operaio internazionale e della sua unit', *Rinascita*, 5 September 1964; Aldo Agosti, *Palmiro Togliatti* (Torino: UTET, 1996) pp. 552–4.

63 Santiago Carrillo, *Discurso ante una asamblea de militantes del Partido* (n.p. [Prague], 1964) p. 39; Semprún, *Autobiografía*, pp. 280–1.

64 Claudín, *Santiago Carrillo*, pp. 181–4.

65 Santiago Carrillo, *Nuevos enfoques a problemas de hoy* (Paris: Éditions Sociales, 1967) pp. 168–79.

66 Carrillo, *Después de Franco, ¿Que?*, pp. 75 –82, 86–7; Carrillo, *Nuevos enfoques*, pp. 54, 116–40.

67 Guy Hermet, *Les Catholiques dans l'Espagne Franquiste*, 2 vols (Paris: Presses de la Fondation Nationale des Sciences Politiques, 1980–1) II, pp. 287–97; Audrey Brassloff, *Religion and Politics in Spain: The Spanish Church in Transition, 1962–96* (London: Macmillan Press, 1998) pp. 7–24. See also Hilari Raguer, *Réquiem por la cristiandad: el Concilio Vaticano II y su impacto en España* (Barcelona: Ediciones Península, 2006) pp. 385–94.

68 Carrillo, *Nuevos enfoques*, pp. 52–4; Santiago Carrillo, *Libertad y socialismo* (Paris: Colección Ebro, 1971) pp. 43–50.

69 Carlos Iniesta Cano, *Memorias y recuerdos* (Barcelona: Editorial Planeta, 1984) pp. 141–2; Julio Busquets, *El militar de carrera en España*, 3rd edn (Barcelona: Ariel, 1967) pp. 107–14, 263; Manuel Balbé, *Orden público y militarismo en la España constitucional 1812–*

1983 (Madrid: Alianza Editorial, 1983) p. 437.

70 Paul Preston, *The Politics of Revenge: Fascism and the Military in Twentieth-Century Spain*, 2nd edn (London: Routledge, 1995) pp. 131–58.

71 Enrique López, *Carrillo: dos caras de una misma moneda* (n.p., n.d.) pp. 26–9.

72 Fernando Claudín, 'La crisis del Partido Comunista de España', *Cuadernos de Ruedo Ibérico*, Nos. 26–27, August–November 1970, p. 54.

73 Hartmut Heine, 'La contribución de la "Nueva Izquierda" al resurgir de la democracia española, 1957–1975', in Fontana, ed., *España bajo el franquismo*, pp. 142–59.

74 Jáuregui and Vega, *Crónica del antifranquismo*, p. 376.

75 *Vanguardia Obrera*, No. 57, August–September 1971; *Accion*, No. 9, November 1972; *Boletín de Información del FRAP*, No. 25, June 1973.

76 'Sobre el reemplazamiento del camarada Jruschov', *Mundo Obrero*, 15 October 1964; Santiago Carrillo, *Informe sobre el XXII Congreso del PCUS* (n.p., n.d.) pp. 15–18, 32–5; Claudín, 'La crisis del PCE', pp. 52–3.

77 Santiago Carrillo, 'China a través del caos maoista', *Nuestra Bandera*, No. 53, 1er trimestre de 1967, pp. 91–100.

78 Carrillo, *Nuevos enfoques*, pp. 140–59.

79 Morán, *Miseria y grandeza*, pp. 432–5; Luis Suárez Fernández, *Franco y la URSS (La diplomacia secreta 1946–1970)* (Madrid: Ediciones Rialp, 1987) pp. 261–72; Claudín, *Santiago Carrillo*, pp. 189–94; articles by Carrillo in *Nuestra Bandera*, Nos. 47–8, January–February 1966, No. 55, 3er trimestre de 1967; *Mundo Obrero*, January 1968.

80 Carrillo, *Demain l'Espagne*, pp. 139–40.

81 Claudín, 'La crisis del PCE', pp. 54–8; Carrillo, *Nuevos enfoques*, pp. 140–59.

82 Claudín, *Santiago Carrillo*, pp. 183–4; Morán, *Miseria y grandeza*, pp. 437–8.

83 Santiago Alvarez, 'La renovación en Checoslovaquia', *Mundo Obrero*, No. 11, 1ª quincena de mayo 1968; *Mundo Obrero*, No. 22, 2ª quincena de Diciembre de 1968, p. 4; Carrillo, *Memorias*, pp. 543–4; Santiago Carrillo, 'La lucha por el socialismo hoy', *Nuestra Bandera*, supplement to No. 58, June 1968, pp. 32, 38–40.

84 Claudín, *Santiago Carrillo*, pp. 194–7; Morán, *Miseria y grandeza*, pp. 438–41; K. S. Karol, 'La déchirure des partis communistes européens', *Le Monde*, 23 October 1970; Jorge Semprún, *Adiós, luz de veranos* (Barcelona: Tusquets Editores, 1998) pp. 123–4; Enrique Líster, *¡Basta! Una aportación a la lucha por la recuperación del Partido*, 2nd edn (Madrid: G. del Toro, 1978) pp. 80–1.

85 Agustín Gómez to Dolores Ibárruri, 27 August 1968, AHPCE, Dirigentes/Dolores Ibárruri/ Correspondencia/.

86 Meeting of the executive committee, 18 September 1968, AHPCE, Dirigentes/Santiago Carrillo/ Documentación política/Comité Ejecutivo/Materia: Dirigentes – informes – comunismo, signatura: 5/1.2.2; 'La cuestión checoslovaca', *Mundo Obrero*, No. 16, September 1968; *L'Humanité*, 7 September 1968; Carrillo, *Demain l'Espagne*, pp. 144–5; Líster, *¡Basta!*, p. 83; Manuel Azcárate, *Luchas y transiciones: memorias de un viaje por el ocaso del comunismo* (Madrid: El País Aguilar, 1998) p. 108.

87 Santiago Carrillo, 'Más problemas actuales del socialismo', *Nuestra Bandera*, No. 59, 3ᵉʳ trimestre, 1968; Morán, *Miseria y grandeza*, pp. 441–7; Claudín, *Santiago Carrillo*, pp. 197–200; Líster, *¡Basta!*, pp. 83–6.

88 On Gómez's career, see Agustín Gómez, 'En manos de la brigada social', *Nuestra Bandera*, No. 30, April 1961. *Mundo Obrero*, No. 18, 2ª quincena de Octubre 1968; No. 22, 2ª quincena de Diciembre de 1968; Morán, *Miseria y grandeza*, pp. 450–1.

89 *Mundo Obrero*, 5 February 1969.

90 *Mundo Obrero*, 15 July 1969.

91 Letters from Eduardo García to the Central Committee, 28 June 1969, and to the executive committee, 8 August 1969; Meeting of Eduardo García with various members of the executive committee, 6 October 1969; Letter from José Bárzana to the executive committee, 5 November 1969, AHPCE, Divergencias/Correspondencia/Caja 108, carp. 3, 4; Líster, *¡Basta!*, pp. 86–95.

92 Azcárate, *Luchas y transiciones*, p. 108.

93 'Intervención de Carrillo en la conferencia', *Mundo Obrero*, 22 June 1969; 'Declaracion de la delegación del PCE al aprobarse el documento', *Mundo Obrero*, 5 July 1969; Azcárate, *Luchas y transiciones*, pp. 109–14; Claudín, *Santiago Carrillo*, pp. 200–2; Carrillo, *Memorias*, pp. 547–51; Morán, *Miseria y grandeza*, pp. 454–5.

94 *Mundo Obrero*, 7 October; 20 December 1969; 8 January 1970; Líster, *¡Basta!*, pp. 51–76, 95–8; Claudín, 'La crisis del PCE', pp. 66–70.

95 *Mundo Obrero* (Líster tendency), No. 1, September 1970; Líster, *¡Basta!*, pp. 47–8, 100–13; *Nuestra Bandera*, No. 65, 3ᵉʳ trimestre de 1970, pp. 3–24; Claudín, 'La crisis del PCE', pp. 74–5; Morán, *Miseria y grandeza*, pp. 457–60.

96 Correspondence with his son, Enrique Líster.

97 *Mundo Obrero*, 30 September, 7 October 1970; Claudín, 'La crisis del PCE', pp. 51–82; *Nuestra Bandera*, No. 65, 3er trimestre de 1970, pp. 3–24; Claudín, *Las divergencias*, pp. 3–5, 94–102; Eduardo García, 'Espagne: le parti communiste consolide ses rangs', *Nouvelle Revue Internationale*, August 1968, pp. 179–80; interview with Santiago Carrillo, and Charles Vanhecke, 'Les "revisions" du p. C. Espagnol: deux ans de crise' in *Le Monde*, 4 November 1970; Líster, *¡Basta!* (these references are to the 1st edn, published by the author in Paris in 1971), pp. 10–41, 62, 83–103.

98 Ignacio Gallego, *El partido de masas que necesitamos* (Paris: Éditions Sociales, 1971) pp. 39–45.

99 Gallego, *El partido de masas*, p. 42.

100 Claudín, 'La crisis del PCE', p. 8l.

Chapter 6: From Public Enemy No. 1 to National Treasure: 1970–2012

1 Fernando Claudín, 'Dos concepciones de "la vía española al socialismo"', in Cuadernos de Ruedo Ibérico, *Horizonte español 1966*, 2 vols (Paris: Éditions Ruedo Iberico, 1966) II, pp. 59–100; Fernando Claudín, 'La crisis del Partido Comunista de España', *Cuadernos de Ruedo Ibérico*, Nos. 26–27, August–November 1970, pp. 79, 82; 1er Congreso del PCE (M–L), *Informe del Comité Central* (Madrid: PCE-ML, 1973), pp. 30–6; *La Voz Comunista* (Portavoz de la Oposición de Izquierdas del PCE), No. 4, 15 January 1974; Santos Juliá Díaz, *Camarada Javier Pradera* (Barcelona: Galaxia Gutenberg, 2012) p. 438.

2 Carrillo's report to the September 1970 *pleno ampliado* (expanded plenary meeting of the Central Committee) was published as *Libertad y socialismo* (Paris: Colección Ebro, 1971). See pp. 56–66.

3 'Promoción Lenin', *Nuestra Bandera*, No. 62, October–November 1969, pp. 22–5; Ignacio Gallego, *El partido de masas que necesitamos* (Paris: Éditions Sociales, 1971) pp. 7–9.

4 Information supplied to the author by Rafael Calvo Serer.

5 'Para devolver la palabra al pueblo', *Mundo Obrero*, 26 November, 10, 24 December 1971; Santiago Carrillo, *Hacia el post-franquismo* (Paris: Colección Ebro, 1974) pp. 57–62; Fernando Claudín, *Santiago Carrillo: crónica de un secretario general* (Barcelona: Editorial Planeta, 1983) pp. 215–16.

6 *Mundo Obrero*, 13 October 1972; PCE, *VIII Congreso del Partido Comunista de España* (Bucharest: '13 de Diciembre 1918', 1972) pp. 29–31, 40–3, 64; Claudín, *Santiago Carrillo*, pp. 211–15; Gregorio Morán, *Miseria y grandeza del Partido Comunista de España 1939–1985* (Barcelona: Editorial Planeta, 1986) pp. 469–71, 489–90.

7 Alejandro Diz, *La sombra del FRAP: génesis y mito de un partido* (Barcelona: Ediciones Actuales, 1977) pp. 69–74; Equipo Adelvec, *FRAP 27 de septiembre de 1975* (Madrid: Ediciones Vanguardia Obrera, 1985) pp. 41–7; Paul Preston, *Juan Carlos: A People's King* (London: HarperCollins, 2004) pp. 274–8.

8 Ismael Fuente, Javier Garcia and Joaquín Prieto, *Golpe mortal: asesinato de Carrero y agonia del franquismo* (Madrid: El País, 1983) pp. 46, 90–1; Carlos Estévez and Francisco Mármol, *Carrero: las razones ocultas de un asesinato* (Madrid: Ediciones Temas de Hoy, 1998) p. 162.

9 *Pueblo*, 22 December 1973; Carlos Iniesta Cano, *Memorias y recuerdos*

(Barcelona: Editorial Planeta, 1984) pp. 218–22; Joaquín Bardavío, *La crisis: historia de quince días* (Madrid: Ediciones Sedmay, 1974) pp. 111–16; Fuente, Garcia and Prieto, *Golpe mortal*, pp. 184–7.

10 *El Periódico*, 26 November 1995.

11 Victoria Prego, *Así se hizo la Transición* (Barcelona: Plaza y Janés, 1995) pp. 13, 28–9; Carrillo, *Hacia el post-franquismo*, pp. 19, 25.

12 'Comunicado sobre la reunión del Pleno del C.C.', *Mundo Obrero*, 5 September 1973; Santiago Carrillo, *Memorias*, 2nd edn (Barcelona: Editorial Planeta, 2006) p. 623; Carrillo, *Hacia el post-franquismo*, pp. 29–30; Fuente, Garcia and Prieto, *Golpe mortal*, pp. 210–13.

13 Manuel Azcárate, 'Sobre la política internacional del Partido', *Nuestra Bandera*, No. 72, 4° trimestre 1973, pp. 15–30; Manuel Azcárate, *Crisis del Eurocomunismo* (Barcelona: Argos Vergara, 1982) pp. 66–71.

14 See Comité Ejecutivo del PCE, *Documentos: Informe de Manuel Azcárate; Artículo publicado en la revista Soviética 'Vida del Partido'; Acotaciónes al artículo* (n.p., n.d. [Paris, 1974]); Manuel Azcárate, *Derrotas y esperanzas* (Barcelona: Editorial Tusquets, 1994) p. 346.

15 Carrillo, *Hacia el post-franquismo*, pp. 98–102; *Mundo Obrero*, 22 May 1974.

16 *Mundo Obrero*, 8 May ('La experiencia de Portugal: Santiago Carrillo por Radio España Independiente'), 22 May (Santiago Carrillo, 'La primavera de Portugal y sus repercusiones en España'), 4, 11, 18, 25 July 1974; *Le Monde*, 23–25 June 1974; Carrillo, *Hacia el post-franquismo*, pp. 5–6; 'Panorama internacional por M. Azcárate: hacia nuevos avances en la lucha antiimperialista y antifascista', *Mundo Obrero*, 4 September 1974.

17 'El espiritu del Ritz', *Cambio 16*, No. 134, 10 June 1974; Ramón Tamames, *Un proyecto de democracia para el futuro de España* (Madrid: Cuadernos para el Diálogo, 1975) pp. 7–10.

18 Carrillo, *Memorias*, pp. 631–6; Luis María Anson, *Don Juan* (Barcelona: Plaza y Janés, 1994) pp. 388–93, 400–2; Teodolfo Lagunero, *Memorias* (Barcelona: Umbriel-Tabla Rasa, 2009) pp. 489–500; Prego, *Así se hizo*, pp. 145–8.

19 *Mundo Obrero*, 4, 19 June, 3 July 1974; Morán, *Miseria y grandeza*, p. 498.

20 *Mundo Obrero*, 24 December 1971, 12 December 1973, 19 June 1974; Carrillo, *Hacia el post-franquismo*, pp. 57–62.

21 *Mundo Obrero*, 31 July 1974; Rafael Calvo Serer, *Mis enfrentamientos con el poder* (Barcelona: Plaza y Janés, 1978) pp. 119–21, 248–65; Carrillo, *Memorias*, pp. 643–52, 661–2.

22 *Mundo Obrero*, 24 December 1974, 19 March 1975; Claudín, *Carrillo*, pp. 221–3.

23 *Frankfurter Allgemeine Zeitung*, 1 August 1974.

24 Lagunero, *Memorias*, pp. 485–9; Carrillo, *Memorias*, pp. 639–42; Prego, *Así se hizo*, pp. 174–6; Anson, *Don Juan*, p. 373.

25 Carrillo, *Hacia el post-franquismo*, pp. 5–6; Santiago Carrillo, *Demain l'Espagne: entretiens avec Régis Debray et Max Gallo* (Paris: Éditions du Seuil, 1974) pp. 15, 136; *Mundo Obrero*, 8, 22 May, 4 June 1974; *Le Monde*, 23–25 June 1974.

26 Lagunero, *Memorias*, pp. 271, 413–16; conversations with Lola Ruiz Ibárruri.

27 Carrillo, *Demain l'Espagne*, pp. 115–17.

28 Claudín, *Carrillo*, p. 218; Morán, *Miseria y grandeza*, pp. 498–9.

29 Carrillo, *Demain l'Espagne*, pp. 186–7.

30 Interview with Carrillo in *Nouvel Observateur*, 23-29 June 1975; 'Carrillo contra Cunhal', *Cambio 16*, 22-28 September 1975.

31 Interview with Carrillo in *Newsweek*, 22 September 1975.

32 *Mundo Obrero*, 8, 22 May 1974.

33 Santiago Carrillo, *Nuevos enfoques a problemas de hoy* (Paris: Éditions Sociales, 1967) pp. 17-18, 140-59.

34 Interview with Carrillo in *Newsweek*, 22 September 1975.

35 Fernando Gómez Peláez, 'Santiago Carrillo o la historia falsificada', *Interrogations*, No. 2, March 1975; Carlos Semprún Maura, '¿Quién es y que pretende Santiago Carrillo?', in Xavier Domingo, ed., *De Carrero Blanco a Eva Forest* (Paris: El Viejo Topo, 1975) pp. 71-89; Felipe Orero, 'Aproximación al mundo político de Santiago Carrillo', *Cuadernos de Ruedo Ibérico*, Nos. 43-5, January–June 1975, pp. 105-27.

36 *Frente Libertario*, No. 45, September 1974; *Vanguardia Obrera*, No. 90, 2ª quincena de agosto, No. 91, September 1974; *Servir al Pueblo*, No. 30, August 1974; *La Voz Comunista*, No. 7, July–August 1974; Nicolás Sartorius and Alberto Sabio, *El final de la dictadura: la conquista de la democracia en España noviembre de 1975–junio de 1977* (Madrid: Temas de Hoy, 2007) pp. 160-1.

37 Enrico Berlinguer and Santiago Carrillo, *Una Spagna libera in un'Europa democratica* (Rome: Editori Riuniti, 1975), contains the complete text of the speeches and of the joint communiqué.

38 *Mundo Obrero*, 1ª & 2ª Semanas de junio de 1975.

39 *Mundo Obrero*, 4ª semana de septiembre de 1975.

40 *Mundo Obrero*, 25 November 1975; *Servir al Pueblo*, No. 45, November 1975; *Correo del Pueblo*, 18 November, 6 December 1975;

41 Víctor Díaz Cardiel *et al.*, *Madrid en huelga: enero 1976* (Madrid: Editorial Ayuso, 1976) pp. 91-150; *Cambio 16*, 19-25 January 1976; *Guardian*, 5, 7, 8, 9, 14, 15, 20 January 1976; *Sunday Times*, 11, 18 January 1976; *Mundo Obrero*, 20, 27 January 1976; 'Las primeras huelgas del post-franquismo', *Cuadernos de Ruedo Ibérico*, Nos. 51-53, May–October 1976, pp. 127-208.

42 *Mundo Obrero*, 4, 11 February 1976; *Cambio 16*, 9-15 February, 1-7 March 1976.

43 Morán, *Miseria y grandeza*, pp. 505-6.

44 Santiago Carrillo, *El año de la peluca* (Barcelona: Ediciones B, 1987) pp. 7-8; Lagunero, *Memorias*, pp. 602-5; Joaquín Bardavío, *Sábado santo rojo* (Madrid: Ediciones Uve, 1980) pp. 27-32; Carrillo, *Memorias*, pp. 671-3, 676-7.

45 Carrillo, *El año de la peluca*, pp. 27-8, 30-2; Simón Sánchez Montero, *Camino de libertad: memorias* (Madrid: Temas de Hoy, 1997) pp. 328-9.

46 Francisco Lasa, 'La oferta de la Junta Democrática: Lenin ha muerto', and Colectivo 70, 'Interpretaciónes políticas en la declaración de la Junta Democrática', *Cuadernos de Ruedo Ibérico*, Nos. 43-45, January–July 1975; *Frente Libertario*, No. 45, September 1974; *Vanguardia Obrera*, No. 90, 2ª quincena de agosto, No. 91, September 1974; *Servir al Pueblo*, No. 30, August 1974.

47 Carrillo, *El año de la peluca*, pp. 8-10.

48 Joaquín Bardavío, *Los silencios del Rey* (Madrid: Strips Editores, 1979) pp. 147-60; Prego, *Así se hizo*, pp. 374-81; Carrillo, *Memorias*, p. 674; Carrillo, *El año de la peluca*, pp. 37-8; author's conversations with

Santiago Carrillo; *Mundo Obrero*, 28 April, 5 May 1976.

49 Carrillo, *Memorias*, pp. 674–5.

50 Carrillo, *El año de la peluca*, pp. 30–1; Carrillo, *Memorias*, pp. 678–80.

51 *Mundo Obrero*, 9 April 1976; Alfonso Osorio, *Trayectoria política de un ministro de la corona* (Barcelona: Editorial Planeta, 1980) pp. 91–4.

52 *Mundo Obrero*, 9, 17 April 1976.

53 For Carrillo's speech, see the supplement to *Mundo Obrero*, 14 July 1976.

54 *Cambio 16*, 12–18, 19–25 July 1976; *Mundo Obrero*, 14 July 1976; Carlos Iniesta Cano, *Memorias y recuerdos* (Barcelona: Editorial Planeta, 1984) pp. 240–1; remarks made by Adolfo Suárez at a private seminar held by the Fundacion Ortega y Gasset in Toledo in May 1984.

55 *Mundo Obrero*, 7 July 1976.

56 Carrillo, *El año de la peluca*, pp. 45–8; *Mundo Obrero*, 1 September 1976; Santiago Carrillo, *De la clandestinidad a la legalidad* (Cheratte, Belgium: M. Levaux, 1976) pp. 26–35, 42–5, 61–5.

57 Carrillo, *Memorias*, pp. 686–8; Bardavío, *Sábado santo rojo*, pp. 42–4.

58 *Cambio 16*, No. 246, 23–29 August 1976; *Mundo Obrero*, 26 July–2 August 1976.

59 Carrillo, *El año de la peluca*, p. 74; Sánchez Montero, *Camino de libertad*, p. 331; Morán, *Miseria y grandeza*, p. 527.

60 Carrillo, *El año de la peluca*, pp. 53–4; Bardavío, *Sábado santo rojo*, pp. 51–8; Prego, *Así se hizo*, pp. 524–9.

61 *Cambio 16*, No. 249, 13–19 September 1976; *Mundo Obrero*, 8 September 1976.

62 *Cambio 16*, No. 250, 20–26 September 1976; Bardavío, *Sábado santo rojo*, pp. 59–60; Gonzalo Fernández de la Mora, *Río arriba:*

memorias (Barcelona: Editorial Planeta, 1995) pp. 261–2; Sabino Fernández Campo, 'Prólogo', in Javier Fernández López, *El Rey y otros militares: los militares en el cambio de régimen político en España (1969–1982)* (Madrid: Editorial Trotta, 1998) pp. 16–18; Fernando Puell de la Villa, *Gutiérrez Mellado: un militar del siglo XX (1912–1995)* (Madrid: Biblioteca Nueva, 1997) pp. 185–6; Prego, *Así se hizo*, pp. 536–8; Miguel Platón, *Hablan los militares: testimonios para la historia* (Barcelona: Editorial Planeta, 2001) pp. 398–400.

63 *Mundo Obrero*, 15–23 September 1976.

64 Prego, *Así se hizo*, pp. 533–5.

65 Diary entries for 22 September, 28 November, 6 December 1976, José María de Areilza, *Cuadernos de la transición* (Barcelona: Editorial Planeta, 1983) pp. 47–8, 71, 78.

66 Carrillo, *El año de la peluca*, pp. 57–60, 66–7; *Mundo Obrero*, 1–7 November 1976.

67 Ana Romero, *Historia de Carmen: memorias de Carmen Díez de Rivera* (Barcelona: Editorial Planeta, 2002) pp. 120–1.

68 *Mundo Obrero*, 1–7, 15–21, 22 November 1976; *Cambio 16*, 22–28 November, 5 December 1976; Osorio, *Trayectoria política*, pp. 208–9; Manuel P. Izquierdo, *De la huelga general a las elecciones generales* (Madrid: Ediciones de la Torre, 1977) pp. 29–30; Rodolfo Martín Villa, *Al servicio del Estado* (Barcelona: Editorial Planeta, 1984) pp. 54–7; Prego, *Así se hizo*, pp. 557–9.

69 Carrillo, *El año de la peluca*, pp. 83–4.

70 *El País*, 18, 28 November 1976; *Mundo Obrero*, 6–12 December 1976; Laureano López Rodó, *Claves de la transición Memorias IV* (Barcelona: Plaza y Janés, 1993) pp.

286–7; Prego, *Así se hizo*, pp. 570–1; Carrillo, *El año de la peluca*, pp. 92–4, 96–104.

71 *El País*, 11 December 1976; *Mundo Obrero*, 20–26 December 1976; Carrillo, *El año de la peluca*, pp. 122–6; Carrillo, *Memorias*, pp. 696–8.

72 *El País*, 14, 15, 16, 17 December 1976; *Cambio 16*, 26 December, 27 December 1976–2 January 1977; Osorio, *Trayectoria*, pp. 252–3; Carrillo, *El año de la peluca*, p. 84.

73 *Mundo Obrero*, 20–26 December 1976; Bardavío, *Sábado santo rojo*, pp. 88–111; Osorio, *Trayectoria*, pp. 254–8; Claudín, *Carrillo*, pp. 2–9, 239–41; Romero, *Historia de Carmen*, pp. 127–9; Carrillo, *El año de la peluca*, pp. 136–43; Carrillo, *Memorias*, pp. 698–706; Sartorius and Sabio, *El final de la dictadura*, p. 319.

74 Manuel Durán, *Martín Villa* (San Sebastián: Hordago Publikapenak, 1979) p. 79; Osorio, *Trayectoria*, pp. 248–9; Alejandro Muñoz Alonso, *El terrorismo en España* (Barcclona: Editorial Planeta, 1982) pp. 76–9; Sánchez Montero, *Camino de libertad*, p. 335; Pío Moa Rodríguez, *Reflexiones sobre el terrorismo* (Madrid: Edición del Autor, 1985) pp. 204–5.

75 *El País*, 12 December 1976; *Cambio 16*, 31 January, 6 February 1977; Pío Moa Rodríguez, *De un tiempo y de un País* (Madrid: Ediciónes de la Torre, 1982) pp. 217–33; Muñoz Alonso, *El terrorismo en España*, pp. 76–85.

76 Consuelo Laiz, *La lucha final: los partidos de la izquierda radical durante la transición española* (Madrid: Libros de la Catarata, 1995) pp. 164–72; Carrillo, *El año de la peluca*, pp. 127, 132, 134.

77 Conversations with Manuel Azcárate, Jaime and Nicolás Sartorius.

78 *Mundo Obrero*, 31 January–6 February 1977; Sánchez Montero, *Camino de libertad*, pp. 337–8; Bardavío, *Sábado santo rojo*, pp. 142–7; Xavier Casals i Meseguer, *La tentación neofascista en España* (Barcelona: Plaza y Janés, 1998) p. 217; Romero, *Historia de Carmen*, pp. 144–8.

79 Romero, *Historia de Carmen*, pp. 134–42, 150–2; Carrillo, *El año de la peluca*, pp. 146–8; Carrillo, *Memorias*, pp. 710–14; Bardavío, *Sábado santo rojo*, pp. 158–71; Claudín, *Carrillo*, pp. 246–7.

80 Azcárate, *Crisis del Eurocomunismo*, p. 98; Morán, *Miseria y grandeza*, p. 538.

81 *Mundo Obrero*, 7–13 March 1977.

82 On the creation of the UCD, see Paul Preston, *The Triumph of Democracy in Spain* (London and New York: Methuen, 1986) pp. 108–14. For Carrillo's expression of approval, *Diario 16*, 24 March 1977; Claudín, *Santiago Carrillo*, p. 248.

83 Claudín, *Carrillo*, p. 249.

84 *Mundo Obrero*, 21–27 March, 4–10, 11–17 April 1977; *Cambio 16*, 18–24 April 1977; Claudín, *Carrillo*, pp. 245–8; Osorio, *Trayectoria*, pp. 286–7; Prego, *Así se hizo*, pp. 643–58; Romero, *Historia de Carmen*, pp. 160, 168, 201; Lagunero, *Memorias*, pp. 662–8.

85 Author's interview with Sabino Fernández Campo, and his 'Prólogo' to Fernández López, *El Rey y otros militares*, pp. 18–19. See also Javier Fernández López, *Sabino Fernández Campo: un hombre de Estado* (Barcelona: Editorial Planeta, 2000) p. 100.

86 *Mundo Obrero*, 20 April 1977; Santiago Carrillo, 'Intervención en el Pleno ampliado del C.C.', in his *Escritos sobre Eurocomunismo*, 2 vols (Madrid: Forma Ediciones, 1977) II, pp. 29–51; Carrillo, *Memorias*, pp. 720–1; Jordi Solé

Tura, *Una historia optimista: memorias* (Madrid: Aguilar/El País, 1999) pp. 375–7; Claudín, *Carrillo*, pp. 250–2; Morán, *Miseria y grandeza*, pp. 541–2.

87 Pedro Vega and Peru Erroteta, *Los herejes del PCE* (Barcelona: Editorial Planeta, 1982) p. 142.

88 Santiago Carrillo, *Memoria de la transición* (Barcelona: Grijalbo, 1983) p. 46; Manuel Azcárate, *Luchas y transiciones: memorias de un viaje por el ocaso del comunismo* (Madrid: El País Aguilar, 1998) pp. 147–8.

89 Santiago Carrillo, *'Eurocomunismo' y Estado* (Barcelona: Editorial Crítica, 1977).

90 Carrillo, *Memorias*, pp. 723–9.

91 Christopher Andrew and Vasili Mitrokhin, *The Sword and the Shield: The Mitrokhin Archive and the Secret History of the KGB* (New York: Basic Books, 1999) pp. 301–2.

92 Comisión de Información y Propaganda del Comité Provincial de Madrid del PCE, *Dossier sobre la polémica en torno al artículo de la revista soviética TIEMPOS NUEVOS* (Madrid: Comité Provincial de Madrid del PCE, 1977) pp. 5–16, 55–60.

93 *Der Spiegel*, 16 May 1977; *Il Manifesto*, 1 November 1975.

94 Julio Luelmo and Henry Winston, *'Eurocomunismo' y Estado o la disintegración del PCE y la ruptura con el movimiento comunista internacional* (Madrid: Akal, 1978). Cf. *Comment*, 4 March 1978, p. 77.

95 *Lodi News Sentinel*, 3 October 1977; *Saratoga Herald Tribune*, 11 October 1977.

96 David Childs, ed., *The Changing Face of Western Communism* (London: Croom Helm, 1980) pp. 52–4.

97 Claudín, *Carrillo*, pp. 252–6.

98 Carrillo, *Memorias*, pp. 729–33; Claudín, *Carrillo*, pp. 259–60;

Eusebio Mujal-León, *Communism and Political Change in Spain* (Bloomington: Indiana University Press, 1983) pp. 157–66.

99 Claudín, *Carrillo*, pp. 262–6.

100 Solé Tura, *Una historia optimista*, pp. 386–8; Carrillo, *Memorias*, pp. 737–8.

101 Cf. Carrillo's speeches in the Cortes on 27 July, 14 and 24 September 1977, reprinted in Carrillo, *Escritos sobre Eurocomunismo*, II, pp. 83–128.

102 *Mundo Obrero*, 16 June, 16 August, 8–14 September, 2–19 December 1977; *Cambio 16*, 17–23, 24–30 October, 31 October–6 November, 7–13 November 1977; Carrillo, *Memorias*, pp. 741–7; Claudín, *Carrillo*, pp. 275–9; Jesús Sánchez Rodríguez, *Teoría y práctica democrática en el PCE (1956–1982)* (Madrid: Fundación de Investigaciones Marxistas, 2004) pp. 286–9; Mujal-León, *Communism*, p. 177; Paul Heywood, 'Mirror Images: The PCE and the PSOE in the Transition to Democracy in Spain', *West European Politics*, Vol. 10, No. 10, April 1987, pp. 193–210.

103 *Mundo Obrero*, 20–26 October 1977; Santiago Carrillo, *El año de la Constitución* (Barcelona: Editorial Crítica, 1978) pp. 115–24; Claudin, *Carrillo*, pp. 279–80; Morán, *Miseria y grandeza*, pp. 553–4.

104 Carrillo, *El año de la constitución*, pp. 136–48.

105 Vega and Erroteta, *Los herejes*, p. 34; Azcárate, *Crisis del Eurocomunismo*, p. 59.

106 For complete membership figures broken down by regions, see Carlos Elordi, 'El PCE por dentro', *La Calle*, No. 95, 15–21 January 1980.

107 Jorge Semprún, *Autobiografía de Federico Sánchez* (Barcelona: Editorial Planeta, 1977), pp. 206–11.

108 Fernando Claudín, *Documentos de una divergencia comunista* (Barcelona: El Viejo Topo, 1978).

109 Rafael Abella, *Semprún–PCE: historia de una polémica* (Barcelona: Editorial Planeta, 1978) p. 27; Carrillo, *Memorias*, pp. 750–6; Claudin, *Carrillo*, pp. 281–2.

110 *Mundo Obrero*, 24 November 1977.

111 *Mundo Obrero*, 8 December 1977.

112 *El País*, 4 January 1978.

113 *El País*, 8 January 1978.

114 López Raimundo and Claudín interviews, and Javier Pradera, 'Las verdades parciales de Jorge Semprún', *Cambio 16*, 8 January 1978; Pradera, interview, *Por Favor*, 16 January 1978.

115 Abella, *Semprún–PCE*, pp. 100–2; Interview with Carrillo in *Cuadernos para el Diálogo*, No. 245, 7–13 January 1978.

116 Santiago Carrillo, 'No nos moverán', *Mundo Obrero*, 19–25 January 1978.

117 *El País*, 22 January 1978; Abella, *Semprún–PCE*, pp. 121–4.

118 Carrillo, *'Eurocomunismo'*, p. 133.

119 Juan Martinez Alier, 'El Pacto de la Moncloa, la lucha sindical y el nuevo corporativismo', *Cuadernos de Ruedo Ibérico*, Nos. 58–60, July–December 1977; G. I. Martí, 'El gran show político o las trampas de la comunicación: las elecciones del 15 de junio de 1977', *Cuadernos de Ruedo Ibérico*, Nos. 61–2, January–April 1979; Rafael Bosch, *La revolucion democrática: ¿Quo vadis, Tamames?* (Madrid: Akal, 1978) pp. 145–81.

120 *El País*, 21 January 1978; *Mundo Obrero*, 26 January 1978.

121 PCE, *9º Congreso del Partido Comunista de España: Resoluciones* (Madrid: PCE, 1978) pp. 71, 154–5; *Nuestra Bandera*, No. 93, March 1978; *El País*, 20–23 April 1978; *Mundo Obrero*, 20, 23 and 27 April 1978. Cf. Fernando Claudín, 'Las tesis del IX Congreso', *Triunfo*, No.

795, 22 April 1978, and Fernando López Agudín, 'Un paso adelante dos pasos atrás', *Triunfo*, No. 796, 27 April 1978; Claudín, *Carrillo*, pp. 293–4.

122 Carrillo, *Memorias*, pp. 752, 764–9; Santiago Carrillo, 'La definición del partido: el marxismo revolucionario hoy', *Mundo Obrero*, 26 January–1 February 1978; Azcárate, *Crisis del Eurocomunismo*, pp. 58–65; Claudin, *Carrillo*, p. 293; Morán, *Miseria y grandeza*, pp. 568–71.

123 PCE, *9º Congreso del Partido Comunista de España*, p. 44.

124 Azcárate, *Crisis del Eurocomunismo*, p. 23.

125 Vega and Erroteta, *Los herejes*, pp. 11–23; Carrillo, *Memorias*, pp. 797–8; Claudín, *Carrillo*, p. 311; Morán, *Miseria y grandeza*, pp. 587–97.

126 *El País*, 30 January 1981.

127 *El País*, 22 February 1981; Carrillo, *Memorias*, pp. 779–82.

128 Sánchez Rodríguez, *Teoría y práctica*, pp. 319–34; Mujal-León, *Communism*, pp. 98–102; Vega and Erroteta, *Los herejes*, pp. 150–1; Carrillo, *Memorias*, pp. 798–800; Azcárate, *Luchas y transiciones*, pp. 183–4.

129 *El País*, 27 July 1981; Vega and Erroteta, *Los herejes*, pp. 101–18; Claudín, *Carrillo*, pp. 334–41.

130 *El País*, 26 July 1981.

131 *Mundo Obrero*, 5–11 June, 24–30 July, 28 July 1981 and supplements 1, 2, 3 and 4. See also *La Calle*, No. 176, 4–10 August 1981; Sánchez Rodríguez, *Teoría y práctica*, pp. 337–43; Azcárate, *Crisis del Eurocomunismo*, pp. 182–3, 225–9; Vega and Erroteta, *Los herejes*, pp. 207–28; Claudín, *Carrillo*, pp. 341–50; Morán, *Miseria y grandeza*, pp. 600–6.

132 *El País*, 25 November 1981; *Mundo Obrero*, 27 November–3 December,

4–10 December 1981; Azcárate, *Crisis del Eurocomunismo*, pp. 249–51, 269–82; Carrillo, *Memorias*, pp. 800–2; Claudín, *Carrillo*, pp. 350–64.

133 Azcárate, *Luchas y transiciones*, pp. 186–95.

134 Azcárate, *Crisis del Eurocomunismo*, pp. 252–62; Carrillo, *Memoria de la transición*, pp. 77, 96–112; Claudín, *Carrillo*, pp. 353–5.

135 Carrillo, *Memoria de la transición*, pp. 213–42; *El País*, 31 July 1982; *Cambio 16*, 26 July, 2 August 1982; Carrillo, *Memorias*, pp. 802–6; Sánchez Montero, *Camino de libertad*, pp. 373–7; Claudín, *Carrillo*, pp. 369–72.

136 *El País*, 29, 30 October 1982; *Cambio 16*, 1 November 1982; Morán, *Miseria y grandeza*, pp. 607–19.

137 Santiago Carrillo, *La memoria en retazos: recuerdos de nuestra historia más reciente española* (Barcelona: Plaza y Janés, 2003) pp. 35–7.

138 *El País*, 17 July 1986; Carrillo, *Memorias*, pp. 808–10; Sánchez Montero, *Camino de libertad*, pp. 379–83; Sánchez Rodríguez, *Teoría y práctica*, p. 337; Sergio Vilar, *Por qué se ha destruido el PCE* (Barcelona: Plaza y Janés, 1986) pp. 221–5.

139 Carrillo, *Memorias*, p. xvii.

140 *El País*, 20 October 2005.

141 *El País*, 23 April 2005.

142 *El País*, 7 June 2008.

143 *El País*, 17 July 2012.

144 *Público*, 15 October 2012.

145 *El País*, 30 October 2012.

Epilogue

1 *El País*, 5 August 1991.

2 *El País*, 9 January 2005.

3 Santiago Carrillo, *Memorias*, 2nd edn (Barcelona: Editorial Planeta, 2006) p. xvi.

4 *El País*, 18 June 1978.

5 *Ibid.*

6 Daniel Arasa, *La invasión de los maquis* (Barcelona: Belacqua de Ediciones, 2004) p. 15; Santiago Carrillo, *Mi testamento político* (Barcelona: Galaxia Gutenberg, 2012) pp. 119–21.

7 Santiago Carrillo, *De la clandestinidad a la legalidad* (Cheratte, Belgium: M. Levaux, 1976) pp. 40–1.

8 Fernando Claudín, *Santiago Carrillo: crónica de un secretario general* (Barcelona: Editorial Planeta, 1983) p. 262.

9 Santiago Carrillo, *Los viejos camaradas* (Barcelona: Editorial Planeta, 2010) p. 72; Carrillo, *Mi testamento político*, p. 237.

10 Santiago Carrillo, *Juez y parte: 15 retratos españoles* (Barcelona: Plaza y Janés, 1996) pp. 255–7; José Luis Losa, 'Cuentas pendientes en el fusilamiento de Grimau', *El Confidencial*, 20 April 2013.

ILLUSTRATION CREDITS

I would like to thank the friends who helped me find these photographs: Emilia Bolinches, Carlos García-Alix, Caroline Hotblack, Enrique Líster López, Manuel Martorell and Irène Tenèze.

Section One
Page 1: EFE/Newscom/lafototeca.com (top); Cañada Blanch Collection (middle); Iberfoto/Photoaisa (bottom)
Page 2: Colección Enrique Líster López (top); EFE/lafototeca.com (bottom)
Page 3: Cañada Blanch Collection (top left); Cañada Blanch Collection (top right); Colección Enrique Líster López (bottom)
Page 4: Ángel Ruiz de Ayúcar (top left); Elvira Gómez Urrutia (top right and bottom)
Page 5: Manuel Martorell (top); Irène Tenèze (middle); Luz Castelló and Emilia Boliches (bottom)
Page 6: EFE/lafototeca.com (top); Colección Enrique Líster López (bottom)
Page 7: Colección Enrique Líster López (top); Irène Tenèze (bottom)
Page 8: Colección Enrique Líster López (top and bottom)

Section Two
Page 1: Colección Enrique Líster López (top and bottom)
Page 2: REX/Sipa Press (top); Colección Enrique Líster López (middle and bottom)
Page 3: Irène Tenèze (top); Gamma-Keystone via Getty Images (bottom)

Page 4: EFE/lafototeca.com (top left, top right and bottom)

Page 5: EFE/Newscom/lafototeca.com (top); CAGP/Iberfoto/ Photoaisa (bottom)

Page 6: epa european pressphoto agency b.v./Alamy (top); EFE/ lafototeca.com (bottom)

Page 7: EFE/lafototeca.com (top and bottom)

Page 8: Christián Gonzalez (top); Juan Carlos Hidalgo/(EPA) EFE/ lafototeca.com (middle); Alberto Morante/(EPA) EFE/lafototeca. com (bottom)

While every effort has been made to trace the owners of copyright material reproduced in this book, the publishers apologise for any omissions or errors and will be pleased to correct future editions.

A NOTE ON PRIMARY SOURCES

In addition to the substantial published literature of memoirs and theoretical works by protagonists listed in the Bibliography, considerable primary material was consulted over a thirty-five-year period from 1976 to 2013. This included letters and diaries of party leaders, secret reports and congress proceedings of the Socialist and Communist parties held in the Archivo Histórico del Partido Comunista de España, Madrid, and in the Archivo Histórico de la Fundación Pablo Iglesias, Madrid; trial records and denunciations of Party members held in the records of the massive state investigation known as the Causa General, held in the Archivo Histórico Nacional in Madrid and the Centro Documental de la Memoria Histórica in Salamanca; and material on relations with the anarchists held in the Archives of the International Institute for Social History, Amsterdam. Exhaustive use was made of the clandestine Communist Party press and the press of the Socialist Party and, to a lesser extent, the French and Spanish national press. Specific references can be found in the Notes.

In addition, interviews were held with Carrillo himself, and other protagonists, between 1976 and 2010. They are named and thanked in the Acknowledgements.

BIBLIOGRAPHY

Abella, Rafael, *Semprún–PCE: historia de una polémica* (Barcelona: Editorial Planeta, 1978)

Agosti, Aldo, *Palmiro Togliatti* (Torino: UTET, 1996)

Aguado Sánchez, Francisco, *El maquis en España* (Madrid: Editorial San Martín, 1975)

Aguado Sánchez, Francisco, *La revolución de octubre de 1934* (Madrid: Editorial San Martín, 1972)

Águila, Juan José del, *El TOP: la represión de la libertad (1963–1977)* (Barcelona: Editorial Planeta, 2001)

Alba, Victor, *El Partido Comunista en España: ensayo de interpretación histórica* (Barcelona: Editorial Planeta, 1979)

Alba, Víctor, *La Alianza Obrera: historia y análisis de una táctica de unidad en España* (Gijón: Ediciones Júcar, 1977)

Álvarez, Ange, Delicado, Iván and Delicado, Roland, *Guérilla antifranquiste du Levant: Crimes et falsifications 1945–1952* (Nîmes: Ardeo, 2014)

Álvarez, Ange, Delicado, Iván and Delicado, Roland, *Royo le guérillero éliminé: frère d'armes de Marcel Bigeard pendant la Libération de l'Ariège* (Nîmes: Ardeo, 2011)

Álvarez, Santiago, Hinojosa, José and Sandoval, José, *El movimiento guerrillero de los años 40*, 2nd edn revised and enlarged (Madrid: Fundación de Investigaciones Marxistas, 2003)

Álvarez, Santiago, *Memorias I: Recuerdos de infancia i de juventud (1920–1936)* (Sada-A Coruña: Ediciós do Castro, 1985)

Álvarez, Santiago, *Memorias II: La Guerra Civil de 1936/1939* (Sada-A Coruña: Ediciós do Castro, 1986)

Álvarez, Santiago, *Memorias III: La lucha continúa … El exílio: la 2ª Guerra Mundial: el regreso clandestino a España (1939–1945)* (Sada-A Coruña: Ediciós do Castro, 1988)

Álvarez, Santiago, *Memorias IV: Más fuertes que la tortura y la pena de muerte (1945–1954)* (Sada-A Coruña: Ediciós do Castro, 1990)

Álvarez, Santiago, *Memorias V: La larga marcha de una lucha sin cuartel (1954–1972)* (Sada-A Coruña: Ediciós do Castro, 1994)

Álvarez, Santiago, *Memorias VI: Largos años de lucha por la libertad (1962–1983)* (Sada-A Coruña: Ediciós do Castro, 1994)

Andrew, Christopher and Mitrokhin, Vasili, *The Sword and the Shield: The Mitrokhin Archive and the Secret History of the KGB* (New York: Basic Books, 1999)

Anson, Beatriz, 'The Limits of Destalinisation: The Spanish Communist Party 1956–1965' (unpublished doctoral thesis, London School of Economics and Political Science, 2002)

Anson, Luis María, *Don Juan* (Barcelona: Plaza y Janés, 1994)

Antón Sanz, Francisco, *Madrid, orgullo de la España antifascista: discurso pronunciado en el Pleno del C.C. del Partido Comunista celebrado en Valencia los días 5, 6, 7 y 8 de Marzo de 1937* (Valencia: Ediciones del Partido Comunista de España, Comisión Nacional de Agit-Prop, 1937)

Araquistáin, Luis, *Sobre la guerra civil y en la emigración* (Madrid: Espasa Calpe, 1983)

Arasa, Daniel, *Años 40: los maquis y el PCE* (Barcelona: Argos Vergara, 1984)

Arasa, Daniel, *La invasión de los maquis* (Barcelona: Belacqua de Ediciones, 2004)

Arasa, Daniel, *Los españoles de Stalin* (Barcelona: Editorial Vorágine, 1993)

Areilza, José María de, *Cuadernos de la transición* (Barcelona: Editorial Planeta, 1983)

Areilza, José María de, *Diario de un ministro de la monarquía* (Barcelona: Editorial Planeta, 1977)

Arnaiz, Aurora, *Retrato hablado de Luisa Julián* (Madrid: Compañía Literaria, 1996)

Aróstegui, Julio and Marco, Jorge, eds, *El último frente: la resistencia armada antifranquista en España 1939–1952* (Madrid: Los Libros de la Catarata, 2008)

Aróstegui, Julio and Martínez, Jesús A., *La Junta de Defensa de Madrid* (Madrid: Comunidad de Madrid, 1984)

Asenjo, Mariano and Ramos, Victoria, *Malagón: autobiografía de un falsificador* (Barcelona: El Viejo Topo, 1999)

Avilés, Gabriel, *Tribunales rojos (Vistbogado defensor)* (Barcelona: Ediciones Destino, 1939)

Avilés, Juan, *Pasionaria, La mujer y el mito* (Barcelona: Plaza y Janés, 2005)

Azaña, Manuel, *Apuntes de memoria inéditos y cartas 1938–1939–1940* (Valencia: Pre-Textos, 1990)

Azaña, Manuel, *Obras completas*, 4 vols (Mexico City: Ediciones Oasis, 1966–8)

Azcárate, Manuel, *Crisis del Eurocomunismo* (Barcelona: Argos Vergara, 1982)

Azcárate, Manuel, *Derrotas y esperanzas* (Barcelona: Editorial Tusquets, 1994)

Azcárate, Manuel, *Luchas y transiciones: memorias de un viaje por el ocaso del comunismo* (Madrid: El País Aguilar, 1998)

Azpíroz Pascual, José María and Elboj Broto, Fernando, *La sublevación de Jaca* (Zaragoza: Guara Editorial, 1984)

Balbé, Manuel, *Orden público y militarismo en la España constitucional 1812–1983* (Madrid: Alianza Editorial, 1983)

Balfour, Sebastian, *Dictatorship, Workers, and the City: Labour in Greater Barcelona since 1939* (Oxford: Clarendon Press, 1989)

Baraibar, Carlos de, *Las Falsas 'posiciones socialistas' de Indalecio Prieto* (Madrid: Ediciones Yunque, 1935)

Bardavío, Joaquín, *El dilema: un pequeño caudillo o un gran Rey* (Madrid: Strips Editores, 1978)

Bardavío, Joaquín, *La crisis: historia de quince dias* (Madrid: Ediciones Sedmay, 1974)

Bardavío, Joaquín, *La rama trágica de los Borbones* (Barcelona: Plaza y Janés, 1989)

Bardavío, Joaquín, *Las claves del Rey: el laberinto de la transición* (Madrid: Espasa Calpe, 1995)

Bardavío, Joaquín, *Los silencios del Rey* (Madrid: Strips Editores, 1979)

Bardavío, Joaquín, *Sábado santo rojo* (Madrid: Ediciones UVE, 1980)

Barrio Alonso, Ángeles, *Anarquismo y anarcosindicalismo en Asturias (1890/1936)* (Madrid: Siglo XXI, 1988)

Berenguer, Dámaso, *De la Dictadura a la República* (Madrid: Editorial Plus Ultra, 1946)

Beria, Sergo, *Beria My Father: Inside Stalin's Kremlin* (London: Duckworth, 2001)

Berlinguer, Enrico and Carrillo, Santiago, *Una Spagna libera in un'Europa democratica* (Rome: Editori Riuniti, 1975)

Besteiro, Julián, *Marxismo y anti-marxismo*, 4th edn (Madrid: Editorial ZYX, 1967)

Bizcarrondo, Marta, ed., *Octubre del 34: reflexiones sobre una revolución* (Madrid: Editorial Ayuso, 1977)

Blinkhorn, Martin, ed., *Spain in Conflict 1931–1939: Democracy and its Enemies* (London: Sage Publications, 1986)

Bolinches, Emilia, *Pilar Soler: rebelde con causas* (Valencia: Publicacions de la Universitat de València, 2013)

Bolloten, Burnett, *The Spanish Civil War: Revolution and Counterrevolution* (Chapel Hill: University of North Carolina Press, 1991)

Bonamusa, Francesc, *El Bloc Obrer i Camperol (1930–1932)* (Barcelona: Curial, 1974)

Borrás, José, *Políticas de los exilados españoles 1944–1950* (Paris: Éditions Ruedo Ibérico, 1976)

Bosch, Rafael, *La revolucion democrática: ¿Quo vadis, Tamames?* (Madrid: Akal, 1978)

Boyd, Carolyn P., *Praetorian Politics in Liberal Spain* (Chapel Hill: University of North Carolina Press, 1979)

Brassloff, Audrey, *Religion and Politics in Spain: The Spanish Church in Transition, 1962–96* (London: Macmillan Press, 1998)

Buckley, Henry, *Life and Death of the Spanish Republic* (London: Hamish Hamilton, 1940)

Busquets, Julio, *El militar de carrera en España*, 3rd edn (Barcelona: Ariel, 1967)

Cabezas, Octavio, *Indalecio Prieto, socialista y español* (Madrid: Algaba Ediciones, 2005)

Cal, Rosa, *A mi no me doblega nadie: Aurora Rodriguez: su vida y su obra (Hildegart)* (Sada-A Coruña: Edicios do Castro, 1991)

Calvo Serer, Rafael, *Mis enfrentamientos con el poder* (Barcelona: Plaza y Janés, 1978)

Caminal, Miquel, *Joan Comorera I: Catalanisme i socialisme (1913–1936)* (Barcelona: Editorial Empúries, 1984)

Caminal, Miquel, *Joan Comorera II: Guerra i revolució (1936–1939)* (Barcelona: Editorial Empúries, 1984)

Caminal, Miquel, *Joan Comorera III: Comunisme i nacionalisme (1939–1958)* (Barcelona: Editorial Empúries, 1985)

Carabantes, Andrés and Cimorra, Eusebio, *Un mito llamado Pasionaria* (Barcelona: Editorial Planeta, 1982)

Carrillo, Santiago, *De la clandestinidad a la legalidad* (Cheratte, Belgium: M. Levaux, 1976)

Carrillo, Santiago, *Deberes del pueblo español en la presente situación internacional y nacional* (Paris: Parti Communiste Français, 1961)

Carrillo, Santiago, *Demain l'Espagne: entretiens avec Régis Debray et Max Gallo* (Paris: Éditions du Seuil, 1974)

Carrillo, Santiago, *Después de Franco, ¿Qué? La democracia política y social que preconizamos los comunistas* (Paris: Éditions Sociales, 1965)

Carrillo, Santiago, *Dialogue on Spain* (London: Lawrence & Wishart, 1976)

Carrillo, Santiago, *Discurso ante una asamblea de militantes del Partido* (n.p. [Prague], 1964)

Carrillo, Santiago, *El año de la Constitución* (Barcelona: Editorial Crítica, 1978)

Carrillo, Santiago, *El año de la peluca* (Barcelona: Ediciones B, 1987)

Carrillo, Santiago, *En marcha hacia la victoria* (Valencia: JSU, 1937)

Carrillo, Santiago, *Entrevistas* (Madrid: El País, 2011)

Carrillo, Santiago, *Escritos sobre Eurocomunismo*, 2 vols (Madrid: Forma Ediciones, 1977)

Carrillo, Santiago, *'Eurocomunismo' y Estado* (Barcelona: Editorial Crítica, 1977)

Carrillo, Santiago, *¿Ha muerto el Comunismo? Ayer y hoy de un movimiento clave para entender la convulsa historia del siglo XX* (Barcelona: Plaza y Janés, 2000)

Carrillo, Santiago, *Hacia el post-franquismo* (Paris: Colección Ebro, 1974)

Carrillo, Santiago, *Informe sobre problemas de organización y los estatutos del Partido* (n.p., n.d.)

Carrillo, Santiago, *Juez y parte: 15 retratos españoles* (Barcelona: Plaza y Janés, 1996)

Carrillo, Santiago, *La juventud, factor de la victoria: discurso pronunciado en el pleno ampliado del C. C. del Partido Comunista de España celebrado en Valencia los días 5, 6, 7 y 8 de marzo de 1937* (Valencia: Ediciones del Partido Comunista de España, Comisión Nacional de Agit-Prop, 1937)

Carrillo, Santiago, *La lucha por el socialismo hoy* (Paris: Colección Ebro, 1969)

Carrillo, Santiago, *La memoria en retazos: recuerdos de nuestra historia más reciente española* (Barcelona: Plaza y Janés, 2003)

Carrillo, Santiago, *La segunda República: recuerdos y reflexiones* (Barcelona: Plaza y Janés, 1999)

Carrillo, Santiago, *La situación en la dirección del Partido y los problemas del reforzamiento del mismo* (Paris: Parti Communiste Français, 1956)

Carrillo, Santiago, *La situación en el Movimiento Comunista* (Paris: P.P.I., 1963)

Carrillo, Santiago, *Libertad y Socialismo* (Paris: Éditions Sociales, 1971)

Carrillo, Santiago, *Los viejos camaradas* (Barcelona: Editorial Planeta, 2010)

Carrillo, Santiago, *Memoria de la transición* (Barcelona: Grijalbo, 1983)

Carrillo, Santiago, *Memorias* (Barcelona: Editorial Planeta, 1993)

Carrillo, Santiago, *Memorias*, 2nd edn (Barcelona: Editorial Planeta, 2006)

Carrillo, Santiago, *Mi testamento político* (Barcelona: Galaxia Gutenberg, 2012)

Carrillo, Santiago, *Nadando a contracorriente* (Madrid: El País, 2012)

Carrillo, Santiago, *Nuevos enfoques a problemas de hoy* (Paris: Éditions Sociales, 1967)

Carrillo, Santiago, *Para echar del poder a Franco y Falange: unidad y lucha*, 'Conferencia de Santiago Carrillo, miembro del buró político del PCE, ante un grupo de militantes del partido emigrados en Francia' (Toulouse: Editorial España Popular, 1944)

Carrillo, Santiago, *Problemas del movimiento comunista* (Paris: P.P.I., 1962)

Carrillo, Santiago, *Problems of Socialism Today* (London: Lawrence & Wishart, 1970)

Casals i Meseguer, Xavier, *La tentación neofascista en España* (Barcelona: Plaza y Janés, 1998)

Casanova, Julián, *De la calle al frente: el anarcosindicalismo en España (1931–1939)* (Barcelona: Editorial Crítica, 1997)

Casas de la Vega, Rafael, *El terror: Madrid 1936: investigación histórica y catálogo de víctimas identificadas* (Madrid: Editorial Fénix, 1994)

Casterás Archidona, Ramón, *Las Juventudes Socialistas Unificadas de Catalunya ante la guerra y la revolución (1936–1939)*, 2nd edn (Barcelona: Hogar del Libro, 1982)

Castro Delgado, Enrique, *Hombres made in Moscú* (Barcelona: Luis de Caralt, 1965)

Castro Delgado, Enrique, *Mi fé se perdió en Moscú* (Barcelona: Luis de Caralt, 1964)

Causa General, *La dominación roja en España* (Madrid: Ministerio de Justicia, 1945)

Cervelló, Josep Sánchez *et al.*, *Maquis: el puño que golpeó al franquismo: la Agrupación Guerrillera de Levante y Aragón (AGLA)* (Barcelona: Flor del Viento Ediciones, 2003)

Cervera Gil, Javier, *Madrid en guerra: la ciudad clandestina 1936–1939*, 2nd edn (Madrid: Alianza Editorial, 2006)

Childs, David, ed., *The Changing Face of Western Communism* (London: Croom Helm, 1980)

Cierva, Ricardo de la, *Carrillo miente: 156 documentos contra 103 falsedades* (Madrid: Editorial Fénix, 1994)

Claudín, Fernando, *Documentos de una divergencia comunista* (Barcelona: El Viejo Topo, 1978)

Claudín, Fernando, *Eurocomunismo y socialismo* (Madrid: Siglo XXI, 1977)

Claudín, Fernando, *La crisis del movimiento comunista: de la Komintern al Kominform* (Paris: Éditions Ruedo Ibérico, 1970)

Claudín, Fernando, 'La crisis del PCE', *Cuadernos de Ruedo Ibérico*, Nos. 26–27, August–November 1970

Claudín, Fernando, *Las divergencias en el partido* (n.p., n.d. [Paris: author, 1965])

Claudín, Fernando, *Santiago Carrillo: crónica de un secretario general* (Barcelona: Editorial Planeta, 1983)

Comisión de Información y Propaganda del Comité Provincial de Madrid del PCE, *Dossier sobre la polémica en torno al artículo de la revista soviética TIEMPOS NUEVOS* (Madrid: Comité Provincial de Madrid del PCE, 1977)

Comité Ejecutivo del PCE, *Documentos: Informe de Manuel Azcárate; Artículo publicado en la revista Soviética 'Vida del Partido'; Acotaciónes al artículo* (n.p., n.d. [Paris, 1974])

Cordón, Antonio, *Trayectoria (Recuerdos de un artillero)* (Seville: Espuela de Plata, 2008)

Cossías, Tomás, *La lucha contra el 'maquis' en España* (Madrid: Editora Nacional, 1956)

Crozier, Brian, *Franco: A Biographical History* (London: Eyre & Spottiswoode, 1967)

Cruz, Rafael, *El Partido Comunista de España en la II República* (Madrid: Alianza, 1987)

Cruz, Rafael, *En el nombre del pueblo: república, rebelión y guerra en la España de 1936* (Madrid: Siglo XXI, 2006)

Cruz, Rafael, *Pasionaria: Dolores Ibárruri, historia y símbolo* (Madrid: Biblioteca Nueva, 1999)

Cuadernos de Ruedo Iberico, *Horizonte español 1966*, 2 vols (Paris: Éditions Ruedo Iberico, 1966)

Cuadernos de Ruedo Iberico, *Horizonte español 1972*, 3 vols (Paris: Éditions Ruedo Iberico, 1972)

Del Valle, José María, *Las instituciones de la República española en exilio* (Paris: Éditions Ruedo Ibérico, 1976)

Díaz, José, *Las enseñanzas de Stalin: guía luminoso para los comunistas españoles* (Mexico City: Editorial Popular, 1940)

Díaz, José, *Tres años de lucha* (Toulouse: Ediciones Nuestro Pueblo, 1947)

Díaz, José and Ibárruri, Dolores, *España y la guerra imperialista: llamamiento del PCE a la emigración española* (Mexico City: Delegación del PCE, 1939)

Díaz Cardiel, Víctor et al., *Madrid en huelga: enero 1976* (Madrid: Editorial Ayuso, 1976)

Diz, Alejandro, *La sombra del FRAP: génesis y mito de un partido* (Barcelona: Ediciones Actuales, 1977)

Documentos inéditos para la historia del Generalísimo Franco, 4 vols (Madrid: Fundación Nacional Francisco Franco, 1992)

Documentos socialistas (Madrid: Publicaciones Índice, 1935)

Domingo, Alfonso, *El ángel rojo: la historia de Melchor Rodríguez, el anarquista que detuvo la represión en el Madrid republicano* (Córdoba: Editorial Almuzara, 2009)

Domingo, Carmen, *Mi querida hija Hildegart* (Barcelona: Editorial Destino, 2008)

Domingo, Xavier, ed., *De Carrero Blanco a Eva Forest* (Paris: El Viejo Topo, 1975)

Dunthorn, David J., *Britain and the Spanish Anti-Franco Opposition, 1940–1950* (London: Palgrave, 2000)

Durán, Manuel, *Martín Villa* (San Sebastián: Hordago Publikapenak, 1979)

Elorza, Antonio and Bizcarrondo, Marta, *Queridos Camaradas: la Internacional Comunista y España, 1919–1939* (Barcelona: Editorial Planeta, 1999)

Encinas Moral, Ángel L., ed., *Las causas de la derrota de la República española: informe elaborado por Stoyán Mínev (Stepanov), Delegado en España de la Komintern (1937–1939)* (Madrid: Miraguano Ediciones, 2003)

Equipo Adelvec, *FRAP 27 de septiembre de 1975* (Madrid: Ediciones Vanguardia Obrera, 1985)

Esparza, José Javier, *El libro negro de Carrillo* (Madrid: Libros Libres, 2010)

Estévez, Carlos and Mármol, Francisco, *Carrero: las razones ocultas de un asesinato* (Madrid: Ediciones Temas de Hoy, 1998)

Estruch Tobella, Joan, *El PCE en la clandestinidad 1939–1956* (Madrid: Siglo XXI, 1982)

Estruch, Joan, *Historia del P.C.E. (1920–1939)* (Barcelona: El Viejo Topo, 1978)

Estruch, Joan, *Historia oculta del PCE* (Madrid: Temas de Hoy, 2000)

Fabre, Jaume, Huertas, Josep M. and Ribas, Antoni, *Vint anys de resistència catalana (1939–1959)* (Barcelona: Edicions de la Magrana, 1978)

Falcón, Irene, *Asalto a los cielos: mi vida junto a Pasionaria* (Madrid: Temas de Hoy, 1996)

Fanés, Félix, *La vaga de tramvies del 1951* (Barcelona: Editorial Laia, 1977)

Federación de Juventudes Socialistas de España, *Resoluciones del IV Congreso* (Madrid: Gráfica Socialista, 1932)

Federación de Juventudes Socialistas de España, *Resoluciones del V Congreso* (Madrid: Gráfica Socialista, 1934)

Fernández Arias, Adelardo (El Duende de la Colegiata), *La agonía de Madrid 1936–1937 (Diario de un superviviente)* (Zaragoza: Librería General, 1938)

Fernández Arias, Adelardo (El Duende de la Colegiata), *Madrid bajo el 'terror' 1936–1937 (Impresiones de un evadido, que estuvo a punto de ser fusilado)* (Zaragoza: Librería General, 1937)

Fernández de Castro, Ignacio, *De las Cortes de Cadiz al Plan de Desarrollo 1808–1966* (Paris: Éditions Ruedo Ibérico, 1968)

Fernández de Castro, Ignacio and Martínez Guerricabeitia, José, *España hoy* (Paris: Éditions Ruedo Ibérico, 1963)

Fernández de la Mora, Gonzalo, *Río arriba: memorias* (Barcelona: Editorial Planeta, 1995)

Fernández López, Javier, *El Rey y otros militares: los militares en el cambio de régimen político en España (1969–1982)* (Madrid: Editorial Trotta, 1998)

Fernández López, Javier, *Sabino Fernández Campo: un hombre de Estado* (Barcelona: Editorial Planeta, 2000)

Fernández Rodríguez, Carlos, *Madrid clandestino: la reestructuración del PCE (1939–1945)* (Madrid: Fundación Domingo Malagón, 2002)

Fernández Santander, Carlos, *Paracuellos del Jarama: ¿Carrillo culpable?* (Barcelona: Argos Vergara, 1983)

Ferri, Llibert, Muixí, Jordi and Sanjuan, Eduardo, *Las huelgas contra Franco (1939–1956)* (Barcelona: Editorial Planeta, 1978)

Fonseca, Carlos, *Trece rosas rojas: la historia más conmovedora de la guerra civil española* (Madrid: Ediciones Temas de Hoy, 2004)

Fontana, Joseph, ed., *España bajo el franquismo* (Barcelona: Editorial Crítica, 1986)

Foreign Relations of the United States 1946, Vol. V (Washington: Government Printing Office, 1969)

Franco Salgado-Araujo, Francisco, *Mis conversaciones privadas con Franco* (Barcelona: Editorial Planeta, 1976)

Fuente, Ismael, Garcia, Javier and Prieto, Joaquín, *Golpe mortal: asesinato de Carrero y agonia del franquismo* (Madrid: El País, 1983)

Fuentes, Juan Francisco, *Largo Caballero: el Lenin español* (Madrid: Editorial Síntesis, 2005)

Fusi, Juan Pablo, *Política obrera en el País Vasco* (Madrid: Ediciones Turner, 1975)

Galíndez, Jesús de, *Los vascos en el Madrid sitiado* (Buenos Aires: Editorial Vasca Ekin, 1945)

Galinsoga, Luis and Franco-Salgado, Francisco, *Centinela de occidente (Semblanza biográfica de Francisco Franco)* (Barcelona: Editorial AHR, 1956)

Gallego, Gregorio, *Madrid, corazón que se desangra* (Madrid: G. del Toro, 1976)

Gallego, Ignacio, *El partido de masas que necesitamos* (Paris: Éditions Sociales, 1971)

García Oliver, Juan, *El eco de los pasos* (Barcelona: Éditions Ruedo Ibérico, 1978)

García Salve, Francisco, *Por qué somos comunistas* (Madrid: Penthalon Ediciones, 1981)

Garrido Caballero, Magdalena, *Resistencia, amnistía libertad: compromiso antifranquista y militancia del PCE en la región de Murcia* (Valencia: Editorial Germania, 2011)

Garrido Caballero, Magdalena, *Compañeros de viaje: historia y memoria de las Asociaciones de Amistad Hispao-Soviéticas* (Murcia: Ediciones de la Universidad de Murcia, 2009)

Gascón, Antonio and Priego, Victoria, *Por hoy y por mañana (Leves comentarios a un libro firmado por Carlos Baraibar* (Madrid: Publicaciones Índice, 1935)

Gibaja Velázquez, José Carlos, *Indalecio Prieto y el socialismo español* (Madrid: Editorial Pablo Iglesias, 1995)

Gibson, Ian, *Paracuellos: cómo fue* (Barcelona: Argos Vergara, 1983)

Gil Robles, José María, *Marginalia política* (Barcelona: Ariel, 1975)

Gil Robles, José María, *No fue posible la paz* (Barcelona: Ariel, 1968)

Ginard i Ferón, David, *Heriberto Quiñones y el movimiento comunista en España (1931–1942)* (Palma de Mallorca and Madrid: Documenta Balear/Compañía Literaria, 2000)

Ginard i Ferón, David, *Matilde Landa: De la Institución Libre de Enseñanza a las prisiones franquistas* (Barcelona: Flor de Viento Ediciones, 2005)

González Cuevas, Pedro Carlos, *Acción Española: teología política y nacionalismo autoritario en España (1913–1936)* (Madrid: Editorial Tecnos, 1998)

González Portilla, Manuel and Garmendía, José María, *La posguerra en el País Vasco: política, acumulación, miseria* (San Sebastián: Kriselu, 1988)

Graham, Helen, *Socialism and War: The Spanish Socialist Party in Power and Crisis, 1936–1939* (Cambridge: Cambridge University Press, 1991)

Graham, Helen, *The Spanish Civil War: A Very Short Introduction* (Oxford: Oxford University Press, 2005)

Graham, Helen, *The Spanish Republic at War 1936–1939* (Cambridge: Cambridge University Press, 2002)

Graham, Helen, *The War and its Shadow: Spain's Long Civil War in Europe's Long Twentieth Century* (Brighton: Sussex Academic Press/Cañada Blanch, 2012)

Graham, Helen and Preston, Paul, eds, *The Popular Front in Europe* (London: Macmillan, 1987)

Grandizo Munis, *Jalones de derrota, promesa de victoria* (Mexico City: Editorial Lucha Obrera, 1948)

Gros, José, *Abriendo camino: relatos de un guerrillero comunista español* (Paris: Colección Ebro, 1971)

Grossi, Manuel, *La insurrección de Asturias (Quince días de revolución socialista)* (Barcelona: Gráficos Alfa, 1935)

Guzmán, Eduardo de, *Mi hija Hildegart* (Barcelona: Plaza y Janés, 1997)

Heine, Hartmut, *A guerrilla antifranquista en Galicia* (Vigo: Edicións Xerais de Galicia, 1980)

Heine, Hartmut, *La oposición política al franquismo* (Barcelona: Editorial Crítica, 1983)

Hermet, Guy, *The Communists in Spain* (Farnborough: Saxon House, 1974)

Hermet, Guy, *Les Catholiques dans l'Espagne Franquiste*, 2 vols (Paris: Presses de la Fondation Nationale des Sciences Politiques, 1980–1)

Hermet, Guy, *Los comunistas en España* (Paris: Éditions Ruedo Ibérico, 1972)

Hernández Sánchez, Fernando, *Comunistas sin partido: Jesús Hernández, Ministro en la guerra civil, disidente en el exilio* (Madrid: Editorial Raíces, 2007)

Hernández Sánchez, Fernando, *Guerra o revolución: el Partido Comunista de España en la guerra civil* (Barcelona: Editorial Crítica, 2010)

Hernández Zancajo, Carlos, *Octubre: segunda etapa* (n.p, n.d. [Madrid, 1935])

Hernández, Jesús, *En el país de la gran mentira* (Madrid: G. del Toro, 1974)

Hernández, Jesús, *La grande trahison* (Paris: Fasquelle Editeurs, 1953)

Hernández, Jesús, *Yo fui un ministro de Stalin* (Madrid: G. del Toro, 1974)

Heywood, Paul, 'Mirror Images: The PCE and the PSOE in the Transition to Democracy in Spain', *West European Politics*, Vol. 10, No. 10, April 1987

Heywood, Paul, *Marxism and the Failure of Organised Socialism in Spain 1879–1936* (Cambridge: Cambridge University Press, 1990)

Ibárruri, Dolores, *El único camino* (Madrid: Editorial Castalia, 1992)

Ibárruri, Dolores, *Informe al Comité Central al 5º Congreso del p. C. de España* (n.p., n.d. [Paris: Parti Communiste Français, 1955])

Ibárruri, Dolores, *Informe pronunciado ante un grupo de dirigentes del Partido, el 25 de octubre de 1951* (n.p.: Edición reservada del autor, 1951)

Ibárruri, Dolores, *Memorias de Pasionaria 1939–1977: me faltaba España* (Barcelona: Editorial Planeta, 1984)

Ibárruri, Dolores, *Por la reconciliación de los españoles hacia la democratización de España* (Paris: Éditions Sociales, 1956)

Ibárruri, Dolores, *Por una España republicana, democrática e independiente: informe al III Pleno* (Paris: Nuestra Bandera, 1947)

Ibárruri, Dolores *et al.*, *Guerra y revolución en España 1936–39*, 4 vols (Moscow: Editorial Progreso, 1966–77)

Ibárruri, Dolores *et al.*, *Historia del Partido Comunista de España (Versión abreviada)* (Warsaw: Ediciones 'Polonia', 1960)

Iniesta Cano, Carlos, *Memorias y recuerdos* (Barcelona: Editorial Planeta, 1984)

Iordache Cârstea, Luiza, 'El exilio español en la URSS: represión y Gulag: entre el acoso comunista, el glacis estalinista y el caparazón franquista' (unpublished doctoral thesis, Universidad Autónoma de Barcelona, 2011)

Jáuregui, Fernando and Vega, Pedro, *Crónica del antifranquismo 1939–1975* (Barcelona: Editorial Planeta, 2007)

Juárez, Javier, *Patria: una española en el KGB* (Barcelona: Editorial Debate, 2008)

Juliá Díaz, Santos, *Camarada Javier Pradera* (Barcelona: Galaxia Gutenberg, 2012)

Juliá Díaz, Santos, ed., *El socialismo en España: desde la fundación del PSOE hasta 1975* (Madrid: Editorial Pablo Iglesias, 1986)

Juliá Díaz, Santos, *Historia del socialismo español (1931–1939)* (Barcelona: Conjunto Editorial, 1989)

Juliá Díaz, Santos, *La izquierda del PSOE (1935–1936)* (Madrid: Siglo XXI, 1977)

Juliá Díaz, Santos, *Los socialistas en la política española 1879–1982* (Madrid: Taurus, 1997)

Juliá Díaz, Santos, *Madrid, 1931–1934: de la fiesta popular a la lucha de clases* (Madrid: Siglo XXI, 1984)

Juliá Díaz, Santos, *Orígenes del Frente Popular en España (1934–1936)* (Madrid: Siglo XXI, 1979)

Juliá Díaz, Santos, ed., *Violencia política en la España del siglo XX* (Madrid: Taurus, 2000)

Karmén, Román, *¡No pasarán!* (Moscow: Editorial Progreso, 1976)

Kolpakidi, Alexander I. and Prokhorov, Dmitri P., *KGB: vsyo o vneshnei razvedke* (Moscow: Olimp, 2002)

Koltsov, Mijail, *Diario de la guerra de España* (Paris: Éditions Ruedo Ibérico, 1963)

Lacomba Avellán, Juan Antonio, *La crisis española de 1917* (Madrid: Editorial Ciencia Nueva, 1970)

Lagunero, Teodolfo, *Memorias* (Barcelona: Umbriel-Tabla Rasa, 2009)

Laiz, Consuelo, *La lucha final: los partidos de la izquierda radical durante la transición española* (Madrid: Libros de la Catarata, 1995)

Lamo de Espinosa, Emilio and Contreras, Manuel, *Filosofía y política en Julián Besteiro*, 2nd edn (Madrid: Editorial Sistema, 1990)

Largo Caballero, Francisco, *Discursos a los trabajadores* (Madrid: Gráfica Socialista, 1934)

Largo Caballero, Francisco, *Escritos de la República* (Madrid: Fundación Pablo Iglesias, 1985)

Largo Caballero, Francisco, *Mis recuerdos: cartas a un amigo* (Mexico City: Editores Unidos, 1954)

Largo Caballero, Francisco, *Obras completas*, 16 vols (Madrid and Barcelona: Fundación Largo Caballero/Instituto Monsa, 2003–9)

Largo Caballero, Francisco, *Presente y futuro de la Unión General de Trabajadores de España* (Madrid: Javier Morata, 1925)

Líster, Enrique, *Así destruyó Carrillo el PCE* (Barcelona: Editorial Planeta, 1983)

Líster, Enrique, *¡Basta! Una aportación a la lucha por la recuperación del Partido* (n.p., n.d. [Paris: author, 1971])

Líster, Enrique, *¡Basta! Una aportación a la lucha por la recuperación del Partido*, 2nd edn (Madrid: G. del Toro, 1978)

Líster, Enrique, *Nuestra guerra* (Paris: Colección Ebro, 1966)

Llaneza, Manuel, *Escritos y discursos* (Oviedo: Fundación José Barreiros, 1985)

Llarch, Joan, *Hildegart: la vírgen roja* (Barcelona: Producciones Editoriales, 1979)

Lleonart y Anselem, Alberto J. and Castiella y Maiz, Fernando María, *España y ONU I (1945–46)* (Madrid: Consejo Superior de Investigaciones Científicas, 1978)

López, Enrique, *Carrillo: dos caras de una misma moneda* (n.p., n.d.)

López Fernández, Antonio, *Defensa de Madrid: relato histórico* (Mexico City: Editorial A. P. Márquez, 1945)

López Raimundo, Gregorio, *Primera clandestinidad: memorias* (Barcelona: Editorial Antártida/Empúries, 1993)

López Raimundo, Gregorio, *Primera clandestinidad: segunda parte* (Barcelona: Editorial Antártida/Empúries, 1995)

López Rodó, Laureano, *Claves de la transición Memorias IV* (Barcelona: Plaza y Janés, 1993)

López Tovar, Vicente, 'Coronel de los guerrilleros españoles en Francia: biografía' (unpublished manuscript)

Losa, José Luis, *Caza de rojos: un relato urbano de la clandestinidad comunista* (Madrid: Espejo de Tinta, 2005)

Loteta, Giuseppe, 'Fratello, mio valoroso compagno …' *Dall'Italia alla Spagna, la vita di Fernando De Rosa, socialista libertario* (Venice: Marsilio, 1998)

Low, Robert, *La Pasionaria: The Spanish Firebrand* (London: Hutchinson, 1992)

Luelmo, Julio and Winston, Henry, *'Eurocomunismo' y Estado o la disintegración del PCE y la ruptura con el movimiento comunista internacional* (Madrid: Akal, 1978)

Marco Carretero, Jorge, *Guerrilleros y vecinos en armas: identidades y culturas de la resistencia antifranquista* (Granada: Editorial Comares, 2012)

Marco Nadal, Enrique, *Todos contra Franco: la Alianza Nacional de Fuerzas Democráticas 1944/1947* (Madrid: Queimada Ediciones, 1982)

Mario de Coca, Gabriel, *Anti-Caballero: una crítica marxista de la bolchevización del Partido Socialista Obrero Español* (Madrid: Ediciones Engels, 1936)

Marsá, Graco, *La sublevación de Jaca: relato de un rebelde* (Madrid: Zeus, 1931)

Martín Ramos, José Luis, *Rojos contra Franco: historia del PSUC, 1939–1947* (Barcelona: Edhasa, 2002)

Martínez de Baños, Fernando, *Hasta su total aniquilación: el Ejército contra el maquis en el Valle de Arán y en el Alto Aragón, 1944–1946* (Madrid: Almena Ediciones, 2002)

Martínez Reverte, Jorge, *La Batalla de Madrid* (Barcelona: Editorial Crítica, 2004)

Martorell, Manuel, *Jesús Monzón: el líder comunista olvidado por la Historia* (Pamplona: Pamiela, 2000)

Maura, Miguel, *Asi cayó Alfonso XIII* (Mexico City: Imprenta Mañez, 1962)

Maurín, Joaquín, *Hacia la segunda revolución: el fracaso de la República y la insurrección de octubre* (Barcelona: Gráficos Alfa, 1935)

Maurín, Joaquín, *Los hombres de la Dictadura* (Madrid: Editorial Cénit, 1930)

Meaker, Gerald H., *The Revolutionary Left in Spain, 1914–1923* (Stanford: Stanford University Press, 1974)

Moa Rodríguez, Pío, *De un tiempo, y de un país* (Madrid: Ediciones de la Torre, 1982)

Moa Rodríguez, Pío, *Reflexiones sobre el terrorismo* (Madrid: Edición del Autor, 1985)

Mola Vidal, Emilio, *Obras completas* (Valladolid: Librería Santarén, 1940)

Monreal, Antoni, *El pensamiento político de Joaquín Maurín* (Barcelona: Ediciones Península, 1984)

Montañés, Enrique, *Anarcosindicalismo y cambio político: Zaragoza, 1930–1936* (Zaragoza: Institución Fernando el Católico, 1989)

Montorio Gonzalvo, José Manuel, *Cordillera ibérica: recuerdos y olvidos de un guerrillero* (Zaragoza: Gobierno de Aragón, 2007)

Moradiellos, Enrique, *El Sindicato de los Obreros Mineros Asturianos 1910–1930* (Oviedo: Universidad de Oviedo, 1986)

Morán, Gregorio, *Miseria y grandeza del Partido Comunista de España 1939–1985* (Barcelona: Editorial Planeta, 1986)

Moreno Gómez, Francisco, *La resistencia armada contra Franco: tragedia del maquis y la guerrilla* (Barcelona: Editorial Crítica, 2001)

Mujal-León, Eusebio, *Communism and Political Change in Spain* (Bloomington: Indiana University Press, 1983)

Munis, Grandizo, *Jalones de derrota, promesa de victoria* (Mexico City: Editorial Lucha Obrera, 1948)

Muñoz Alonso, Alejandro, *El terrorismo en España* (Barcelona: Editorial Planeta, 1982)

Nin, Andrés, *Los problemas de la revolución española* (Paris: Éditions Ruedo Ibérico, 1971)

Novales, Félix, *El tazón de hierro: memoria personal de un militante de los GRAPO* (Barcelona: Editorial Crítica, 1989)

Núñez, Miguel, *La revolución y el deseo: memorias* (Barcelona: Ediciones Península, 2002)

Ojeda, Germán, ed., *Octubre 1934: cincuenta años para la reflexión* (Madrid: Siglo XXI, 1985)

Ortiz, Jean, ed., *Rouges: maquis de France et d'Espagne: les guerrilleros* (Biarritz: Atlantica-Séguier, 2006)

Osorio, Alfonso, *Trayectoria política de un ministro de la corona* (Barcelona: Editorial Planeta, 1980)

Pagès i Blanch, Pelai, *Andreu Nin: una vida al servicio de la clase obrera* (Barcelona: Laertes, 2011)

Pàmies, Teresa, *Quan érem capitans: memòries d'aquella guerra* (Barcelona: Dopesa, 1974)

Parti Communiste Français, *2 meses de huelgas* (Paris: Parti Communiste Français, 1962)

PCE, *¡Adelante por la libertad y la independencia de España!* (Santiago de Chile: DIAP, 1942)

PCE, *Carta a las organizaciones y militantes del Partido* (Mexico City: Ediciones España Popular, 1952)

PCE, *Declaración por la reconciliación nacional, por una solución democrática y pacífica del problema español* (n.p., n.d. [Paris, 1956])

PCE, *El heroico pueblo español lucha contra el franquismo y por la victoria de la Unión Soviética* (Bogotá: Ediciones Sociales, 1941)

PCE, *9º Congreso del Partido Comunista de España: Resoluciones* (Madrid: PCE, 1978)

PCE, *VIII Congreso del Partido Comunista de España* (Bucharest: '13 de Diciembre 1918', 1972)

PCE, *¡Por la Unión Nacional de todos los españoles contra Franco, los invasores germano-italianos y los traidores!* (n.p., n.d. [Mexico City, 1941])

Pike, David Wingeate, *In the Service of Stalin: The Spanish Communists in Exile 1939–1945* (Oxford: Clarendon Press, 1993)

Pike, David Wingeate, *Jours de gloire, jours de honte: le Parti Communiste d'Espagne en France depuis son arrivée en 1939 jusqu'à son départ en 1950* (Paris: Société d'Édition d'Enseignement Supérieur, 1984)

Pike, David Wingeate, *Spaniards in the Holocaust: Mauthausen, the Horror on the Danube* (London: Routledge, 2000)

Pike, David Wingeate, *Vae Victis! Los republicanos españoles refugiados en Francia 1939–1944* (Paris: Éditions Ruedo Ibérico, 1969)

Piñuel, José Luis, *El terrorismo en la transición española* (Madrid: Editorial Fundamentos, 1986)

Platón, Miguel, *Hablan los militares: testimonios para la historia* (Barcelona: Editorial Planeta, 2001)

Prego, Victoria, *Así se hizo la Transición* (Barcelona: Plaza y Janés, 1995)

Preston, Paul, *The Coming of the Spanish Civil War: Reform, Reaction and Revolution in the Second Spanish Republic*, 2nd edn (London: Routledge, 1994)

Preston, Paul, *¡Comrades! Portraits from the Spanish Civil War* (London: HarperCollins, 1999)

Preston, Paul, *Franco: A Biography* (HarperCollins, London, 1993)

Preston, Paul, *Juan Carlos: A People's King* (London: HarperCollins, 2004)

Preston, Paul, *The Politics of Revenge: Fascism and the Military in Twentieth-Century Spain* 2nd edn (London: Routledge, 1995)

Preston, Paul, *The Spanish Civil War: Reaction, Revolution, Revenge* (London: HarperCollins, 2006)

Preston, Paul, *The Spanish Holocaust: Inquisition and Extermination in Twentieth-Century Spain* (London: HarperCollins, 2012)

Preston, Paul, *The Triumph of Democracy in Spain* (London and New York: Methuen, 1986)

Prieto, Indalecio, *Convulsiones de España: pequeños detalles de grandes sucesos*, 3 vols (Mexico City: Ediciones Oasis, 1967–9)

Prieto, Indalecio, *Discursos fundamentales* (Madrid: Ediciones Turner, 1975)

Prieto, Indalecio, *Posiciones socialistas: del momento* (Madrid: Publicaciones Índice, n.d. [1935]) 1er Congreso del PCE (M–L), *Informe del Comité Central* (Madrid: PCE-ML, 1973)

Primo de Rivera, José Antonio, 'Discurso de la fundación de Falange Española', in *Textos de doctrina política*, 4th edn (Madrid: Sección Femenina de FET y de las JONS, 1966)

PSOE, *XII Congreso del Partido Socialista Obrero Español, 28 de junio al 4 de julio de 1928* (Madrid: Gráfica Socialista, 1929)

PSOE, *Convocatoria y orden del día para el XII congreso ordinario del Partido Socialista Obrero Español* (Madrid: Gráfica Socialista, 1927)

Puell de la Villa, Fernando, *Gutiérrez Mellado: un militar del siglo XX (1912–1995)* (Madrid: Biblioteca Nueva, 1997)

Quiñonero, Llum, *Nosotras que perdimos la paz* (Madrid: Foca, 2005)

Quintanilla, Luis, 'Pasatiempo': la vida de un pintor (Memorias) (Sada-A Coruña: Ediciós do Castro, 2004)

Quintanilla, Paul, Waiting at the Shore: Art, Revolution, War and Exile in the Life of the Spanish Artist Luis Quintanilla (Rhode Island: Lulu Press, 2003)

Radosh, Ronald, Habeck, Mary R. and Sevostianov, Grigory, eds, Spain Betrayed: The Soviet Union in the Spanish Civil War (New Haven: Yale University Press, 2001)

Raguer, Hilari, El quadern de Montjuïc: records de la vaga de tramvies (Barcelona: Editorial Claret, 2001)

Raguer, Hilari, Réquiem por la cristiandad: el Concilio Vaticano II y su impacto en España (Barcelona: Ediciones Península, 2006)

Ramírez, Luis, Nuestros primeros veinticinco años (Paris: Éditions Ruedo Ibérico, 1964)

Ramos Oliveira, Antonio, Nosotros los marxistas: Lenin contra Marx, 2nd edn (Madrid: Ediciones Júcar, 1979)

Rayfield, Donald, Stalin and his Hangmen: An Authoritative Portrait of a Tyrant and Those Who Served Him (London: Viking, 2004)

Riambau, Esteve, Ricardo Muñoz Suay: una vida en sombras (Barcelona: Ediciones Tusquets, 2007)

Ribelles de la Vega, Silvia, Luis Montero Sabugo: en los abismos de la historia: vida y muerte de un comunista (Oviedo: Pentalfa Ediciones, 2011)

Richards, Michael, 'Falange, Autarky and Crisis: The Barcelona General Strike of 1951', European History Quarterly, October 1999

Richards, Michael, A Time of Silence: Civil War and the Culture of Repression in Franco's Spain, 1936–1945 (Cambridge: Cambridge University Press, 1998)

Rico, Eduardo G., Queríamos la revolución: crónicas del FELIPE (Frente de Liberación Popular) (Barcelona: Flor del Viento, 1998)

Rico, José Antonio, En los dominios del Kremlin (Mexico City: Atlántico, 1952)

Rodríguez Armada, Amandino and Novais, José Antonio, ¿Quién mató a Julián Grimau? (Madrid: Ediciones 99, 1976)

Roig, Montserrat, Noche y niebla: los catalanes en los campos nazis (Barcelona: Ediciones Península, 1978)

Rojo, General Vicente, Así fue la defensa de Madrid (Mexico City: Ediciones Era, 1967)

Romero, Ana, Historia de Carmen: memorias de Carmen Díez de Rivera (Barcelona: Editorial Planeta, 2002)

Romeu Alfaro, Fernanda, El silencio roto: mujeres contra el franquismo (Madrid: Edición de la autora, 1994)

Romeu Alfaro, Fernanda, Más allá de la utopía: perfil histórico de la Agrupación Guerrillera de Levante (Valencia: Edicions Alfons el Magnànim, 1987)

Romeu Alfaro, Fernanda, *Más allá de la utopía: Agrupación Guerrillera de Levante* (Cuenca: Ediciones de la Universidad de Castilla-La Mancha, 2002)

Rosal, Amaro del, *1934: el movimiento revolucionario de octubre* (Madrid: Akal, 1983)

Rosal, Amaro del, *Historia de la UGT de España 1901–1939*, 2 vols (Barcelona: Grijalbo, 1977)

Ross, Marjorie, *El secreto encanto de la KGB: las cinco vidas de Iósif Griguliévich* (Heredia, Costa Rica: Farben Grupo Editorial Norma, 2004)

Rossanda, Rossana, *Un viaje inútil* (Barcelona: Laia, 1984)

Ruiz Ayúcar, Ángel, *Crónica agitada de ocho años tranquilos 1963–1970* (Madrid: Editorial San Martín, 1974)

Ruiz Ayúcar, Ángel, *El partido comunista: treinta y siete años de clandestinidad* (Madrid: Editorial San Martín, 1976)

[Ruiz de Ayúcar, Ángel], *¿Crimen o castigo? Documentos inéditos sobre Julián Grimau* (Madrid: Servicio de Información Española, 1963)

Saborit, Andrés, *Julián Besteiro* (Buenos Aires: Losada, 1967)

Sala, Antonio and Durán, Eduardo, *Crítica de la izquierda autoritaria en Cataluña* (Paris: Éditions Ruedo Ibérico, 1975)

Salazar Alonso, Rafael, *Bajo el signo de la revolución* (Madrid: Librería de San Martín, 1935)

Salvador Maranón, Alicia, *De ¡Bienvenido, Mr. Marshall! a Viridiana: Historia de UNINCI, una productora cinematográfica española bajo el franquismo* (Madrid: Egeda, 2006)

Sánchez Montero, Simón, *Camino de la libertad: memorias* (Madrid: Ediciones Temas de Hoy, 1997)

Sánchez Rodríguez, Jesús, *Teoría y práctica democrática en el PCE (1956–1982)* (Madrid: Fundación de Investigaciones Marxistas, 2004)

Santiago, Enrique de, *La Unión General de Trabajadores ante la revolución* (Madrid: Tipografía Sáez Hermanos, 1932)

Sartorius, Nicolás and Sabio, Alberto, *El final de la dictadura: la conquista de la democracia en España noviembre de 1975–junio de 1977* (Madrid: Temas de Hoy, 2007)

Satrústegui, Joaquín *et al.*, eds, *Cuando la transición se hizo posible: el 'contubernio de Munich'* (Madrid: Editorial Tecnos, 1993)

Sanz Oller, Julio, *Entre el fraude y la esperanza* (Paris: Éditions Ruedo Ibérico, 1972)

Schlayer, Félix, *Diplomático en el Madrid rojo* (Seville: Espuela de Plata, 2008)

Semprún, Jorge, *Adiós, luz de veranos* (Barcelona: Tusquets Editores, 1998)

Semprún, Jorge, *Autobiografía de Federico Sánchez* (Barcelona: Editorial Planeta, 1977)

Semprún, Jorge, *Communism in Spain in the Franco Era: The Autobiography of Federico Sánchez* (Brighton: Harvester Press, 1980)

Semprún, Jorge, *Federico Sánchez se despide de ustedes* (Barcelona: Tusquets Editores, 1993)

Semprún, Jorge, *Montand, la vida continua* (Barcelona: Editorial Planeta, 1983)

Semprún Maura, Carlos, *El exilio fue una fiesta: memoria informal de un español de París* (Barcelona: Editorial Planeta, 1998)

Semprun Maura, Carlos, 'La "oposición" y sus militantes', *Cuadernos de Ruedo Ibérico*, Nos. 33–35, March 1972

Semprun Maura, Carlos, '¿Quién es y qué pretende Santiago Carrillo?', in El Viejo Topo, *De Carrero Blanco a Eva Forest* (Paris: El Viejo Topo, 1975)

Serrano Poncela, Segundo, *El Partido Socialista y la conquista del poder* (Barcelona: Ediciones L'Hora, 1935)

Serrano, Secundino, *Maquis: historia de la guerrilla antifranquista* (Madrid: Ediciones Temas de Hoy, 2001)

VI Congreso del Partido Comunista de España, Informe del Comité Central presentado por Santiago Carrillo (Prague: Ediciones 'Boletín de Información', 1960)

Sinclair, Alison, *Sex and Society in Early Twentieth-Century Spain: Hildegart Rodríguez and the World League for Sexual Reform* (Cardiff: University of Wales Press, 2007)

Sinova, Justino, ed., *Historia del Franquismo*, 2 vols (Madrid: Información y Prensa, 1985)

Solé Tura, Jordi, *Una historia optimista: memorias* (Madrid: Aguilar/El País, 1999)

Sorel, Andrés, *Búsqueda, reconstrucción e historia de la guerrilla española del siglo XX a través de sus documentos, relatos y protagonistas* (Paris: Éditions de la Librairie du Globe, 1970)

Soriano, Ramón, *La mano izquierda de Franco* (Barcelona: Editorial Planeta, 1981)

Souto Kustrín, Sandra, *Paso a la juventud: movilización democrática, estalinismo y revolución en la República Española* (Valencia: Publicacions de la Universitat de València, 2013)

Souto Kustrín, Sandra, *'Y ¿Madrid? ¿Qué hace Madrid?' Movimiento revolucionario y acción colectiva (1933–1936)* (Madrid: Siglo XXI, 2004)

Suárez Fernández, Luis, *Franco y la URSS (La diplomacia secreta 1946–1970)* (Madrid: Ediciones Rialp, 1987)

Sudoplatov, Pavel, *Special Tasks: Memoirs of an Unwanted Witness* (London: Little, Brown, 1994)

Tagüeña Lacorte, Manuel, *Testimonio de dos guerras* (Mexico City: Ediciones Oasis, 1973)

Tamames, Ramón, *Un proyecto de democracia para el futuro de España* (Madrid: Cuadernos para el Diálogo, 1975)

Togliatti, Palmiro, *Escritos sobre la guerra de España* (Barcelona: Editorial Crítica, 1980)

Togliatti, Palmiro, *Opere 1935–1944* (Rome: Editori Riuniti, 1979)

Tuñón de Lara, Manuel, *El movimiento obrero en la historia de España* (Madrid: Taurus, 1972)

Tuñón de Lara, Manuel, *La España del siglo XX*, 2nd edn (Paris: Librería Española, 1973)

Tusell, Xavier, *La oposición democrática al franquismo 1939–1962* (Barcelona: Editorial Planeta, 1977)

Ucelay Da Cal, Enric, *La Catalunya populista: imatge, cultura i política en l'etapa republicana (1931–1939)* (Barcelona: Edicions de La Magrana, 1982)

Urban, G. R., ed., *Communist Reformation: Nationalism, Internationalism and Change in the World Communist Movement* (New York: St Martin's Press, 1979)

Vaksberg, Arkadi, *Hotel Lux: les partis frères au service de l'Internationale Communiste* (Paris: Éditions Fayard, 1993)

Vayo, Julio Álvarez del, *The Last Optimist* (London: Putnam, 1950)

Vázquez Montalbán, Manuel, *Pasionaria y los siete enanitos* (Barcelona: Editorial Planeta, 1995)

Vega, Eulàlia, *Anarquistas y sindicalistas durante la segunda República: la CNT y los Sindicatos de Oposición en el País Valenciano* (Valencia: Edicions Alfons el Magnànim, 1987)

Vega, Pedro and Erroteta, Peru, *Los herejes del PCE* (Barcelona: Editorial Planeta, 1982)

Vegas Latapie, Eugenio, *El pensamiento político de Calvo Sotelo* (Madrid: Cultura Española, 1941)

Vegas Latapie, Eugenio, *Escritos políticos* (Madrid: Cultura Española, 1941)

Vicuña, Padre Carlos, OSA, *Mártires Agustinos de El Escorial* (El Escorial: Imprenta del Monasterio de El Escorial, 1943)

Vidal Castaño, José Antonio, *La memoria reprimida: historias orales del maquis* (Valencia: Publicacions de la Universitat de València, 2004)

Vidali, Vittorio, *Diary of the Twentieth Congress of the Communist Party of the Soviet Union* (Westport, Conn.: Lawrence Hill, 1984)

Vidarte, Juan-Simeón, *El bienio negro y la insurrección de Asturias* (Barcelona: Grijalbo, 1978)

Vidarte, Juan-Simeón, *Las Cortes Constituyentes de 1931–1933* (Barcelona: Grijalbo, 1976)

Vidarte, Juan-Simeón, *Todos fuimos culpables* (Mexico City: Grijalbo, 1973)

Vilanova, Antonio, *Los olvidados: los exilados españoles en la segunda guerra mundial* (Paris: Éditions Ruedo Ibérico, 1969)

Vilar, Sergio, *Historia del anti-franquismo 1939–1975* (Barcelona: Plaza y Janés, 1984)

Vilar, Sergio, *La oposición a la dictadura: protagonistas de la España democrática: la oposición a la dictadura* (Paris: Ediciones Sociales/Librería Española, 1968)

Vilar, Sergio, *Por qué se ha destruido el PCE* (Barcelona: Plaza y Janés, 1986)

Viñas, Ángel, *El escudo de la República: el oro de España, la apuesta soviética y los hechos de mayo de 1937* (Barcelona: Editorial Crítica, 2007)

Viñas, Ángel and Hernández Sánchez, Fernando, *El desplome de la República* (Barcelona: Editorial Crítica, 2009)

Viñas, Ricard, *La formación de las Juventudes Socialistas Unificadas (1934–1936)* (Madrid: Siglo XXI, 1978)

Volkogonov, Dmitri, *Stalin: Triumph and Tragedy* (London: Weidenfeld & Nicolson, 1991)

Volodarsky, Boris, *El caso Orlov: los servicios secretos soviéticos en la guerra civil española* (Barcelona: Editorial Crítica, 2013)

Volodarsky, Boris, 'Soviet Intelligence Services in the Spanish Civil War, 1936–1939' (unpublished doctoral thesis, London School of Economics and Political Science, 2010)

Yagüe, María Eugenia, *Santiago Carrillo: perfil humano y político* (Madrid: Editorial Cambio 16, 1977)

Yusta Rodrigo, Mercedes, *Guerrilla y resistencia campesina: la resistencia armada contra el franquismo en Aragón (1939–1952)* (Zaragoza: Prensas Universitarias de Zaragoza, 2003)

Yusta Rodrigo, Mercedes, *La guerra de los vencidos: el maquis en el Maestrazgo turolense, 1940–1950*, 2nd edn (Zaragoza: Institución Fernando el Católico, 2005)

Zugazagoitia, Julián, *Guerra y vicisitudes de los españoles*, 2nd edn, 2 vols (Paris: Librería Española, 1968)

INDEX

SC indicates Santiago Carrillo